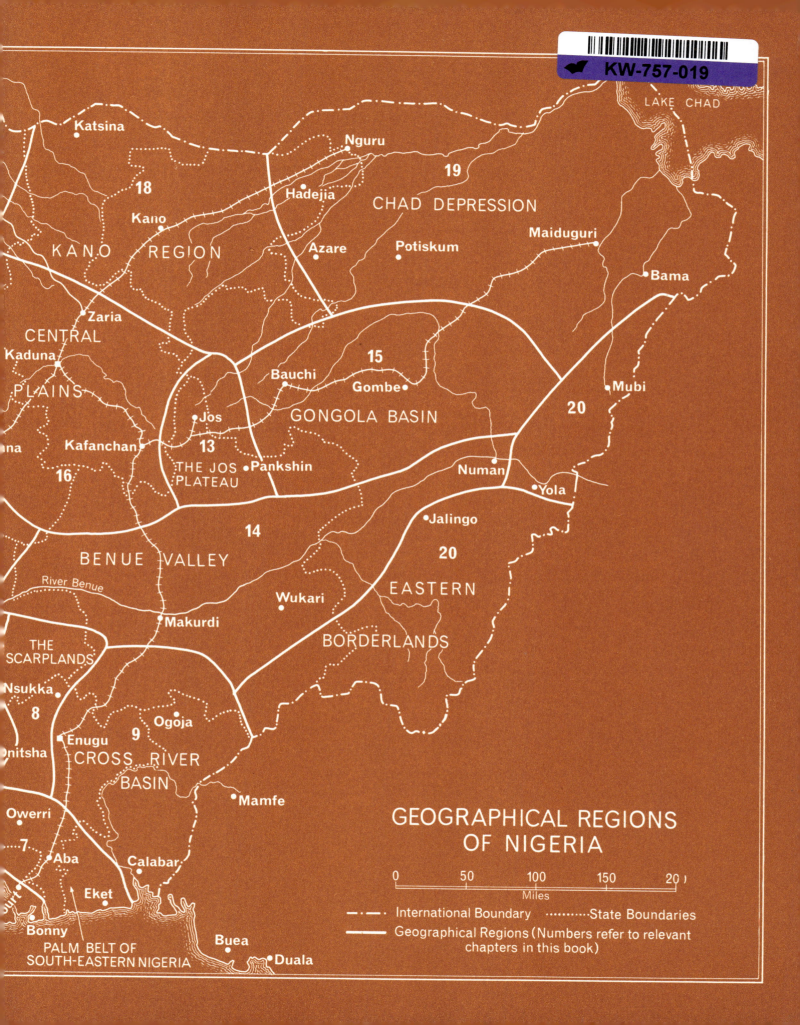

LAKE CHAD

Katsina

Nguru

19

18

Hadejia

CHAD DEPRESSION

Kano

Azare

Potiskum

Maiduguri

KANO REGION

Bama

Zaria

CENTRAL

Kaduna

15

Mubi

PLAINS

Bauchi

Gombe

20

Jos

GONGOLA BASIN

Kafanchan

13

16

THE JOS
PLATEAU

Pankshin

Numan

Yola

14

Jalingo

BENUE VALLEY

20

River Benue

Wukari

EASTERN

Makurdi

THE
SCARPLANDS

BORDERLANDS

Nsukka

8

Ogoja

9

Enugu

Onitsha

CROSS RIVER

BASIN

Mamfe

Owerri

**GEOGRAPHICAL REGIONS
OF NIGERIA**

7

Aba

Calabar

0   50   100   150   20
Miles

Eket

Bonny

Buea

—·—·— International Boundary   ·········· State Boundaries

PALM BELT OF
SOUTH-EASTERN NIGERIA

Duala

——— Geographical Regions (Numbers refer to relevant
chapters in this book)

Geographical Regions
of Nigeria

REUBEN K. UDO

Senior Lecturer in Geography
University of Ibadan

Geographical Regions of Nigeria

HEINEMANN
LONDON / NAIROBI / IBADAN

DEDICATION

To the memory of those who died
in the fight to keep Nigeria one

Heinemann Educational Books Ltd.

48 Charles Street, London W1X 8AH

PMB 5205 Ibadan. POB 25080 Nairobi

MELBOURNE TORONTO AUCKLAND

SINGAPORE HONG KONG JOHANNESBURG

SBN 435 34913 9 (hardback)

SBN 435 34914 7 (paperback)

© R. K. Udo 1970

First Published 1970

Printed in Great Britain by
Morrison & Gibb Ltd., London and Edinburgh

CONTENTS

MAPS AND DIAGRAMS

PHOTOGRAPHS

ACKNOWLEDGEMENTS

The author and publisher are grateful to the following for permission to reproduce the photographs: Federal Information Service, Lagos, for Plates 1, 2, 3, 4, 11, 19, 24, 29, 30, 31, 33, 36, 38, 39, 40, 43, 44 and 46; Ministry of Information, Kaduna, for Plates 34, 41, 42, 45 and 47; the Editor, *Nigeria Magazine,* for Plates 6, 7, 9, 35, 51 and 52; the Management, Bacita Sugar Estate for Plate 25; The Editor, *The Daily Times of Nigeria* for Plate 27. Other photographs were taken by the author.

PREFACE

The only standard text on the geography of Nigeria was published in 1955, that is about thirteen years ago, and has never been revised. It is therefore very much out-of-date in respect of various developments in the country, particularly in the fields of agriculture and industry. But even if Buchanan and Pugh's *Land and People in Nigeria* were revised it is not designed to serve the needs of the student or general reader who wants to learn about the land, people and economy of such an area as the lower Niger Valley, the Jos Plateau or the Kano region. *Geographical Regions of Nigeria* which is based on a course of lectures given to undergraduates at the University of Ibadan is designed to meet such a need.

As Chief Examiner for Geography II in the West African School Certificate Examination, I have been conscious of the need to provide teachers and students with the necessary information and sketch maps which will help candidates in answering questions intelligibly. *Geographical Regions of Nigeria* will help satisfy this need. It is intended primarily for students in sixth forms and teacher training colleges as well as university students, but those preparing for the School Certificate Examination will find the maps and diagrams particularly useful. The foreigner who intends to learn about or work amongst the people of any part of Nigeria will also benefit from reading this book.

The presentation is in three parts which fit in with the traditional division of the country into three zones—a southern zone or the coastlands of Guinea, a central zone or the middle belt, and a northern zone or the Nigerian Sudan. The chapter dealing with the eastern borderlands is included in the section on the Sudan although in actual fact the borderlands cover areas which are representative of the coastlands, the middle belt and the Sudan.

The departure of this volume from the stereotype pattern of regional texts, which normally feature introductory chapters on aspects of the systematic geography of the country or group of countries concerned, is deliberate. Rather, a short review of the essential features of the geography of Nigeria, followed by a commentary on the traditional division of the country into the three broad zones named in the previous paragraph, is presented as a necessary introduction to the volume.

My major sources include annual reports of government departments and statutory corporations, several research papers, a few of which are unpublished, and the *Statistical and Economic Review* of the United Africa Company. I have also found some of the B.A. dissertations of my former students very useful. My extensive tour of the Northern States in 1965 has also been of great help in the writing of this book.

I am grateful to the Geography Department at the University of Ibadan for providing the funds for travel and other research expenses which have made the production of this book possible. I am also grateful to Dr W. B. Morgan and Mr H. P. White, both my former teachers, for reading through and offering useful comments on the manuscript.

Most of the maps and diagrams were drawn by Messrs T. K. S. P. Amachree and A. Faoye of the Department of Geography at the University of Ibadan.

Reuben K. Udo

Evanston, Illinois

Introduction to Nigeria

Nigeria came into being in 1914, when the two protectorates of Northern and Southern Nigeria were amalgamated under the governorship of Sir Frederick Lugard. She became independent in 1960, after more than half a century of British rule. Three years later, she adopted a republican constitution but remained a member of the British Commonwealth. Today, the relics of British rule are to be seen in every aspect of Nigerian life. Her monetary and educational systems are patterned after those of the British, and her official language, which is English, is likely to remain unchanged since the many national groups speak more than two hundred different languages. Trade and cultural contacts with her immediate francophone neighbours of Dahomey, Niger and Cameroon have been very slight, while similar ties with the more distant anglophone countries of Ghana and Sierra Leone are much stronger. This situation is likely to change in the future when French becomes as widely spoken as English.

With a population of about 56 million (1963), the Federal Republic of Nigeria is the most densely populated country in Africa. The area which is 356,700 square miles, about four times the size of the United Kingdom, is equally impressive; and so is the wide range of her natural resources which include groundnuts, cocoa, palm produce, rubber, petroleum and tin.

Physiographically, the country consists of several extensive plateau surfaces including the Jos Plateau, the Udi Plateau and the north central high plains. The coastal areas, including the Niger Delta, are covered with young soft rocks which are also common in the Niger-Benue trough and the Lake Chad basin. In most parts of the western state and the six northern states, the underlying rocks are very old and hard. Extensive plains with broad valleys and numerous hills, usually survivals of erosion called inselbergs, occur in areas of old hard rocks. These inselbergs occur singly or in groups and are to be found in various stages of disintegration. In the Igalla-Udi plateau area, which is underlain by young sedimentary rocks, several of these inselbergs have flat tops with a thick layer of indurated ironstone. Dome-shaped hills as well as long ridges, which resemble those of the Ilesha area, also occur in the plateau area around Nsukka.

Volcanic hills, consisting of the remains of extinct volcanoes appear in the Jos and Biu Plateaux, as well as in the Eastern borderlands. The craters of these extinct volcanoes are usually well-preserved and several of them contain crater lakes. The nearest active volcano is Mount Cameroon (13,350 feet), which lies just outside Nigeria. Another prominent landform is the Enugu escarpment,

Plate 1. Wading through floods caused by torrential rain at Abeokuta. In 1963 a similar flood interrupted for two weeks road transportation between Lagos and the rest of the country.

Plate 2. Weathered Inselberg on the Jos Plateau. This is a partially collapsed dome of Precambrean granite. Notice the scanty vegetation on the rock, the walled compounds at the foot of the rock and the grain fields in the foreground.

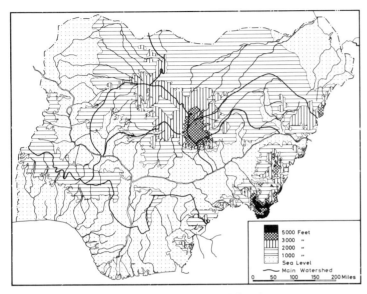

Figure 1. The Relief and Drainage of Nigeria

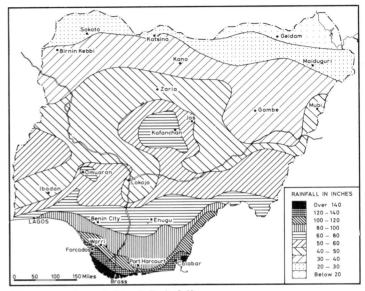

Figure 2. Annual Total Rainfall

which rises abruptly for about 600 feet above the Enugu plains, and whose slope is beautifully cut up by fast streams.

The River Niger, after which the country is named and the Benue, its largest tributary, are the main rivers. Both rivers rise outside the country but meet at the Lokoja confluence and later enter the Gulf of Guinea through a large network of creeks and distributaries which form the Niger Delta. A few short rivers flowing directly into the ocean, rise south of the Niger-Benue watershed; but all rivers draining the area north of Niger-Benue trough rise from the Jos Plateau. These rivers include the rivers Sokoto, Kaduna and Gongola, and rivers draining into Lake Chad. As in other parts of Africa, rapids and falls are common along Nigerian rivers and are partly responsible for the fact that navigation is not possible along certain parts of these rivers.

The climate is influenced mainly by two wind systems. These are the rain-bearing south-west monsoon, which blows from the ocean; and the dry, dusty north-east trades or harmattan which come from the Sahara Desert. There are two seasons: the rainy season and the dry season; the lengths of which vary from north to south. In the south, for example, the rainy season lasts for nine months (March to November), but in the far north, it lasts for only four and a half months (mid-May to September). Along the coast, where there is usually a short break in the rains, four seasons are usually recognized. These are the long rainy season (March to early August), the short dry season (August), the short rainy

season (September to early November) and the long dry season (mid-November to February). One important effect of this break in the rains is that it makes it possible for some southern farmers to grow two crops of maize in a year.

Rainfall is a critical factor in farming and delays in the onset of the rains have been known to cause crop failures and famine. The beginning of the rainy season is marked by great heat and destructive storms, accompanied by lightning. Crops as well as mat-thatched houses are often destroyed during these thunderstorms, when as much as one-and-a-half inches of rain may fall in less than one hour. The actual amount of rainfall (Figure 2) as well as the length of the rainy season decreases from south to north. It is also significant that the rains become less reliable as one moves northwards, away from the ocean.

Shade temperatures exceeding 100°F. have been recorded in the north-east, where frosts have also occurred during the dry season. Elsewhere, but particularly in the south, the temperatures are fairly constant (Table 1). The idea that the sun always shines very fiercely in Nigeria is inaccurate because during the rainy season, clouds usually hide the sun, while dust-haze plays the same role during the dry season. What makes the climate of Nigeria so trying is not the high temperatures, but the relative humidity which exceeds eighty per cent along the coast for most of the year.

The harmattan, which blows during the dry season, is a cold, dry and dusty wind. It brings about a considerable drop in the relative humidity, making the weather rather

Table 1 CLIMATIC DATA FOR SELECTED STATIONS

Station	Elements		Jan.	Feb.	Mar.	Apr.	May	June	July	Aug.	Sept.	Oct.	Nov.	Dec.	Year
Port Harcourt	Rainfall (inches)		1·2	2·3	5·0	7·5	9·9	13·3	12·9	12·3	15·5	10·7	5·5	1·8	97
	Temp. (° F.)	Max.	88·7	90·6	90·3	89·3	87·7	85·3	82·9	83·7	84·4	85·6	87·3	88·2	87·0
		Min.	72·7	73·5	74·5	74·5	73·8	73·4	72·7	72·2	72·7	72·7	73·1	73·1	73·3
	Relative Humidity (%)	6 a.m.	94	95	95	95	95	95	95	95	95	96	96	95	95
		12 noon	65	60	67	70	73	76	78	75	75	76	71	69	71
Lagos	Rainfall (inches)		1·1	1·6	3·8	5·6	10·8	18·1	11·1	2·7	5·5	8·1	2·7	1·0	72·0
	Temp. (° F.)	Max.	90·5	91·0	91·5	90·2	87·9	84·2	82·2	81·7	83·9	85·7	89·3	89·3	87·3
		Min.	69·8	72·6	73·1	71·7	72·1	71·2	70·0	69·7	70·5	71·0	71·7	70·9	71·2
	Relative Humidity (%)	6 a.m.	98	97	98	98	98	98	97	97	97	98	98	98	98
		12 noon	62	64	65	73	78	82	79	78	77	77	70	69	73
Enugu	Rainfall (inches)		0·7	1·1	2·6	5·9	10·4	11·4	7·6	6·7	12·8	9·8	2·1	0·5	71·5
	Temp. (° F.)	Max.	89·7	92·1	92·7	91·1	88·1	85·1	82·9	83·0	84·5	86·5	89·2	89·3	87·8
		Min.	72·2	73·3	75·0	74·8	72·9	71·6	71·5	71·1	70·8	71·0	72·6	72·1	72·4
	Relative Humidity (%)	6 a.m.	82	80	86	88	91	92	92	91	93	93	91	83	89
		12 noon	46	46	54	62	69	73	75	73	73	70	58	50	62
Ibadan	Rainfall (inches)		0·4	0·9	3·5	5·5	5·9	7·5	6·3	3·4	7·0	6·1	1·6	0·4	48·4
	Temp. (° F.)	Max.	91·2	93·5	93·9	92·4	88·8	85·6	82·2	82·1	84·7	86·7	89·5	90·3	88·5
		Min.	69·2	70·5	72·7	72·5	71·9	71·0	70·0	70·0	70·0	69·7	69·9	69·2	70·5
	Relative Humidity (%)	6 a.m.	94	92	95	95	96	97	97	97	97	98	97	96	96
		12 noon	51	49	54	60	67	74	78	78	75	79	63	56	65
Yola	Rainfall (inches)		0·0	0·0	0·3	1·9	4·9	6·2	6·8	7·7	7·8	3·2	0·2	0·0	39·0
	Temp. (° F.)	Max.	95·1	98·4	102·0	103·0	96·9	90·5	87·4	86·2	87·2	91·1	96·9	96·0	94·2
		Min.	65·2	69·4	75·5	78·8	76·1	73·4	72·4	72·5	71·5	71·9	67·5	65·1	71·6
	Relative Humidity (%)	6 a.m.	35	33	34	55	76	87	90	92	93	91	71	47	67
		12 noon	16	15	17	26	39	61	66	68	69	60	29	19	40
Jos	Rainfall (inches)		0·1	0·1	1·0	3·5	7·9	9·1	12·9	11·6	8·4	1·6	0·1	0·1	56·4
	Temp. (° F.)	Max.	82·1	85·6	87·2	88·5	85·0	80·9	76·4	74·9	78·6	82·2	83·4	82·4	82·2
		Min.	57·0	59·3	64·1	66·3	65·4	63·4	62·7	62·3	62·2	62·2	60·3	57·2	61·9
	Relative Humidity (%)	6 a.m.	33	40	45	66	83	92	95	97	96	86	51	40	69
		12 noon	14	17	18	24	46	62	71	76	63	45	21	17	39
Sokoto	Rainfall (inches)		0·0	0·0	0·0	0·4	2·0	3·5	5·8	9·3	5·7	0·5	0·0	0·0	27·3
	Temp. (° F.)	Max.	96·1	95·5	100·7	104·9	102·8	97·6	90·7	86·3	89·4	96·1	97·7	92·6	95·5
		Min.	59·6	62·9	70·2	76·2	78·6	76·4	72·5	72·1	71·6	70·5	64·3	59·8	69·6
	Relative Humidity (%)	6 a.m.	28	31	23	33	56	71	81	90	90	82	47	38	56
		12 noon	12	16	10	17	29	41	55	68	63	41	16	17	32
Kano	Rainfall (inches)		0·0	0·0	0·1	0·4	2·5	4·4	8·0	12·4	5·0	0·5	0·0	0·0	33·3
	Temp. (° F.)	Max.	85·6	89·9	95·7	100·8	99·3	94·5	87·2	85·1	88·0	93·5	92·5	87·1	91·6
		Min.	56·1	59·5	65·9	72·4	74·6	73·9	71·1	69·6	69·4	68·1	61·1	56·9	66·6
	Relative Humidity (%)	6 a.m.	37	33	31	42	63	74	88	94	92	80	48	43	60
		12 noon	13	12	12	19	32	46	60	71	61	36	15	12	32
Maiduguri	Rainfall (inches)		0·0	0·0	0·0	0·3	1·6	2·7	6·9	8·8	4·1	0·8	0·0	0·0	25·2
	Temp. (° F.)	Max.	88·9	92·9	98·2	104·1	102·1	97·4	89·4	85·6	89·4	95·3	95·1	90·3	94·0
		Min.	54·7	58·0	64·9	71·1	75·4	74·8	72·7	71·2	70·9	68·5	59·6	55·4	66·4
	Relative Humidity (%)	6 a.m.	48	41	34	32	53	73	87	94	93	83	60	56	63
		12 noon	17	13	11	12	25	40	60	69	59	37	18	20	32

Notes—For each station the data given are:

    (1) Mean monthly rainfall in inches
    (2) Mean daily maximum temperatures (° F.)
    (3) Mean daily minimum temperatures (° F.)
    (4) Mean relative humidity at 6 a.m. (%)
    (5) Mean relative humidity at 12 noon (%)

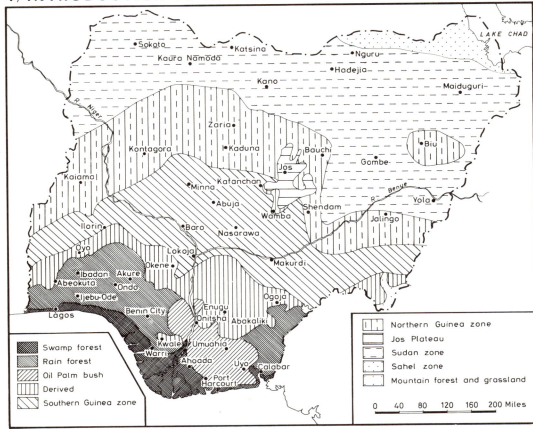

Figure 3. Vegetation zones

invigorating. Unpleasant aspects of this wind include very cold nights, cracked lips and furniture as well as thick deposits of dust all over the house. Bush fires, which are very destructive of woodland and occasionally of human settlements, are common during the harmattan.

In several districts, water for domestic use and for cattle is difficult to obtain during the dry season, when streams and wells may dry up. At this time of year, many villagers may travel three to seven miles to fetch water from the nearest stream. The water problem is particularly acute in the drier savannalands of the far north and in those parts of the south which are underlain by thick layers of porous sands. Water shortage during the dry season is responsible for the seasonal migrations of the cattle Fulani and his herd to the better watered districts of the Niger-Benue trough and the Lake Chad depression. Recent efforts to combat the water problem include the tapping of underground water resources through the digging of wells and pressure pumps, as well as the construction of puddle dams across streams.

The distribution of rainfall is the most important factor influencing the vegetation of Nigeria, although topography and ground water conditions are also of local importance. The east to west arrangement of the main vegetation belt (Figure 3) is clearly a reflection of the fact that the rainfall as well as the length of the rainy season decreases from south to north. Mangrove swamps and high rain forests which occur in the south, give way northwards to less dense forests and a progressively more open savanna vegetation. In the more densely settled parts of

the palm belt, the original high forest vegetation has been completely replaced by open palm bush.

Climate and parent materials are the most important factors influencing the character of soils, although slope is important in several localities. Soils developed on sandstones are usually less fertile than soils in areas underlain by rocks of the Basement Complex. Thus, although climatic conditions would permit cocoa cultivation over most of southern Nigeria, good cocoa soil is only to be found in areas of Basement Complex rocks. The limit of the cotton belt in the far north (Figure 7) is also set by soil conditions. Lateritic ironstone is common, except on the alluvium of river flood plains.

In various parts of the country overcropping, due to increasing demand for farmland, and overgrazing have resulted in soil impoverishment and soil erosion. Sheet erosion by wind and running water is widespread, particularly in the drier areas of the far north; but it is less spectacular and probably less destructive than gully erosion, which has laid waste vast areas of Sokoto, Katsina, Awka and Enugu provinces. Physical factors, including the torrential nature of the rains and steep slopes have also contributed to accelerated soil erosion.

Animals, both wild and domestic, vary with the vegetation belts with the exception of hippopotami, crocodiles, snakes, goats, sheep and chicken, which are to be found all over the country. In the forests of the south, monkeys, elephants and leopards are common; while several species of antelope and lion are found in the drier north. Cattle rearing is restricted to the far north because

Plate 3. (a) Savana landscape near Jalingo.

Plate 3. (b) A sand quarry near Lagos. The sandstone hill which is quarried for road building is one of the areas of high relief in this region of lagoons and swamps.

of the presence in the south and middle belt of the tsetse fly, which carries a deadly cattle disease called trypanosomiasis. A few dwarf cattle may, however, be found in parts of the midwestern and eastern states, where they are kept mainly for ritual purposes. Other domestic animals which are restricted to grassland areas are the horse, the donkey and in the far north, the camel. The famous Moroccan leather of the caravan trade across the Sahara Desert came from the red-skin Sokoto goat, which is let loose to fend for itself, unlike the more robust southern Nigeria goat, which is usually penned and fed.

THE PEOPLE AND THEIR WAYS OF LIFE

The 56 million people of Nigeria belong to many ethnic groups, each of which has its own customs, traditions, costumes and language. The larger groups are the Hausas, Fulanis and Kanuris in the north, the Tivs and Nupes in the middle belt, and the Yorubas, Ibos, Ibibios and Edos in the south (Figure 4). The greatest concentration of the smaller ethnic groups is in the middle belt, where the more isolated groups still lead a relatively primitive life. In pre-British days, the northern groups were organized into large states with an effective system of government; and so were the Yorubas and the Edos of the south. The Ibos and the Ibibios, on the other hand, were rather disorganized; the largest political grouping amongst them being the village-group. The extended family system was, however, a common aspect of the traditional society of all ethnic groups.

Less than ten per cent of the population live in towns which have more than 50,000 inhabitants; and most of these towns are concentrated in Yorubaland (Figure 6), where there are six urban centres with more than 100,000 people. Yoruba towns are all indigenous, as distinct from the new towns of the colonial period. The larger ones include Ibadan (627,000), Ife (111,000) and Ogbomosho (146,000). A few large indigenous cities such as Kano (295,000), Zaria (166,000) and Katsina (91,000) also exist in the north; but most towns in the middle belt and the eastern states, including Jos, Enugu and Port Harcourt,

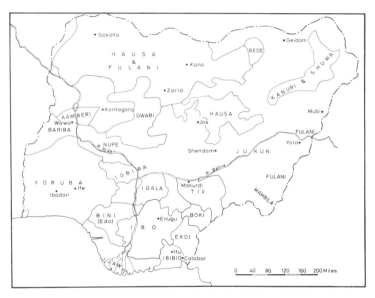

Figure 4. Major Ethnic (Tribal) Groups

Figure 5. Rural Population Density (1952/3 Census)

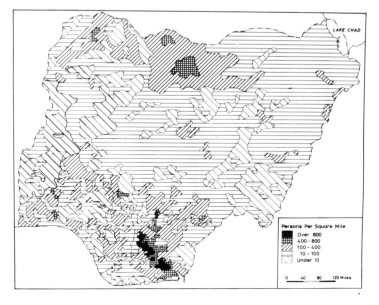

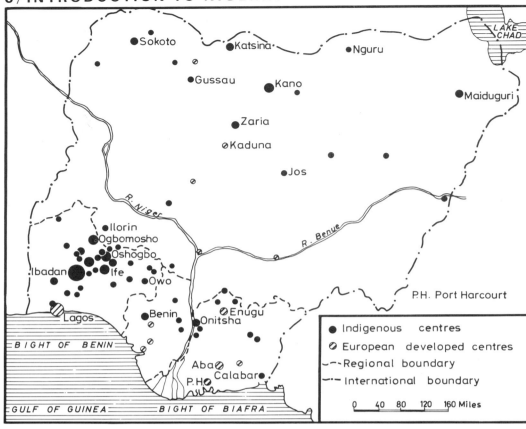

Figure 6. Urban Centres (1952/3 Census)

are creations of the colonial period. Several others including Ikot Ekpene and Umuahia are indigenous villages which were transformed into urban centres during the period of British rule.

The majority of Nigerians, therefore, live in rural villages in which the compound (Figure 31), which is an enclosure containing the houses of a man, his wives and in some cases the houses of his brothers, is the unit of settlement. Except in such large urban areas as Ibadan or Kano, the land area within the compound, as well as the immediate surroundings of the compound, is farmed every year. It is called the compoundland and is usually distinguished from the main or distant farmlands. The acreage of the compoundland which rarely exceeds a quarter of an acre is invariably smaller than that of the main farmland.

Islam is the predominant religion in the far north, but the south is predominantly Christian, although Moslems outnumber Christians in parts of Yorubaland. Christianity has also made great inroads into the middle belt, but by far the greater majority of Nigerians are pagans, worshipping several gods and practising polygamy.

Figure 5 gives an idea of the distribution of the population. The most densely settled areas are in parts of the Ibo and Ibibio areas of the eastern states, the central parts of Kano emirate, the immediate suburbs of Sokoto town and southern Tivland. These areas experience considerable pressure on farmland, such that many of the inhabitants are obliged to migrate to other tribal areas, where they rent and cultivate relatively large farms. The very sparsely settled areas of the middle belt, the lower

Niger valley and the cross river district are some of the centres of absorption of these migrant tenant farmers. There is also a considerable movement of people from rural areas into the cities, as well as to other rural areas such as the cocoa belt, the Jos tin fields and the Benin rubber belt.

Almost seventy per cent of the adult working population are employed in primary occupations of which farming is the most important. Land was formerly held in common by the village or the extended family; but today, individual land tenure is the rule in many areas. The land inheritance system is largely responsible for the extreme fragmentation of farmland, but it does not offer an adequate explanation for the small size of holdings cultivated; since farm sizes in several sparsely settled areas, with no land problem, are not necessarily larger than those in the overcrowded districts. Most farmers cultivate every year two or more holdings, each of which may be a mile or two away from the other. Food farms in the south rarely exceed one acre, but in the north, it is common to find farmers cultivating fields measuring two or more acres. One reason for this difference is that farms are less difficult to prepare in the open grassland areas of the north.

The traditional systems of bush fallows in which the farmland is rotated about a fixed settlement is still the rule, although permanent cultivation based on the use of household manure and crop rotation is practised in the Kano area and parts of the eastern states. Irrigated agriculture is of growing importance in the drier parts of the middle belt and the far north, but the development of mixed farming has been hampered by the fact that the

Commodity	Purchases (thousand tons)			Producer Price (£ per ton)			Producer Income (£ million)		
	1963/4	1964/5	1965/6	1963/4	1964/5	1965/6	1963/4	1964/5	1965/6
Cocoa	216	294	182	106	116	61	22·9	34·1	11·1
Seed cotton	129	131	127	41	46	47	5·7	6·0	5·0
Groundnuts	787	679	977	39	41	42	30·5	28·0	41·1
Beniseed	20	24	23	45	46	46	0·9	1·1	1·1
Soya beans	11	19	19	23	23	23	0·3	0·4	0·4
Palm oil	148	164	130	40	40	41	5·9	6·5	5·3
Palm kernels	401	449	416	27	27	28	10·8	12·1	11·6

SOURCE: Federal Office of Statistics Lagos

cattle population belongs to the nomadic Fulani who also take charge of the few cattle owned by the settled Hausa farmer. The need to obtain cash for tax, school fees and an increasing range of goods has induced the Nigerian farmer to produce for the market rather than for subsistence.

Table 3 PRODUCTION OF PRINCIPAL ECONOMIC MINERALS 1956/6

Year	Coal	Tin Ore	Columbite	Crude Petroleum	Natural Gas
	Thousand Tons	Tons	Tons	Thousand Tons	Million Cubic Feet
1956	787	12,507	2,604	—	—
1957	815	13,151	1,923	—	—
1958	925	8,412	806	256	—
1959	742	7,481	1,588	533	—
1960	562	10,374	2,047	837	5,095
1961	597	10,513	2,346	2,234	10,943
1962	624	11,096	2,264	3,274	17,179
1963	568	11,698	2,011	3,712	22,106
1964	688	11,785	2,339	5,859	36,333
1965	728	12,884	2,548	13,324	94,287
1966	630	12,566	2,221	20,668	101,582

SOURCE: *Annual Abstract of Statistics 1965* p. 37 Lagos

Like the rest of tropical Africa, Nigeria is poor in indigenous food plants, staples such as maize, cassava, groundnuts, some varieties of yams and several fruits having been introduced during the last two hundred years. Guinea corn and the oil palm are, however, indigenous food plants. Food habits vary with various ethnic groups, grains being the staple in the north, while root crops, such as yams and cassava, form the staple foods of the south. There is therefore a considerable internal trade in foodstuffs to meet the demands of migrant groups, such as the Hausa communities in Yoruba towns. There is also a considerable flow of foodstuffs from food surplus areas of the middle Niger valley and the Benin Forests to such food deficit areas as the cocoa belt and the Jos tin fields.

An increasing number of farmers earn their income from the sale of export crops, of which the most important are groundnuts, cocoa, palm produce, cotton and rubber (Table 2). In several countries, these crops are usually grown on plantations but in Nigeria, peasants control the production of agricultural exports. Indeed, almost all the plantations shown in Figure 7 were established after 1951, when the anti-plantation policy of the colonial administration was reversed. The contribution of the plantation to the country's agricultural export is, however, still insignificant.

The major economic minerals of Nigeria are tin ore, crude petroleum, coal and natural gas. Tin and coal have been mined for more than half a century but the exploitation of the delta oil fields (Figure 8) started during the late 1950's. Almost all the tin is exported, while the coal which is considered to be of poor quality is consumed locally. Petroleum is now the most important mineral and is of major importance as a foreign exchange earner. In 1966 the value of petroleum export was almost £92 million and this may be compared with figures for other exports (Table 11).

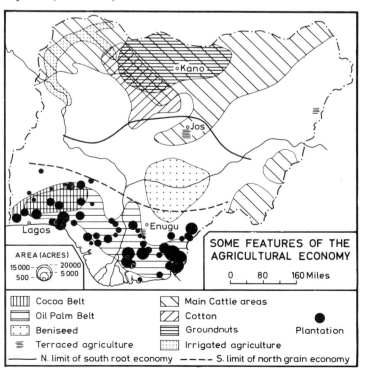

Figure 7. *Features of the Agricultural Economy*

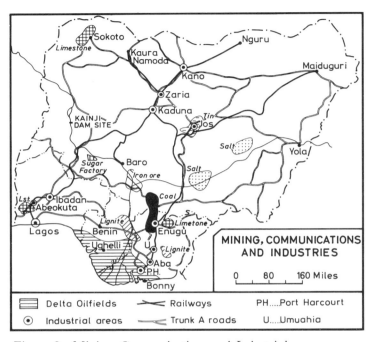

Key:

- Delta Oilfields — Railways — PH....Port Harcourt
- ⊙ Industrial areas — Trunk A roads — U....Umuahia

MINING, COMMUNICATIONS AND INDUSTRIES

0   80   160 Miles

Figure 8. Mining, Communications and Industrial areas

Nigeria's consumption of petroleum fuels is now met from locally refined crude oil, while an increasing amount of natural gas is being used for generating electric power for industry and lighting. The £85 million hydro-electric power plant at Kainji which is expected to go into production sometime in 1969, will produce enough power to meet the power requirements of the main industrial areas for another ten years.

Modern manufacturing industry is recent in Nigeria although a number of craft industries including weaving, pottery-making, and smelting of iron as well as glass blowing have been practised for several centuries in many parts of the country. The scale of operation of these cottage industries was small and almost every indigenous manufacturer suffered a setback following the importation of cheaper but better quality products from abroad. Immediately before and during the Second World War there was a flowering of modern small-scale manufacturers featuring the processing of local raw materials. Examples of these industries, which were financed by local capital, include the first soap-making factories at Aba, making use of the local palm oil; the making of rough cotton cloth in parts of northern Nigeria and the manufacture, in various parts of the Niger Delta, of gin from fermented palm wine.

Large-scale manufacturing industries started during the years immediately after the Second World War and have consisted mainly of import-substitution manufactures. The major manufacturing establishments have tended to concentrate on the production of food and drinks such as beer and soft drinks; meat processing and sugar refining; textiles and footwears, as well as light engineering, including vehicle assembly. The processing of local raw material has been largely for the home market, with the exception of tin smelting, rubber processing and oil-seed crushing; the products of which are largely meant for foreign markets. A wide range of products meant for the home market, but based on imported raw materials, include plastics, steel products, enamel-ware and gramophone records. Many other products like foam rubber, cement and textiles, also for the home market, are produced from local raw materials. The main industrial centres are shown in Figure 8.

THE BASIS OF REGIONAL DIVISION

It is quite clear that several fundamental differences exist between north and south in respect of the physical environment, social organization and agricultural practices. These differences, which derive partly from location relative to the sea and from historical antecedents, form the basis of the three-zone division of Nigeria, and indeed of the whole of West Africa, into the coastlands of the south, the Sudan in the far north and the middle belt which separates these two zones.

This three-zone division of West Africa into east-west macro-regions is particularly clear in Nigeria because of the latitudinal extent of the country from about $4\frac{1}{2}°$ N. to about $13\frac{1}{2}°$ N. Beginning from the south, the first major zone is the coastlands of Guinea which, by its location, comes under the full influence of the sea. Heavy rainfall exceeding 150 inches per annum in several parts and featuring a two-maxima regime is characteristic. The climax vegetation of this zone is high forest vegetation with mangrove swamps predominating along the coast. It is a zone of intense exploitation of forest resources, of large-scale expansion of tree-crops by peasants and lately, on commercial plantations. Nigeria's oil fields are located in this zone and so are her ports and major industrial establishments. This is the home of such large ethnic groups as the Yorubas, Binis, Ibos and Ibibios who together provide about three-quarters of the country's skilled man power. The coastlands are the most populous and most developed parts of the country.

North of the coastlands of Guinea lies a rather broad central zone or middle belt which extends from $7\frac{1}{2}°$ to 11° N. Aspects of its climate, vegetation and agricultural practices mark out the middle belt as a zone of transition between the coastlands and the Sudan. Its sparse population, poor communication and limited resources are the main factors which make the middle belt the poorest and least developed zone in the country. It covers about two-fifths of the area of Nigeria but has a population of less than one-fifth and, apart from tin, contributes very little towards the export trade of the country. The middle belt is, however, a major food surplus store with vast areas awaiting settlement and development. Its future appears to lie in the expansion of food, and fortunately climatic and ecological conditions permit the propagation of both the root crops of the coastlands and the grains of the Sudan. The post-independence period has witnessed the development of such large-scale projects as the Bacita Sugar Estate, the Niger Dams Project and the expansion of irrigated rice.

Finally, there is the northern zone or the Nigerian Sudan which has a relatively dry climate largely because of its interior location. The main concentration of the cattle population of the country occurs in this zone, which is the home of the nomadic cattle Fulani and the settled Hausa cultivator. The main concentrations of the human population are in the immediate vicinity of Sokoto, Katsina and Kano City. In pre-colonial days, the Nigerian Sudan was the most developed part of the country; a situation which was made possible by its long trade and cultural contact across the Sahara with the Mediterranean world and its relatively developed transport system featuring the use of the horse, the camel and the donkey. Today the Nigerian Sudan is the most important producer of groundnuts and cotton in the country.

Each of these macro-regions is divided into a number of smaller parts called geographical regions. The boundaries of each region are defined as a necessary introduction to the study of that region and will be found to include physical divides as well as cultural and economic divides. The regions are essentially cultural and economic in character, although such titles as the Niger Delta or the Jos Plateau may appear to emphasize the physical element. Each is a composite region in that there is considerable area variation in regard to relief, climate and ways of life. Yet each possesses a high degree of 'unity in diversity' and is in some ways different from other neighbouring regions.

Twenty regions are recognized and the reader will notice that nine of these are in the south, seven in the middle belt and four in the north, including the eastern borderlands. In terms of land area, the middle belt is the most extensive, but the south which has a much larger population and a much more developed and varied economy is areally more diversified. The north is a vast area but is culturally more integrated than the other two macro-regions. The physical landscape of the north is also more uniform in character; hence the recognition of only three regions, based on historical antecedents and the pattern of modern development.

Works consulted and suggestions for further reading:
1. Buchanan, K. M. & Pugh, J. C., *Land and People in Nigeria* London 1955
2. Floyd, B. N., 'The Federal Republic of Nigeria' *Focus* Vol. 15 No. 2 October 1964
3. Forde, D. & Scott, R., *The Native Economies of Nigeria* London 1946
4. Grove, A. T., 'Soil Erosion and populations problems in Southeast Nigeria' *Geographical Journal* 117 pp. 291–306 1951
5. Helleiner, G. K., *Peasant Agriculture, Government and Economic Growth in Nigeria* Homewood, Illinois: Richard Irwin 1966
6. Miller, R. R., 'The Climate of Nigeria' *Geography* 37 1952
7. Morgan, W. B., 'Agriculture in Southern Nigeria' *Economic Geography* 35 pp. 138–50 1959
8. Report on the Sample Census of Agriculture 1950–1 Lagos 1952

Part One The Coastlands of Nigeria

1 The Lagos Metropolitan District

The Lagos Metropolitan District is defined as the area served by the Lagos Municipal Transport Service. It consists of Lagos municipality and a number of suburban towns such as Shomolu, Mushin, Ikeja and Ajegunle which now constitute one continuous built-up residential area. Administratively, the municipality, which has a population of about 600,000, constitutes the Federal Capital of Nigeria, while the neighbouring suburbs with another quarter of a million people form part of the newly created Lagos State. As the principal seat of government and commerce, Lagos houses the head offices of most government departments and leading business firms, foreign embassies and international organizations. As Nigeria's premier and best developed port, Lagos handles about seventy per cent of the country's total imports and exports.

THE SITUATION AND SITE OF LAGOS

Lagos is situated on the far western part of the Nigerian coastline and is the nearest Nigerian port to America and

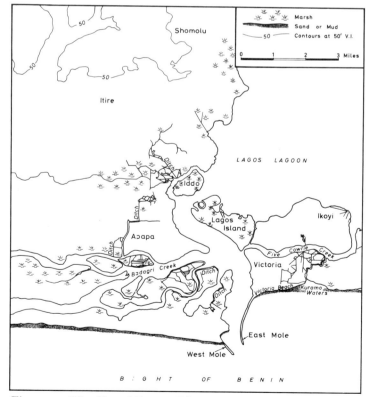

Figure 9. The Site of Lagos. The swamps on the mainland, in parts of Apapa and the islands of Lagos, Iddo, Ikoyi and Victoria have since been reclaimed

Western Europe. As the capital of Nigeria, its location has been strongly critized on the grounds that it is not central as compared with a place like Lokoja. It is however within easy reach by road, rail and air of various parts of the country and is likely to remain the financial and possibly the political metropolis of the country.

Lagoons, islands and sandbars are the dominant features of the physical landscape of Lagos and indeed Lagos was so named because of the lagoon system in the area. The lagoon and sandbar system extends inland for about twenty miles and dates from the late pleistocene times, when a rise in sea level led to submergence along the Nigerian coast. Submergence resulted in the drowning of the lower reaches of such rivers as the Ogun and the creation of an indented coastline and islands. The deposition of sandy materials brought by longshore drift led to the development of a sandbar which enclosed part of the seas to form the lagoon.

The site of Lagos is shown in Figure 9. The more prominent islands include Lagos Island, Iddo, Ikoyi and Victoria Islands. Iddo is linked to the mainland settlement of Ebute Metta by the Denton Causeway while all the islands are linked to one another by bridges, the longest being the Carter bridge linking Lagos to Iddo. Considerable parts of these islands remain flooded after heavy rainstorms but a series of drainage channels have successfully been used to keep dry a featureless area like Victoria Island which overlooks the open sea. West of the main entrance to the Lagos quays, the islands remain swampy and relatively uninhabited. Future reclamation of these areas cannot be ruled out although with the creation of Lagos State, Lagos can now expand landwards without encroaching on the territory of the Western State.

THE ORIGIN AND EARLY GROWTH OF LAGOS

The island city of Lagos, known locally as Eko, was founded more than 300 years ago by the Aworis, a Yoruba subgroup, who found the island to be a good defensible site. By 1880 the settlement, whose economy was initially based on fishing and farming on both Lagos and Iddo islands, had grown to become one of the leading slave ports of West Africa. Its location near to the only permanent break through the sandspit into the main lagoon along the Bight of Benin, and its position near to the war-torn Yoruba mainland which was a major source region for slaves, played an important part in its early growth. The natural handicaps of Lagos as a port at this time were considerable. The offshore bar at the mouth of the Lagos

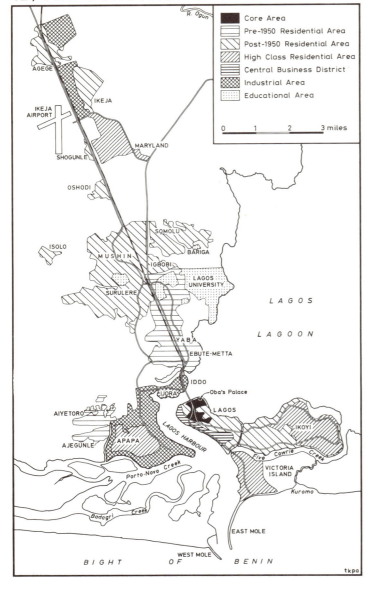

Figure 10. Urban Land use in the Lagos Metropolitan District

entrance restricted the carrying trade of the port until the early part of this century, when major development works were undertaken after Lagos had been selected as the terminus of the Western Railway.

In 1800 the population of Lagos, excluding Ebute Metta and other settlements north of the lagoon, was estimated at 5,000 but fifty years later Lagos, Iddo and Ebute Metta had a population of about 20,000. This rapid growth was due to the influx of freed Yoruba slaves from Brazil and Sierra Leone, as well as to the increasing number of domestic slaves kept in the town. The growth of Lagos has been even more rapid since the beginning of this century, increase through immigration being invariably greater than natural increase.

Like the city-states of the Niger Delta and the Calabar area, Lagos owed its early growth and prosperity to trade. In the words of Captain John Adams, an early trader in West Africa, it was 'the policy of the Lagos people, like

those of Bonny, to be themselves the traders and not brokers'. They therefore went in their canoes to Whydah, Badagry, and to towns like Ikorodu, Epe, Ejirin and Ikosi to purchase slaves, cloths and foodstuffs for sale.[1] The town benefitted considerably from the wealth and education of ex-slaves who had made good in Brazil and Freetown, but the impact of this group was not fully felt until after 1851 when King Kosoko, who was not favourably disposed toward them, fled the town as a result of British aggression.

THE GROWTH OF RESIDENTIAL DISTRICTS

The oldest residential district of Lagos lies to the north and west of Idumagbo lagoon. The Oba's palace, which overlooks Ebute Ero market, is located north of this lagoon. Like the old residential area south of Idumagbo lagoon and extending westwards to Alakoro, housing conditions in the district are very poor, Lagos Island still constituting one of the worst slums in Nigeria. It is still largely inhabited by Lagos indigenes and descendants of the freed slaves who immigrated from Brazil and Freetown. This is the only part of Lagos which has any semblance to the traditional Yoruba town, the palace and the Oba's market being located in the heart of the core area.

As the nearest low grade residential area to the Central Business District (CBD), the core area of Lagos is rather congested. Increasing demand for housing by the low income group has led to the construction of wooden or corrugated iron sheet structures in small spaces formerly left open. Like other low grade residential areas such as Shomolu, Mushin and Ajegunle, Old Lagos is characterized by narrow, confused lanes, access to many houses being through these winding footpaths which often serve as drains for household water. Housing conditions are generally so poor that in spite of its nearness to the CBD, rents remain the lowest in Lagos. Much of this area has been affected by the recent slum clearance scheme undertaken by the Lagos Executive Development Board.

In the spirit of Colonial Nigeria, the high grade residential areas of East Marina and Ikoyi grew up to house the colonial administrative staff. The first of these segregated residential areas was East Marina where the State House and the Prime Minister's residence are built and Victoria Island, which now provides the home for foreign ambassadors, may be regarded as a seaward extension of this

[1] Adams, John, *Sketches taken during ten voyages to Africa between the years 1786 and 1800* p. 27 London 1823

Plate 4. A View of Lagos Island. The Central Business district with its multi-storied buildings can be seen in the background.

residential area. Newer high grade residential districts include Apapa, Railway Compound, Itire Estate and Palm Grove Estate. Housing density at Ikoyi remains very low, some houses occupying as much as an acre of garden space. In the newer estates developed during the post-war years, there are more houses to the acre, although conditions here cannot be compared with the relatively congested medium grade residential areas of Yaba and Surulere (Figure 10).

In spite of the rapid expansion of the mainland residential areas of Ebute Metta, Yaba and Surulere, Lagos has found it impossible to accommodate all who work or provide essential services within the Municipality. Hence the growth of large suburbs like Shomolu, Mushin and Ajegunle, which until recently had the worst roads in the metropolitan area. The fact that until 1967 these suburbs were administered by the Government of Western Nigeria proved a great handicap in developing them or extending some facilities from Lagos municipality to them. Rather the suburbs became large slums and notorious hideouts for criminals and Indian hemp peddlers. The recent creation of the Lagos State will go a long way to eliminating some of the problems inhibiting the development of these suburban residential areas.

The newest residential areas include the Surulere Estate developed by the Lagos Executive Development Board (LEDB) for the purpose of resettling Lagosians displaced in connection with the slum clearance scheme in central Lagos. There are about fourteen houses per acre as compared with over twenty houses per acre in the low grade residential areas.

THE CENTRAL BUSINESS DISTRICT

The most impressive part of the city is the Central Business District (CBD), which includes all the southern part of Lagos Island. Its distinctive features include an increasing number of skyscrapers rising to over twenty-five floors and the great intensity of land use, particularly in the retail and administrative subdistricts. The retail subdistrict, which occupies the central portions of Broad Street and the Marina, is the heart of the CBD. It is usually congested during the daytime when thousands of shoppers and visitors come in from all over the Greater Lagos area as well as from distant cities like Ibadan, Abeokuta and Ijebu-Ode.

Other important functions of the CBD include wholesaling, financing, administration and education. There is the Anglican Cathedral of Lagos in this area and the Methodist Boys' High School and the Anglican Girls' School located along the east end of Broad Street. These institutions, which are more than one hundred years old, are now faced with the problem of traffic congestion and lack of space for expansion. At the same time, there has been a great increase in land and property value in the subdistrict. A few of these institutions have therefore sold their CBD sites and moved to the peripheral areas of the Lagos Metropolitan District. This development is matched by the expansion of the retail and administrative subdistricts, particularly in the slum clearance scheme area enclosed by Balogun, Nnamdi Azikiwe and Broad Streets.

Some of the functions of the CBD are also performed in a few outlying business centres including Idumota in Lagos Island, Iddo Island, Onyibo in Ebute Metta and Sabo in Yaba. Each outlying business centre, with the exception

Plate 5. Idumota Square, Lagos. Carter bridge, the first mainland bridge, appears in the background.

of Iddo Island, also has an open-air market, while street trading and small shops dominate the business life of the principal thoroughfares of Ereko and Nnamdi Azikiwe Streets.

INDUSTRIAL DEVELOPMENT IN THE GREATER LAGOS AREA

The greatest concentration of manufacturing industries in Nigeria occurs in the Lagos area where a number of industrial estates have been established since 1950. These estates constitute parts of the legislative encouragement meant to attract foreign investors, who are also given considerable tax concessions and reliefs. Other factors which explain the rapid growth of new and large industrial establishments in the Lagos area include the large reserve of semi-skilled and skilled labour, good transportation, a relatively high standard of available public utilities and a large local market.

In 1966 there were five industrial estates in the Lagos area and these were Apapa, Ijora, Yaba, Ikeja and Mushin, the last two of which are still owned by the Government of the Western State of Nigeria. The oldest of these is the 1,000 acre Apapa Industrial Estate located close to the harbour facilities at Apapa. Industries on this estate include automobile assembly, flour milling, metal windows and doors, paints, radio assembly and the manufacture of soaps and detergents. Most of the large-scale manufacturing establishments are located in the peripheral areas of Greater Lagos and since 1966 a number of factories including the Palm Kernel Crushing Mill have been established in the newly developing industrial site on the road to Ikorodu.

One of the most developed large-scale industries is the food and drinks, which employs a relatively high proportion of females. The large beer factory near Apapa was built about 1946 and has expanded so much during the post-independence period that it now employs about 680 persons. In addition to its main product, Star Lager Beer, this factory also produces mineral waters, orange drinks and, since 1966, Heinekens Beer. There are also a number of other factories producing drinks like Pepsi-Cola and Seven-Up. Another old industrial establishment is the large soap and margarine factory of the West African Soap Company which employs more than 700 workers. This factory produces about 20,000 tons of soap and 750 tons of margarine annually. Other industries include the motor vehicle assembly plants of C.F.A.O., A.G. Leventis and Co., B.E.W.A.C. and S.C.O.A. Motors, all of which are located at Apapa, the textile mills at Ikeja, steel fabricating plants and paints as well as cosmetics and pharmaceutical industries.

EXPANSION OF TRADE AND PORT DEVELOPMENT

During the early days of shipping along the Nigerian coast, Lagos was never considered to be an important port largely because of the offshore bar which blocked the entrance to its harbour. As early as 1505, Pereira described the Lagos entrance as 'really dangerous' and capable of admitting vessels of no more than thirty-five tons. The surf trans-shipment system used at the port was not only dangerous to life and property, but also costly in time and money. The importance of Lagos as a port started during the nineteenth century, when the lagoons of the Lagos area were used as hiding places for slave ships trying to avoid the naval patrol of the British West Coast Squadron. By 1850, Lagos had become so notorious as a slave port that the British decided on permanent occupation of the port.

The real turning point in the development of Lagos as a first class port started with its selection, in preference to Warri or Sapele, as the coastal terminal of the railway to the Northern States. This was followed by the construction in 1917 of moles designed to solve the problems of poor approach and entrance and since then, Lagos has grown to become the main focus of transport routes in the country. It is the main outlet for Nigeria's products to the world markets, its main exports consisting of cocoa, groundnuts, palm kernels, groundnut cakes, tin and columbite, cotton lint and seed, scrap iron and hides and skin. The main imports include iron, steel plates and bars, salt, textiles, chemicals, vehicles and flour. Beginning from 1964, over seventy-five per cent of the imports have been evacuated by road while the road is responsible for handling fifty-eight per cent of the exports.

Lagos is served by two quays—the customs quay which overlooks the Marina Street and was established about 1870, and Apapa quay. Apapa is usually identified as the port of Lagos. It has an 8,000 foot long wharf with a depth at low water of twenty-seven feet, nine berths, thirteen covered transit sheds for general cargo and railway facilities. By comparison customs quay, which has been losing traffic to Apapa since 1960, has a wharf 1,250 feet long, which provides three berths for general cargo and one berth for lighters, with a depth at low water of twenty-four feet, but has no railway facilities. Both quays are approached by a dredged channel having a draught of twenty-eight feet, the channel being protected by two moles—the 10,423-foot East Mole and the 5,175 foot West Mole. There is also a floating dock at Apapa which can accommodate ships up to 4,000 tons.

The port is administered by the Nigerian Ports Authority

Table 4 VALUE OF TRADE THROUGH LAGOS PORT 1954/64 (£ THOUSANDS)

YEAR	Exports		Imports	
	LAGOS	ALL NIGERIAN PORTS	LAGOS	ALL NIGERIAN PORTS
1954	87,233	149,532	79,143	114,069
1955	76,211	132,534	96,217	136,117
1956	74,589	134,573	108,691	152,770
1957	67,360	127,534	101,611	152,468
1958	70,241	135,550	112,926	166,274
1959	87,319	163,497	119,902	178,405
1960	83,685	169,714	150,226	215,891
1961	88,472	173,628	158,020	222,519
1962	81,709	168,536	145,489	203,217
1963	89,106	189,672	143,477	207,556
1964	103,304	214,650	171,933	253,880

SOURCE: *Annual Abstracts of Statistics 1965* p. 86 Lagos

Table 5 TONNAGE OF CARGO HANDLED AT LAGOS PORT (THOUSAND TONS)

YEAR	Exports (Cargo Loaded)		Imports (Cargo Unloaded)	
	LAGOS	ALL NIGERIAN PORTS	LAGOS	ALL NIGERIAN PORTS
1954	962	2,096	1,268	1,841
1955	1,000	2,248	1,538	2,252
1956	1,334	2,461	1,708	2,571
1957	1,011	2,314	1,787	2,590
1958	1,111	2,675	2,081	2,788
1959	1,262	3,048	2,107	2,910
1960	1,081	3,201	2,141	3,041
1961	1,272	4,831	2,299	3,187
1962	1,198	5,843	2,263	3,179
1963	1,303	6,297	2,203	3,126
1964	1,319	8,434	2,514	3,505

SOURCE: *Annual Abstract of Statistics 1965* pp. 60–1 Lagos

Note: Tonnage for crude oil exported from Bonny is included in total for all Nigerian ports

which was established in 1954, but shorehandling labour is supplied by private contractors. The handling of cargo is highly mechanized. Mobile cranes and duty forks are used for loading and offloading cargo, and in the warehouses bagged produce is stacked with the aid of powered mobile bag conveyors. The Atlantic Terminal at Apapa caters for passengers and provides such facilities as a modern waiting lounge, a refreshment bar and a customs baggage examination hall.

Most ships calling at Lagos are cargo liners drawing not more than twenty feet, although ships drawing twenty-five feet can now use the port. The tonnage handled has increased from a quarter of a million in 1911 to about three million since 1960. Tonnage handled has shown an overall increase over the years, but considerable variations have occurred in certain export commodities partly as a result of harvest conditions and partly as a result of delays in delivering cargo to the port of export. Until 1949, export tonnages were higher than import tonnages but the growing demand for machinery and construction materials during the last fifteen years has led to a rapid increase in import tonnages. Lagos also handles a considerable amount of coastal traffic which is likely to decrease now that large vessels can take full load at the Benin ports (see pages 42 and 60).

TRANSPORT PROBLEMS

The fact that Lagos Island, where most of the government offices and the department stores are located, is linked to the mainland where the bulk of the workers live by only one bridge, is the main cause of traffic hold-up during the rush hours. A second bridge costing £9 million was opened to traffic on 8 February 1969, and will go a long way to reducing congestion on the Carter bridge, although the increasing number of vehicles on the road might well frustrate the hope that the heavy and irritatingly slow rush hour traffic will be prevented. A monorail from Lagos to the suburbs has been proposed as a means of solving traffic congestion in the municipality.

One of the greatest problems facing the motorist in central Lagos is lack of parking space. The car parks provided by the City Council are inadequate and a time is drawing near when motorists will be obliged to leave their cars in mainland garages and take a bus to Lagos. There are several one-way streets and very few traffic lights.

Lagos is well served by taxis, most of which have meters. The Lagos Municipal Transport Service also operates a fleet of buses and air-charter services are available. The airport, which is located at Ikeja, is, however, rather removed from the town and is not served by Lagos buses. The railway terminus is located on Iddo Island which lies between Lagos Island and the mainland.

EDUCATION AND RECREATION

Primary education, which is free, is the responsibility of the City Council, which has built modern and well-equipped schools in various parts of Lagos. There are also several secondary and commercial schools most of which are run by private establishments including the Christian and Ahmadiya Missions. The University of Lagos, together with its large modern teaching hospital, was established in 1962. There is also a post-graduate law school and several public libraries.

The non-tidal Lagos Lagoon, which encircles Lagos Island, provides an excellent resort for sailing in small private craft. This is particularly true of the narrow lagoon separating Ikoyi from Victoria Island. Here small boats owned largely by foreign nationals working in Lagos can be seen plying every evening. It is the Victoria beach, however, which provides the most popular holiday resort both for the Nigerian population and foreigners.

In recent years, this excellent resort has been infested by numerous self-proclaimed prophets whose places of worship consist of open spaces enclosed by low mounds of beach sand. Signposts inviting passersby to take their worries and illnesses to these prophets, and small sheds constructed with palm fronds, constitute the main accessories to these praying sheds. Attempts by the City Council to eject these 'prophets', who appear to derive inspiration from the Atlantic waves and the sand of the sea coast, have so far failed.

Works consulted and suggestions for further reading:
1. Earl, A. K., 'Nigeria's Ports' *Nigeria Magazine* No. 72 pp. 27–30 March 1962
2. Mabogunje, A. L., 'Evolution and Analysis of Retail Structure of Lagos, Nigeria' *Economic Geography* 40 pp. 304–23 1964
3. Mabogunje, A. L., 'Lagos, A Study in Urban Geography' unpublished Ph.D. thesis University of London 1961
4. Ogundana, B., 'Lagos: Nigeria's Premier Port' *Nigerian Geographical Journal* Vol. 4 pp. 26–40 1961
5. Webb, J. E., *The Erosion of Victoria Beach: Its Causes and Cure* Ibadan 1960

2 The Creeks and Lagoons of South-western Nigeria

The maze of creeks, rivers and lagoons which provide a cheap and in some localities the only means of transportation, constitute the most distinguishing physical feature of the coastal areas of Yorubaland. Important features of the human geography of the region include its sparse population, the pattern and character of recent migrations into the area, and the great impact which Lagos is making on the development of transportation, as well as on the changing pattern of economic activities in the region. By definition, the region consists of the Colony Province, Ijebu waterside and the coastal area of Okitipupa Division of Western Nigeria, and represents only a part of the system of creeks and lagoons which borders parts of the West African coast.

Historically, the region has much in common with other coastal areas of West Africa, including the Niger Delta and the creeks bordering the Cross River estuary. The continued contact, for many centuries, of this region with European traders, has had similar effects on the local economy and traditional life as in the Niger Delta and Calabar region. Trading centres such as Badagry, Lagos and Epe remind one of the Ijaw city-states of the Niger Delta or the Efik trading settlements along the Calabar River. But unlike these two other areas, which have suffered considerable loss in population during the last fifty years, the creeks and lagoons area of western Nigeria has been gaining population, and is currently witnessing considerable growth in its economy. Further investigations reveal that this situation is largely a result of the rapid growth of Lagos, which provides an adequate and growing market for primary products from the rural parts of this region.

THE PHYSICAL LANDSCAPE AND CLIMATIC CONDITIONS

The creeks and lagoons area of western Nigeria is a low-lying region with a general elevation of about 100 feet above sea level, rising to over 150 feet along the northern boundary. A coastal strip of fine unconsolidated sand fronts the open sea and seen from the air, this strip stands out clearly as an open sandy tract which is completely devoid of vegetal cover. The sands give way to silty soil and swamps with considerable vegetation as one approaches the southern edge of the lagoons. West of Epe, the width of the land area separating the lagoons from the open sea exceeds ten miles, but in scme places such as the stretch between Badagry and the Lagos entrance it is only about one mile. A few miles away from the swampy and low-lying area immediately north of the lagoons, the land becomes much firmer, and is closely dissected by the rivers draining southwards into the region.

This region is often described as a featureless plain but there is considerable variation in the topography of the area east of Ikorodu town. The road from Ikorodu to Ijede for example passes through a dissected sandstone tract and is characterized by steep gradients which are completely absent in the Lagos and Badagry areas. The lagoonside at the now disused Ikorodu beach market, where the land rises very gently from the water's edge, contrasts markedly with the steep rise at Ijede, where a sandstone cliff overlooks the Lagos lagoon (Figure 11). Compared with the swampy land west of the Lagos lagoon, the Ikorodu-Ejirin area which consists of firmer land provides more varied scenery and better soil conditions.

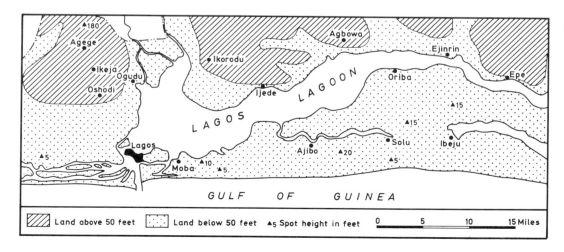

Figure 11. Relief of the Lagos Lagoon Area

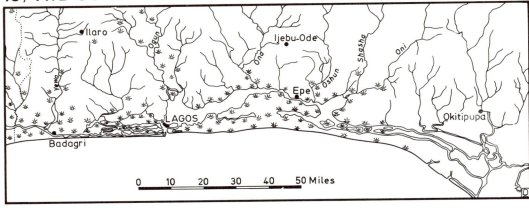

Figure 12. Drainage of the Lagoon and Creeks Area of South-Western Nigeria

One of the main physical characteristics of this region is its poor drainage (Figure 12). Excepting such major rivers as the Ogun, Oshun and Shasha which flow directly into the lagoons, the numerous short streams draining this region get lost in the freshwater swamps north of the lagoons where they wander about as a system of creeks. The delta formation at the mouth of the Ogun, which empties into the Lagos lagoon, confirms the difficulties the rivers encounter in traversing the zone.

Towards the middle of the rainy season, that is about the month of August, when the rivers overflow their banks, the countryside presents an even duller landscape following the submergence of the riverside vegetation of grass and shrubs. The footpaths linking the various farm huts to one another, as well as to the main roads or lagoonside, become inundated, thereby increasing the degree of isolation.

The Lagos lagoon is the most extensive of the lagoons of this region and constitutes an important waterway for the surrounding villages and farmsteads. Its depth is generally below ten feet, being much deeper in the west, but rather shallow east of Lekki, where the lagoon narrows down to assume the character of a creek. The depth of water varies with the season of the year, while certain parts of it are known to be silting up rapidly.

Soil types throughout the region are closely related to parent materials. Porous sandy soils occur along the narrow stretch of the coastal zone which is bare of vegetal cover, except for the plantations of coconut palms which occur on the landward side. Further inland, the sandy coastal strip gives way to a densely forested zone of mangrove swamps in which the soil is often masked by undecomposed leaf fall. Both the northern and southern border of the lagoons have clayey and muddy soils which support lowland rain forest and very dense stands of the oil palm. This soil type provides the most fertile and most cultivated land in the region and it is along the lagoon sides that numerous migrants settle to cultivate cassava on a large scale for the Lagos markets.

In Okitipupa Division the creeks or waterside areas are aptly referred to as Igbekun which means 'beside the sea', and their surface features and economic pattern contrast markedly with those of the mainland. Okitipupa itself, like Ikeja and Abia, is located in the drier mainland which carries out a considerable trade in local foodstuffs with the Waterside areas.

The whole region has a very rainy climate which only goes to worsen the soil conditions in the waterside areas, where there is already a superabundance of surface water. The rains come mainly between May and September, July being the wettest month. Compared with the Niger Delta and the coastlands of the South-eastern State, the rainfall which ranges from eighty to one hundred inches is not too heavy. The only months when the rainfall is less than four inches are December, January and February. The short dry season or August break which occurs all over southern Nigeria is particularly marked in this region.

Soil conditions are largely responsible for areal differences in the vegetation of this region. Mangrove forests grow along the banks of lagoons and creeks which are washed by brackish water while freshwater swamp forest dominates the freshwater swamps along the Lagos-Ikorodu road. Unlike the rainforest belt further inland, the freshwater swamp forest presents a very irregular and broken appearance, featuring dense growth of trees separated by extensive gaps of open grass and shrubs on seasonally flooded land. Patches of open water are not uncommon even during the dry season. In the immediate hinterland of Lagos, the vegetation of the flood plains has been completely altered as a result of intensive cultivation of market garden vegetables.

Extensive communities of the raffia palm dominate the banks of some creeks in the freshwater swamp zone in much the same way as the coconut palm is the dominant tree along the Atlantic coast. The freshwater swamp zone also supports a considerably dense growth of oil palm trees, but these palms are rarely exploited since their fruits are considered to yield much less oil than palms growing wild in the rainforest belt. Of the three palms, the coconut palm appears to be the most important in the economy of the creeks and lagoons area. Thus, while the oil palm and the

Plate 6. A View of West Mahin creek. Notice that the water surface is almost totally hidden from view by dense growth of aquarian plants.

raffia palm grow wild in the swamps, several farmers have established extensive coconut plantations along the sand-spit fronting the open sea.

POPULATION AND SETTLEMENT

One of the most striking features of the distribution of population in this region is the greater concentration of people in the west, that is the area between the Dahomey border and the Lagos lagoon, and the relative emptiness of the central area (between Lagos lagoon and the Lekki lagoon) and the eastern area. Both the coastal strip and the banks of creeks and lagoons appear to provide the most favourable sites for settlement, particularly in the Ilaye District of Okitipupa where fishing is the dominant economic activity. The great diversity in the ethnic composition of the population is also significant and is partly explained by the fact that this region, as a pioneer fringe, has attracted population from various parts of the Yoruba mainland, from the territories of Old Benin as well as from the fishing tribes of the coastlands stretching from Ghana to the Cross River estuary. The mainland areas of Okitipupa District, for example, are settled by Ikale Yorubas and people of Benin descent, while the waterside areas are settled by Ilaye Yorubas and Eastern Ijaws.

Ijebu Yorubas dominate the central areas where a number of Binis, as well as Ewes and Kitas from Ghana

and Dahomey are to be found. Ijaws from the delta are also found as far west as the Badagry district and in recent years there has been an increasing influx of Urhobos, Ibos and Ibibios into the creeks and lagoons region of south-western Nigeria. In Ikale and the Bini confederation districts of Okitipupa, Urhobo migrant farmers make up about half the population of 94,000 and 13,000 respectively (1953 census figures).

Most of this region appears to have been settled only in the recent historical past. The earliest settlements such as Badagry, Epe and Ketu Agbowa were founded during the early part of the eighteenth century, but the bulk of the population as well as most of the existing settlements are associated with immigration during the present century. The present concentration of population in the area west of the Lagos lagoon is also a recent development, dating from the first decade of this century. About 1850, the main concentration of population was in the Epe District, not around Ikeja or the Badagry region which had suffered considerably from slave raids and economic decline. In 1851 there was a sudden drop in the population of Badagry and its environs following the decline in the slave trade and the collapse of the local trade in palm oil. British operations in Lagos during the same period also led to the migration of King Kosoko and a large number of Lagosians into Epe in 1851. Today, population movement is directed mainly towards Lagos and the Lagos area.

Before 1900, many of the settlements established south of the main lagoon between Lagos and Lekki were founded by political refugees. Sites which were not easily approached from the Yoruba mainland or easily defensible sites appeared more suitable to the refugees whose main consideration at the time was security rather than economic. Some of these refugee settlements are Oriba, Lekki, Ibeju, Ajiran and Ikate. Ikosi and a few other settlements on the mainland side of the lagoon are also said to have been founded by Ijebu refugees fleeing from Epe, after an open conflict between the Ijebu and the Lagos Yorubas resident at Epe Town. Since 1900, the motive for migration into the areas south of the main lagoon has been primarily economic and unlike the past, non-Yorubas constitute a very large proportion of the migrants.

Lagos (600,000) is by far the most important settlement in the region. The next class of settlements is the small towns with population ranging from 5,000 to 40,000 persons. Badagry, Ikeja, Ikorodu, Epe, Agege and Okitipupa are some of the more important of these small towns which serve as collecting and service centres for the surrounding districts. An important feature of these towns is that they are all located north of the main lagoon and therefore have direct road contact with the Yoruba mainland and Lagos.

The tendency for particular ethnic groups to congregate in separate quarters of a village or town, as well as in distinct hamlets and camps arises from the fact that certain ethnic groups have come to be identified with particular economic activities. Ijaws, Ewes and Kitas who engage mainly in sea fishing often settle in small hamlets and fishing camps located along the sandy tract fronting the Bight of Benin; while Ilayes, Ijebus and some Ijaws who engage mainly in creek and lagoon fishing live in small hamlets and villages located along the lagoons and creeks. The small farm camps, which have between two and fifteen inhabitants and tend to be temporary in character, are occupied mainly by the Urhobos and Ibos who cultivate cassava and collect firewood for the Lagos market in addition to their dominant economic activity, which consists of harvesting and processing palm fruits for oil as well as tapping and selling palm wine. The mainland villages, on the other hand, consist of quarters occupied by Hausas engaged in the kola trade as well as Igbirras, Ibos and Yorubas who constitute the main source of hired farm labour. Many of the smaller settlements or camps are deserted during the flood season when all but the highest land is inundated.

The new settlements of Ugbonla and Aiyetoro, founded during the Second World War by religious sects of the Christian faith are an interesting development in the settlement history of the waterside area of Okitipupa District. Ugbonla which was founded by the Cherubim and Seraphim sect has been described as a neat and well-planned town with a large church and community school built by community effort. Like Aiyetoro, which was founded by another sect, the Holy Apostles, it has a sound economy based on fishing and is a communistic society in which all earnings go to a central purse.[1]

Houses erected on stilts are a common feature in this region of swamps and creeks. Mud houses are common in the mainland area of the region but in the waterside areas, walls of houses are usually made with bamboos. In the more permanent settlements such as the apostles' town of Ugbonla, corrugated iron sheets are often used to roof even bamboo huts.

THE GROWTH AND DECLINE OF BADAGRY

Badagry[2] (6,000) is one of the smaller towns located on the north bank of the main lagoon; and therefore has direct contact by road with Lagos and the rest of the country. It was founded in the late 1720's by Popo refugees who had been forced into the creeks by the Fons of Dahomey, during the latter's drive to subjugate the coastal settlements so as to have free access to the salt pans as well as to European traders at the coast. Like other coastal towns such as Bonny and Calabar, Badagry was favourably located to handle the trade in slaves which, during its first hundred years of existence, was to dominate all other economic activities in the town and environs. Like Bonny, but unlike Calabar, Badagry depended on outside sources for most of its food supply owing largely to the limitation imposed on food farming by the barren and sandy soil of the locality. This was a major weakness which hastened the destruction of the town in 1784, after a short siege by the Fon people of Dahomey.

Regular raids by the Fon tribesmen ended about the turn of the century, after which Badagry started to recover as a slave port, and later as a trading centre for palm oil and imported cloth. In 1851, the town was again attacked and much of it burnt down after some quarrel with the king of Lagos. This attack, followed by persistent threat of revived hostility from Dahomey, led to a large-scale exodus of traders, missionaries and ordinary citizens to Lagos. Hence the rapid drop in the population of the town from about 12,500 in 1800 to less than 2,000 in 1851.

[1] Duckworth, E. H., 'A visit to the Apostles and the Town of Aiyetoro' *Nigeria Magazine* No. 36 1951

[2] Hodder, B. W., 'Badagry I: Slave Port and Mission Centre' *Nigerian Geographical Journal* Vol. V No. 2 p. 75

Since then, the population of the town has increased gradually to 6,000 in 1911, but declined to 5,970 in 1952. The recent decline of the town is due to the growing influence of Lagos on the whole of this region of lagoons and creeks.

At the same time the rural population of Badagry District has shown considerable increase since 1931, as a result of immigration of tenant farmers. The number of settlements has also increased and the tendency has been to establish small settlements of less than one hundred persons. Settlements showing a decrease in population during the last sixty years are generally those located immediately north and south of the main lagoon while settlements on the mainland show an increase in population. This is partly explained by the decline in the carrying trade of the lagoons as well as the growing emphasis on food farming at the expense of fishing.

The tribal composition of Badagry town is still predominantly Popo although up to a third of it is now Yoruba. Housing in many quarters still keeps to the form which prevailed more than a century ago, walls of bamboos with roofing of thatch or iron sheets. The tarring of the road from Lagos to Badagry has brought great opportunities to the town which is likely to be developed into a tourist centre and seaside resort.

RUDIMENTARY IRRIGATION IN BADAGRY

A visit to a number of vegetable farms in the immediate outskirts of Badagry and cassava farms on the sandy island separating Badagry lagoon from the open sea will convince any one that farming cannot be highly developed in an area with such poor soils. The development of vegetable gardens which are watered by hand scoops is therefore of great interest to the geographer. Onions, garden eggs, water leaves (*Talinum triangulare*) are the most common vegetables cultivated in the fields which consist of a large number of raised flat-topped mounds, each with a surface area of about one hundred square yards. The mounds which are about three feet above the ground have irregular shapes and are separated by narrow paths. Each mound is built up with sand from pits dug nearby

Plate 7. A Street in the Holy Apostles town of Aiyetoro. Both the houses and the street are raised on stilts. Both the bamboos used for the walls and the mats used for the roof come from the raffia palm.

to provide water for irrigation and since the water table is very close to the surface, such pits rarely exceed three feet in depth.

The flat mounds, when completed, consist of sand rather than soil. A thick carpet of grass is laid on it and covered lightly with sandy soil after which the crops are sown. A large-scale application of manure including human waste helps in raising good crops which are watered from time to time by a man standing in the water pit with a small basin which he uses to transfer water on to the vegetable mounds. The porous nature of the mounds demands frequent watering and it is fortunate that the water supply is obtained on the spot.

It is quite clear that the limiting factor to the expansion of irrigation in the Badagry area is the poor soils rather than availability of water. The black colour assumed by some of the soils under damp conditions is deceptive and is not an indication of a high humus content usually associated with dark soils. Rather, on exposure to the sun, the soils turn grey and dusty. Some muturu cattle are kept but they are too few to provide adequate manure for the expansion of this primitive form of irrigated agriculture.

ASPECTS OF THE CHANGING AGRICULTURAL ECONOMY

The last hundred years have witnessed considerable changes in the pattern of economic activities in the creeks and lagoons area of south-western Nigeria. During the days of the slave and palm oil trade, settlements like Badagry and Epe, but particularly those located south of the main lagoon, depended largely on food produced on the mainland. The inhabitants of the creeks concentrated on fishing which yields more immediate returns than cropping. But in recent years agriculture has assumed an increasing role in the growing economy of the region and today, food production is a highly commercialized venture featuring the cultivation of maize and cassava, as well as a number of market garden vegetables destined for the Lagos urban market. This remarkable change has been brought about by the demands of the ever growing population of the greater Lagos area.

By 1865, much of Colony Province had come under the direct administration of the British, who made great efforts to develop coconut cultivation on a commercial scale. In 1887, coconut nurseries were established in the Badagry area and in spite of the destruction of young palms by

tornadoes and pests, a number of coconut plantations were successfully established. New plantations of coconut trees abound in the Lekki area; and in many parts of the central and eastern parts of the region, farming consists of growing coconut and cassava for sale in Lagos. A pilot factory for producing coir fibre from coconut fruits was established in Badagry in 1960, and when fully developed will probably lead to a further expansion of coconut culture in the area.

Crop combinations, field sizes and intensity of cultivation vary with distance from Lagos. Cassava and maize are by far the most important crops throughout the region but between Lagos and Ikorodu and about the same distance east and west of Lagos, market gardening, horticulture and commercial production of flowers feature prominently in the farming system. Holdings are small and often located along the banks of the main river valleys. The observant traveller will not fail to notice the intensity of the cultivation of the Ogun river floodplains on both side of the Lagos–Ikorodu road. In some cases, these crops are cultivated in very large estates which supply the main department stores in the city. Such large farms, which may exceed ten acres, are often joint vegetable and poultry farms and are usually owned by well-to-do Lagos citizens who run the farms exclusively by hired labour. Tomatoes, cabbages, pineapples, okro (*Hibiscus esculens*), pawpaw, ewedu and bananas are some of the crops produced on these farms and gardens. Maize and cassava, the staples of the region, are also important.

In the middle and far east of the area lying between Lagos and the Benin River, agriculture becomes more extensive, field sizes are larger and instead of permanent cultivation practised along the river valleys near Lagos, the common-place system of the rotation of bush fallows predominates. The farms feature such crop combinations as cassava, maize and melon or cassava and maize and rarely yam, beans and vegetables. Tree crops feature prominently immediately north of the main lagoon, kola being the main crop.

Rice production on the swamps bordering the lagoons and creeks has started, but the quantity produced is as yet insignificant and is sold almost entirely in the local markets of Epe and Okitipupa. The swamps, however, offer great prospects for the expansion of rice culture; hence the present efforts of the Western Nigeria Ministry of Agriculture to popularize the cultivation of swamp rice.

Many of the food farmers in the creeks and lagoons region are strangers who have migrated into the area for the sole purpose of cultivating food crops as well as exploiting the wild palm-trees growing all over the region. North of the main lagoon, these migrants who are mainly Urhobos and Ibos, combine crop farming with the exploitation of palm fruits but tend to concentrate on food crop production in the areas south of the lagoon where cassava is the main crop.

According to Daryll Forde, Isoko migrants in Ijebu waterside area paid an entrance fee of six shillings in addition to an annual rent of fifteen shillings in 1950, at which time the rent in Ikale District of Okitipupa was thirty shillings per annum; excluding an entrance fee of ten shillings. Field enquiries in 1965, in the Epe area, revealed that Isoko migrants still dominated the creek oil palm industry, but that the rents in this area had gone up to between twenty and thirty pounds per annum depending on the size of the area and the number of palms within the area allocated to the migrant tenant.

Double cropping, which is made possible by the local climate, is one of the most distinguishing features of food farming in the region. The two cropping seasons are January to March and August to September. Maize is invariably the first crop on newly cleared farmland except when groundnuts are grown, while cassava is planted just before the land reverts to fallow. New farms may be cleared either in January to March or August to September and so young plants of both maize and cassava are to be found in both seasons. Yam is rarely cultivated except by Urhobo and Ibo migrants whose yam crops are for domestic consumption rather than for the Lagos markets. Lagos therefore receives its yam supplies from outside this region.

In the face of all these changes, farming implements have remained primitive. The short-handled hoe is still in vogue and the traditional system of bush clearing and firing remains intact. Prospects exist for mechanized cultivation of rice in the area south of the main lagoon and of tree crops in the area bordering the Yoruba mainland.

FISHING ACTIVITIES AND ASSOCIATED CRAFT INDUSTRIES

In spite of growing emphasis on the production of food-crops, fishing remains the most important economic activity in the region. It involves greater capital invest-ment than farming, but has come to be preferred largely because fishing is a ready cash earner, whereas the farmer has to wait many months before his crops are ready for harvest and sale. The quantity and variety of fish caught

have increased over the years owing to the adoption of improved fishing techniques and the growing importance of sea fishing. At the same time, the market area for dis-tribution of fresh fish caught in the region has extended to include such inland consuming centres as Ibadan, Ife, Oshogbo, Ondo and Ijebu-Ode.

Like market garden vegetables, fresh fish is highly prized in the Lagos metropolitan area and is equally perishable. The main areas supplying fresh fish to Lagos are therefore similarly restricted to within twenty to twenty-five miles. Beyond this zone the bulk of the fish caught is smoked, although a sizeable amount is sold fresh to Epe and Ikorodu markets for transmission to the mainland towns.

Fishing is carried out either as a full-time job or on a part-time basis. In the past people engaged in lagoon and sea fishing were essentially full-time fishermen while those who fished in the creeks did so on a part-time basis. At present the situation is not as simple as that, since many lagoon and sea fishers have turned part-time, following the growing emphasis on the cultivation of coconuts and food crops. The seasonal character of the fishing industry, which is a result of marked fluctuations in the level of water in the creeks and lagoons, has also contributed to the increase in the number of part-time fishermen.

Although the local inhabitants of the region have become increasingly interested in sea fishing, the broad division in which people from particular ethnic groups are associated with creek, lagoon or sea fishing still remains. In the district which supplies fresh fish to the Lagos market, for instance, the Ewes and Ketas of Ghana are the main sea fishermen while the Ijaws, Ilajes and Ijebus fish mainly on the lagoons but also on the sea. Creek fishing in this area is restricted to migrant farmers who only take to fishing as a spare time occupation.

Improvements in the fishing industry have taken the form of adoption of better fishing methods, the use of bigger vessels and improved means of transportation of fish from the fishing grounds to the consuming centres. Cast nets, set nets and hook-and-line are the most popular fishing equipment in use; although the use of fish traps and sudd-cutting are common in the swamps. Larger and powered canoes are now in common use both for fishing and for transporting the fish.

In Okitipupa and other distant areas, the fish caught are smoked by fishermen who live in huts having two partitions—one for sleeping and the other for smoking the fish. But in the Lagos area and as far east as Epe, women traders who dominate the distribution of fish in the main-land markets take canoes or send representatives to the creeks to buy fish which they smoke before transporting to Ibadan, Ijebu-Ode and Lagos. Lesser middlemen traders at Ibadan are often seen smoking fresh fish from Epe, Ikorodu or Lagos in the open market-place.

Those who concentrate on sea fishing generally fish in groups of four or more. Group fishing was also a feature of creek and lagoon fishing in the past, but the tendency today is for people to fish individually, since many of them now combine fishing with farming. What is needed today is the establishment of co-operative societies which will, amongst other things, make it possible for fishermen to use more efficient and modern equipment, which will make for increase in the quantity of fish caught per man. Such fish co-operatives will also aid in the efficient marketing of fish to the mutual benefit of both the fishermen and the consumers.

COLLECTING FOREST PRODUCTS

In addition to harvesting and processing oil palm fruits, Isoko migrants, as well as the local Yoruba population, earn some cash by collecting firewood, charcoal and building poles for sale in the Lagos markets. These products are in great demand in the Lagos area by the low income groups, who cannot afford to cook with electricity or gas. Bundles of wood cut from the forests and swamps of the region are commonly seen piled up along motorable roads awaiting shipment to Lagos. Other forest products which feature in the collecting economy include leaves for wrapping cooked food for sale, and a special type of leaf for preserving kola nuts. These leaves are collected mostly in the areas south of the main lagoon and are ferried by canoes to Epe, Ikosi and Ejinrin to be loaded into lorries bound for Ijebu-Ode, Mamu and Shagamu and other important kola markets.

Collecting forest products is a part-time occupation. Isoko migrants are known to restrict this activity to the morning hours, that is before going on to do the day's job of farming or processing palm fruits, or in the evening after the day's farm work. The peak collecting period is between October and December, which is the slack season in the farming calendar. During this time of the year those engaged in collecting are known to earn between two and four pounds every week depending on the particular product collected.

The creeks also provide an important product in the form of building sand which is collected and transported by tippers to the main towns. Heaps of sand collected for use in the Lagos area may be found along the creeks on both sides of Ikorodu road. The collectors usually go far out into the creeks where they dive to collect the sand which is loaded into canoes for delivery to the collecting base.

THE DEVELOPMENT OF TRADE AND TRANSPORTATION

As in the Niger Delta, differences in economic activities and the products obtained from the waterside areas and the mainland led to an early trade contact between the two zones. The only means of transportation at the disposal of the waterside people at this time was canoe transport, while the people of the mainland depended on human porterage along the numerous footpaths which still exist in the region. Commercial production of fish and cassava started on a large scale in response to the growing urban markets of Lagos. The lagoons and creeks remained the main trade route to the Lagos markets from such distant producing centres as Okitipupa District and Ijebu waterside. Today, these creeks and lagoons are still used in transporting goods to Lagos but much of the passenger traffic as well as food products destined for Lagos are transported by road.

The period after the Second World War witnessed a remarkable development not only in road transport, but also in water transport, which is still important for ferrying goods from the waterside areas to the road termini at Ikorodu, Epe, Okitipupa and Badagry, as well as for direct haulage to Lagos. Improvement in water transport has been in the form of introducing powered motor boats and launches which operate fast passenger services between the main settlements in the region. Dredging and sudd clearance along the major creeks have been carried out to allow tugs to pull heavily laden barges plying between Lagos and Okitipupa or Sapele. These large barges often carry palm produce and timber to Lagos from the Mid-west and Okitipupa, while the return cargo includes hardware, building materials and other imported articles from Lagos.

A considerable decline in water transport to Lagos followed the opening in 1953 of the Lagos-Ikorodu road which also made it possible to travel by road from Epe to Lagos. This was followed by the tarring of existing roads including the Epe to Ijebu-Ode road in 1956, the Agbowa to Shagamu road in 1956 and the Agbowa to Ikorodu road in 1958. Transportation from various parts of the region to Lagos became much quicker and, surprisingly, also cheaper by road than by water. A journey from Ikorodu to Lagos (twenty miles), for example, costs from ninepence to one shilling by road and takes about thirty-five minutes as compared with two shillings charged by outboard-engined canoes which take two hours to do the journey. The same situation holds for the more distant journey from Epe or Okitipupa which also costs less and is much faster by road.

Environmental factors have also operated to the disadvantage of water transport. The blocking of waterways by weeds, fallen trees, but most commonly by sudd is a common occurrence and constitutes a serious handicap to navigation. The marked drop in water level during the dry season also constitutes another problem for water transport. At this time of the year the smaller creeks dry up completely or become impassable even for small canoes. Free movements of persons and goods become restricted, giving rise to an increase in the prices of foodstuffs.

Today, much of the canoe traffic in the creeks and lagoons is concerned with the production sector of the economy rather than with transportation. Many of the canoes are still propelled by paddles, but there has also been a large increase in the number of canoes fitted with small 'Archimedes' or 'Johnson' outboard engines. In all cases the small canoes are engaged in transporting men and goods for short distances. They are indispensable for collecting and assembling such goods as local handicrafts, palm produce, garri, fish and other produce at the major collecting points, where they are shipped to Lagos by launches or by road.

Improved accessibility, following road development in the region during the decade ending in 1960, was followed by the withdrawal of the main trading firms such as the U.A.C. and P.Z. from the distribution of consumer goods. Shops belonging to these and other firms were closed down and transferred to Ijebu-Ode, Shagamu and Ikeja areas. The carrying trade of the lagoons declined in consequence, since the local petty traders who took over the distributive trade preferred the faster and cheaper service provided by the new road link with Lagos. John Holt, G. B. Ollivant and a few other firms still maintain wholesale stores in Okitipupa hence the continuing traffic by barges and launches carrying hardwares, printed cotton cloth, cement and other goods from Lagos.

The period of foreign firms' participation in the distributive trade in consumer goods was also marked by the prevalence of the mobile trader, who travelled from one market to another to sell his wares. In Okitipupa District the mobile traders, who are commonly referred to as 'Osomalo', consist of young men from Akure and Ijesha. They sell their wares on credit but at high prices, and payment is usually by instalments and may involve mort-gaging of landed property or harvests. This local system of hire-purchase arrangement came about as a result of the inability of the peasant to travel to distant markets to buy, owing to his limited cash income.

Trade in locally distilled or illicit gin appears to be on the increase and this has been facilitated by canoe transport. Some of the huts found along the Ogun flood plains on both sides of the Lagos-Ikorodu road are surprisingly not farm huts, even though they are located in the midst of cultivated land. Rather, these huts are occupied by large-scale dealers in illicit gin distilled from palm wine. One of the dealers interviewed in March 1966 indicated that the gin is usually distilled in the Niger Delta area and transported in hundred-gallon drums by large canoes to the Lagos area. It appears however, that a small amount of gin is also distilled in the region by migrants from the Niger Delta.

It is still illegal to distil and distribute locally made gin although it has always been difficult to enforce the law. Dealers in the distribution of the liquor have since discovered that it is easier to outwit the police along the creeks than on roads, hence the preference for canoe transport. The liquor which consists of raw alcohol is sent to the Lagos black market in kerosine tins where it is distributed at about two shillings a pint. There is no doubt that there is a great demand for the liquor amongst the low income group in the Lagos area but the boldness with which the dealers carry on this trade is surprising.

Works consulted and suggestions for further reading:
1. Ajaegbu, H. I., 'The Impact of Lagos on the Changing Rural Economy of the Creeks and Lagoon Areas of Epe and Ikeja Divisions, Western Nigeria' unpublished Ph.D. thesis, University of Ibadan 1968
2. Duckworth, E. H., 'A visit to the Apostles and the Town of Aiyetoro' *Nigeria Magazine* No. 36 1951
3. Forde, D., *The Yoruba speaking peoples of south-western Nigeria* London 1962
4. Hodder, B. W., 'Badagry I: Slave Port and Mission Centre' *Nigerian Geographical Journal* Vol. 5 pp. 75–86 1962
5. Hodder, B. W., 'Badagry II: One Hundred Years of Change' *Nigerian Geographical Journal* Vol. 6 pp. 3–16 1963

3 The Cocoa Belt of Yorubaland

The Nigerian cocoa belt (Figure 13) which covers a total area of over 10,000 square miles, a tenth of which is planted with cocoa, is the most developed area of its size in the country. It produces over ninety-five per cent of the country's cocoa, the rest coming from the South-eastern and Midwestern States. In the west and north, the limits of the region are set by inadequate rainfall and follow approximately the forty-five inch rainfall isohyet, while unsuitable soil combined with excessive rainfall are the limiting factors in the east and south. In Ibadan and Ife-Ilesha Divisions of Oyo Province and in parts of Ondo, Abeokuta and Ijebu Provinces where cocoa production is concentrated, *per capita* income is more than double the national average and the high standard of living is obvious from the expensive houses and dresses of the local people. The indigenous people, the Yorubas, who are one of the most sophisticated groups in Nigeria, have a rich culture and a relatively long period of recorded history. Bronze and terracotta figures from Ife, reputed to be the cradle of Yoruba civilization are known all over the world of arts. Brass and iron working are of long-standing importance and so is weaving, which is the most widespread traditional craft industry.

Compared with other groups in southern Nigeria, the Yorubas are organized into large sub-groups such as Egba, Ekiti and Ijebu. Large, but loosely connected chiefdoms of many centuries standing replace the small independent village-groups of the Eastern States. Traditional respect for elders remains intact but tribal integration is less pronounced. The Yorubas thus have a history of more independent thinking in politics than the other peoples of southern Nigeria. By tradition, the Yorubas live in towns and it is in the cocoa belt that these towns are concentrated.

The emphasis placed on cocoa and kola cultivation as well as the growth of towns in this region has converted the cocoa belt into a food deficit area. But unlike other such food deficit areas as the Jos Plateau, and parts of Owerri and Onitsha Provinces, the cocoa belt has much cultivable but as yet uncultivated land. Wherever suitable land for cocoa exists, local farmers concentrate on cultivating cocoa, and grow practically no food crops, particularly when the trees are in full bearing. The general belief appears to be that no food farmer can prosper as much as the cocoa farmer and so the bulk of the yams and other foodstuffs sold in Ibadan and Ondo comes from

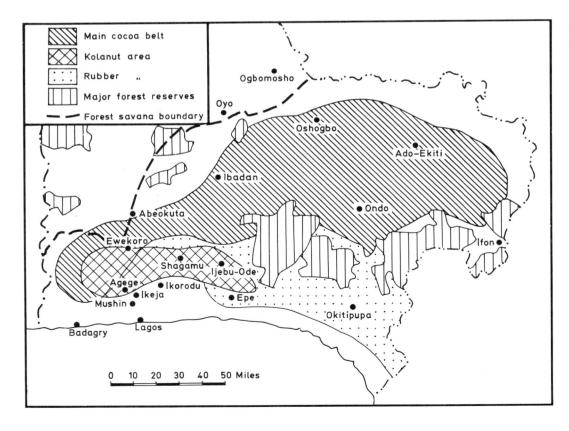

Figure 13. Crop Regions and Forest Reserves in the Cocoa Belt

Table 6 MEAN MONTHLY RAINFALL (UP TO 1957) FOR SELECTED STATIONS

Station	Altitude in Feet	No. of Years	Jan.	Feb.	Mar.	April	May	June	July	Aug.	Sept.	Oct.	Nov.	Dec.	Total
Ondo	940	49	0·4	1·4	4·3	6·2	6·7	8·4	9·3	5·2	9·3	7·7	2·9	0·7	62·5
Owo	1,053	22	0·3	1·3	3·7	4·9	6·4	6·5	7·7	6·2	9·8	5·3	1·7	0·9	54·7
Ibadan	745	53	0·4	0·9	3·6	5·3	5·9	7·4	6·1	3·3	7·0	6·2	1·8	0·4	48·3
Ado-Ekiti	1,650	23	0·4	1·3	4·0	4·7	6·2	6·8	5·1	3·5	8·7	7·0	2·9	0·6	51·2
Oshogbo	1,000	14	0·3	1·2	2·9	4·3	5·5	5·5	4·9	5·1	7·3	6·7	1·8	0·4	45·8

non-cocoa growing parts of Oyo, Iseyin, Ekiti and Owo Divisions.

LANDFORMS, CLIMATE, VEGETATION AND SOILS

Excepting along the south-western margin, the cocoa belt lies wholly within the area underlain by metamorphic rocks of the Basement Complex, which outcrop over most of the Western State. The land-surface is generally undulating and descends gradually from an altitude of over 1,600 feet in Ekiti Division in the north to 400 feet farther south in Ondo and Ijebu Provinces. In the southern part of the region the landscape, which is heavily forested, consists of a dissected plain developed on tertiary sediments. Elsewhere, but particularly in areas of very resistant rocks or rocks protected from weathering by a capping of lateritic ironstone, the characteristic landscape consists of old plains broken by steep-sided inselbergs which may occur singly or in groups. The inselbergs which are to be found in various stages of disintegration are very numerous in Ekti, Akure and Ondo Divisions where they assume much greater heights than in the Ibadan area. One of the most prominent groups of these inselbergs occurs in Idanre just east of Ondo, where the highest points in Yorubaland are encountered in the Idanre hills, which rise well above 3,000 feet.

In most areas the hills show a north-south trend, thus reflecting the general strike of the underlying rocks. Some form of vegetation is found on all but the steepest and smoothest of these inselbergs. The quartz ridge area east of Ilesha features many prominent ridges rising abruptly from the surrounding country and elongated in a north-south direction. These ridges, including the giant Oke Messi-Efon Alaiye ridge with summit levels above 2,000 feet rising to 2,400 feet in the south, are usually densely wooded. An isolated and smaller chain of quartz ridges

passes through Ibadan town where it provides the site for the Bower Tower, Mapo Hall and the new Premier Hotel at Mokola.

The region is drained by many north-south flowing rivers of which the Ogun, the Oshun, the Shasha and the Owena are the more important. The main rivers normally flow all round the year, but there is a marked seasonal variation in their volume and in exceptionally dry years many of them may be reduced to a series of pools maintained by sub-surface flow. The smaller tributaries are dry each year for periods varying from a few weeks to several months. Navigability of the main river channels is restricted to their lower reaches where they form part of the coastal creeks, but in general these rivers constitute an impediment to east-west road communications.

In general, the climate is cooler and drier than in corresponding areas in the Eastern States. The main characteristic features are a high but uniform temperature, heavy rainfall decreasing to moderate in the north, a high relative humidity and intense cloud cover. The short dry season, which lasts from late July to early September, is much longer than in other parts of southern Nigeria and, as can be detected from Table 6, this drier period tends to become less marked from south to north.

Under present climatic conditions, lowland rain forest is the natural vegetation, even in the northern districts of Ekiti. A heavy biotic pressure due to centuries of human occupation has, however, reduced the forests to derived savanna, particularly in the drier northern fringes and in areas having soils with poor moisture retaining qualities. Substantial areas of Ibadan and Ondo Provinces are now under this grassy vegetation but recent field investigations by Morgan and Moss (1966)[1] confirm that the forest-savanna boundary has been relatively stable in the last few decades. Gallery forests along streamsides are common

[1] Personal discussion with W. B. Morgan at Ibadan in 1966

Plate 8. (a) Old Idanre.

Plate 8. (b) New Idanre.

in the derived savanna of Ibadan, Ede-Oshogbo and Ikirun Districts. These forests feature such conspicuous species as the *Brachystegia eurycoma* which has flaming red young foliage during the months of January and February.

Large forest reserves exist in Ondo and Ijebu Provinces and are exploited in much the same way as the forests of the Benin Lowlands. Afforestation with teak is practised by the Forestry Department as well as by local farmers, the tree plantations being concentrated in the derived savanna areas where they are intended to provide building poles and fuel. The Olokomeji teak plantation near Ibadan has been an important source of telegraph poles since the early 1950's.

The character of soil profiles in the region is determined largely by the nature of the parent rock and good cocoa soils are generally limited to areas where the parent material consists of rocks of the Basement Complex. The great variety of Basement Complex rocks give rise to a large number of ferruginous soil groups, which are acidic but much more fertile than the acid sands of the Udi Plateau. These ferruginous soils also have a high clay content and good drainage.

PRODUCTION AND MARKETING OF COCOA

Cocoa was introduced into Nigeria from Fernando Po in the latter part of the nineteenth century, and has since been developed almost exclusively by peasant farmers. The first year of export was in 1895 when twenty-one tons of cocoa were shipped. Cocoa export exceeded 10,000 tons for the first time in 1917 and from then, production grew very rapidly to reach 114,000 tons in 1939, thanks to the energy and initiative of the Nigerian peasant farmer. But the quality of Nigerian cocoa was very poor owing to lack of scientific guidance in preparing the beans for export. Great improvements in quality followed the expansion of the Produce Inspection Service established in 1928 and the payment of price differentials on different grades of cocoa. Since 1960, the quantity of cocoa exported every year has exceeded 150,000 tons per annum; Nigeria being the third world producer of cocoa (after Ghana and Brazil).

Cocoa differs significantly from other food-crops in that a piece of land is not used for two or three years and then allowed to revert to fallow, but is kept under cocoa for as long as forty years. It introduces the need for security of tenure on land cropped with cocoa, particularly in view of the initial investment which even small-scale farmers of cocoa have to make. This is one reason why the traditional Yoruba system of communal land rights has undergone considerable modifications in parts of the cocoa belt, where outright sales of land are now common.

The cost of establishing a cocoa farm often depends on the size of the farm, which varies between an acre or two worked by family labour, to small plantations of fifty acres, which employ regular labour. The majority of the farms are about 2·5 acres. Cocoa is best planted on newly cleared forest land and hired labour is generally required in clearing the bush and felling trees. This is done between January and March. Some farmers plant cocoa seedlings as soon as the land is ready for cultivation, while others prefer to raise a crop of yams first. In all cases, food-crops are also raised on the cocoa farm during the first four years when the cocoa is not bearing any fruit.

Cocoa seedlings are easily damaged by too much sun and by heavy rainstorms such as are common at the beginning and end of the rainy season. This is why a few trees are left behind while clearing the bush so that some shade may be provided. More shade is provided by planting banana and food-crops. At the present rate of wage labour (about two shillings and sixpence per man per day) the total establishment cost for a farm of one acre, including initial clearing and fourth-year weeding may be put at about forty pounds.

Flowering begins in December and the main cocoa harvest takes place between October and February. Ninety to ninety-five per cent of the total crop is harvested during this main crop season while the remainder, the 'light crop', is gathered from April to August. The main harvest is a very busy time for the cocoa farmer who is usually obliged to employ hired labour to gather the crops, and tend the beans during fermentation, which lasts about a week. The quality of the crop depends largely on proper fermentation, which consists of heaping beans from newly harvested pods together and covering them with plantain leaves so that white pulp round the beans can turn into liquid and be drained away. Care is required in turning the heap at least twice so as to ensure even fermentation. Fermented beans are dried in the open-air either on mats laid on the ground or on a specially made table called the *tarage*, the latter producing better and cleaner cocoa.

In 1963 (*Nigerian Trade Journal* Vol. 11 No. 2 p. 69) it was estimated that over 300,000 farmers in Western Nigeria were directly engaged in cocoa production and that about a third of the Region's population of over ten million were dependent on one or the other of the various processes of cocoa production. Those engaged in the marketing and transporting of cocoa are more numerous than the actual farmers, and taken as a group they receive a substantial part of the income from cocoa production. But this income, which in fact is the difference between local price and price at the port of shipment, is spread over a very large number of traders. As in the case of the rubber trade in the Benin Lowlands, there is a hierarchy of middlemen between the grower and the exporting firms. Most of these middlemen operate on a system of cash advances and commissions. Petty local pan-buyers, about half of which are women, buy the picked cocoa pods and undertake the work of fermenting, drying and transporting the beans from the farm. Their profit is small, being about three shillings per hundredweight, but many of them make considerable profits from the interests on loans which they usually give to farmers 'against cocoa crops.

On the higher rung of the middleman ladder is the African wholesaler who often controls a large number of lesser middlemen, including the scalemen, who depend on him for cash advances and commissions. The wholesaler is himself generally tied to one of the exporting firms by advances and makes additional profit by transporting, in his own lorry, the crop which he buys.

The Cocoa Marketing Board was first established in 1947 and continued to function as a commodity Marketing Board until 1954, when a single Marketing Board was established for cocoa, palm produce and seed cotton from the Western State. The Board appoints licensed buying agents and arranges for the evacuation of the produce to the port of export, and for the sale of the produce in the world market.

PROBLEMS OF THE NIGERIAN COCOA INDUSTRY

The importance of cocoa to the economy of the Western State has been indicated in terms of the number of people involved in cultivating and marketing the crop. The economy of the state and the higher living standard enjoyed by its people depend on cocoa, which accounted for about £40 million or ninety per cent of the export earnings of the state in 1965. Problems facing the cocoa industry cannot therefore be overlooked by anyone interested in, or seeking to understand, the economic situation in this state.

One of the greatest problems of cocoa growing is presented by diseases and pests, notably swollen shoot (sometimes referred to as 'die-back'), blackpod and capsid. Swollen shoot starts with falling leaves and loss of fruit, followed by the death of the tree, and it is caused by a virus which is readily transmitted from tree to tree by a small insect, the mealy bug. There are two areas of mass infection, an area of about 100,000 acres near Ibadan and another with 25,000 acres near Ilaro, where the elimination of the disease will require destroying the bulk of cocoa trees in the area. The difficulties facing the administrator in a bid to reclaim areas infected by swollen shoot have been ably presented in a recent novel *One Man One Matchet* by T. M. Aluko (Heinemann Educational Books 1965), who is himself the son of a cocoa farmer. Large scale spraying against blackpod and capsid started in 1956 and 1957 respectively, and today all farmers are capable of using spraying equipment which may be purchased in any central place within the cocoa belt.

Another important problem has to do with the fluctuation in the price of cocoa, which still varies considerably, in spite of the stabilizing effect of the State Marketing Board. In 1963 for instance, the gazetted price for Grade I cocoa in western Nigeria was £110 per ton rising to £181 in 1964 and falling to £130 in 1965. The average yield of 500 pounds per acre on peasant-farms compares favourably with about 400 pounds in the plantations of Trinidad, but higher yields of 800 to 1,200 pounds per acre have been recorded in experimental plots in the region. The problem of declining yield becomes more serious every year since by far the greater number of cocoa trees are over the age of maximum yield.[1] In 1965–6 for example, almost fifty per cent (470,000 acres) of the cocoa acreage were declining in production (twenty-eight to thirty-seven years) while another twenty-six per cent (250,000 acres) were thirty-seven years of age.[2]

THE RISE AND EXPANSION OF KOLA-NUT CULTIVATION

Unlike cocoa, the kola-nut is indigenous to Nigeria and is grown all over the forest belt of southern Nigeria, although the main producing area is to be found in the south-western part of the cocoa belt around Otta, Ilaro, in Remo Division and Ijebu southern district. In these areas, the crop dominates the local economy in much the same way as cocoa does in other parts of the forestland of Yorubaland; but in other areas like Irun in Ekiti, Kola is still intercropped with cocoa. Indeed, around Otta, where kola cultivation has proved more profitable than cocoa, the latter crop has since been completely displaced. Kola is also found to be more tolerant of the relatively poor soils derived from sedimentary rocks, hence the dominance of kola along the southern part of the cocoa belt.

Two varities of kola are cultivated—'cola acuminata' (Abata) which is indigenous to the region and the kola

[1] Peak production is recorded between eighteen and twenty-five years after which there is a rapid decline in yield
[2] United Nations (FAO), *Agricultural Development in Nigeria 1965–1980* p. 55 Rome 1966

of commerce or 'cola nitida' (Gbanja), which was introduced into the region from Ghana. This was in 1910 when the Department of Agriculture obtained large quantities of kola seed from Ghana for sale to Nigerian farmers. Before then, Nigeria had depended largely on kola exports from Ghana.

Like cocoa, the kola-nut is a tree crop and therefore presents very similar problems of land use. Also like cocoa, the crop is grown in small plots which rarely exceed three acres. Even in Remo Division where kola is the dominant cash crop, the impressive and continuous plantations, which cover rather extensive areas, are in fact made up of a number of small plots belonging to several persons. Often, food crops like cassava and vegetables are grown in the kola fields during the first four to seven years, when the trees are not mature enough to bear fruits. Labour requirements are also similar but there is no direct competition for labour between the two crops, except during the harvest season (mid-July to January for kola).

Kola pods are usually harvested by men, while children extract the nuts from the pod. Curing then takes place during which time the seeds are made to dry gradually in such a way that they do not harden up, but remain succulent for chewing. The seeds are then packed in baskets lined with Abura (*Micragyna stipulosa*) leaves and spiced with a special type of solution in order to prevent insects from damaging them.

THE KOLA TRADE BETWEEN NORTHERN AND WESTERN NIGERIA

The main difference between kola and cocoa is that kola is marketed in the country while cocoa is exported. The main consuming centres for kola are in the drier savanna lands of Nigeria and the neighbouring territories, and the most established traders and transporters are Hausas. It is proper to mention here that the kola trade between the forest and the Sudan is of long-standing importance in West Africa, and that before this century, almost all the kola came from Ghana, the Ivory Coast and Guinea.

As in the case of other commodities produced and traded locally, there are no figures of production or of the quantity of kola exported to the Northern States. A recent report of the FAO (1965) on Agricultural Development in Nigeria between 1965 and 1980 indicates that kola produced in Yorubaland is worth some £13 million and that there are about 18 million trees in the area.[1] Smith and Hay (1966) estimate that in 1964, 50,800 tons of kola were exported from western Nigeria to the north and that the value of this was about £5·3 million.[2]

Kola nut traders are mainly Hausas who are to be found in large numbers in the main kola growing areas where they have established some hamlets. In the larger towns such as Shagamu and Ijebu-Ode, Hausa kola traders live in special wards called Sabo. The unit of trade in the centres of production is the *Kondo* (= basket) measure, each of which contains 500–700 seeds, and cost between thirty and seventy shillings depending on the variety and the season of the year. The sale of the crop is in the hands of Yoruba women and middlemen may buy from house to house or in the village market. The nuts are packed in specially-made containers and exported by road or rail to the Northern States. The flexibility of road transport is largely responsible for the growing preference, by kola traders, of road transportation.

A number of ancillary industries have sprung up to provide full-time employment to many people living in the kola districts. These include rope-making for tying the kola parcels, basket-making and the collection, in the forest, of special leaves used for packing the nuts.

THE KOLA-NUT TOWN OF SHAGAMU

Shagamu (51,000 in 1963) is situated almost midway between Lagos and Ibadan. It was founded about the middle of the nineteenth century and for several decades it maintained, together with Ijebu-Ode, a strict control of the trade routes between the lagoon ports and the Yoruba mainland. This trade monopoly was broken in 1892 following British penetration. The trunk road and railway from Lagos to the then Northern Provinces of Nigeria passed through Abeokuta while Shagamu was completely by-passed and remained an insignificant rural town for the next half-century. In 1953, however Shagamu regained its former control of the trade between the Lagos area and the north following the building of the Lagos-Shagamu-Ibadan road which is about twenty-five miles shorter than the Lagos-Abeokuta-Ibadan road. Shagamu's position as a road centre has been strengthened recently by the opening in 1964 of the new Lagos-Benin road which branches off at Shagamu.

The mainstay of the economy of Shagamu is the trade in kola-nuts, Shagamu being the largest kola collecting point in Nigeria. As a return cargo, trucks carrying kola to the Northern States bring yams, rice, beans and onions to Shagamu, which has thus become an important food distributing centre, serving a district which is no longer

[1] United Nations (FAO) *Agricultural Development in Nigeria 1965–1980* p. 173 Rome 1966
[2] Hay, A. H. & Smith, H. T., 'Preliminary Estimates of Nigeria's Interregional Trade and Associated Money Flows' *Nigerian Journal of Economics and Social Studies* VIII pp. 9–35 (reference on p. 28) 1966

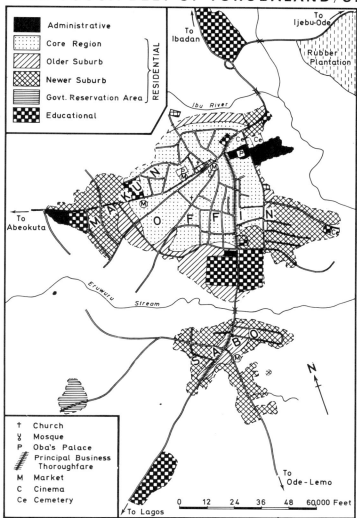

Figure 14. The Town of Shagamu

self-sufficient in local food-crops owing to the growing emphasis on kola-nut production.

Unlike other important Yoruba towns, Shagamu has never been walled, but the layout of its core area is similar to those of other Yoruba towns. In 1962, it had a Hausa population of over 2,000 almost all of whom live in the Hausa section called Sabo. The Eruwuru stream separates the main town from Sabo which was founded in 1942 and which is now the busiest part of the town. Sabo market and the near-by lorry park are the scene of bustle and activity involving the marketing, packing and loading of kola packages into lorries bound for towns in the Northern States. The rapid growth of residential areas has almost resulted in the merging of Sabo with the original town of Shagamu (Figure 14).

OTHER CASH CROPS PRODUCED IN THE COCOA BELT

Apart from cocoa and kola, the cocoa belt produces palm oil and kernels, citrus fruit, cotton and recently rubber, which has been introduced in the extreme south of the region. Up to the middle of the nineteenth century, palm trees which grew wild on farmland and in the forests were felled indiscriminately for palm wine, but by 1877 it was reported that the trees were carefully and jealously guarded on account of the oils which they produced for home and overseas markets. But although palm produce is an important export from the Western State it has since been relegated to a secondary position by cocoa.

Excepting in the few plantations which are a recent development, palm trees in western Nigeria and indeed in the whole country are very old and grow to heights of over forty feet. Yield of oil from trees, especially those in the south-west of the cocoa belt, is poor largely because most of the fruits here have a thin mesocarp and a large kernel. These fruits have, however, continued to supply a steady export of kernels.

Citrus growing has featured prominently in Ikeja and Agege areas for many decades. In Ibadan the expansion of citrus since 1950 has been caused by two factors, the first of which is the necessity of supplying a crop to rehabilitate areas from which cocoa suffering from swollen shoot disease has been cut out. Secondly, small plantations of citrus fruits owned by local farmers or by the Western Nigeria Development Corporation established around Ibadan are meant to supply the modern canning factory opened at Ibadan in 1954, to prepare concentrated citrus juices for the home and export markets.

Coffee is grown in Abeokuta and Ondo Provinces. Both the Robusta type (*Coffea canephora*) and Liberica type (*Coffea liberica*) are grown, the latter mainly for local consumption.

At present, western Nigeria is a very small producer of rubber, its total contribution to the total Nigerian rubber output being about three per cent. There are, however, great prospects for large-scale expansion of rubber in the forests of Ondo and Ijebu Provinces, where climatic conditions are very similar to those of the Benin rubber belt. In 1964, there were just about 5,000 acres cropped with rubber and half of this was still immature. Cropping is mainly on small farms of under three acres but there is an increasing number of farms ranging from fifty to a hundred acres as well as a few large plantations owned by the Western Nigeria Development Corporation.

Cotton is another cash crop which is grown in parts of the region. Its propagation in western Nigeria was inspired by early missionaries who supervised the cultivation of cotton in the Abeokuta area as far back as 1852. By 1862 cotton farms were widespread in Abeokuta and in that year the district exported as many as 3.7 million bales, each of which weighed 130 pounds. A sudden decline followed, and by the end of the century very little cotton was produced. Today, the bulk of Nigeria's cotton export comes from the Northern States; but the last ten years have witnessed a rapid expansion of cotton in the Western State, which owns the large textile mill at Ikeja.

SOME ASPECTS OF FOOD CROP PRODUCTION IN THE COCOA BELT

The main features of food farming in the region are the same as for other parts of the forested areas of southern Nigeria excepting that much of the farmwork is done by men. Bush fallowing is the farming system and each farmer cultivates several plots every year, only a few of which exceed a quarter of an acre in area. Mixed cropping is the rule and, as in other parts of the south and middle belt, yam is usually the first crop of a newly cleared patch, with cassava as the last crop before the land reverts to fallow. Fallow periods vary considerably, depending mainly on availability of farmland and on soil fertility. In Ibadan, Ilesha and parts of Ife Districts, where land for food-crops has been very much restricted as a result of the expansion of tree crops, farmland is usually cropped for three years at a time and then left fallow for three to five years. Much longer fallow periods are common in the less densely settled parts of Ondo Province.

Yams (*Dioscorea spp.*), maize (*Zea mays*) and cassava (*Manihot spp.*) are the principal food-crops, but a variety of minor crops such as pumpkins, beans, melon and okro are also planted. In wetter parts of the region and in heavily shaded areas such as the forested areas of Ijebu and Ondo, cocoyam is important. Upland rice is of increasing importance in Ondo and Abeokuta Provinces, where the crop is gradually displacing both yams and cassava.

Until about the end of the Second World War, the yam was the staple item of diet in the forest areas of Yorubaland, but since then there has been a steady increase in the production and consumption of cassava in the forms of *garri* or *amala*. This is particularly true of the areas with reduced fallows, since cassava is less sensitive than the yam to the relatively less fertile soils.

As in the Creeks and Lagoons region farther south, two crops of maize can be harvested, the first being between July and the end of August, while late maize which is planted in August is harvested in late December or early January. In the northern and drier parts of the region, late maize yields are much poorer and in some cases the crop may fail completely.

Yams are planted in February after which pumpkins, groundnuts and maize are planted in the same plot.

Amongst the Yorubas, white yam (*Dioscorea rotundata*) is very popular, but yellow yam (*Dioscorea cayanensis*) is also cultivated. Unfortunately, white yam which shows greater response to fertiliser is more susceptible to virus disease and eelworm attack than yellow yam. Yam harvest is a busy period in the farming calendar and comes in November, although this main harvest is always preceded by an early harvest in late July and August.

TOWN-FARM RELATIONSHIPS IN THE COCOA BELT

Like other Nigerians, the Yorubas are essentially farmers, but the fact that they live in very large towns has necessitated the cropping of farmlands which are rather far from their homes. Two types of farmlands are usually recognized amongst these people—farms in the outskirt of the settlement (*oko etile*) and farms in the forest or bush (*oko egan*). Farmlands lying up to four or five miles from such large towns as Ibadan, Ijebu-Ode and Idanre constitute the *oko etile* and are cultivated mainly by part-time farmers who travel on foot or by bicycle to their farms. Beyond this limit lies the *oko egan*, which is so far away that many hamlets and villages (*aba*) have sprung up to house farming families, who stay out in their farms for most of the farming season, although some return to the town during the weekends.

Soil impoverishment in the *oko etile* and the expansion of cocoa have been largely responsible for the growing importance of the *oko egan*. Initially, only temporary huts were built in the farming villages, but today, many permanent buildings are common, particularly on distant cocoa farms. In Ibadan District, where there were over 3,000 of these farming villages in 1960, some of them have grown into large villages such as Moniya, Olode and Odo-Ona. Like the inhabitants of the Calabar farm villages, the *oko egan* settlements have strong ties with the main towns, where each farmer has a house or room, where he usually spends the weekends or the off-farm season. These distant farm villages provide a considerable proportion of the food requirements of the urban markets and look to the urban centres for services such as education, shopping and amusements.

COMMERCIAL PLANTATIONS AND FARM SETTLEMENTS

Almost all the plantations shown in Figure 15 were established after 1950, while the farm settlement scheme started in 1960. Throughout the first half of this century, the

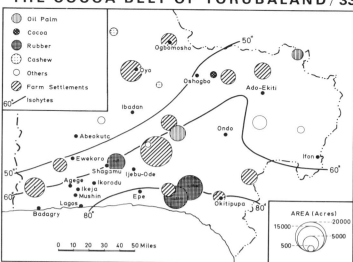

Figure 15. Farm Settlements and Tree Crop Plantations in the Cocoa Belt

Nigerian colonial government was against plantation agriculture which it rejected in preference for peasant-type farming. This explains why cocoa is grown almost exclusively by peasants rather than in plantations.

The way in which the people live, grouped together in large nucleated settlements, leaves vast areas of land open for mechanized or plantation agriculture and both climatic and edaphic conditions confirm that plantations of oil palm trees, cocoa, rubber and citrus can be established in various parts of the region. At present, however, emphasis appears to be on oil palm and rubber plantations, while cocoa, which is successfully grown on a large scale by peasants, is not given much consideration. One reason for this is the desire to diversify the economy of the Western State, which now suffers from an over-dependence on one crop, cocoa.

Farm settlements, most of which produce tree crops under plantation conditions are designed to combine the good aspects of both plantation and peasant type agriculture. There are at least seven farm settlements in the forested areas based on such crop combinations as cocoa and oil palms, cocoa and citrus, oil palm and rubber or cocoa, oil palm and citrus. The size of the settlements varies from the 3,000 acres Okitipupa farm settlement to the 6,000 acres Orin Ekiti settlement; but they are much smaller than those in the Eastern States.

All settlers are given a two-year post-primary school training in farm institutes before they are allocated some farmland. In a tree crop farm settlement such as that at Ibiade each settler is allocated twenty acres, twelve of which are devoted to oil palm and eight to rubber. In addition each settler is allocated a two-acre plot for raising food-crops. For such settlements, the cost of establishing each settler is estimated at three thousand pounds and it is expected that when the farm is in full production the settler will be able to make a net income of six hundred pounds per annum. He is expected to pay back the capital invested in his farm over a period of about fifteen years but may be ejected from the farm if he does not cultivate it in the proper way. He may not fragment his holding and is in a position to make use of machinery supplied through the settlement authority.

The capital outlay on these farm settlements is certainly high but it is too early yet to question the investment of so much money on each farmer. It may well turn out that farm settlements will lead to an agricultural revolution in Nigeria, but even at this early stage we are in a position to observe that the farm settlement cannot do much to arrest the growing movement of young school leavers to the main towns of the cocoa belt.

SOME ASPECTS OF THE POPULATION AND SETTLEMENTS

In 1952, about four million or ninety per cent of the Yorubas of Nigeria lived in the forest region, but today, the figure is about seven million. Such a rapid increase within a period of just over ten years appears unusual, but may be accounted for partly by the undercount of the 1952 census and partly by large numbers of immigrants from other parts of Nigeria.

The Yorubas live in large towns and the cocoa belt is the most urbanised region of its size in Nigeria. In 1952, forty-eight per cent of the population lived in settlements with over 5,000 persons compared with twenty-eight per cent in the north and east, while twenty-three per cent of the total population lived in towns with more than 50,000 persons (compared with three per cent in the east and two per cent in the north).

Urbanisation amongst the Yorubas dates from the remote past, but apart from such ancient towns as Ife and Ijebu-Ode, from where pioneers colonised such parts of Yorubaland as Ekiti, Ondo and Ijebu sub-tribal areas, most of the other larger towns are a product of nineteenth-century warfare in the area. Abeokuta and Ibadan for example were founded as camps for the army engaged in, and for refugees fleeing from, nineteenth-century wars with Dahomey and the Fulanis respectively. The warriors of Dahomey and the Fulanis approached Yorubaland from the west and north, hence the general shift in the centres of concentration of people towards the east and south.

One interesting fact about the distribution of Yoruba towns is that all the five indigenous towns with over 100,000 persons are located in the derived savanna or open forests of Oyo and Ibadan Provinces, while towns in the high forest zone have less than 50,000 persons. Yet the forest offers a natural defence against the mounted Fulani from the north. The main reason for this avoidance of the forest appears to lie in the fact that farming is more tedious under forest conditions.

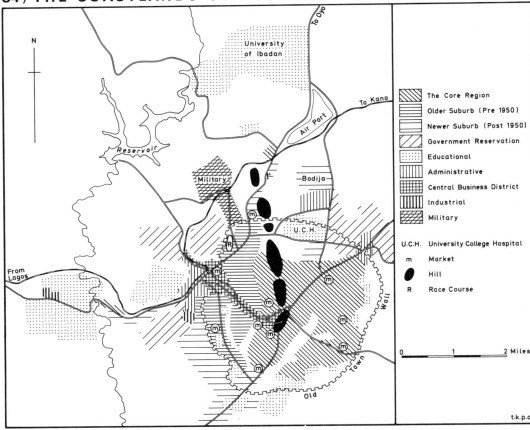

Figure 16. The City and Suburbs of Ibadan

IBADAN

Ibadan (627,380 in 1963), the largest indigenous African town is located in the heart of the cocoa-producing area of the Western State of Nigeria. It started as a military camp during the second decade of the nineteenth century and was later settled by refugees from Old Oyo as well as from other parts of Yorubaland. Drawing its population from various parts of Yorubaland, Ibadan was even at this early stage a scene of political rivalry and struggle by the various groups for leadership. This struggle continues, and it was the desperate acts of an unpopular government at Ibadan that were among the causes of the military takeover in January 1966. The population today is even more heterogeneous, almost every Nigerian tribe being represented. There are also a large number of Syrians and Lebanese who dominate the retail trade in textiles.

In 1851, the population was estimated at between 60,000 and 100,000, and the town was surrounded by a wall about ten miles in circumference. The town wall enclosed not only the settlement but also some farmland, although the main farms were outside the walls. In 1953, about thirty-five per cent of the population was engaged in agriculture as compared with twenty-one per cent in trading and clerical and nine per cent in administration and the professions.

The large number of farmers in the city suggests that the transition to urban industrialism is slow. Nevertheless Ibadan is an important centre of commerce, administration, learning and industry. Its location near to Lagos,

eighty-five miles by road and 120 miles by rail, and the fact that Ibadan is linked to all parts of the Western State by good roads accounts for the dominant position of Ibadan in the distributive trade of this part of the country. Thousands of inhabitants, both indigenous and foreigners are engaged in one kind of trade or another; business being carried out in the local markets, open-air stalls, shops and department stores.

The range of quartzite hills running through the heart of Ibadan (Figure 16) is the most prominent feature of the physical landscape of the city. These hills have provided sites for such landmarks as Mapo Town Hall, Bower Tower, and the new Premier Hotel at Mokola. Other prominent buildings include the ten-storey Co-operative building and the twenty-seven storey Cocoa House which is the tallest building in Nigeria. Ibadan's £500,000 Liberty Stadium, with a sitting capacity of 35,000 spectators, is the largest and best equipped in Nigeria.

Considering the level of technology of the people and the resources at the disposal of government and individuals, it is not difficult to appreciate the serious problems of sanitation posed by the congregation of such a large number of people as at Ibadan. The squalor of such old parts of the city as Inalende, Ogunpa and Adeoyo as well as of the newer residential areas of Sabo, Agbeni and Kongi provide some of the worst slums in the country. High-grade residential areas such as Links Reservation, Bodija Housing Estate and Ibadan University are located at least a couple of miles from the congested parts of the city.

It is in connection with its famous university that Ibadan is known all over the world of learning. The university, the first in Nigeria, was established in 1948 and by 1966 it had a student population of about 3,000. The University College Teaching Hospital together with the Nursing School offers the most elaborate and up-to-date medical facilities in West Africa.

Ibadan is the administrative capital of the Western State of Nigeria and like Kaduna and Enugu its administrative hinterland has been reduced as a result of the reorganization of Nigeria into twelve states. Its growing industries include the large Nigeria Tobacco Company's factory, the Nigerian plastics factory and the Pepsi-Cola factory.

POST-WAR MIGRATIONS INTO THE COCOA BELT

Employment of hired labour for bush clearing, felling trees and preparing the ground for cultivating cocoa has always been a common feature of cocoa farming in western Nigeria. Before the Second World War hired labour in Ibadan area was largely local, and consisted of men who preferred to work for wages rather than farm themselves. In Colony Province and parts of Abeokuta, the hired labourers came from distant places like Shaki, Ekiti and various parts of the Northern States. Such distant migrants came only for a season or two and worked for a purpose such as to get money for marriage payments. The rate of pay in 1938 was about seven pounds and ten shillings per annum.

Since 1945, the volume and pattern of population movements into the cocoa belt have changed. There has been an increase in the number of migrant labourers to meet the growing demand for labour following the free primary education scheme and the consequent withdrawal of family labour from the farms. Expansion of cocoa farms has also increased the demand for labour and each of the main cocoa areas appears to have its own labour hinterland. Thus Ijebu draws its labour mainly from Oyo, Oshogbo and parts of Ekiti while Ibadan area obtains its labour from Igbira, Semorika, Oshogbo and Ila.

Yorubas from the northern edge of the cocoa belt are known to travel long distances into the cocoa belt where they settle and acquire land for cocoa farming. Atan farmers in Ife are examples of these tenant farmers. The spread of cocoa farms in the early 1920's into the southern savannalands immediately north of the main cocoa belt has, however, tended to reduce and indeed stop migrants from places like Irun coming into the main cocoa-growing areas. In Irun, the people now employ wage labour on their cocoa farms, instead of travelling out as labourers as in the past.

A share-cropping arrangement between indigenous cocoa-farmers and migrants is one of the new developments in cocoa farming in parts of Ekiti. At Ikere Ekiti, sons of the soil who cannot find suitable land for establishing their own cocoa farms enter into this arrangement whereby they manage cocoa farms in return for a share of the proceeds of the sales of cocoa beans. The arrangement is simple. The labourer is entitled to two-thirds of the proceeds if he is responsible for spraying expenses, that is in addition to providing labour for harvesting and processing the beans for marketing. If the owner of the farm is responsible for spraying expenses, the labourer gets only a third of the proceeds.

The ubiquitous Isoko migrant palm cutter is found all over the cocoa belt where he also provides occasional labour in cocoa farms. His main occupation, however, is harvesting palm fruits and producing palm oil. Isoko and Bini migrants also settle as food farmers, while Ibos come in both as farmhands and as traders in palm wine tapped by Isoko migrants. The western part of the cocoa belt, which is also an important kola producing area, attracts many Hausas who dominate the kola trade and the transportation of kola-nuts to the main market centres in the Northern States.

As the most urbanised geographical region of Nigeria, the cocoa belt is a centre of attraction for population from various parts of the country. The urban migrants are often not associated with the cocoa industry, at least not directly. They are attracted by employment opportunities in such growing towns as Ibadan, Ife and Ondo; and consist mainly of school leavers looking for urban employment.

TRADITIONAL CRAFT INDUSTRIES

Local cottage industries which still feature prominently in the economy of many districts include weaving, dyeing, pottery and metal-work. These industries are organized on a compound basis and are generally carried on in the verandah or courtyard of houses owned by workers, who are often also the proprietors.

The cloth industry—weaving, spinning and dyeing—is the most widespread of the cottage industries. Men and women take part in weaving, the women using vertical hand-looms to produce cloths which are usually thirty inches wide and six feet long, while the men use horizontal belt-looms to produce narrow strips of cloth about fourteen inches wide and from fifty to sixty feet long. These narrow strips are later sewn together to produce the desired width. Materials used include home-spun cotton, wild silk which is produced locally, and imported threads. The dominant traditional colours consist of varying tones of indigo but brigher colours are now available as a result of increasing use of imported dye and bright-coloured silk threads.

The making of adire cloth (adire = to tie and dye), which suffered some setback between 1940–60 owing to the importation of more attractively manufactured and cheaper imitation adire from Europe, has received a new impetus since 1960. This has been brought about by an unprecedented demand for locally-made adire which is considered to be thicker and more durable, and the growing tendency for men to use adire for making shirts as well as local Yoruba attire and, in some cases, for furnishings.

Potteries are located by streams where adequate supplies of clay and water are found. Production is in the hands of women and is declining owing to competition by aluminium cooking pots which are more durable and very economical of fuel. The use of earthen pots for storing drinking water, for cooking and serving food is now confined to the least progressive or remote villages.

Blacksmithing, formerly based on locally smelted iron but now dependent on scrap and imported metal bars, is the principal form of metal-working. It serves the farming population and is mainly concerned with producing hoe blades, cutlasses, knives and axes. Charcoal is still used as fuel, while traditional tools include bellows constructed with goat or sheep skin and bamboo sticks, anvils of stone and hammers as well as pincers made from locally smelted iron. In the past most smithies were built on or close to granitic outcrops, where weathered rock boulders provided some of the basic tools.

MODERN SMALL-SCALE AND FACTORY INDUSTRIES

Small-scale industries employing less than ten people and having an investment capital of about fifty pounds include light engineering (vulcanizing and goldsmithing), food (cornmills and bakeries) and service industries featuring printing, hairdressing and beer parlours. These are all to be found in the major towns and some of them are also common in smaller central places. Cornmills, for example, which are used for grinding corn, beans and dried yam into amala and melon are located near market squares.

The metal industry, featuring the manufacture of boxes of various sizes, kerosene lanterns, buckets and basins, became important during the Second World War when imported goods were scarce. There is still a great demand for small boxes which school children prefer to use in place of school bags since they have to walk long distances to school in a rainy climate. Buckets and basins, on the other hand, have had to compete against aluminium wares now produced in large factories in the country. The metal industry depends for its raw materials on kerosene tins, petrol drums and discarded corrugated iron sheets.

Large-scale factory industries are to be found in the state capital of Ibadan and in the great industrial estate at Ikeja, on the outskirts of Lagos. There is also a large cement factory at Ewekoro, near Abeokuta, and the Top beer brewery at Abeokuta.

With the exception of the Nigerian Tobacco Co.'s cigarette factory, there is government participation in all the large industrial establishments. Indeed, many manufacturing industries in the state were started off with funds made available to the Western Nigeria Development Corporation by the State Marketing Board.

Works consulted and suggestions for further reading:
1. Akinola, R. A., 'The Ibadan Region' *Nigerian Geographical Journal* No. VI pp. 102–15 1963
2. Akinola, R. A., 'The Industrial Structure of Ibadan' *Nigerian Geographical Journal* No. VII pp. 115–30 1964
3. Forde, Daryll, *The Yoruba Speaking Peoples of South-Western Nigeria* London 1962
4. Forde, D. & Scott, R., *The Native Economies of Nigeria* Chapter 7 and relevant sections of Chapter 2 London 1946
5. Galleti, R., Baldwin, K. O. S. & Dina, I. O., *Nigerian Cocoa Farmers* London 1956
6. Hay, A. H. & Smith, H. T., 'Preliminary Estimates of Nigeria's Inter-regional Trade and Associated Money Flows' *Nigerian Journal of Economics & Social Studies* No. VIII pp. 9–35 1966
7. Hodder, B. W., 'Rural Periodic day markets in part of Yorubaland, Western Nigeria' *Transaction of the Institute of British Geographers* No. XXIX pp. 149–69 1961
8. Morgan, W. B., 'The Influence of European Contacts in the Landscape of Southern Nigeria' *Geographical Journal* No. 125 pp. 48–64 1959
9. Ojo, G. J. A., *Yoruba Culture: A Geographical Analysis* London 1966

4 The Benin Lowlands

The Lowlands of Benin are part of the vast coastal plains which form the southern half of the Southern Provinces of Nigeria. The main features of its present-day geography include the extensive blocks of luxuriant high forest which occur in the central and western parts of the region, the rapid expansion of plantation agriculture, the development of timber and rubber and the large influx of immigrants who settle to work as farm labourers or tenant farmers. It is bounded in the north by a narrow but distinctive west-east clay vale, which separates the Afenmai hill region in the north from the Ishan Plateau in the south. The scrub and savanna vegetation of this clay vale also makes it a veritable regional boundary separating the forested lowlands in the south from the grassy hills of Afenmai. In the south, the region is bordered by the Niger Delta while the Lower Niger valley forms the eastern limit. The western boundary is not very distinctive, owing to the westward extension of certain features of its physical and cultural landscape into southern Ondo and Ijebu Provinces of Yorubaland.

This lowland region covers only a small part of the ancient kingdom of Benin. Benin cultural influence is still obvious amongst the various linguistic groups who often claim to have migrated from Benin city. The Ibos of Asaba and Aboh Division for instance, are culturally more akin to the people of Benin than to the other Ibo-speaking groups east of the Niger. For this reason, and because of the greater opportunities which they have in their less crowded state, as well as the fear of being out-numbered by Ibo migrants from east of the Niger, any move directed at administering the western or Ika Ibos from Enugu would meet with stiff opposition from the people themselves.

A journey from Asaba through Benin to Ijebu-Ode reveals some of the contrasts between east and west in the region. The older road linking Asaba to Benin is lined with oil bean trees and a number of street villages in which houses are built along both sides of the road. Farmlands and palm bush, rather than high forest, appear as far as the eye can see; but a few miles west of Benin city, the landscape changes as the traveller enters the new Benin-Ijebu-Ode highway, which traverses a very sparsely settled forest country. The new road has not yet made any noticeable impact on the arrangement of houses in near-by

Plate 9. A bathing pool. Drinking water is drawn farther upstream while clothes are washed where the stream is shallow.

settlements, but there are numerous wayside racks which display crops like cocoyams, plantains and other forest products for sale to the motorist.

RELIEF AND DRAINAGE

The Benin region (Figure 17) is a tilted plain which slopes in a south-west direction, its highest elevation occurring in the Ishan Plateau which is located in the north-east. Like its southern component, the Asaba Plateau, the Ishan Plateau rises steeply from the Niger Valley and is bordered on the northern edge by a steep slope overlooking the clay vale which separates the Benin Lowlands from the hills of Afenmai. The physical characteristics of these plateau areas remind one of the Udi Plateau on the other side of the Niger. Some of the more striking similarities in the character of both areas include the level topography, the easily worked sandy soils which attracted the early settlers to occupy the interfluves, and the paucity of surface drainage. Water shortage during the dry season is particularly acute along the densely settled broad ridge, which constitutes a local watershed in the northern part of the Ishan Plateau.

In the west and south, the region consists of a sandy coastal plain generally below 400 hundred feet above sea level. Excepting the high hill immediately east of Benin city and in the river valleys, abrupt changes of slope are rare. The marked uniformity in the topography of the southern part is clearly seen in the Sobo Plains near Sapele, where a vast grass island occurs in the heart of the rain forests of the Benin lowlands.

With the exception of the Osse River which rises in the Kabba Plateau, rivers draining the Lowlands of Benin rise within the region; the Ishan Plateau being the source of many streams. The upper courses of the rivers are characterised by steeply incised valleys which give way to extensive broad valleys a few miles before the rivers join the Ethiope River, which drains into the ocean through the estuary called the Benin River. As a result of the long dry season and the geological conditions of the Ishan and Asaba areas, the local streams usually dry up during the dry seasons. Further south, particularly in the area lying between the Jamieson and Oroghoda Rivers, the seasonal character of the streams is largely caused by the depth and porous character of the coastal plain sands which allows water to percolate a long way.

No observant traveller from Benin to Ijebu-Ode will fail to notice the wide floodplain of the Osse River which until recently constituted an effective barrier to east-west movement. It is the largest river in the region and is now crossed by a bridge on the new Benin—Ijebu-Ode road.

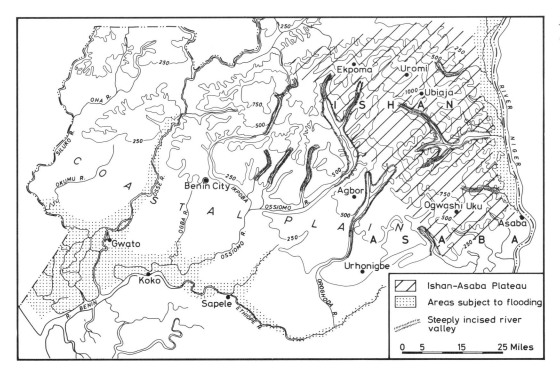

Figure 17. Relief and Drainage of the Benin Lowlands

Its rise during the rainy season is rather sudden, and so is the fall in water level during the dry season, when it may be reduced to a series of water holes connected by a small trickle of water.

In parts of Urhobo Division there are several lakes many of which dry out completely during the dry season. These lakes occur in depressions in areas where the soil is clayey. A few large lakes which contain water all the year round can still be found in the Sobo Plains, and their occurrence may be explained in terms of the theory which suggests that the Sobo Plains were formed by the drying up of large areas of swamps or a shallow lake.

CLIMATE AND VEGETATION

Climatic conditions are similar to other parts of southern Nigeria. There is a marked dry season, the duration of which increases from three months in the south to five months in the Ishan Plateau. Mean daily temperatures also increase northwards, but the rainfall decreases inland from ninety-six inches at Sapele to less than fifty inches in the Ishan Plateau. The short dry season, usually referred to as the August break in the rains, is more marked here than in south-eastern Nigeria but its duration decreases as one approaches the Ishan Plateau. The slight seasonal variation in the temperature is striking, the difference between the coldest month and the hottest month being no more than 6° F.

The natural vegetation of the region is lowland rain forest with swamp vegetation in the south and west. In the more mature high forests areas now restricted to the forest reserves, the forest consists of three strata of trees. The first or top stratum consists of trees of about a hundred and twenty feet or more high, and is made up of widespread and often isolated crowns, while the second or middle stratum is made up of trees from fifty to a hundred and twenty feet high. Trees in this stratum often have smaller crowns but those in the third stratum or understorey have spreading crowns. The understorey consists of trees of about fifty feet high and forms a rather dense canopy which protects the ground from the direct rays of the sun. Grass is generally absent although there are several exceptions, the most notable one being on the Sobo Plains which is one of the more extensive gaps found in the high rainforest of the Benin Lowlands. The origin of the Sobo Plains is still obscure. The flat surface of the plains and the prevelance of swamp and waterside species in the forest fringing the plains tend to support the view that the Sobo Plains grassland occupy a former swampy area now dried up. There is, however, an alternative theory which

explains the grass plains as a product of repeated and excessive farming.

In the north and east of Benin, the forest becomes thinner and the trees less gigantic. It is however in the more densely settled parts of Asaba Division such as Ogwashi Uku, Umunede and near Asaba town that the forest is completely replaced by secondary bush. Along the Benin-Sapele road, large tracts of man-made forests of para rubber predominate. The large acreage under forest reserves (Figure 20) is striking. Tropical hardwood for export as well as for the Sapele timber industry comes mainly from these reserves which produce a large number of well-known tropical species including sapelewood, mahogany, walnut and opepe.

POPULATION AND SETTLEMENT

Although the Binis have close cultural ties with the Yorubas with whom they share a common boundary, the Binis do not live in large towns as the Yorubas do. Rather, the bulk of the population live in rural areas in villages

Figure 18. A Street Village along the Benin-Ogba Road

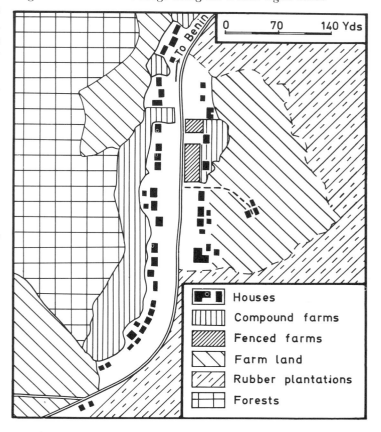

	Houses
	Compound farms
	Fenced farms
	Farm land
	Rubber plantations
	Forests

which rarely have more than 2,000 inhabitants. The largest city and oldest urban settlement is the historical capital of Benin city, but in recent years, a few of the larger villages have grown up into administrative and market towns. Such towns include Agbor, Uromi, Urhonigbe and Ogwashi Uku.

The main concentration of population is in the Ishan Plateau, where rural densities may exceed 600 persons per square mile. Vast stretches of the region which are under forest reserves are closed to farming, and are therefore uninhabited. But although the existence of these forest reserves has tended to restrict the spread of people, their size and location were determined by the absence of population in the areas which were set aside as reserves.

Ribbon development along the roads is the charcteristic form of settlement amongst the various groups of this region. Even the formerly well-fortified Egwale or chief villages of the Ishan Plateau area have been affected by this change. In the past, Ishan people lived in compact settlements built in forest clearings, but far removed from the streams. But since the first decade of this century, there has been a growing tendency for villages to move from their older sites in the forest to more accessible positions on the roads. Similar ribbon developments may be found along the road from Asaba to Benin, where the arrangement is so perfected that in many of these road-side villages it is rare to find any house which is not directly facing the road. Figure 18 shows ribbon development along the Benin-Ogba road.

In Urhobo Division transport facilities offered by the road as well as waterways like the Ethiope River have led to the movement of population of these highways. Several villages have grown up along the Sapele-Obiaruku road which runs along the Ethiope River; and during the inter censal period of 1953 to 1963, some of these villages have grown in size from less than 1,000 persons to over 4,000 persons. Some of these roadside villages have offshoots, called 'watersides' which have grown up along the bank of the Ethiope River. One such settlement is Okpara Waterside (4,940 in 1963) which originated as a small oil palm trading beach of the main village now called Okpara Inland (6,720 in 1963). Today, Okpara Waterside, which is the largest rubber collecting centre in Western Urhobo, has a crepe factory and is an important market town.

RECENT MIGRATIONS INTO THE BENIN LOWLANDS

As an area of large-scale cropping of rubber in commercial plantations as well as in small peasant holdings

and of forest exploitation, the Benin Lowlands offer considerable attraction to migrants from the Eastern Ibo Districts of Awka, Udi, Orlu and Onitsha and parts of Urhobo and Ishan Divisions of the Midwestern State. As in the creeks and lagoons region of south-western Nigeria, there is a tendency to ethnic specialization in the various economic activities pursued by migrants in this region. In the rubber farms west and south of Benin city, for example, Ishan migrants engage primarily in cultivating the land for food-crops while the Ibos concentrate on rubber tapping. Migrants from Urhobo Division carry out their traditional occupation of harvesting and processing palm fruits. In addition, paid labourers engaged in the various timber concessions come from all sections of the population.

As a result of the movements of stranger farmers into all parts of the Benin Lowlands, many of the villages have a rather mixed population in which migrants may outnumber the indigenous people (Figure 19). A number of small camps providing accommodation for two to ten people have also sprung up to house migrants like the Isokos, who prefer to live close to their place of work. The large proportion of males in the migrant population is largely explained by the fact that many of the migrants are bachelors who hope to get married after raising sufficient

Figure 19. Ogba—An Edo village with a predominantly Migrant Population

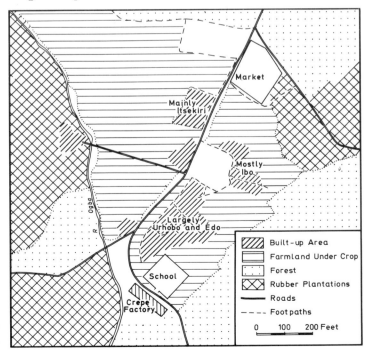

money for the bride price. It is also true that in many districts, the jobs available for migrants such as rubber tapping, climbing palm trees and timber jobs are essentially masculine in character.

Migrants working in the rubber farms are engaged directly as paid labourers or as share-tappers and live mainly in small camps in the farms. Many of them also operate as leaseholders, who obtain rights to tap the trees in a farm for a fixed number of years on payment of a lump sum. Broken farmers also pledge their farms to migrants.

Around Ogwashi and many other parts of Asaba Division, there are a large number of migrant palm wine tappers who have spent as many as twenty years in their present place of work. Some of these migrants operate on a large scale, employing as many as six labourers to tap for them on salaries of up to twenty-five pounds per annum per tapper, who is also fed by the employer.

THE BENIN RUBBER INDUSTRY

Rubber is the most important and a rapidly expanding economic crop in the Benin Lowlands. Production is concentrated in Benin Division. In 1958, for example, rubber export from Nigeria was valued at £7 million, the Benin forests accounting for over £6·2 million. The situation today is slightly different owing to the expansion, during the last ten years, of rubber cultivation in the Calabar district of the Southeastern State and in the forests of Ondo and Ijebu-Ode in the Western State. In these latter areas rubber is produced in commercial planatations, but in the Benin Lowlands peasant production predominates. Numerous families take part in cultivating, tapping and trading rubber. Many farmers have started investing in small rubber plantations and in districts like Ukuani in Aboh Division rubber cultivation is expanding at the expense of food crops. This is one way in which rubber affects the economy of the Benin area in much the same way as cocoa does in parts of Ibadan and Ondo Provinces. Also, like cocoa in Western Nigeria, rubber is attracting a large number of migrants to the Benin area.

In its early stages, the Benin rubber industry was based on the tapping of indigenous rubber bearing trees, the *Funtumia elastica* and the vines, *Landolphia* and *Clintandara* which grow wild in the forests. In 1895 the value of rubber exports from this source was £2·3 million, but as a result of reckless tapping and the consequent depletion of the resources the value of rubber export dropped to a mere £0·13 million in 1900. For the next ten years, a number of communal farms of *Funtumia* were established such that at the end of 1910 there were about one and a quarter million cultivated trees in 700 villages. The Para rubber tree (*Hevea brasiliensis*), upon which the world natural rubber industry is based, was introduced about 1913, and today *Hevea* has completely replaced *Funtumia* as a source of rubber in the Benin forest region.

Only a small proportion of the rubber produced in the region comes from commercial plantations. This is largely explained by the fact that the colonial administration of Nigeria did not favour the plantation system of agriculture, but believed and insisted that tree crops in the country could and should be developed by the indigenous population. The oldest plantation in Nigeria, the 2,000 acre rubber plantation established near Sapele by Miller Brothers in 1905 is located in the southern border of the Benin rubber belt. The government's anti-plantation policy was reversed about 1951 and since then the State Government Development Corporation has invested considerable sums of money in rubber plantations.

In 1963, there were only 25,000 acres of plantation rubber as compared with 350,000 acres under peasant management. The present situation in which the peasant farmer is the chief producer of rubber in the Benin region is likely to remain unaltered for many decades. But peasant production is fraught with many problems of which the most disturbing is the poor quality of rubber sheets caused by poor smoking or by deliberate adulteration. Peasant farmers operate on a very small scale, their farms varying from one to about twenty-five acres. They depend essentially on family labour, although those with larger estates generally employ tappers. Such tappers work for an agreed wage with the exception of share-tappers whose remuneration depends on the proceeds of the day's job. Abuses associated with share-tappers include slaughter tapping and conversion of latex into rubber lumps, which are sold without the knowledge of the owner of the farm. Share-tappers often tap the trees every day instead of every other day and in many cases tapping is started before the trees are of age. Some are known to tap the trees almost to the roots. These practises which are injurious to the trees lead to low yields per acre and constitute a serious threat to the peasant rubber industry.

Attempts made by government to improve the quality of rubber sheets from peasant farms include payment of different prices for different grades of rubber sheets and the organization of government sponsored Rubber Improvement Campaigns. Government has also given assistance in building smoke-houses where better rubber sheets can be produced. The need for establishing farmer co-operatives has since been recognized, but very little has been done in this direction.

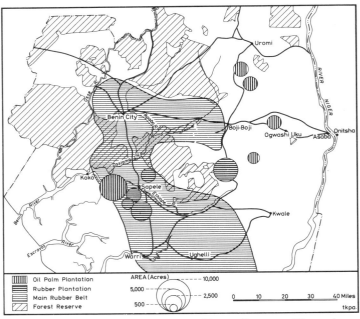

Figure 20. The Benin Lowlands—Forest Reserves, Plantations and the Benin Rubber Belt

	Total Export from Nigeria		Export from Sapele	
Year	Tonnage	Value	Tonnage	Value
1961	55,093	£11,019,000	30,201	£5,095,000
1962	59,620	£11,356,000	31,216	£5,647,000
1963	63,239	£11,788,000	42,423	£9,024,000
1964	72,069	£12,166,000	46,835	£11,463,000
1965	67,874	£10,988,000	39,927	£6,324,021

Table 7 RUBBER EXPORTS FROM NIGERIA 1961–5

SOURCE: *Federation of Nigeria Trade Report 1966*

Unlike cocoa, groundnuts or palm produce, Nigerian rubber is not marketed through a marketing board. Rather, there are a number of exporting firms who obtain their rubber from agents and sub-agents stationed at important settlements. But probably the most interesting character in the rubber trade is the itinerant buyer who goes into remote areas to buy small quantities of rubber sheet and lump rubber. He is often an assistant to an agent or sub-agent and sometimes combines his trading activities with rubber tapping. His job as a buyer is carried out mainly in the evenings, when he goes from house to house.

Producer price for rubber is fixed every month by the exporters at Sapele; an arrangement which differs significantly from those for crops like cotton, cocoa and groundnuts which are handled by marketing boards responsible for fixing producer prices for each year. This arrangement results in greater price fluctuation in the marketing of rubber sheets. Usually the prices are high during the rainy season, especially from May to July, when the weather makes tapping a rather unpleasant job, while very low prices feature during the dry season. The price of lump rubber which is not graded remains stable at three pence per pound all through the year.

Most of the rubber produced in the Benin forests is exported to the United Kingdom, the United States of America, Western Germany and the Netherlands. Table 7 shows the tonnage and value of rubber exports from Nigeria and from Sapele between 1961 and 1965. The fall in export figures for 1965 is partly due to actual fall in production of sheet rubber as well as to increasing demand for rubber sheets by local industries. The fall in production of sheet rubber is itself a result of fall in producer price which has led to some share tappers deserting the rubber farms to look for better jobs in the towns and thereby creating labour shortages in the rubber farms. Increasing demand for lump rubber, used in making crepe for local shoe factories, has also resulted in actual fall in the production of sheet rubber.

Since 1960 Benin rubber has found a growing internal market in the shoe factories at Sapele, Lagos and Kano. The Kano factory in particular produces rubber sandals which are in great demand by the local population since they are cheaper, though much less comfortable, than leather sandals. Benin rubber is also used in the manufacture of automobile tyres and Dunlopillo mattresses, both of which are now made in Nigeria. The expansion of these and other industries making use of rubber or rubber products means an increase in the local consumption of rubber which is therefore not likely to suffer, at least not to the same extent, the reverses that plague the Nigerian cocoa industry.

FORESTRY AND THE TIMBER INDUSTRY

Timber exports from the timber port of Sapele which serves the Benin forest region was valued at £3·6 million in 1962. This represented fifty per cent by value of the total timber exports from Nigeria in that year. A considerable quantity of logs from this region is also exported from Lagos harbour. Logs for shipment at Lagos are carried to the port by road or by large barges plying the creeks and lagoons which link the Benin ports with Lagos harbour. The Benin forests, therefore, constitute the most important source of timber for the Nigerian export as well as the home market. In the past, this dominant position was even greater and as late as 1948, the forests of this region accounted for sixty per cent of all the timber fellings in Nigeria and eighty per cent of the exports. Ease of access by waterways and roads to the main lumber areas and the relative wealth of economic species in the region are responsible for the large proportion of timber exports from the area.

The bulk of the timber comes from areas set aside as forest reserves (Figure 20) by the Government Department of Forestry, which supervises the exploitation of the reserves. Only large firms may obtain and work timber concessions which are usually granted for twenty-five years at a time. The Nigerian forestry law demands that in these concessions timber should be treated as a crop, in order to ensure the preservation of the forest resources of the country for posterity. Exploited tracts of the reserves are therefore replanted with timber trees so as to preserve certain species and prevent complete destruction of trees in such areas. Concession owners pay to the Government a fee of threepence per cubic foot of tree felled in addition to a ground rent for the area of the concession.

Some timber also comes from the free forest areas which are areas not under reservation, and where trees are felled without any regard to regeneration. The Forestry Department can declare any part of an existing reserve as a free area in order to make such an area available for things like road development or urban expansion. Free forests are usually exploited by individuals or small partnerships who do not qualify for concessions. Such entrepreneurs are always obliged to pay a permit fee of five pounds for every tree stump felled.

Although a saw mill was established at Koko as long ago as 1917 and a plywood factory at Sapele in 1948, logs, which are timber in its raw and crude form, constituted over eighty per cent of the total timber export in 1960. Sawn timber and plywood accounted for the remaining fraction. Both the large saw mills and the plywood factory are located at the timber port of Sapele which is therefore a collecting point for most of the logs cut in the Benin forests. The larger companies such as the African Timber and Plywood Co. invest large sums of money at various stages of the industry. In parts of the Benin forests, logs are carried by wheeled tractors to the nearest waterside to be floated to Sapele or direct to Sapele by road. Since some logs float while others sink, it was necessary at a certain time to adjust the extraction rate in such a way that two floaters were extracted for every sinker. By securing the sinker between two floaters it was possible to float all three to their destination at Sapele. But this meant that the extraction of sinkers which are the harder and more durable wood was conditioned to some extent by the rate of extraction of floaters. To overcome this situation, lighters are now used for transporting excess sinkers.

Operations at the larger mills are highly mechanized, but indigenous firms like Jothomas and Asaboro still depend largely on human labour. Pit sawing is still common in the free forest areas, where individual prospectors operate; but this is essentially a seasonal occupation since the forests may become so waterlogged during the rains as to slacken or even prevent felling operations.

THE TIMBER TOWN OF SAPELE

Sapele is the centre of the timber industry in Nigeria, a fact which is largely explained by its location close to one of the most wooded areas in Africa. Sapele port handles over fifty per cent by volume of all timber products exported from Nigeria and timber contributes about fourteen per cent of the total export of the port (1964). The impact of the industry on the townscape and economy of the town is readily appreciated by a visit to the main saw mills and plywood factory, and by the fact that the development of the town has depended largely on the growth of the timber industry. The employment opportunities provided are obvious from the fact that the United Africa Timber Co. alone employed 3,192 people in 1963 while three other saw mills employed a total of 300 workers. In 1960 as much as a third of Sapele's population of 33,638 was dependent in one way or the other on the timber industry.

The rapid growth of the town has been made possible by the influx of job seekers from all over the country, and the only supply of electricity for the town comes from a plant owned by the largest saw-mill factory in town. There is no piped water except the little extra which the timber companies can spare and the two local technical institutes were established by the United African Timber Co. which also has a hospital.

The rapid growth of Sapele town is due partly to the facilities it provides for exporting logs but primarily to the establishment of saw mills and the plywood mill. The first saw mill at Sapele was established in 1935 but today there are over one hundred large and small saw mills in the town and in 1964, sawn timber made up about twelve per cent of the total timber exports from the port.

The manufacture of plywood is the most economical way of converting logs to usable wood; and so the opening of the plywood factory in 1948 was a bold step forward. Compared with sawn timber, plywood is virtually a stable and homogeneous material which does not shrink or warp. Unlike solid timber, it does not split or shear and can be manufactured in panels of a size rarely attained in solid wood. It has a wide variety of uses including the manufacture of tea chests and furniture. The factories at Sapele also make floor tiles.

FOOD FARMING, HUNTING AND GATHERING

Although large areas of land in the region have been set aside as forest reserves, farmland is abundant except in the Ishan Plateau and parts of Asaba Division, where the large influx of stranger farmers from the East Central State has brought about considerable pressure on the land. In Benin Division and Western Asaba, there is sufficient land for everyone. Fallow periods of over fifteen years are not uncommon, although seven to eight years is usual in the more densely settled areas. This longer period of rest, not the use of artificial or household manure, is responsible for the much better yields of yams in the area as compared with the yields in the overcrowded areas of Iboland.

Although farmland is not a limiting factor in food farming in this region, farm sizes are not larger than in other parts of southern Nigeria. This is largely a result of difficulty in clearing the forest as well as in keeping the farm clear of weeds, owing to the fact that farm implements in use are still primitive and the fact that food farmers have to compete for labour with the timber companies as well as rubber and cocoa farmers. Another factor limiting the size of farmlands in Benin Division is the amount of seed-yams the farmer has in store or can afford to buy.

The farming calendar is similar to those of other parts of south-western Nigeria, except that the only crop grown during the second cropping season in September is maize. Throughout the region yam is the first crop of the rotation, the man's crop and the main staple food. Both in Benin and Asaba Division men do most of the farm work while women, who are mainly traders, assist in weeding as well as in planting the lesser crops such as maize, cocoyam, pepper and melons which are inter-cropped with yams. The sample agricultural census of 1950, carried out by the Department of Statistics, revealed that on the basis of the area under cultivation of each crop cassava, yams, cocoyams and maize, in that order, were the main crops grown in Asaba and Benin Divisions. The figures showed that 42 per cent of farmlands in Asaba was under cassava as compared with 35 per cent in Benin and that 7 per cent of the land in Asaba was cultivated with cocoyam as compared with 20 per cent in Benin Division.

Hunting is an important occupation, particularly in Benin Division where there are a number of hunters who specialize in hunting big game like elephant and leopard. Many hunters are essentially farmers who take to hunting during the slack season in the farming calendar. Ivory from elephants was one of the important items of trade between the Portuguese and ancient Benin, and past rulers of the kingdom are known to have kept a band of elephant hunters in a village near the capital city. Traps, dane guns and dogs are employed in hunting and bush meat is often seen displayed for sale along the Benin-Ifon and the Benin-Ore roads. Bush meat provides the main source of protein since livestock—goats, sheep and fowls which are widespread are rarely killed except for sacrificial purposes or during festive occasions. Dwarf cattle are found in many villages, Ibusa in Asaba Division having as many as about 500 herds (1963) which roam about the settlement zone. Unfortunately, in this village, these cows are only meant for sacrifice to the dead and may not be eaten under any circumstances.

Collecting of forest products such as snails, tortoises, firewood and wild fruits and greens is the work of women and children. Along the new Benin-Ijebu-Ode road, large quantities of snails are displayed for sales to passersby to Lagos, Ibadan or Benin where five snails are sold for a shilling in the open-air market or for two shillings and sixpence in the night clubs. The collection of other wild foods is particularly important during the hunger season when wild yams, cassava and vegetables are sought and collected to help tide over the period of food shortage.

CRAFTS AND INDUSTRIES

The organization of small craft industries in ancient Benin was similar to that in pre-industrial European cities. Almost all the indigenous crafts were in the hands of special gilds such as the gilds of blacksmiths, wood and ivory carvers, leather workers and drum-makers. Some of these gilds still function today.

Brass-casting and the carving of wood and ivory were confined to certain wards in the city of Benin and are still almost non-existent outside the capital city. Brass works as well as ivory carving were under the control of the *Oba* and figures produced were largely ritual or representing the *Oba* in ceremonial attire. Carpenters producing carved door frames and drum parts were the major group of artisans living outside the city walls.

Ceremonial cloth was woven in the city but the cloth requirements of the people of Benin were met by imports from outside the kingdom. In Ishan weaving is an important occupation amongst the women folk, who use both local and European thread on simple upright broad looms. Pottery is another important occupation and is carried out both within and outside Benin city. Benin city has a longstanding tradition of iron working, but much of its iron implements came from the Ishan Plateau, where there are still smiths who trace their origins to the smith's ward of Benin city.

The survival and recent expansion in small craft industries is in response to the growing demand by tourists and the Nigerian elite. Many of the crafts are still carried on in small workshops which often consist of the verandah of the proprietor's house. The labour requirement is small and consists mainly of young apprentices.

Modern factory industry is not yet well developed in Benin city. Large factories producing crepe rubber and furniture exist in addition to smaller establishments such as grinding mills for pepper, cassava and beans. The proposed £250,000 distillery, which is expected to produce pure alcohol from palm wine, will go a long way to replacing a long standing traditional industry—the distillation of illicit gin—in the southern parts of the region. The factory, which is expected to refine ten million tons of native gin in addition to processing palm wine for gin, will create employment for over 2,000 palm wine tappers in the region.[1]

BENIN CITY

The ancient city of Benin is reputed to date from the tenth century A.D. It was the seat of government of one of the most powerful states in West Africa, the frontiers of which extended westwards in the sixteenth century to include Lagos and Dahomey, and eastward to the banks of the Niger. It was a well fortified city and traces of the earthworks built round the city can still be identified.

Trade between Benin and Portugal started in the

[1] *Nigerian Review* p. 51 March 1967

fifteenth century, when the Benin empire supplied Portugal with such trade goods as pepper, coral beads, elephant tusks and, later, slaves in return for guns and gunpowder as well as other European manufactures. The supply of metal from Portugal was an important factor in the development of the celebrated brasswork of the city. Its port of trade was Gwato on the Benin river, a port which suffered absolute decline following the British conquest of Benin in 1897.

The creation in 1963 of the Midwest State, which is administered from Benin, has restored in some way the administrative functions of the city. Employment opportunities have increased following the establishment of many more government departments, but industrial development has been very slow. Apart from the traditional cottage industries featuring woodwork and ivory carving, the larger industrial establishments are based on local raw materials such as rubber and timber.

Compared with Enugu, Lagos and Kano, the growth of Benin city has not been impressive. Yet it services an extensive rural area and lies on the major road linking the east and Lagos. The Benin Lowlands are, however, sparsely peopled and the position of Benin city is rather distant from the scene of oil exploration to permit as much impact as is the case with Port Harcourt.

Works consulted and suggestions for further reading:

1. Blanckenburg, P., 'Rubber farming in Benin Area, A study of some socio-economic factors influencing rubber production.' Preliminary Report of Nigerian Institute of Social and Economic Research Ibadan Mimeo 1965.
2. Bradbury, R. E., *The Benin Kingdom and the Edo speaking peoples of southwestern Nigeria* (Ethnographic Survey of Africa) London 1957
3. Keay, R. W. J. & Onochie, C. F., 'Some Observations on the Sobo Plains' *Farm and Forest* No. VIII p. 71 1947
4. Nzekwu, O., 'Nigeria's Timber Industry' *Nigeria Magazine* No. 75 pp. 47–56 1962
5. Udo, R. K., 'Sixty Years of Plantation Agriculture in Southern Nigeria: 1902–62' *Economic Geography* No. 41 pp. 356–68 1965
6. United Nations (FAO), *Agricultural Development in Nigeria: 1965–1980* Chapter 5 deals with 'Policies and Programmes For Rubber Development'

5 The Lower Niger Valley

The Lower Niger begins below Lokoja and extends for a distance of about 185 miles in a southerly direction to the town of Aboh, which is considered as the apex of the Niger Delta. Over this stretch, (Figure 21) the Niger flows through a valley cut in the Basement Complex in the so-called rocky section (Lokoja to Itobe) and then through sedimentary rocks up to Aboh. The character of the valley, narrow and rocky above Idah, but wide with extensive flood plains south of Idah (except around Onitsha), is a reflection of the resistance of the rock foundation through which the valley is cut. In this stretch of the Niger valley, the number of islands of sand and clay, usually elongated in the direction of the flow of the river drops to forty-three islands per 100 miles as compared with not less than 100 islands per 100 miles in the Middle Niger Valley. This change has been explained by the fact that between Lokoja and Aboh, the Niger develops more meanders, thereby diminishing the number of islands, since islands are rarely found in meandering rivers.[1] Around Atani and in other parts, these islands are cultivated by local inhabitants or by migrant farmers from parts of the East Central State.

THE LOKOJA CONFLUENCE

Figure 22 shows that the dominating feature of the Lokoja confluence where the Benue meets the Niger is not the channel of the Niger, but that of the Benue which at this point is divided into two channels—the North Channel and the South Channel. The North Channel provides the normal shipping route but occasionally the South Channel, which draws at least sixty per cent of the Benue discharge, provides a better way. These two channels have come into being as a result of the formation of Benue Island which is thought to be recent. The description of the confluence by the Lander brothers, who passed through it in 1830, gives the impression that Benue Island did not exist then or was so low that the entire island including its vegetation was completely inundated. The position today is quite different because even the highest flood leaves parts of the island uncovered. Observations over the years indicate that at the confluence, both banks of the Benue as well as the left bank of the Niger have undergone considerable changes since the days of the Lander brothers. The right bank of the Niger which consists entirely of rock and stone has however suffered no noticeable changes during the period.

[1] N.E.D.E.C.O. *River Studies and Recommendations on Improvement of Niger and Benue* Amsterdam p. 565 1959

Local information confirms that the North Channel has been the normal shipping route in the past, possibly because it is the shortest way from Lokoja and because rocks occur in the entrance to the South Channel. Yet the confluence of the North Channel is blocked by the Benue Bar whilst the South Channel meets the Niger at a reasonable depth, and would have provided the main shipping route but for the occurrence of the Lokoja Flats immediately below the confluence of the South Channel and the Niger. These Flats remain shallow at the time of the first rise in the Benue thereby making it hard to find a good crossing channel. Fortunately they can be avoided completely by using the North Channel via the sacrifice channel, which lies between Duck Island and the right bank of the Niger. Recent investigations of the Lokoja confluence point to the future deterioration of the South Channel and this suggests that the North Channel will continue to be the main shipping route.

Figure 21. The Lower Niger Valley

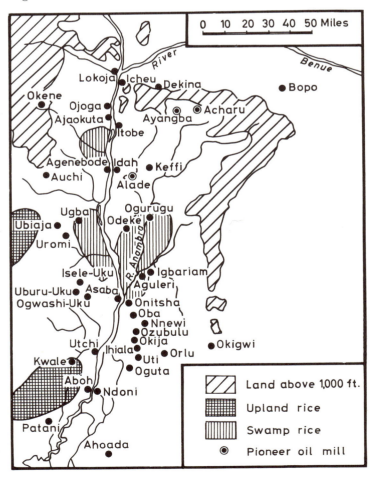

THE NIGER ROCKY SECTION

Just below the confluence at Lokoja the hills close in rapidly and the channel of the Niger becomes narrow and rocky. High granite domes and rounded hills separated by wooded valleys rise up on each bank, while a few rocks protrude into the shipping channel. Sandbanks are practically absent and the cross sections show a trough-like profile. South of Itobe, the valley broadens (332 miles from the sea) through a short stretch of broken plain, after which the hills close in again as the river flows, for the last time, in a valley cut through rocks of the Basement Complex. The next narrowing point is at Idah, where the river flows between cliffs of false-bedded sandstones.

A rapid increase in the speed of the current normally follows a channel contraction such as that presented by the rocky section of the Lower Niger. Between Lokoja and Itobe, this has been prevented as a result of the ability of the combined volume of the Niger and Benue waters to cut a deep channel into the rocks of the Basement Complex. Rocks which protrude in the shipping channels (Figure 23) have been marked by buoys and navigation through this section is said to be relatively easy.

Below the narrowing at Idah, the Niger flows through a more open valley until it reaches the defile at Onitsha, the largest and most important port on the Niger, where the valley narrows for the last time. The left bank is bordered by a wide plain of alluvium, twenty miles in width and extending eastwards to incorporate the course of the Anambra River while the right bank is bordered by low sandstone hills. In this stretch both banks are sandy, covered with dense vegetation and are populated by numerous villages and towns. The river bed itself is littered with sandbanks which rise above the river at low-water.

THE NIGER AT ONITSHA

Between Asaba and Onitsha, the Niger valley narrows considerably as hills close in to the river bank or its flood-plains (Figure 24). Down to the confluence with the Anambra, the east bank is a low wide plain, through which the Anambra flows, and is completely flooded at high-water season. At Onitsha, the dip slope of the Orlu cuesta formation terminates at the river bank. This upland area, which varies between 500 and 800 feet in height, is dissected by a number of small streams draining into the Niger. Flat-topped hills capped by lateritic sandstones characterize the surface of this upland which dips slightly to the south-west; hence the fact that the height

of the residual hills decreases in a south-westerly direction. North of the road from Asaba to Benin, the hilly country west of the Niger presents a similar relief as that around Onitsha; but south of Asaba, the hills recede and give way to another floodplain, which shows remnants of several ancient river arms and meanders and which, like the Anambra plain, is flooded at high-water season.

South of Onitsha, no less than three terraces and alluvial plains have been recognized between the river bed and the eastern hilly country. Each terrace is several hundred feet wide and the lowest, which is thirty feet above the high-water level of the Niger, is represented at Onitsha by a shallow depression draining into the marshy pond which divides the town into two separate parts. The second terrace is about 100 feet above the highest water level while the third is 260 feet. Only the lowest terrace is related to the present River Niger while the 100-feet and the 260-feet terraces are said to represent erosion stages of an older Niger.

After this last obstruction at Onitsha, the Niger flows in its own alluvial deposits which are now bordered on both sides by the Coastal Plains sands. Few islands occur

Figure 22. The Niger-Benue Confluence at Lokoja

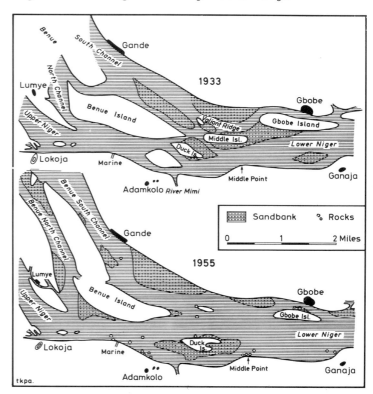

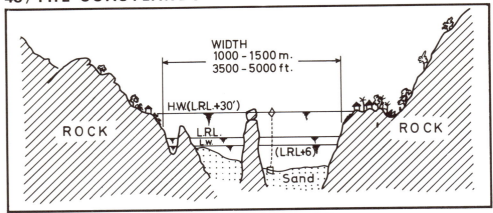

THE ROCKY SECTION

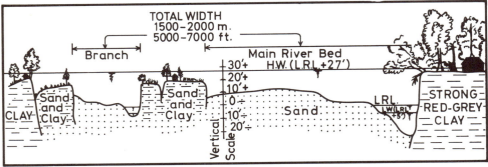

THE NIGER BETWEEN ILLUSHI AND ONITSHA

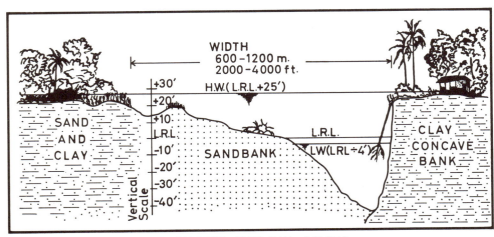

THE NIGER BELOW ABOH

Figure 23. Sections across the Lower Niger Valley

in this last stretch which is characterized by pronounced meanders and deferred tributary junctions.

THE ANAMBRA DRAINAGE BASIN

The River Anambra is the largest tributary of the Niger below Lokoja and its valley is so close to that of the Niger that it can properly be regarded as a component part of the Lower Niger lowlands. Indeed below Illushi, the floodplains of the Niger merge imperceptibly into that of the Anambra and farther north, the Ofu River which meets the Anambra at Ogurugu runs very close to the

Niger. The watershed between the Anambra and the Benue basins is of great topographical interest. It consists of a plateau surface which is in effect the northern limb of the Udi-Nsukka Plateau. The relief of this plateau surface which runs east-west through Igala Division is similar to that around Udi and consists of sandstone hills such as those which occur along the road between Dekina and Ayangba. The acid sand soils of the Nsukka-Udi area also occur along the Igala Plateau surface and since the rainfall figures are similar, it is not surprising that the vegetation presents the same aspect of open orchard bush.

The change in the vegetation as one leaves the plateau in the direction of Ayangba is impressive. Rich forests of wild oil palm trees replace the orchard bush on the plateau surface and these have given rise to a long-standing oil palm industry in an area generally considered to be outside the palm belt.

THE LOWER NIGER WATERWAY

Before the development of rail and road transportation in Nigeria, the Lower Niger provided the only means of contact between the outside world and a large part of the country. Forcados (which is located on one of the Niger distributaries), not Lagos or Port Harcourt, was the mail boat stop and principal gateway into Nigeria up to and including the first decade of this century. Palm oil markets and primitive ports, where oil from the immediate hinterland was collected for delivery to the delta ports, lined both banks of the Lower Niger. Tin from the Jos Plateau and beniseed from the Benue valley were almost exclusively exported through this waterway, which also handled a considerable tonnage of groundnuts from the far north. Today, these commodities are largely evacuated by road and railway to Port Harcourt, resulting in a considerable loss of traffic to the Lower Niger waterway. Hence the decline of many riverine ports and trading beaches, some of which have completely ceased to exist. But day by day, the Lower Niger port of Onitsha is growing as its trade and traffic increases. The growth of this port town is discussed later, but the point can well be made here that much of the trade goods distributed from Onitsha come to the town not by way of the Niger, but by road from the north, Lagos and Port Harcourt.

The limit of all season navigation on the Niger is Onitsha which is 232 miles from the open sea; while up to Lokoja (362 miles), the river is navigable from June to March. Defects of navigability including deficient discharge at low water, retarded scour after rapid drop in water-levels and fast shifting of sand-banks during high-water, which characterize the Benue and the Niger above Lokoja, are common in the Lower Niger waterway but are less pronounced. Increase in the duration of navigation below the confluence is made possible by the fact that the rise of the Benue in June makes up for part of the low-water period in the Niger, while the low-water discharges of the Benue are overlapped by the Black Flood of the Niger. The result of these differences in the hydrograph of the Benue and the Middle Niger is that high-water period on the Lower Niger starts a month earlier than on the Niger above Lokoja; while low-water period is at least a month shorter, since the rains also start earlier in the south. This is why the effect on navigability of the August fall on the Benue, which is also noticeable on the Niger below Lokoja, is minimal in the Lower Niger, where the discharges are already large.[1]

TRADE AND POLITICS IN PRE-COLONIAL DAYS

Between Aboh and Asaba, both sides of the Niger valley are inhabited by the riverine Ibo who, like most other groups inhabiting the Lower Niger valley, claim Benin descent. Above Asaba, the people on the west coast are a mixture of Ibo and Bini while the east bank is inhabited by a mixed population of Ibo and Igala. The cultural life of the entire Lower Niger valley is dominated by Bini and Igala influences, hence the claims and counter-claims that such Ibo settlements as Aboh and Ossomari were founded and settled initially by migrants from Benin and Igala territories. Even the people of Ozubulu who live a few miles away from the left bank of the Niger claim to have crossed over from the Midwest.

A considerable trade, as well as political contact, existed between the peoples of the Lower Niger valley in pre-colonial days. Politically the Igalas were the dominant ethnic group and it is known that they made many successful incursions into Ibo territory along the east bank of the Niger and in the Nsukka area. According to Lander and other explorers in this region, trade between Ibos and Igalas was carried on at periodic markets held at fixed points along the Niger; usually on uninhabited islands, or on relatively deserted stretches of the riverbank. During the rainy season, when the islands and sandbanks were flooded, trading was carried on in canoes moored close together in much the same way as the early Europeans in the delta traded from hulks. This trade arrangement reminds one of the silent trade in gold between the forest people and the Moors in the western Sudan. The reasons for selecting a neutral trading ground are not quite clear. It may well be that both groups were rather suspicious of one another, while recognizing at the same time, the need for exchange of goods.

Aboh and Idah appear to have been the lower and upper limit respectively of the common trade zone, whereby both the Ibos and the Igalas could trade freely. In 1858 Bishop Crowther observed that Igala canoes were not allowed to go beyond Aboh while Ibo canoes were not allowed to ply beyond Idah. Just as the Ijaws and other coastal peoples prevented the interior groups from

[1] *River Studies and Recommendations on Improvement of Niger and Benue* p. 748

trading directly with European vessels at the coast, the Ibos of Aboh prevented a direct trade intercourse between the Igalas and the coastal people, while the Igalas maintained a strict monopoly over markets north of Idah. Today, Igala people are to be found all over the banks of the Lower Niger where they settle to fish, farm and trade. It is thought that many settlements such as Okpaiye, Umolu and Udoni were Igala outposts which later adopted Ibo culture.

The free trade zone between Aboh and Idah was also opened to Ijaw traders from the delta, whose trade organization was very similar to that of the Efiks of Calabar in that they established many trading outposts along the Lower Niger valley in much the same way as the Efiks did in the Cross River valley. One of such Ijaw trading settlements was located on the south side of Oguta Lake, opposite the lake town of Oguta which, until the beginning of the Second World War, was one of the most important palm oil collecting centres in the East Central State. From Oguta oil was ferried in canoes and barges to Abonnema, and even today that part of the southern shore of the lake which is directly opposite Oguta town beach is called Kalabari Beach (after the Ijaws or Kalabari people). Oguta District, which like the other parts of the Niger floodplains is an important yam-producing area, also traded this food-crop to the delta people.

In Igala District, the main item of external trade during the closing years of the last century was rubber, although palm oil was also produced and marketed by the women-folk. The rubber came from indigenous rubber-bearing plants including the *Funtimia elastica* tree and the *Landolphia* vine. Rubber from Igala contributed considerably to Nigeria's rubber export which was valued at £2·4 million in 1895; declining rapidly to £131,000 five years later as a result of reckless tapping.

It is hardly necessary to recall that the trade in palm oil, which dates to the middle of the nineteenth century, as well as the rubber trade came up as substitutes to the lucrative but inhuman trade in slaves. Igala men also traded in horses and other livestock which were reared locally, the main customers being the northern Ibos who required horses for various ceremonies. The view has been expressed that Igala maintained in the past a more considerable horse population than it does today and that since this is tsetse-fly country, it is possible that the fly may not have been so heavily infected with sleeping sickness at the time. Trade in foodstuffs and other items such as cloth, pots and locally-made knives were directed by women who still dominate the distributive trade.

FOOD PRODUCTION AND OTHER ECONOMIC ACTIVITIES

The production of food for the home, as well as for the Onitsha urban market, constitutes the most important economic activity in the central part of the Lower Niger valley. Yam, which is produced on a large scale in Anam, Aguleri and Asaba areas, is the most important crop amongst the riverain Ibo, who also cultivate cassava, maize and sweet potatoes along the flood plains. Swamp rice is also of growing importance in the Anambra plains and around Ilushi. In order to beat the annual floods, and since soil conditions are favourable, crops are planted much earlier on the flood plains. Hence the early yams and maize which appear at Onitsha market from June to August, when food is relatively very scarce.

Early yams from the Niger flood plains are very large in size, good in taste but cannot keep long in store. They are transported to the market in canoes some of which are motorized. From Onitsha the early yam is distributed to various parts of the country, particularly those areas still experiencing food problems. One significant fact about the distribution of these early yams, and indeed of early maize and greens from the Niger-Anambra flood plains, is that they sell much cheaper at Onitsha food market than at Asaba or in the periodic markets of the villages where they are produced. One reason for this paradox is the fact that the farmers have a better chance of selling canoe loads of their produce within a short time at Onitsha. Another reason is that at Onitsha the farmer can use some of the proceeds of his sales to buy a greater range of imported goods.

Outside the floodplains, cassava has replaced yams as the main food-crop, and is cultivated on a large scale by both the local people and by stranger farmers. Some farmers cultivate well over four acres of cassava which, like yam, is bulky but costs much less per unit weight. In order to save themselves the labour of harvesting the cassava crop or of carrying it to the market, and as a result of the desire of middlemen and contractors to obtain the crop as cheaply as possible, matured cassava is now sold on the field at so much per head load. The buyer harvests as many headloads as she wants (this being the job of women) and heaps these up by the nearest motorable road from where they are conveyed to the market or to be fermented before sale.

An important aspect of the rural economy of Asaba Division and of the Anambra District is the large influx of stranger farmers from the overcrowded areas of Udi and Awka in the East Central State, as well as from the Isoko District of the Niger Delta. These migrant farmers

Plate 10. A Street in Umueze Anam.

cross the Niger at Onitsha, and engage primarily in the cultivation of yams and cassava for sale to the neighbouring urban markets of Onitsha and Asaba. Many of them also work as farm labourers, while others exploit palm fruits for oil and kernel. Around Ogwashi-Uku it is common to find migrants who have been away from home for over fifteen years. Thousands of such migrant farmers are also found south of Onitsha, particularly in the flood plains lying between the Niger and Orashi Rivers. These migrants usually go in groups to negotiate the right to farm or harvest palm fruits, and the rents they pay vary from district to district.

Migrants from Okigwi and Orlu Divisions usually leave their wives behind to cultivate the small gardens at their home village. The Isokos, who come from Delta Province, build permanent settlements of their own and appear very much at home in their new environments. They are found as far north as the Anambra lowlands, where they cultivate yams, groundnuts and cassava, in addition to fishing. The isolated farmsteads of these migrants contrast markedly with the large nucleated villages of the local Anam people. Anam people themselves usually migrate to farm in areas which are located at great distances from their villages and normally spend a greater part of the year in such distant farmlands. Umueze Anam village, for example, is virtually deserted during the farming season and is only repopulated after the yam harvest which takes place just before the Anambra floods its plains.

Fishing is an important occupation amongst the Anams and Kwale Ibos, but most of the dried fish handled at Onitsha market comes from Lake Chad. In most areas, the rivers and ponds are free for fishing to local inhabitants while strangers like the Ijaws and Isokos are obliged to pay rents in order to obtain fishing rights. In the Niger-Anambra area rent is paid annually, although a case has been reported of a group of Isoko migrants who paid one hundred pounds at a time for fishing rights over a period of three years.[1] Fishing in the Oguta lake, excepting in the immediate borders of the lake, is free to anyone.

Although fishing is carried out by men, women and children, the main function of the women in the fishing economy is that of selling the catch. Fishing methods used by the various ethnic groups are similar and consist of using nets and other traps in the open river as well as the use of fish poison in damned portions of the river bed or the creeks. In Anam district, the fishing season begins during the floods when the rivers and creeks are full and when the people have returned to their villages from their distant farm outposts.

Canoe-making is probably the most important ancillary craft industry associated with fishing and the carrying trade of the people of Anam and Asaba. The main canoe-making settlements include Onitsha, Idah, Umueze Anam and Osomari. At Onitsha the Hausas take an active part in building canoes for local use, as well as for export to Lake Chad, which depends on the lower Niger valley for wooden canoes.[2] The practise of fixing a twelve horse-power or thirty horse-power archimedes engine in canoes is now very common, although the greater number of canoes plying the lower Niger are still paddle-propelled. The manufacture of fishing nets, traps and baskets is associated with the fishing industry but the Igalas also manufacture soap as well as waist beads from the shell of the fan palm tree.

THE IGALA OIL PALM INDUSTRY

The position of the oil palm in the Igala economy is very different from its position in the economy of the Ibo or Ibibio farmer of the forest belt. Amongst the latter, palm produce is the major source of income and an important factor which permits the survival of as many as one thousand persons per square mile in rural districts with relatively impoverished soils. In Igala, however, there is abundant farmland and a ready market for other produce so that the people do not have to depend on the oil palm as is the case further south. Indeed according to J. S. Boston it is considered a sign of social failure if a man, who is above thirty-five years of age, engages extensively in cutting palm fruit for sale as a means of obtaining a livelihood. Rather, the oil palm industry is controlled by the women folk who, traditionally, do not take a very active part in agriculture, and by young men who are still struggling for economic independence.[3] Amongst the Ibos and Ibibios, oil palm traders are amongst the wealthiest men in the society; but in Igala, this trade is carried on by women who, indeed, dominate all aspects of marketing and exploitation of wild produce, leaving farming and hunting to the men.

[1] Chubb, L. T., *Ibo Land Tenure* p. 54 Ibadan

[2] This statement is true for the period before the 1966–8 political crises in the country

[3] Boston, J. S., 'The Igala Oil-Palm Industry' *Nigerian Institute of Social and Economic Research* Conference Proceedings pp. 100–10 March 1962

Rights of ownership over palms, and rights of access to communal palm groves, are broadly similar to those in the Ibibio area. Palms on compoundlands belong to the owner of the compound and this applies to palms on farmland under cultivation. Such palms are exempt from the usual annual prohibition of two to three months duration, during which no one is expected to harvest palms in the village territory. At the expiry of the ban, the first fruits go to the land-owning group in the village. This annual ban is similar in some ways to the less regular bans imposed in the Ibibio area, except that in the latter case the proceeds from fruits harvested during the ban go to the common purse of the village for community development projects. In Igala palm trees revert to common ownership once the farmland reverts to fallow or the compoundland ceases to be occupied.

Igala methods of processing palm fruits are similar to those of the Yorubas of Western Nigeria, but the usual arrangement whereby the oil belongs to the man, while the woman takes the kernel, does not apply. Where a wife processes the fruits cut by her husband, such work is regarded as part of her normal domestic duty; although a husband may reward his wife with fruits which then belong entirely to her.

Attempts to modernise the oil palm industry in Igala have met with the same problems as in the palm belt further south. The pioneer oil mills introduced in 1951 are faced with the same problem of inadequate and irregular supply of fruits, and are therefore finding it difficult to pay their way. The scheme of establishing communal plantations, which was started in 1951, met with no response and had to be abandoned four years later. In terms of national output, palm oil from Igala is insignificant and tonnage graded for export has maintained a steady decline from 3,851 tons in 1956 to 384 tons in 1961. The quantity of palm kernel on the other hand increased from 11,600 tons in 1956 to 18,000 tons in 1961.

TRAFFIC ACROSS THE NIGER[1]

Until the opening of the Niger bridge at Onitsha in January 1966, there was no through road connection between the Eastern States and the provinces west of the Lower Niger valley. Rather, there were motorized ferries at Onitsha, Idah and Lokoja for crossing lorries and cars as well as passengers. These ferries operated side by side with the primitive but more ancient canoe ferry services.

[1] Based on Nwankwo, E. C., 'Traffic Across the Niger' unpublished B.A. dissertation Dept. of Geography University of Ibadan June 1966

The busiest ferry point was at Onitsha, and many of the observations in this section refer to traffic across the Niger at the Onitsha-Asaba crossing.

Onitsha and Asaba lie on the trunk road linking the Eastern States to Lagos, and this explains in part the large volume of traffic handled at this crossing. Another important factor is that in this area the Niger valley creates a barrier between the Western and Eastern Ibos, hence the greater rate of contact, particularly since Eastern Ibos have long found it necessary to cross over the Niger to farm the western banks. The fact that these migrant farmers and others from the Asaba end have always preferred to market their produce at Onitsha, constitutes another reason for the heavy ferry traffic between Asaba and Onitsha.

Before the government motor-launch was introduced in 1927, canoes and engine-boats were the only means of carrying goods and persons from one side of the river to another. Traffic was very small and the fare for crossing was about two pence per head. The goods transported consisted mainly of foodstuffs from the Asaba end and imported goods coming in from Lagos. But canoe ferrying is essentially slow and unsafe. Accidents involving loss of lives and property were common. Another problem arose from the fact that most of the canoes were owned and operated by Anam people who usually returned to their farms during the farming season. In later years, big outboard engine boats like the Errico were used for ferrying passengers and goods. A traveller to Lagos and the West was obliged to stop at Onitsha, cross the river by these boats and at the Asaba end, he had to negotiate for another lorry or taxi to take him to his destination. The gap created by the absence of reliable or established travel agencies, which could have minimised the difficulties confronting the traveller along this route, was filled by dishonest motor touts, who contrived to rob passengers while pretending to help them.

In 1952 motor ferries capable of carrying lorries replaced the launches which could only carry cars. Loaded lorries were now able to cross the Niger in about forty minutes without breaking bulk, and the demand for the service was so great that there were ten services between Onitsha and Asaba every week-day, and four on Sundays. Passengers still preferred the Errico launch service, whose landing stage at Onitsha market made it more suitable for the food traders, who are the most regular users of any ferry service between Onitsha and Asaba. But there were still as many as 2,400 passengers using the Inland Waterways ferry every day while the number of vehicles per day averaged 200 (1960–4). Ferrying, however, still involved a huge wastage of time, particularly during the annual period of congestion in December, when cars were delayed for over twelve hours and lorries for five days at the Asaba end. Often one of the two ferries operating at this crossing was withdrawn for repairs and servicing and, in order to cater for its customers, the Inland Waterways on one such occasion in 1964 was obliged to hire a Shell-BP vessel at a loss of £40 per day. Besides, the operation of the ferry service was limited to the day since there was no sailing after 8pm. At the period of the opening of the Niger bridge, an average of 7,000 vehicles crossed the Niger by ferry each month (1964) and this yielded a cash income of about £15,000 per month.

The character of the seasonal fluctuation in the volume of traffic across the Niger at Onitsha is indicated in the reference made to the withdrawal of Anam canoes during the farming season, as well as to the congestion experienced every December at the motor-ferry of the Inland Waterways Department. This seasonal fluctuation persisted even at a time when the Anams were no longer in control of the trans-Niger canoe traffic. The greatest volume of traffic occurred in the dry season when part-time traders, who had taken off time to farm their land, were back in the trading business. In addition, the main harvest season starts at the beginning of the dry seasons; hence the large traffic in foodstuff from the Asaba end, where Onitsha traders buy food in bulk to store up for resale during the hunger period.

The £5 million Niger bridge which was completed in December 1965 is a toll bridge which has proved a welcome relief to those crossing the Niger at Onitsha.[1] Apart from gains in time, the tariff for crossing vehicles is not more than fifty per cent of the tariff levied by the Inland Waterways ferry. The location of the bridge is shown in Figure 24. The opening of the bridge has had a considerable impact on trans-Niger traffic at Onitsha. The first few months of its operation has confirmed the anticipated phenomenal increase in the number of vehicles crossing the Niger. The Inland Waterways ferry service and several motor boats have already been withdrawn, but since the bridge heads are far from the markets at Onitsha and Asaba, local food traders still prefer the motor boats which land at the market beaches. But these boats have lost much of their traffic and may be completely withdrawn in the near future. It appears, however, that as in the pre-ferry days, canoes will continue to be used for transporting yams from Anam, Atani and other areas to Onitsha market as well as for conveying sand from the exposed sandbanks in the middle of the Niger bed and firewood, all of which are low value goods, to the main consuming centre at Onitsha.

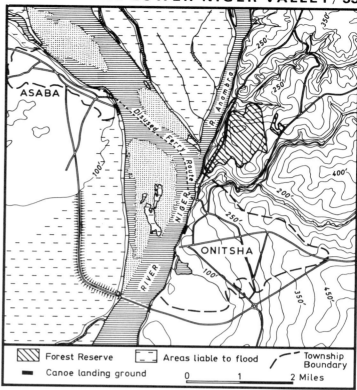

Figure 24. The Niger at Onitsha

Forest Reserve	Areas liable to flood
Canoe landing ground	Township Boundary
0 1 2 Miles	

THE TOWN AND MARKET OF ONITSHA

Onitsha is known all over Nigeria for its market which is by far the largest and most modern in the country, if not in West Africa and for the variety of goods obtainable from this market. The value of goods handled at Onitsha market per annum has been put at about ten million pounds, and only a few people who visit this market will doubt the veracity of the common saying that if there is any merchandise that cannot be obtained at Onitsha, then that merchandise cannot be obtained anywhere else in Nigeria. The market which occupies a fifteen acre site was built in 1955 at a cost of about £530,000 and has a total of 3,264 stalls almost one half of which are in the covered sections, intended for the sales of textiles and certain perishable goods.[2] The layout of the market is impressive, the grain dealers stores are, for ease of access, located close to the river front; the meat and fish stalls are next to the slaughter house, other stalls are grouped into sections, each of which caters for traders dealing in the same commodities.

During the last three to four hundred years, Onitsha has been the focus point of canoe traffic bringing yams, beans, maize, rice and imported merchandise from the Upper Niger, the Benue valley and from the coast through Burutu, Warri and Sapele. Onitsha has in effect been a collecting and distributing centre rather than a producer-distributor one and this explains the vast extent of its

[1] This bridge was destroyed in September 1967 by retreating troops of the secessionist regime in the East Central State
[2] 'Onitsha Market' *Nigeria Trade Journal* Vol. 5 pp. 88–91 1957

hinterland which includes such distant places as Kano, Sokoto, Maiduguri and Jos. Products of the Nigerian Sudan such as beans, millet, guinea corn, dried fish, cotton and shea butter arrive at Onitsha by road or river, from where they are distributed to other parts of south-eastern Nigeria.[1] Its immediate hinterland, which includes the Anambra floodplains, Asaba Division and the flood-plains below Onitsha, is also a rich food surplus region which supplies quantities of yams and fruits through Onitsha market to various parts of the East Central State.

When in 1857 the Niger Trade expedition of McGregor Laird visited Onitsha the market was a small market which, like other nieghbouring Ibo markets, was held every four days. Its position in the heart of the palm belt was an important factor in the growth of the early trade, which was largely in the hands of the womenfolk who operated mainly as middlemen between the upland villages of Obosi, Ogidi, Umudioka and Nkwelle and the riverine people of Anam, Aboh, Asaba and Ogbaru. Trade with Britain brought about the growth of the 'Waterside Town' as distinct from 'Onitsha Proper' which at that time was a small village off the bank of the river. The uninhabited space between the two settlements has since been built up, but even today the river bank is still dominated by the settler elements as distinct from the Onitsha indigenes who live away from the river bank. The spatial growth of both the town and market followed the formal occupation of Southern Nigeria by the British when Onitsha market, like those of many other settle-ments, became a daily market rather than a four-day cycle market.

Although it is formal to talk of 'Onitsha market', there is in fact more than one market in Onitsha. Apart from the main market, there is the Ochanja market which now serves as an extension of the former as well as other smaller markets including Nde-nde market and Ogbe Umuase. Yet stall space is still insufficient as is evidenced by the high rent of from £4 to £7 per stall per month which traders are obliged to pay to stall-owners who in turn pay only £2 per month per stall to the market authority. The growing demand for more stalls has also led to the conversion of the immediate residential neigh-bourhood to permanent extensions of the market, through a system whereby enterprising traders replace existing houses by a two- or three-storey building, the ground floor of which serves as a trading stall. In most cases, the owners of the plots are financially incapable of building such houses and in that case, the trader enters into a tenancy agreement whereby he can lease the ground floor on a long-term basis (usually over thirty years) for a much reduced rent while the landlord lives upstairs.

The influx of traders from all parts of the country and the Cameroons to buy at Onitsha is another important aspect of the market functions of Onitsha. Amongst the factors responsible for this attraction are the low prices of commodities in Onitsha, the wide range of goods on sale, and the ease and low cost of transportation to and from Onitsha. Many people are baffled by the fact that Onitsha market offers the lowest prices for most imported com-modities but there are many reasons for this, one of which is the keen competition in the market. Low prices are also a result of large scale smuggling which make it possible to sell high-quality goods at about half the shop price since this permits the dealer who paid no customs duty to make a considerable profit. The sale of imitation goods is also another factor which makes for the low prices at Onitsha market. Onitsha traders often send samples of British or European goods to Japanese manufacturers, who are generally able to produce a much cheaper imitation which bears so close a resemblance to the original that most consumers are not able to distinguish which is which. Onitsha market is also notorious for the barbaric law of its traders, who have repeatedly beaten to death, in broad daylight, anyone suspected of being a thief.

Selected references

1. N.E.D.E.C.O. *River Studies and Recommendations on Improvement of Niger and Benue* Amsterdam 1959
2. Chubb, L. T., *Ibo Land Tenure* Ibadan 1961
3. Boston, J. S., 'The Igala Oil-Palm Industry' Nigerian Institute of Social and Economic Research Conference Proceedings pp. 100–10 March 1962
4. Nwankwo, E. C., 'Traffic Across the Niger' unpublished B.A. dissertation. Dept. of Geography University of Ibadan 1966
5. Unigwe, A. V., 'Fishing Among the Anams' *Nigeria* No. 18 p. 171 1939
6. Nzekwu, O., 'Onitsha' *Nigeria* No. 50 pp. 200–3 1956

---

[1] This is true of the pre-civil war period. The indication is that this trade will be resumed at the end of hostilities

6 The Niger Delta

Along the coast, the Niger Delta extends from the Benin River in the west to the Bonny River in the east. Inland, it begins a few miles below the village of Aboh at a point where the Niger forks into the Nun and Forcados Rivers. It is a low-lying region riddled with an intricate system of natural water channels through which the Niger finds its way into the sea. Before the mouths of these channels were blocked by bars the delta provided the largest number of sheltered port sites along the coastline of West Africa, and such historic ports as Bonny, Warri, Brass and Forcados were located in this region. In the seventeenth and eighteenth centuries, the combined trade of these ports made the Niger Delta the most important slave mart along the West African coast and in the early part of the nineteenth century, when palm oil became the main item of trade, these ports exported more oil than the rest of West Africa put together.

The Niger Delta is a region of difficulty. Its prosperity in pre-colonial days was based not on local resources but on the middleman role of its port towns in the trade in slaves and palm oil between the European traders of the coast and the people of the rainforest belt. This trade monopoly was broken by the establishment of British administration, which was followed by the economic decline of the region. As a result of its physical handicap, the delta is a region which is unlikely ever to be highly developed. So far, there is no indication that the recent mineral oil boom which has transformed the landscape of the immediate hinterland of Port Harcourt will have any great impact on the delta which produces the crude oil.

It is significant that the commodities of trade which brought wealth to pre-colonial delta society were produced outside the delta and that today, areas close to, but definitely outside the delta, stand to profit more from the petroleum in the delta. Already, there are loud grumblings that so far the delta has benefited least from the oil industry. The righteous indignation of the people to this situation might appear to be misplaced since the neglect of the delta can properly be blamed on its difficult terrain. There is, however, no doubt that the local people would have had more cash from the oil companies except for the fact that under Nigerian law, sub-surface or mining rights in land belong to the national government and not to individuals or the local government authority. The local inhabitants own the surface rights and are entitled to a rental fee as well as compensation for crops and trees destroyed at drilling sites.

PHYSICAL CHARACTERISTICS OF THE NIGER DELTA

The erroneous idea that the Niger Delta is a vast area with numerous creeks which are bordered by mangrove trees arises from the fact that most people who come in contact with the delta do so at Port Harcourt, Sapele or Warri; each of which is located at the landward edge of the mangrove swamps. There are, however, three main physical divisions in the region and these are: the freshwater zone; the mangrove swamps; and the coastal sand ridges zone.

Considering the size of its population and the varied nature of the local resources the freshwater zone, that is the plain extending northwards from the mangrove swamps to the apex of the delta, is the most important physical division of the region. The northern part of this zone may be regarded as a southward extension of the Lower Niger floodplain, except for the fact that it has a greater silt and clay foundation and is more susceptible to the yearly inundation by river floods. The southern part, on the other hand, is given to great tidal influence but is not much affected by river floods. Most water channels in this freshwater zone are bordered by natural levees, which are of great topographical interest and of great economic importance to the local people. Those levees, which are high enough to escape from the effects of river floods, provide the site for most of the settlements in this zone. Other levees are used for cultivating such crops as cassava, yam, cocoyam, vegetables and plantains, which are usually harvested before the river floods come up.

Away from the river, the level of the land falls gently with the result that the land between two levees is liable to flooding. The soil also changes from the brown loams and sandy loams at the crest of the levee to more acidic and more clayey soils on the slopes. Flooding prevents the cultivation of levee slope soils which are closely populated by oil palm trees.

Large swamps, many of which are silted water courses, occur in several areas particularly in the Isoko and Yenegoa districts. Drainage is poor, especially in the eastern districts where pools of standing water persist from March to December. A mixture of raffia palms and broad-leaved trees in which the former predominates is the chief type of vegetation; hence the fact that the main products of these swamps are palm wine, the raw material of illicit gin and some timber.

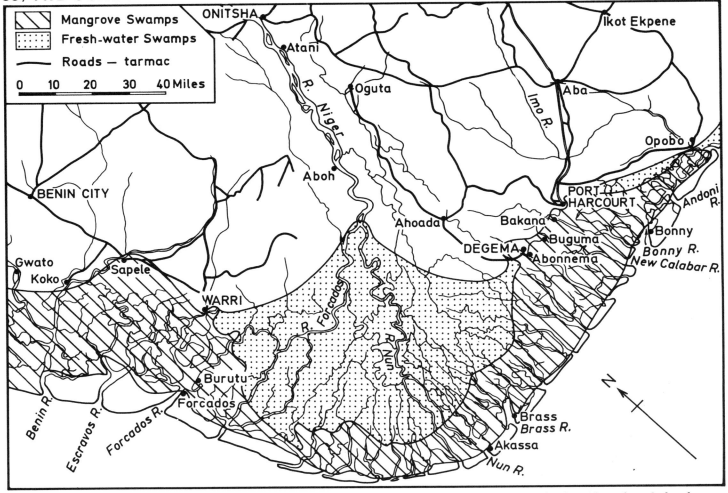

Figure 25. Physical Regions of the Niger Delta. The unshaded narrow strip fronting the open sea is the region of sandy beaches and abandoned beach ridges

In the central part of the Niger Delta, mangrove swamps, which are largely muddy and uninhabitable, occur south of the freshwater swamps. Elsewhere, but particularly in the Sapele-Warri and the Port Harcourt-Abonnema areas, where the widest stretches of the mangrove swamps occur, these swamps are bordered on the landward side by firm sedimentary rock of the coastal plain formation and not by freshwater swamps (Figure 25). There are about 4,000 square miles of mangrove swamps in the delta. Within these swamps may be found a number of fairly high lands which are dry throughout the year. Such patches of dry land provide sites on which settlements like Buguma, Bakana, Degema and Tombia are built. But these islands are often plagued by creek erosion, which is said to occur when the level of the sea falls, at which time the creeks erode their lowest part and begin to cut back gradually. At Opobo Town, creek erosion is threatening the main building of St Paul's church, the playing field of which has already been submerged by advancing swamps. Soils of the swamps are rich in organic matter in the top layer, but contain too much salt, especially in the dry season.

The third physical division of the delta is the narrow strip of sandy ridges and beach ridges which lie very close to the open sea. The width of the strip varies from a few yards to ten miles and is bordered on the landward side by swampy areas containing many creeks. As a result of the heavy rainfall in this area, the swamps are covered with freshwater vegetation, but further inland, these swamps give way to mangrove swamps. The soils of the sandy ridges are mostly sandy or sandy loams which sometimes have an underlying layer of impervious pan. The high rainfall also causes much leaching in the soils, which are rather poor but do support crops like mangoes, coconuts, cashew nuts and oil palm trees.

Excepting the region of the mangrove swamps where trees grow only close to the banks of the creeks, the whole delta is covered with a dense vegetation. Extensive forest tracts in which the oil palm is the predominant species occur in the north of the mangrove swamps. Viewed from the air, the scenery is one of great natural beauty and calm. Here and there occurs a cluster of huts marking a fishing outpost or a larger cluster with permanent structures being the remnants of an old trading port. These features, together with the occasional canoe, boat or ship, and the drilling rigs of the oil companies help to break the endless view of water, swamps and trees. Both the siesmic lines of the Shell-BP exploratory teams and the perpetual flames of natural gas at the various oil wells and flowstations can be clearly discerned from the air.

Human activities are still largely controlled by natural conditions, which in some areas limit the occupation of the people to fishing. In a region which already has too much surface water, a high rainfall, ranging from 120 inches in the region of Aboh to 200 inches at the coast, creates considerable problems to settlement and land use. Much difficulty is experienced and time wasted in transporting heavy drilling rig equipment from one location to another; and large sums of money and labour are expended in laying pipelines across swamps and wide channels like the Forcados and Nun Rivers. The use of helicopters to transport supplies to drilling sites has been necessitated by the difficult environment which makes it impossible to build access roads to sites within the delta. For the same reason, there is no direct road from Port Harcourt to Ughelli except through Onitsha—a distance of 280 miles as compared with only seventy-five miles by helicopter.

CAUSES AND CONSEQUENCES OF THE ANNUAL FLOODING OF THE DELTA

Almost every part of the delta is under water at one time of the year or another, but the northern part, which is the habitable part, remains dry after the rains and the Niger floods except for the large swamps referred to above. In Isoko and the Ahoada area of the delta, flooding is so extensive that the aspect of the landscape is entirely different in January and February, when the water in the Niger and its distributaries is at its lowest, to the high-water period, which is also the flood season.

Two separate and distinct annual floods are distinguished both by their cause and the period of occurrence. The first is due to local rainfall, while the other is caused by floodwater coming down the Niger. The rain floods (Ovo in Isoko) are caused by local rains, about ninety inches of which are concentrated within a few months of the year. Since the sandy soils are porous and very pervious, there is a rapid rise in the ground-water level, a process which subsequently floods the lowlands. Since the rains also cause a corresponding rise in the level of local rivers, the Ovo floodwater from the creeks cannot escape and the result is a prolonged and disastrous flood as the creeks fill up and are ponded back to overflow their banks.

The other annual flood, the river flood (Owhe in Isoko) is in effect caused by the arrival in the area of the Black Flood from the upper reaches of the Niger. It has nothing to do with local rains and is thought to be due to last year's rain coming down the River Niger from the hinterland of Sierra Leone and Guinea. At the Lokoja confluence, it is joined by the Benue Flood, caused by the current year's rainfall in that river-basin; and together the flood sweeps down the Lower Niger valley, submerging all sandbanks and washing downstream vast quantities of sand which form new sandbanks when the flood subsides. The low-lying lands beginning from the region of Aboh southwards are always exposed to the full force of this flood as it surges down the Niger distributaries, bursting their banks and flooding the lowlands.

A common geomorphic feature associated with these annual floods is the continual changing of the river courses in the delta. Indeed it is the resulting abandoned meander loops which make up a large number of the lakes and swamps in the delta.

These floods have a tremendous influence on the pattern of human life and economic activities in the delta. For practical purposes our interest here is on the effects of the floods on those areas of the northern delta like Urhobo, Isoko and Ahoada districts where much development is possible if the floods can be controlled. At present crops like yams, cassava and maize are restricted to the drier parts of this area, but the acreage under them can be extended if the floods are controlled.

Drilling operations of the Shell-BP exploratory team in the upper reaches of this delta have also been affected by the floods. Since land-rigs are used in this part of the delta, drilling is not possible when the land is flooded.

ASPECTS OF THE TRADITIONAL ECONOMY

The traditional economy of the delta may be discussed under two broad categories—the economy of the 'landsmen' who occupy the drier land at the head of the delta, and the simpler economy of the 'watermen' farther south. The landsmen consist of the Urhobos, Isokos and riverain Ibos whose occupations include farming, fishing, collecting and processing palm fruits and hunting. In contrast the watermen, the Ijaws and Itsekiris, are essentially fishermen and traders with a less diversified economy; and they depend on the landsmen for such essential food items as yams, grains and fruits. In the past, they produced salt which they traded with the landsmen for food-crops.

Yams and cassava are the main food-crops grown by the landsmen. Farming activities begin around mid-December, when the floods are receding. Yams are the first crop to be planted and later maize, beans and groundnuts are interplanted in the same fields. As in other parts of the country yams, of which many varieties exist, are the crop of the men and here, the water yam is of particular importance, being the first main crop to be harvested after maize. Cassava and the other crops are cultivated by the womenfolk. The sandy nature of the soils in this area appears quite suited to groundnuts which the Isokos grow for local consumption and not for export.

Another important occupation of the landsmen, and one for which they are best known in areas where they migrate to settle for a time, is the collecting of palm fruits which they process and sell. We shall come across these delta migrants from time to time in other regions, but it is convenient at this stage to comment on their methods of extracting palm oil. After cutting, the fruits are softened under a leaf cover in the sun for a few days before being stripped off from the bunch. They are then thrown into large canoe-like wooden troughs, about twelve feet long, and trodden on by two to four men until the fruits are reduced to pulp, nuts and oil. The oil is scooped out at one end of the trough and stored in kerosene tins or calabashes. Water is then added to the remaining pulp, which is retreaded so that the oil comes to the surface to be collected. The oil is then boiled to remove impurities, the whole operation taking about three days or about a week from the cutting of the fruits.

The landsmen of the delta also fish, but many of them do so part-time. Canoe building is an important industry since canoes are the only means of transportation in many areas. Canoes are also important in the local fishing industry and fortunately, this part of the delta provides the necessary trees for the industry. Other crafts include pottery, basket-making and mat-making.

The environment of the watermen precludes farming except in a few districts like Ozobo in Western Ijaw Division where the levees lining the creeks are cultivated with water yams, cocoyams, cassava, plantains and maize. In Itsekiri area, where some cultivable land exists, there is virtually no cultivation since the Itsekiris look down on agriculture as 'slaves' work', their main occupations being trading and creek fishing. Fishing rights are as important to them as land rights are to the people farther inland and disputes over fishing rights occasion much litigation.

Nearer the open sea, the watermen specialize in sea-fishing and may travel considerable distances away from their home. Ijaw fishermen are found as far east as the Cross River estuary and the southern Cameroons coast, and westwards they may be found around Badagry and Dahomey. Fishermen who travel to fish in distant waters usually stay away from home for many months.

The distillation of gin from wine obtained from the raffia palm is a longstanding traditional industry, which has now become the main source of income to some Ijaw groups in the western delta. At Ozobo in Midwestern Nigeria, this industry is the main source of money for taxes, school fees and even for community development projects.[1] The gin is produced in large quantities and exported in bulk by canoes to riverine ports like Onitsha, Jebba, Lokoja and Yola as well as to the seaports of Warri, Lagos, Tiko and Duala in the Cameroon.

Plantain is a common crop found all over the delta. It is therefore not surprising that plantain and fish form the staple food of the area. Coconut palms also abound as far south as Bonny where the state government corporation has a 1,200-acre coconut plantation.

Rubber is an important cash crop in the northern part of the western delta which forms part of Benin rubber belt (see Figure 20). In western Urhobo District, as much as seventy-five per cent of land under cultivation in 1965 was cropped with rubber. Peasant rubber holdings, only a few of which exceed ten acres, stretch for miles and miles on both sides of roads passing through this district, where rubber forests, created by man, have virtually displaced the dense natural rain forest of the area.

One significant effect of the development of rubber production in the western delta is the reduction in the volume of rural migrants from the district. Many would-be

[1] Brisibe, A., 'Retail Trade and Transportation at Ozobo' unpublished B.A. dissertation Dept. of Geography University of Ibadan 1967

Figure 26. Morphology of the Eastern Delta

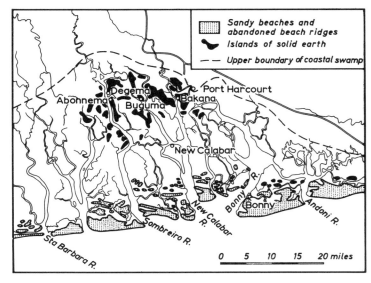

migrants are now engaged as labourers in the rubber farms which also depend for labour on the large influx of stranger elements who serve mainly as rubber tappers.

EARLY TRADE WITH EUROPE AND THE DEVELOPMENT OF DELTA PORTS

On the basis of their location relative to the sea and of their rock foundation, which is actually a function of the distance from the sea, port sites in the Niger Delta may be divided into two groups. Sandy beaches and abandoned beach-ridges provide the first group of port sites, while the second or inland group of port sites is provided by islands of solid earth rising above the mangrove swamps, which have invaded the upper reaches of many of the Niger distributaries, as well as by salients of the mainland projecting into the mangrove swamps. Ports which have grown up on the first site group include Forcados, Burutu, Bonny and Brass and by their location may be referred to as ' exterior ' ports; while ports like Bakana, Abonnema, Warri and Port Harcourt which have grown up on the inland or second site group may be called 'interior' ports (Figure 26).

In the early days of shipping along the delta coast, that is during the period of the slave-trade and the palm-oil trade, local kings like Peppel of Bonny and Jaja of Opobo held jurisdiction over the waters within their kingdom. European vessels could only trade in such areas with the permission of these kings and even then, the trade was confined to the coast towns. Contact with the producer was through middlemen and generally, the king who controlled a river-mouth also controlled the trade up that river. Indeed, delta politics at this time were dominated by the struggle to control the trade of the various river entrances and their immediate hinterland. The most favourable location for ports at this time was on the exterior sites.

The fierceness with which the delta people guarded the trade monopoly is best appreciated when one remembers that the prosperity of the watermen derived primarily from their middlemen position in the European trade in slaves and palm oil, both commodities of which came from outside the delta. The delta itself had little to offer in this trade, and even the food taken by the delta people, with the exception of fish, came from the interior.

One of the physical handicaps facing ports in the delta has been the limited area of dry land available for expanding port facilities on those sites which occur south of the inland border of the mangrove swamps. In the past, when trading ships usually anchored off the creeks and remained long enough to dispose of their merchandise and reload with cargo from the interior, there was no provision for such port terminal facilities as quays, transit sheds, warehouses, passenger accommodation, offices, road and rail approaches; all of which are necessary for modern shipping. By their location, the exterior ports of the delta cannot provide all or even most of these necessary terminal facilities.

The turning point in the fortunes of these old delta ports came with the building of roads and railways which followed the establishment of British rule. For various reasons, the termini of these land transportation media proved more suitable as port sites. One such reason was that inland ports like Port Harcourt, Warri and Sapele had access to the hinterlands through land transportation as well as through water transport unlike the exterior ports. These inland ports have therefore been able to expand their hinterland at the expense of other ports.

Another great handicap confronting ports in the delta is the gradual shoaling (or silting up) of all the entrances to the River Niger. The western delta ports have been particularly handicapped since the submarine bars at the mouth of their approaches are growing at a fast rate. The entrance to these ports, at the end of the last century, was through the Forcados River, on whose banks grew the ports of Forcados and Burutu. In 1899, the draught on the Forcados Bar was twenty feet, but by 1928 this had decreased to seventeen-and-a-half-feet. In 1960, it was only eleven feet and its length, which was half a mile across in 1899, increased to three-and-a-quarter miles in 1960. The Forcados entrance has, in consequence, been closed to ocean liners (since 1939), and Forcados has since ceased to function as a port. Other ports similarly affected are Brass, Akassa and Opobo.

In practical terms, the deterioration of both the bars and river channels increased shipping costs partly because considerable time was wasted in waiting for high tide to cross the flats and partly because ships had to be lightly laden if they were to cross the bars safely even at high tide. In the case of the western delta ports, which handle the Niger-Benue traffic, the latter factor meant that much of the produce coming down these rivers was not loaded direct on to ocean-going ships, but was carried by coasters to Lagos for loading. To meet the cost of this coastal freight a surcharge of twelve shillings and six pence per ton was levied on all exports from the western delta ports. This contributed to diverting groundnuts and cotton exports from the western delta ports to Lagos.

THE ESCRAVOS BAR PROJECT

This project[1] which involved the dredging of the estuary of the Escravos River and the construction of a five-and-a-half mile long mole from the mainland, together with an island mole which is 3,000 feet long was completed in 1964 at a cost of thirteen million pounds. It was designed to keep open the entrance to that river and expand the trade of the western delta ports by removing most of the obstacles discussed above.

For the first 11,100 feet, the main mole runs south-westerly at an angle of 45° from the shoreline. It then turns west, crossing the Escravos bar at almost a right angle. The purpose of this mole is to deflect the littoral drift and the flow of water from the Escravos River, and this it does by turning out to sea the ocean and river currents which flow along the coast, and were largely responsible for the formation of the bars. The 3,000-feet island mole is designed to force the current to move faster. The channel has been dredged to a depth of twenty-two feet and the flow of water through it is fast enough to prevent sand and silt being dropped. It is estimated that ships carrying 6,000–8,000 tons will be able to use the entrance which was formerly restricted to ships carrying 2,000–3,000 tons.

Some of the real problems which faced this project deserve to be mentioned in passing. One of these was getting an adequate supply of granite at the nearest location to the construction site. A quarry at Otu, between Ondo and Okitipupa was opened to supply the granite and a seventeen-and-a-half mile railway was built to transport the rocks to the nearest creek port from where they were loaded on barges and carried 125 miles through various creeks to the Escravos bar.

Labour for the job had to be brought from outside the delta which is thinly populated. At the peak of the job, as many as 2,150 Nigerians and eighty expatriates were employed, all of them being camped in a town built on Escravos Island by the contractors, who provided shopping and medical facilities as well as free transport to Warri and back every week.

THE PORT AND TOWN OF PORT HARCOURT

Port Harcourt, the second largest port in Nigeria, was founded in 1912 as a coal port and is now the operational headquarters of the Nigerian petroleum industry. In 1953, it had a population of 59,000 but the population of the greater Port Harcourt area in 1966 is believed to be more than 100,000. Its rapid growth in recent years is largely due to the expansion of the oil industry which has also attracted many varied manufacturing industries to this promising port town. The port is equipped with modern facilities for loading, unloading and distribution of goods. At present, it handles about twenty per cent of Nigeria's total imports and exports.

One of the greatest problems of the port in post-war years has been increasing congestion leading to long delays in the clearance of ships. The great expansion of Nigeria's overseas trade, and the development of road transport and cash crop production since the war, placed too much strain on the limited facilities of the port which was originally planned as a railway port. Congestion at the port was so bad that in 1956 a total of 284 ship-days were lost to shipping in spite of efforts to relieve congestion by clearing cargo by road. The cost of these delays in monetary terms was put at £500 a day and in 1957 a £4 million port extension contract was awarded. This project was completed in 1964 and proved a great relief in easing congestion. Rapid increase in cargo handled at the port, including industrial machinery, has since led to further congestion and another plan for further expansion is under consideration.

Port Harcourt is one of the most industrialized towns in Nigeria and has been mentioned as a possible site for the proposed iron and steel industry. Its locational advantages include easy access to markets and raw materials from Nigeria or abroad and proximity to the supply of petroleum and gas from the neighbouring oil fields. The local oil refinery will also provide raw materials for petro-chemical industries. Industrial opportunities at Port Harcourt appear unlimited and the new trans-Amadi industrial layout may be built up within the next ten years. Its main industries include glass-making and the manufacture of aluminium wares, paints, automobile tyres, pressed concrete, tiles and cigarettes.

THE DEVELOPMENT OF THE DELTA OIL FIELDS

The search for oil in Nigeria started in 1937, but it was not until January 1956 that oil was found in appreciable quantities at Oloibiri in the Niger Delta. At this time, the Shell-BP Petroleum Development Company, which spearheaded the search for crude oil in Nigeria, had spent more than £15 million. About the end of 1956 and in 1958, more promising discoveries were made at Afam and Bomu respectively. These first finds were in the eastern delta but in 1959 and again in 1961, major oil finds

---

[1] 'The Escravos Bar Project' *Nigeria Trade Journal* Vol. XII No. 4 pp. 130–133 1964

Table 8 VALUE OF IMPORTS THROUGH DELTA PORTS
1960/4 £ THOUSAND

Year	Port Harcourt	Sapele	Warri	Burutu	Degema	All Nigerian Ports
1960	46,260	4,008	4,445	2,378	58	215,891
1961	47,759	3,747	3,229	2,589	58	222,519
1962	47,651	2,536	2,171	997	11	203,217
1964	52,359	2,015	1,627	760	7	207,556
1964	60,115	2,316	3,529	6,726	—	253,880

Table 9 VALUE OF EXPORTS THROUGH DELTA PORTS
1960/4 £ THOUSAND

Year	Port Harcourt	Sapele	Warri	Burutu	Degema	All Nigerian Ports
1960	38,027	22,571	3,052	4,879	1,435	169,714
1961	38,405	20,535	3,164	3,820	1,071	173,628
1962	33,203	21,417	4,123	3,449	567	168,536
1963	37,217	22,614	4,416	4,129	713	189,672
1964	38,115	26,544	3,973	2,589	756	214,650

SOURCE: *Annual Abstracts of Statistics 1965* p. 86 Lagos

were made at Ughelli and off Burutu, both in the western delta. Today, the Niger delta is going through a second oil age, but one with a difference. In the past the delta was largely a trading zone for palm oil, but today it is a producer of crude mineral oil.

During the last ten years, the delta oilfields have witnessed considerable development. Production activities of Shell-BP, the most important petroleum development company in the country, are centred in two main areas— the Greater Port Harcourt area which includes Bomu, Oloibiri, Afam, Ebubu, Imo River and Obigbo oil fields; and the Greater Ughelli area in Midwestern Nigeria. The Port Harcourt area is the more developed, and is already provided with hundreds of miles of pipelines, booster stations or pump stations and flow stations. Production started in the Greater Ughelli area in June 1965 when the trans-Niger pipeline system linking the Midwest fields to the Bonny Terminal was completed. Current production (1966) is now over 300,000 barrels per day, and this approximates to 15 million tons a year.

The first shipment of Nigerian crude oil was in 1958 and the port of shipment was Port Harcourt. But Port Harcourt had a number of disadvantages as a crude oil terminal[1] and so Bonny, a former palm oil port, was chosen after a study of eleven possible outlets to the sea along the Nigeria coast. In 1961, the first phase of the new terminal was completed at a cost of £1·5 million. It consisted of four storage tanks with a combined storage capacity of 330,000 barrels. By August 1966 there were fourteen storage tanks with a total capacity of 3·5 million barrels. The Bonny Terminal which is completely automated is described as one of the most modern in the world. All operations of loading, emptying, measuring and so on are electronically controlled from a central point. This explains why the operational staff at Bonny is very small and why the reviving effect of the oil industry on Bonny is unlikely to be tremendous. But Bonny is alive once again, and is doing brisk business in smuggled goods from the tankers which call regularly.

Table 10 shows the figures for the crude oil exports since 1958. Much of this oil goes to refineries in Britain, Holland and Germany. In October 1965 the local refinery at Alesa-Eleme near Port Harcourt started production with a daily intake capacity of 30,000 barrels which totals up to 1·5 million tons per annum. So far, the refinery is catering for Nigeria's local needs for petrol, diesel and kerosene.

Table 10 CRUDE OIL EXPORTS 1958/66

Year	Export in thousand tons	Value in £ thousands
1958	245	979
1959	538	2,702
1960	828	4,408
1961	2,224	11,546
1962	3,368	16,739
1963	3,695	20,176
1964	5,783	32,057
1965	13,019	68,097
1966	18,945	91,973

SOURCE: Federal Office of Statistics Lagos

By far the greater proportion of natural gas produced along with Nigerian crude oil is burnt off and wasted. Yet natural gas itself is an important source of energy. But the demand for it in Nigeria is at present very restricted, hence the need to burn the excess gas, since oil production cannot be kept down simply because of a desire to ensure the consumption of the gas produced along with the oil. There is a great potential market for industrial use of natural gas in the Port Harcourt area where the Electricity Corporation of Nigeria (ECN) has been the chief customer since 1963. Both the Afam power station and the power plant serving the trans-Amadi area of Port Harcourt are driven by natural gas supplied from the Afam and Apara oil fields. Natural gas is also supplied

[1] The disadvantages included restriction of the size of tankers as a result of the depth of water in the channel.

Plate 11. The Oil Refinery near Port Harcourt.

Plate 12. The Shell-BP Oil Terminal at Bonny.

to industries based at Aba as well as to the Alesa refinery and the ECN power plant at Ughelli.

Negotiations to sell Nigerian gas in Western Europe have been overtaken by the important event of the discovery of natural gas in the North Sea. The idea of bottling the gas for domestic purposes was at first considered to be uneconomical but gas bottled in the Port Harcourt area has been on the market since the early part of 1967.

Since the discovery of oil ten years ago by the Shell-BP Development Company, about seven other oil companies have applied and obtained oil concessions in the delta (Figure 27). These include the American Overseas Petroleum Limited whose discoveries include the Pen-

nington area; Nigeria Agip Oil Company with discoveries at Ebocha; Mobil Exploration and Tennessee Nigeria Incorporated.

Offshore oil searching started in 1960 and by 1966 every company to drill offshore had found oil. In normal circumstances it is much cheaper to find oil under the land than the sea. But the cost of working in the delta swamps is so great that the Nigerian Gulf Oil Company is reported to say that 'in Nigeria offshore drilling is quicker and more effective than wrestling with the swamps'.[1] Another factor which has contributed to the high cost of drilling for oil in the delta is that conditions below the ground are considered to be as difficult as on the surface. In place of immense underground oil pools which occur in the Middle East, Nigerian oil occurs in small fragmented pools. The result of this is that for full exploitation, a small oilfield in Nigeria needs many more wells than a much larger field in the Middle East, and this in turn means extra cost.

IMPACT OF THE OIL INDUSTRY ON THE AREAS OF OPERATION

Apart from the remarkable changes at the Bonny Terminal and the modern refinery at Alesa-Eleme together with the tract of ten pipes linking the refinery to the jetty on Okrika island, the oil industry has not made many visible changes in the delta landscape. Rather it is in the immediate hinterland of Port Harcourt, at Umuokoroshe and Umumasi, that a lasting and impressive monument of the oil industry has been planted. In these two neighbouring areas Shell has literally built a town overnight, where most of its 4,000 employees in the Port Harcourt area live and work. Delta clinic, a well-staffed specialist hospital originally built for the Company's staff at Port Harcourt,

[1] *The Times* London 3 May 1966 p. 25

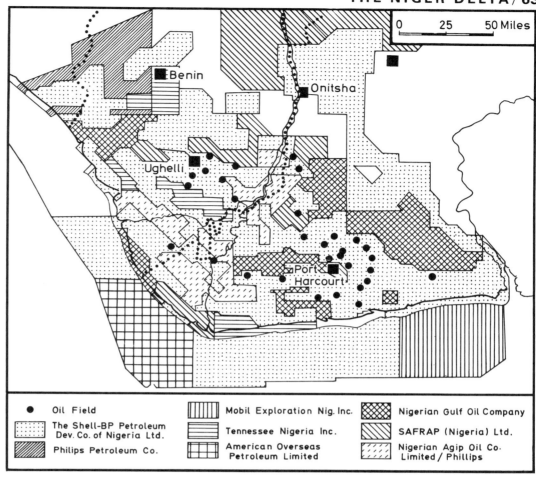

*Figure 27. Oil Concessions in
the Niger Delta*

but now converted into a community hospital, is another
of the numerous services which have been provided by
Shell.

In spite of these innovations people from the delta feel
that they have not benefited enough from the oil which
comes out of their land and that the proceeds from the oil
go towards the development of other areas. To a large
extent this grievance is true, but the problem lies more
with the delta environment. The Niger Delta Development Board is, however, doing a lot to improve living
conditions in the delta and the best the oil companies can
do is to channel their financial aid through this Board.

Fringe benefits accruing to villages in the oil-producing
areas include well-built bridges and tarmac roads leading
from Port Harcourt to the various remote drilling sites.
These roads are amongst the best in the country and are
built so that they can cope with the movement of heavy
drilling equipment. They are abandoned after the drilling
operations, but although they may not link one village to
another, these roads have opened up large areas of
cultivated land. Large cassava and maize farms are found

along both sides of such roads, and lorries from Port
Harcourt may be seen transporting harvested crops from
the more distant farms to the main consuming centres.

OIL IN THE NIGERIAN ECONOMY

The development of oil and gas resources in the Niger
Delta has been the most significant economic event in
Nigeria in recent years. It is now certain that for many
decades oil exports will represent a substantial foreign exchange injection into the Nigerian economy. As shown in
Table 11 (Nigeria's main exports 1957–66), oil is now the
leading export by value in Nigeria. But it is not expected
that oil will ever have the same dominant position in the
economy that it has, for example, in Kuwait or Saudi
Arabia, where oil supplies about ninety per cent of both
exports and government revenues. In Nigeria, the
traditional exports such as cocoa, palm produce, groundnuts, tin and rubber will continue to play an important
part in the country's foreign trade. This is a fortunate
situation since the oil industry is bound to come to an end

Table 11 NIGERIA'S PRINCIPAL EXPORTS BY VALUE
1957/66 £ THOUSANDS

Period	Cocoa	Palm Produce	Groundnuts	Timber Products	Raw Cotton	Rubber	Tin and Columbite	Petroleum Oil
1957	26,036	31,760	24,739	4,992	6,337	7,022	8,390	—
1958	26,668	33,113	30,695	6,262	7,845	7,627	4,394	979
1959	38,289	39,779	32,098	7,009	7,301	11,608	5,340	2,702
1960	36,772	40,044	28,198	8,136	6,207	14,239	8,166	4,408
1961	33,746	33,117	37,225	7,912	11,120	11,024	7,808	11,546
1962	33,847	25,824	38,603	6,970	5,857	11,356	?	16,739
1963	32,359	30,183	43,142	7,848	9,516	11,788	?	20,176
1964	40,100	31,717	42,392	8,882	6,105	12,166	13,805	32,057
1965	42,691	40,132	47,818	6,562	3,298	10,988	16,073	68,097
1966	28,260	33,392	45,510	6,451	3,422	11,474	15,466	91,973

SOURCE: Federal Office of Statistics Lagos

some day. But unlike these other commodities, oil has the major advantage of a relatively stable price. The price of cocoa in the world market for instance, has varied since the war from £500 per ton to as low as £100 per ton as compared with a variation of only twelve per cent in Nigerian oil between 1958 and 1965.

The working and refining of oil (and gas) in Nigeria is also making a direct contribution to the economy by providing readily available sources of energy. The £10 million refinery is now under production and it is expected that all of Nigeria's requirements of major petroleum products such as petrol, kerosene, diesel oil, heavy fuel oil and bottled gas will soon be met from local sources. The saving which this will mean to our foreign exchange can be appreciated when it is realized that in 1965, Nigeria spent £15 million on net imports of these products.

Another way in which the oil industry benefits Nigeria is that it provides employment to many people in various aspects of its operations. In 1966 at least 5,000 Nigerians and 600 expatriates were employed directly by the oil industry or by contractors working exclusively for the industry. The industry has also contributed significantly to developing the local human resources through the training of mechanics, drillers, seismic operators and laboratory technicians for its own services.

The most important financial contribution of the oil industry to the country as a whole comes from direct payments to the Government. In the past, the principal contributions amounting in all to £40 million by 1965 have been rentals for concession areas in which to explore, and royalties on the oil actually produced. The principal contributions in the future will, however, be tax payments under the petroleum profits tax ordinance. In 1965 Shell-

BP alone paid a total of £14·6 million to the Government as compared with £7·4 million in 1964.

THE WORK OF THE NIGER DELTA DEVELOPMENT BOARD

The Niger Delta Development Board which was formally established in 1960 came into being as a result of the recommendations of the Minorities Commission, whose report was published two years earlier. The Ijaw people of the Niger Delta had represented to the Commission that a separate state should be created for the delta area but while rejecting this view, the Commission held that the delta area merited special consideration and therefore recommended a special Federal Board to consider and advise upon the problems of development in the area. As at present constituted, the Board's area of operation consists of Yenagoa Province and Ogoni Division in the Rivers State and the Western Ijaw Division of Delta Province in the Midwest State.

Field investigations into the agricultural potential of the delta, the means of developing forestry, fisheries and transportation occupied the most part of the first half of the 1960's. Soil and other pilot surveys have since been carried out and work has already started on a number of development schemes. Experimental farms have been established at various points where the yield of economic crops including rubber, cocoa and oil palm is being investigated.

Rice is considered to be the crop best suited to the swamps and the BG 79 variety is already widely cultivated in the delta. The Board has started trying different varieties of rice at Igbematoru, with the view to exploring the possibility of getting two rice crops in a year by planting the Japonica variety immediately before or after BG 79 on the same piece of land. A good water control system such as building dykes is considered to be a necessary step for double cropping and the first trial polder of 300 acres at Peremabiri is doing well. A rice mill with a capacity of 3,600 tons of paddy has been installed in Peremabiri to process rice from the Board's polder and the surrounding villages. The plan is to buy the paddy from local farmers and to feed the residues to livestock which will produce dung for fertilising the land.

Rice, jute, maize, soya beans and cowpeas have been successfully grown during the dry season of 1965–6 and 1966–7 in the Board's observation farm in Amassoma. Cultivation of these crops at this time of the year is made possible through basin irrigation, whereby flood water is entrapped in specially constructed basins which are later drained off for cropping. A number of different varieties of sugar cane have been introduced in different observation farms as part of the investigation on the possibilities of producing sugar cane on a large scale. Many problems confront mechanical cultivation in the delta, but investments in water control measures may yet turn the Niger Delta into a large food surplus region.

The Niger Delta Development Board has also carried out investigations on conservation and scientific exploitation of forest resources. It is now known that pulp from mangroves cannot produce good quality paper unless mixed with a stronger pulp and that tannin samples from mangrove barks have not been well received by leather workers, due principally to the colour and the low tannin content. Concerning the fishing industry, the problems which the Board seeks to solve include fish preservation, the establishment of freshwater fish ponds to ensure better harvests, transportation of fresh fish and the formation of fisheries cooperatives which will help fishermen to take advantage of modern fishing methods by pooling their resources to purchase modern equipments.

Works consulted and suggestions for further reading

1. Dike, K. O., *Trade and Politics in the Niger Delta, 1830–1885* (Oxford Studies in African Affairs) London 1956
2. Earl, A. K., 'Nigeria's Ports' *Nigeria* No. 72 pp. 27–33 1962
3. Gallway, H., 'The Rising of the Brassmen' *African Affairs* No. 34 p. 144 1935
4. Johnston, H. H., 'The Niger Delta' *Proceeding of the Royal Geographical Society* No. 10 pp. 750–61 1888
5. Melamid, A., 'The Geography of the Nigerian Petroleum Industry' *Economic Geography* No. 44 pp. 37–56 1968
6. NEDECO *Western Niger Delta—Report on Investigation* The Hague 1954
7. Udo R. K. & Ogundana B., 'Factors Influencing the Fortunes of Ports in the Niger Delta' *Scottish Geographical Magazine* No. 82 pp. 169–83 1966
8. United Africa Company 'Forcados and Escravos Bar' *Statistical and Economic Review* No. 6 September 1950
9. United Africa Company 'Port Capacity and Shipping Turnround in West Africa' *Statistical and Economic Review* No. 19 1957

7 The Palm Belt
of South-Eastern Nigeria

Compared with the coastal areas west of the Lower Niger valley, the palm belt is remarkable for the open character of its vegetation and the predominance of the oil palm, which is the most important cash crop in the region. The uniformity of its terrain, which is almost completely devoid of physiographic differentiation is unique, and so is the fact that parts of this region support a rural population of over 1,000 persons per square mile. Farming practices are also very similar all over the region, in spite of the fact that it is occupied by a variety of ethnic groups including the Owerri Ibos, the Annangs and Ibibios as well as the Ogonis and Oron people who live nearer the coast.

Palm produce is the basis of the export trade of this region, which is now one of the most developed parts of the country. It makes it possible for large numbers of people to survive in districts which produce very little food. But few people invest in palm plantations, unlike the case with cocoa in Yorubaland or rubber in the Benin Forests. Rather, the inhabitants of this region tend to invest more in education, in transportation and trade in manufactured goods which, in this part of the country, is carried on mainly by men rather than by women. Skilled and semi-skilled labour is plentiful and is exported in large numbers to other parts of the country. Unskilled labour goes mainly to the nearby island of Fernando Po as well as to the plantations of the Cross River district and the Midwest.

RELIEF AND DRAINAGE CHARACTERISTICS

The entire region is underlain by one main geological formation, the Coastal Plain Sands. This formation which is of late tertiary age is rather deep and the soils developed on it are porous, highly leached and usually infertile. In certain districts like Ikot Ekpene and Afara in Umuahia, impermeable layers of clay occur near the surface and in many other areas the soils consist of lateritic material under a superficial layer of fine-grained sands. Rivers are few and far between, the vast interfluves being characterized by dry valleys which carry surface drainage in years with exceptionally high rainfall. The phenomenal monotony of the terrain and the very straight river courses may be accounted for by the absence of any tectonic disturbances since the sands were laid down and by the homogeneity of the rock structure.

With the exception of the Imo River, the few rivers draining the region rise within the Coastal Plain Sands

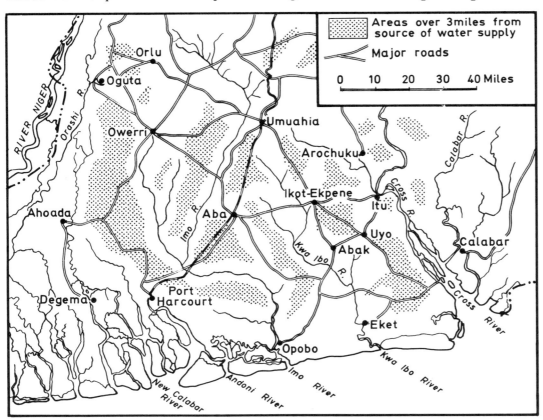

Figure 28. The Palm Belt of South-Eastern Nigeria

formation. Their water is clear and sparkling, unlike that of the Imo which rises in an area underlain by the Imo shales and whose water is muddy and largely contaminated. The main streams draining the region are the Imo, the Otamiri, the Aba and Kwa Ibo Rivers; all of which have very few tributaries as compared with rivers of the Cross River basin or the scarplands of Onitsha and Enugu Provinces. In this respect the Imo behaves in a rather curious way in that its upper course, which rises in and flows over the Imo shales, takes about eight tributaries during its thirty-mile traverse of this geological formation, while its middle course which flows through the Coastal Plains Sand in an extraordinarily straight valley, and has no tributaries throughout its length of about fifty miles. The upper Imo is a captured headwater of the Enyong Creek which flows into the Cross River at Itu.

In view of the rather uniform aspect of the landscape, river valleys constitute the major relief features in the region. Even such rivers as the Kwa Ibo and the Aba River which are of recent origin have eroded considerable valleys for themselves, their courses being devoid of cliff-sections or gorge-like tracts. Extensive stretches of these valleys are often very marshy, supporting dense growths of raffia palms.

The undulating nature of the interfluves gives rise to numerous depressions and low hills. Many of these depressions become inundated during the rainy season but consist of heaps of sand when the water subsides. Roads passing through such depressions may be completely covered with sand and present more difficulty to the cyclist and motorist than the small intervening hills. Where these depressions are underlain by clay, they may contain water for several months.

CLIMATE AND VEGETATION

The mean annual rainfall decreases inland from about 125 inches at Eket to about ninety inches north of Owerri. In the north and central parts the onset of the rains may be delayed, and this is injurious to crops planted in anticipation of the rains; otherwise the rains come mostly during the growing season. The rainy season begins in March and lasts till October or early November. At Owerri and in the area farther north, the heaviest rain falls in September but in the south and central parts of the region, a slight break of about two weeks occurs in August, giving rise to a two-maxima regime in which the rainiest months are July and September.

In March, April and May, the rains come in violent storms, destroying crops, especially maize plants, and roofs of houses. There is a heavy downpour of short duration when several inches may be recorded within an hour. As in other parts of West Africa, the sudden and torrential run-off which usually accompanies a thunderstorm may give rise to widespread sheet erosion on slopes; while farms situated at the depressions become flooded, resulting in a considerable loss of crops.

Temperature conditions are similar all over the region. The hottest months are February and March, when the mean annual temperature is above 80° F. Heavy rain clouds, which may remain unbroken for weeks, have the effect of lowering the day temperatures for July, August and September. The influence of the harmattan is not severe and lasts for only a few weeks in December and January. It is a general belief amongst the Ibibios that the severer the harmattan, the better the yield of such fruits as the mango, the African pear and the kola-nut. The relative humidity remains high all through the year excepting during the short harmattan spell. It averages about eighty per cent in the south, being much higher along the coast.

The high temperature and high humidity favour quick plant growth but although the natural climax vegetation is the tropical rainforest, parts of the region have been so farmed that traces of the true vegetation are only to be found in juju groves or forbidden bush which are rarely more than one acre in extent. Larger patches of forests occur in the sparsely settled areas, but over most of the region, a secondary vegetation—the palm bush predominates. Fallowed bush is characterized by dense shrubs of *Acioa barterii* (*Akan* in Ibibio) and *Macrolobium macrophyllum* (*Nya* in Ibibio) which are planted for the purpose of restoring soil fertility.

RURAL WATER SUPPLIES

Water for domestic use is in short supply during the dry season (November-February), when the only source of water is from springs and streams. As in other parts of the Eastern States, the population is concentrated on the interfluves and many villagers are obliged to travel distances of up to seven miles to fetch water for domestic use. Fortunately, in this region, access to the streams is easier since the rivers are less incised than in the scarplands of Enugu and Onitsha Province; but distance to the stream is often much greater. The quality of the water here appears much better, except that villagers downstream are obliged to drink water which has been contaminated in various ways by those occupying the upper reaches.

During the rainy season, water for domestic use is obtained from rain dripping down the roof of houses and the stems of coconut trees. Open pits located within the compound provide water for washing as well as for preparing palm oil but in the dry season the long trek to the streams begins. As a rule, the job of fetching water falls to women and children and this is usually done in the early hours of the morning or after the day's work has been completed, particularly when the evening is lit by the moon.

Today the trade in water is an established occupation in those areas which are still to be supplied with pipe-borne water. A trader requires a bicycle which may be rented and two kerosene tins which are conveyed in a wooden tray tied to the carrier of the bicycle. There is the prospect of immediate cash and many young men take to the water trade during the dry season, which is also a slack season in the farming calendar. A tin of water costs three to six pence depending on the demand and the distance of the selling point from the stream.

Pits dug in clay depressions still provide water for part of the dry season to villages like Abak Ifia which have not yet benefited from the Rural Water Scheme of the Government. The quality of water from such pits is usually poor and the spread of guinea-worm has been associated with water from such ponds. A number of wells varying in depth from sixty to a hundred and twenty feet have been provided in many districts by communal effort, by local councils or by the Government.

POPULATION AND SETTLEMENT

Some of the most densely settled areas in Nigeria are found in this region, where a direct relationship exists between the density of population and the degree of dispersion of rural settlement as well as the importance attached to the oil palm *vis-à-vis* food production in the local economy. The most densely populated areas include Mbaise and Ikeduru-Mbaitole Districts of Owerri Division, northern Ngwaland and the Annang areas of Ikot Ekpene and Abak Divisions, where rural densities of over one thousand persons per square mile are common. The most sparsely settled areas occur along the coast, as well as along the central and lower Imo valley, where there are less than one hundred persons to the square mile.

The general conception that land belongs to the community no longer applies to the very densely populated areas where all land, excepting juju groves, market squares and a few palm groves, belong to individuals or to families rather than to the village community. Land acquisition is hereditary, each male child being entitled to a share of his father's land. This has led to extreme fragmentation and the proliferation of uneconomic holdings. The communal spirit of old can still be seen in operation when the village community is called upon to raise funds for a school or church building. All palm trees excluding those on compoundlands are declared reserved during a period of three to six months, when all fruits harvested are sold and the money used for the project in hand. What is striking is that Roman Catholics will co-operate in raising funds for a Protestant church or school building and vice versa, although there have been cases of open disputes on the question of which denomination should be called upon to administer community schools.

The close relationship between population density and settlement pattern is clearly brought out in Owerri Division (Figures 29 and 30) where dispersed compounds are the dominant type of settlement in Mbaise and Ikeduru-Mbaitoli (800 persons per square mile), while compact hamlets and villages occur in sparsely settled areas. The main reason for dispersion in overcrowded areas is connected with the breakdown of traditional land tenure systems in such areas. With the spread of individual tenure and continued fragmentation of farmland, the compoundland has encroached on farmlands, resulting in a rural landscape which is very similar to that of Ogidi, Nnewi and Ozubulu in Onitsha Division (Figure 36).

Considering the number of oil palm trees per acre of land, the number of local people who obtain their living from palm produce, and the quantity of oil exported per head of the population, this region emerges as the most important palm oil producing area in Nigeria. Detailed studies of the oil palm economy in such parts of the region as Ngwaland show, however, that the importance of the oil palm in the local economy increases with increasing pressure of population on available farmland. In northern Ngwaland, where farmland is so scarce that fallow periods of about two to three years are common, the oil palm plays an all-important role in the local economy. The situation is different in the sparsely settled southern Ngwaland, where fallow periods of about five years are still common and where food-crop production is still the primary occupation of the people, who often rent out their palm plots to migrant farmers.

The multiplicity of Christian religious sects is another interesting development amongst the varied ethnic groups occupying this region. A village of about 2,000 inhabitants may have as many as seven of these spiritual churches,

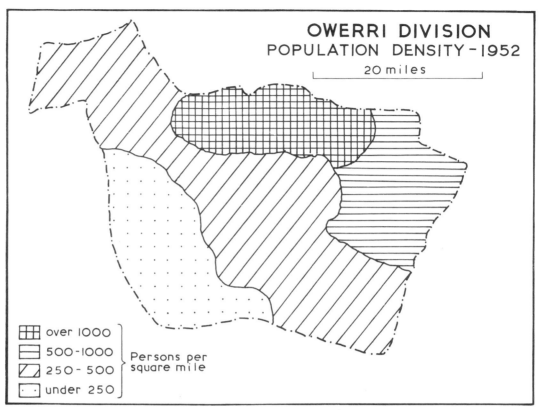

Figure 29. Population Density of Owerri Division (1952 Census)

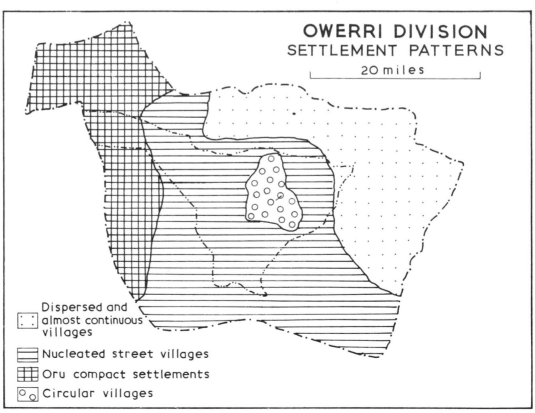

Figure 30. Settlement Patterns in Owerri Division

the congregations of which are predominantly of the female sex. Their spread appears to serve an economic as well as a social need, in that they provide opportunities for absorbing some unemployed young men, as well as providing emotional satisfaction through the pseudo-religious services, which combine elements of Christianity with ritualistic displays formerly associated with the worship of local gods. The main drawback to the spread of this type of worship, which appeals most to the poorest in the society, is the fact that members may be called upon at regular intervals to fast and pray for up to three days in a week. Time best used in doing productive work is thus spent in idle supplication but fortunately, the ability of such people to stay hungry for several days often saves them the embarrassment of how to feed themselves.

Settlements are usually named after the founder. Amongst the Ibos a village founded by a Mr Agu will be called Ndi Agu (= people of Agu) or Umuagu (= children of Agu) and in the same way, the name of an Ibibio village such as Nto Akpan (= children of Akpan) or Ikot Osukpong (= followers of Osukpong) indicates that the village was founded by a Mr Akpan or a Mr Osukpong as the case may be. Settlements may also be named after relief features such as a hill, a stream or swampy ground.

Small communities of Aro Ibos are a common feature of rural settlements in this region. The Aros are a group of Ibo-speaking people whose traditional home is at Arochuku, near the Cross River. These Aro settlements date from the period of the slave trade, when the Long Juju of Arochuku served as an important medium in acquiring slaves in this part of Nigeria. The spread of these Aro colonies at the time was essential for the efficient and continued projection of the authority of the oracle. Some of them like Ndikelionwu grew up on conquered territories, but by far the greater number were founded on land 'shown' to Aro families by the groups amongst whom they resided. Ottenberg recognizes three types of Aro colonies based mainly on the size of the settlement as well as on the political link of the original village-group with Arochuku. Firstly, there were the small settlements which were scattered all over the region, some being located along the major slave routes. The Aro quarters at Ifuho and Urua Otu at Ikot Ekpene come under this category. Settlers in such colonies interfered very little in the local village-group politics and although they now appear to be identified with the local community, they still look back to Arochuku in much the same way as the Jews regard Jerusalem.

Ottenberg's second group of Aro settlements consists of larger colonies which sprang up close to large central markets. Although such colonies dominated the markets, the local people were still left with some autonomy in their affairs. Uzuakoli and Uburu which may be cited as two good examples of these market colonies lie outside this region, being located in the Cross River basin. Finally there were areas like Afikpo and Otanchara in Okigwi where the Aros established, in addition to oracular and trading activities, political control over the people. At Aro-Ndizorgu in Orlu, for example, the Aros established a colony which is now double the size of the population of the combined parent villages of Arochuku.

Roads have played an important part in modifying the pattern of rural settlements in the region, particularly in the densely settled areas where dispersed compounds are the rule. The tendency has been for people to build close to the road with the result that, over the years, ribbon or wayside settlements have emerged. Compoundlands in this region, including those along the roadside are fenced

Figure 31. A Wayside Compound near Ikot Ekpene

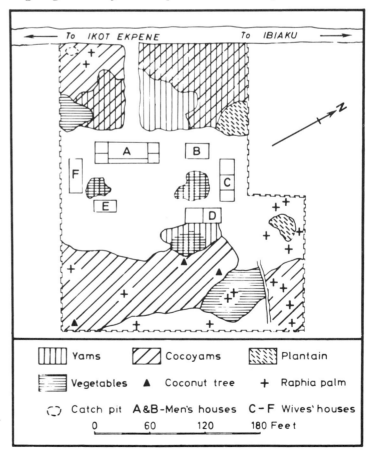

round with livesticks, while those in Onitsha and Enugu areas are usually surrounded by short walls. A typical wayside compound is shown in Figure 31. In addition to the houses and fruit trees, the enclosure serves as a cemetry, beautifully decorated tombstones being a common feature of compounds which are old enough to record the death of an adult member. The enclosure as well as the land immediately outside the fence are cropped every year and it is common to see yam tendrils climbing tombstones located on compoundlands.

THE MARKET AND INDUSTRIAL TOWN OF ABA

Aba is one of those new towns in the Eastern States which owes its rapid growth to the functional transformation of pre-British villages into administrative headquarters of various political units created during the colonial period. At the beginning of this century Aba was a large market village on the trade route from Bende to Okrika and Bonny. Its position as a rural central place was strengthened following the establishment of a garrison there in 1901 and a native court in 1904. As the seat of administration of Ngwa District, other establishments like the post office, prisons, a hospital and offices as well as residential quarters for the administrative staff were built. The coming of the railway in 1915 and the development of road transportation strengthened the position of Aba as a route centre, and today Aba is one of the four largest towns in the Eastern States, with a market only second in size and range of goods to that at Onitsha.

The busiest and noisiest parts of Aba in the daytime are the motor park and the Aba main market. Aba motor park is one of the largest in the country and is kept very lively by the numerous touts who expend much energy trying to persuade and at times force a passenger to travel by a particular taxi, bus or mammy-waggon. Retail traders come to Aba from Ikot Ekpene, Uyo, Oron, Owerri, Umuahia, Opobo and Uzuakoli to buy goods like sugar, cloth, stock fish and lanterns which many Aba traders import direct from the manufacturing countries.

Ethnic specialization is a long-standing feature of trading in Aba. Ibos from Nkwerre in Orlu Division specialize in the tobacco trade while Cross River Ibos from Abiriba, Ohafia and Item specialize in textiles, including singlets and ready-made garments. In recent years, these eastern Ibo traders have done very brisk business in second-hand clothing which finds a ready market amongst the poorer peasants of Nigeria. Most of the imposing residential buildings along Asa Road and in

other parts of the town belong to successful traders, who have since taken over the retail trade from such commercial firms as the United Africa Co., Paterson Zechonis and G. B. Ollivant.

The development of factory industries, based largely on local raw material and skill, has made remarkable progress since 1950. Some of the more important factories which are located in the main industrial estate which occupies the northern part of the town are the Star Beer factory, which produces mineral waters, soap factories belonging to Lever Brothers and other enterpreneurs, and a pharmaceutical factory for producing drugs. There is also a large textile factory which uses cotton from the Northern States.

Soap-making is based on local palm oil and is not new to this part of the country. Indeed, the making of black soap is one of the most widespread village industries of this part of the country. Today, there are at least four large soap factories at Aba, the smallest of which is owned by a Nigerian businessman. In 1961, three of these factories produced about 76,000 cases of soap almost all of which were sold without delay.

THE NIGERIAN OIL PALM INDUSTRY

Although the Nigerian palm belt stretches right through the breadth of the southern provinces, the main producing area of palm oil and palm kernel is in south-eastern Nigeria. The density of palm per acre which may be up to 150 is greatest in this region and so is the importance which the peasant attaches to the fruits of the palm. This is why the problems of the Nigerian oil palm industry are discussed along with the economic importance of this tree to the inhabitants of this region.

Unlike the other major export crops of Nigeria—cocoa, groundnuts and rubber—the oil palm is indigenous to the forest belt of Nigeria. Also unlike these crops which are cultivated and tended by the Nigerian peasant, the present supply of palm produce in the country comes almost entirely from palm trees growing wild or semi-wild in compoundlands, in farmlands or in special groves around the village. A few farmers now cultivate palm trees, but by far the greater majority are not impressed by the idea of cultivated palms and although a few commercial plantations have been established in recent years, the source of Nigerian palm produce is bound to remain unchanged for several decades.

During the nineteenth century palm oil was the most important commodity of trade from Nigeria, and today it remains the most important cash crop of the Eastern States. In the 1830's, the value of the palm oil export averaged about £500,000 per annum and at the beginning of this century, Nigeria was the largest exporter of palm produce in the world. But the quality of the oil was poor, owing to the primitive methods of extraction. Attempts to introduce the plantation system were turned down by the Colonial administration and by 1923, the plantations of Malaya and the Congo were already producing greater quantities and better oil than Nigeria.

It is important to realize that about fifty per cent of the oil produced in the palm belt is consumed locally. Export figures for palm oil which have averaged about 170,000 tons for Nigeria since 1950 must be viewed against this background. Palm kernel export during this period averaged about 400,000 per annum, but in this case, virtually all the kernel was exported. At least eighty-five per cent of the palm oil exported from Nigeria since 1950 comes from the Eastern States.

OWNERSHIP AND HARVESTING OF PALMS

In most parts of the Eastern States, palms which grow on compoundlands belong to the owner of the compound and there is no restriction as to when and how he exploits such trees. Palms growing on farmland under cultivation usually belong to the owner of the farm, except that a farmer who rents land for growing crops may not harvest palms on the land unless there is specific provision to that effect in the terms of the lease. Palms on fallow bush belong to individuals in the very densely settled areas but to extended families or village communities in the sparsely settled areas. Finally, there are special communal groves which, like palms growing along stream valleys, can be exploited by any member of the village community.

Rights in palms except those in compoundlands are usually restricted. This is particularly true of Ibibio areas where the system of declaring palm trees 'closed' to individual exploitation is common. Rather than asking members of the community to make cash contributions towards such projects as building a village school or church or a community scholarship scheme, it is usual for village councils to declare all palms in the village closed for three to six months. During this period, the palms are harvested at regular intervals and on set days, by members who pay a fixed deposit of about ten shillings per palm cutter per day. There is no restriction on the number of trees a cutter may exploit for that day, but the money so collected goes into the general pool for the project in hand.

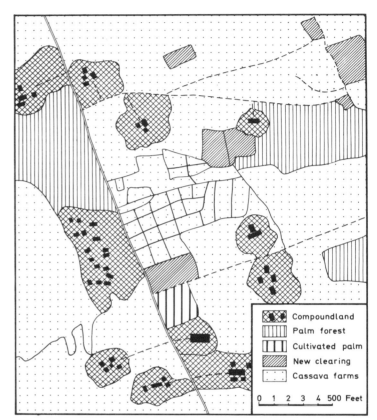

Figure 32. Land Use in the Palm Belt (near Aba)

Some Ngwa villages are reported to adopt this system of declaring all palms communal for three months and arranging for specific harvesting days so as to enable every adult male to raise money to pay his tax. In Ikot Ekpene, a man who has incurred much expenditure through his father's funeral or daughter's marriage may ask for and obtain the exclusive right to harvest for three months all palms growing in a communal grove.

These restrictive methods of exploitation have tended to inhibit the successful operation of pioneer oil mills. At the same time so much fruit may be harvested on these set days that it is impossible to process it all before it goes bad. For good quality oil the fruit must be processed not more than forty-eight hours after cutting, but in most villages it takes as much as five to seven days to extract the fruits from the bunch in readiness for steaming. The fatty acid which forms during this period, in which considerable fermentation takes place, is largely responsible for the poor quality of the oil produced by local peasants.

METHODS OF PRODUCTION

The extraction of palm oil by traditional methods is the

work of women, although men often help in pounding the steamed fruits. Pounding separates the pulp from the nuts, the former being squeezed by hand to produce the oil. This method results in the production of much better oil than that obtained by the Yorubas or the Isoko migrant oil palm exploiters. It yields Grade I oil, but if the fruits are boiled much sooner it will be possible to produce Special Grade oil by this method. Its other main handicap is that it extracts only about fifty-five to sixty per cent of the oil content of the fruit. In this part of the country the oil extracted in a normal home belongs to the man, the woman's share being the nuts which she and her children crack between stones to obtain the kernels.

In the early 1930's, the hand press was introduced into the region in the hope that it would lead to a higher extraction rate compared with the traditional methods. But although the press extracts up to sixty-five per cent of the oil, it is still necessary to steam and pound the fruits before feeding the pulp to the press. The economics of using the press therefore depend largely on whether the two hours saved per gallon of oil extracted is worth the tariff paid for using the press.

Pioneer oil mills which were introduced after the Second World War extract up to eighty-five per cent of the oil content of the fruit, but initially they met with great opposition from the women-folk who feared the inevitable loss in their traditional share of the proceeds of the oil palm economy. The mills were established by the Eastern Nigeria Development Corporation. Many of the mills failed to pay their way and have since been demolished.

THE TRADE IN PALM PRODUCE

Palm oil and kernels are purchased by agents licensed by State Produce Marketing Boards which control the export of palm produce from each state. The link between the producer and the Marketing Board is very similar to that for cocoa and groundnuts. Each licensed buying agent has a number of middlemen of all grades who supply him with produce. Usually the middlemen depend on cash advances made to them by such agents as John Holt, Miller Brothers, Fraser and Shephard and G. B. Ollivant. They set up at sheds along the major roads and make purchases either direct from producers or from itinerant buyers who go about from house to house and from one village market to another to buy oil and kernel. Usually, there is some degree of specialization at this scale of buying, in that itinerant buyers concentrate either on oil or kernels. Itinerant buyers, each carrying a basket con-

taining as many as six kerosene tins of oil or a sack of kernels on a bicycle, are commonly seen along bush tracks and major roads in this part of the country.

Licensed buying agents and their wayside agents deliver the oil in large drums with a capacity of 120 or 100 gallons to bulk plants at Opobo or Port Harcourt, where the oil is stored awaiting shipment. The agents are responsible for arranging to transport the oil and kernels to the port of shipment; but the gazetted price for each commodity takes care of this fact in that the prices paid for a ton of produce varies with distance from the port of export, being greatest at such ports.

THE PALM GROVE REHABILITATON SCHEME

The palm grove rehabilitation scheme of the Ministry of Agriculture is directed at improving the agricultural aspects of the oil palm industry, in much the same way as the hand press and the pioneer oil mills have sought to tackle the mechanical problems associated with peasant oil production. Fruits from trees growing wild or semi-wild produce less oil than plantation fruits because their pericarp is thin while the shell which has little value is thick. Also wild palms take up to twelve years before yielding and by this time they become so tall that they have to be climbed to be harvested. This is a laborious job made more difficult by the often irregular and scattered nature of palm in natural palmeries. The rehabilitation scheme therefore aims at replacing existing wild palms with improved seedlings from the Ministry of Agriculture.

The scheme requires a minimum acreage of five acres per rehabilitation unit, which must be made up of not more than two separate plots near to one another. Farmers taking part in the scheme obtain grants of £18 per acre, £10 to be paid in cash while the balance represents the value of seedlings and fertilizers supplied to farmers. Since it takes cultivated palms about four or five years to bear the first fruits, the cutting down of existing wild palms entails a temporary loss of revenue to the peasant. The cash payment of £10 is made partly to offset such loss and also to cover the farmer's expenditure in cutting down existing wild palms and clearing the bush. When the palms mature, it is estimated that a replanted grove will yield about £45 per acre per year as compared with £8 for natural palmeries.

FARMING ACTIVITIES AND LIVESTOCK

Since the main economic crop, the oil palm, is very rarely cultivated, farming in this region still consists of growing foodcrops for subsistence as well as for sale. The main food-crops are cassava, yams, cocoyams, maize, fluted pumpkins and plantain. The size of holdings rarely exceeds an acre and most households farm four to six holdings in any one year. As in other parts of the country these holdings are scattered about, such that a distance of about two miles may separate any two holdings. Land disputes are very frequent, particularly in the densely settled areas where outright sale of land is now common, although it is more usual for those in need of farmland to lease some for a rent which is equivalent to about thirty shillings an acre. The lease usually lasts for one crop year and in some cases, owners of land have prohibited the cultivation of cassava which takes much longer to mature and is thought to be a very exhausting crop.

Bush clearing takes place in January and February and is done both by men and women. Hired labour is usually employed by widows or those who have more land than they can cope with. Young men still turn up to clear farmland for their prospective mothers-in-law. About a fortnight after clearing the bush, the brush is fired and the land cleared of burnt sticks in preparation for hoeing. After the yams have been planted the man who has more then one wife proceeds to divide his plots between his wives who then interplant such crops as maize, okro, melon and other vegetables.

Mixed cropping and crop succession ensure maximum use of the land and gives the soil some protection from sheet erosion. Yams, maize and pumpkins are planted at the same time and are allowed to germinate and grow before cocoyam, calabash and later, cassava are planted. Maize is harvested in June-July after which the farm becomes less crowded. In the sparsely settled areas of Asa and Ahoada, it is not uncommon to find migrant farmers planting newly cleared farmland with cassava which is later processed and sold in the form of garri to the urban markets of Aba and Port Harcourt. Cassava, unlike yam, is planted any time between February and September, and there is hardly a time of the year in which matured cassava is not found in the farms.

Farming implements include the matchet used for bush clearing, the native spade used for making yam holes and the short-handled hoe used by women for weeding. Seeds for planting as well as harvested crops are conveyed in baskets loaded on to bicycles but usually the carrying of goods is done by women and children, head-loading being the normal method. Human carriers or the bicycle therefore replace the donkey which performs the same job in the Kano region and other areas of the Nigerian Sudan.

Most women keep goats and chickens but pigs, sheep and ducks are less common while the ownership of dwarf cattle is restricted to prominent men in the village community. The breed of goat in this region is very different from that in the far north of Nigeria and unlike Sokoto, where the goat is left to fend for itself, the Ibos and Ibibios usually pen their goats in sheds, partly to protect the crops. Chickens are left entirely to fend for themselves.

ECONOMIC PRODUCTS OF THE RAFFIA PALM

The raffia palm grows wild along stream beds or in swampy areas all over southern Nigeria but amongst the Ibibios, most of the palms are cultivated on compound-lands or in near-by farmlands. It may appear strange that up till today few people plant oil palm trees while the same people will plant raffia palms. One reason for this is probably connected with the fact that the productive life of the raffia palm is very short. Indeed after a harvest of palm wine lasting about two months the palm withers and dies, usually in its tenth or eleventh year. In addition the raffia palm provides most of the traditional building materials; that is in addition to wine, raffia and piassava. The leaves are made into mats, the ribs used for rafters as well as constructing the walls of houses while piassava is used in place of nails and twines.

It is significant that the palm wine taken in this part of the country is tapped not from the oil palm but from the raffia palm, which produces a more tasty wine which is rich in yeast. There is now a growing internal trade in the local palm wine or tombo, which can now be preserved for several months. Tombo merchants are seen at various village markets where they collect and load the wines in chartered lorries bound for Aba, Port Harcourt, Onitsha, Umuahia and Enugu.

The raffia palm is the basis of the export trade in piassava which is used for making a number of items including brooms and hard brush. It also provides raffia for the local weaving industry which produces fanciful mats and bags, but has since given way to cloth weaving in Akwete.

CREEK AND SEA FISHING IN EKET

The coastal area between Ibeno and Jamestown in Eket Division is one of the most important areas of commercial fishing in Nigeria. As in the Okitipupa area of the Western State of Nigeria, fishing is carried out along the creeks, along the coast and in distant waters. Rainfall in this coastal area exceeds one hundred inches per annum and the soil, which is waterlogged for most of the year, is

Plate 13. Walled compounds in the Palm belt. Plantains and other crops are cultivated within the compounds.

Plate 14. Esuk Mma. A fishing settlement near Oron.

unsuitable for farming. Apart from small plots of plantains, bananas and coconuts as well as small vegetable gardens around the compounds, the people depend on outside sources for their food, their main occupation being fishing.

In addition to the indigenous people, there are a number of stranger fishermen from the Niger Delta, Ogoni, Okitipupa and Ghana. Most indigenous fishermen whose base is at Ibeno or Jamestown fish individually, and unlike the foreigners who are full-time fishermen, they take to fishing as a part-time occupation. One reason for this disparity is that the strangers are not permitted to exploit any forest produce except firewood and sticks used for drying fish. They therefore depend on the local people for fishing traps, raffia nets used mainly for shrimps, cray-fish and lobsters, canoes and roofing mats, the raw materials of which come from the forest. Many local fishermen, on the other hand, spend part of the year making or repairing this equipment.

There are a growing number of Ibeno people who take to fishing as a full-time occupation, but most of them migrate to distant fishing grounds of which the Cameroon coast is the most popular. These migrants usually return home during festive occasions when they bring back large quantities of dried fish for sale, since there is a much greater demand for fish in Eket than in the Cameroons.

A variety of fishing methods is employed, including the use of traps, nets and water poisoning but weirs are not allowed except across small creeks. The one-inch mesh net may only be used to catch small-sized fish like ekpai (*Ethmalosa sardinella*). Women take part in creek fishing and gathering of periwinkles, but their main job in the fishing economy is to sell the catch which is usually disposed of in the form of dried fish.

Recent innovations in the local fishing industry include the use of nylon nets which are lighter but stronger and more durable and the establishment of a fishing co-operative society which plans to introduce a trawler in the near future. The use of out-board engines and nylon nets has resulted in larger catches, but the problem of preserving the fish remains. Smoking is the acceptable method of preserving fish not sold fresh, but a considerable quantity goes to waste because of poor smoking. The Ilaje

method of drying sliced bits of fish in the sun is not very popular, and in any case the weather does not very much favour this method. Salting has also been introduced, but is equally unpopular because, amongst other things, it involves some expenditure in purchasing the salt as well as containers.

TRADITIONAL CRAFT INDUSTRIES

Carving, cane work and raffia work are important crafts in the Annang areas of Ikot Ekpene and Abak. Carved figures include masks of various shapes, toys and doors while chairs, stools and trays are made from cane. A wider range of goods comes from raffia and these include bags, mats, toys and hats. These products are made in rural areas and in scattered homesteads and their distribution was not organized until recently, when a dealers' co-operative society was formed at Ikot Ekpene. The war-time Ikot Ekpene raffia guild, which produced toys and school bags for export flourished only for a few years, after which it was liquidated owing to mismanagement.

Another important craft industry is the cloth-weaving industry centred at Akwete on the Imo River. Raffia and sisal hemp were used in the past but today the main weaving fibre is cotton, although silk is also used. The weaving of cloth at Akwete is dominated by the women-folk but it is striking to note that in the neighbouring Annang areas, where raffia weaving is still important, it is the men that practise the craft. Akwete cloth is in great demand by the Nigerian *élite* as well as by foreign tourists. But the modest organization of production which is still largely by the sole proprietor and her family, is a limiting factor in the quantity produced.

ROAD TRANSPORTATION

The development of road transportation in the palm belt of south-eastern Nigeria is unrivalled in any part of the country. It has the most developed road network in West Africa and roads converging at Aba are amongst the busiest roads in the country. The pace in transport services is usually set by this region which started the use of estate Peugeot cars for long-distance passenger transport. Today, the dual purpose mammy-wagon is on the way out and is essentially restricted to carrying goods. Most passengers now travel by buses and mini-buses, while the more well-to-do usually travel in seven-seater estate cars, which are used as taxis for intertown transport. This is a part of the country where travellers have become very time conscious and the transport situation may be judged from the fact that it is possible to travel to Aba and back from such towns as Port Harcourt, Uyo, Ikot Ekpene, Umuahia, Owerri and Onitsha between 4 a.m. and 11 p.m. every day, including Sunday.

There is no doubt that the state of development of transportation reflects the rapid growth of the economy of this part of the country. The main problem at present is that most vehicles are operated by individuals or groups of persons who obtain them on hire purchase and whose aim is to raise enough money to pay off the monthly instalments. The struggle to induce passengers to travel by particular vehicles has often taken the form of physical combat between two opposing groups of touts. Many passengers have lost their luggage in the process, while some touts have landed in jail. The high rate of road accidents also derives from the rush to do many trips a day. It is therefore not uncommon to find commercial vehicles doing seventy miles per hour even though all of them carry the inscription 'Maximum Speed: 35 m.p.h.'

Works consulted and suggestions for further reading:

1. Chubb, L. T., *Ibo Land Tenure* Ibadan 1961
2. Forde, D. & Jones, G. I., *The Ibo and Ibibio-Speaking Peoples of South-eastern Nigeria.* (Ethnographic Survey of Africa) London 1950
3. Martin, Anne, *The Oil Palm Economy of the Ibibio Farmer* (Colonial Research Studies No. 19 Ibadan, 1956
4. Morgan, W. B., 'Farming Practice, Settlement Pattern and Population Density in South-East Nigeria' *Geographical Journal* Vol. 121 pp. 320–33 1955
5. Udo, R. K., 'Disintegration of Nucleated Settlement in Eastern Nigeria' *Geographical Review* Vol. 60 pp. 53–67 1965
6. Udo, R. K., 'Land and Population in Otoro District' *Nigerian Geographical Journal* Vol. 4 pp. 3–19 1961

8 The Scarplands of South-Eastern Nigeria

A few miles south-east of the Niger-Benue confluence at Lokoja, the land rises to form an elongated west-east highland which divides Igala Division into two unequal lowland areas—a northern plain draining into the lower Benue and a southern plain draining into the Niger. In a relief map of Nigeria, this highland appears as a dimunitive eastern counterpart of the uplands of Afenmai and Western Kabba. The observant traveller through Okene or Kabba to Oturkpo, by way of Lokoja, will notice that apart from the occurrence of residual hills, many of which are capped with lateritic ironstones, on the plateau surfaces of both upland areas, the two highlands are essentially different. The uplands of Afenmai and Western Kabba are developed almost exclusively on rocks of the Basement Complex, while the uplands east of the Lower Niger valley are underlain by cretaceous sandstones.

East of the Lower Niger valley, the highland occurs as a plateau marked by precipitous escarpments. Both the plateau surface and the escarpments constitute two of the main morphological units of the scarplands of south-eastern Nigeria. Other morphological units of this composite region include the Awka-Orlu uplands, and the Ebenebe sandstone ridge. The scarpland region is one of the most documented regions in the country, but much of the literature is concerned only with areas within the East Central State, where the main upland is identified with the well-known Udi Plateau, and the scarp surface with the Enugu escarpment.

For its size, this region provides the most varied landscapes and scenic beauty in Nigeria. Some of the more fascinating landscapes include the scarp slopes at Enugu and Awgu, the terraced hill farms at Maku and the impressive though destructive monuments carved out by gully erosion at Nsudde, Agulu and other places. Farmland is insufficient for the local population and many parts of the region are food deficit areas. This is the main reason why this region exports a considerable percentage of its adult population to towns and rural areas in other parts of the country.

LANDFORMS AND DRAINAGE CHARACTERISTICS

A close relationship exists between geological formations and morphological units in the region. The surface of the main plateau for example is associated with Falsebedded Sandstones while the middle and lower slopes of the north and east facing escarpments bordering this plateau are associated with rocks of the Lower Coal Measures. Geology plays a dominant role in determining the drainage

characteristics as well as the landforms of the major geomorphic units.

The main highland area which is by far the most prominent morphological unit in the region is shaped like an inverted L. Its north-south limb which is usually referred to as the Udi Plateau is very well documented but not so the east-west limb which is called the Igala Plateau. Steep escarpments characterize the eastern and northern ends of the Udi and Igala Plateaux respectively; the former dipping gently towards the west and south-west while the latter dips southwards. The general elevation of the plateau surface is 1,000 feet above sea level.

The scenic beauty of these plateaux which are underlain by Falsebedded Sandstones is impressive particularly during the rainy season, when the open landscape is carpeted with green grass. Erosional survivals (Figure 33) which appear as flat-topped ridges, flat-topped as well as dome-shaped hills, dominate the plateau landscape especially in the area lying west of the highway linking Ukehe to Nsukka. West and south-west of Nsukka, as well as around Aku, the hills and ridges occur in groups enclosing saucer-shaped depressions, the perimeters of

Figure 33. The Scarplands of Northern Iboland

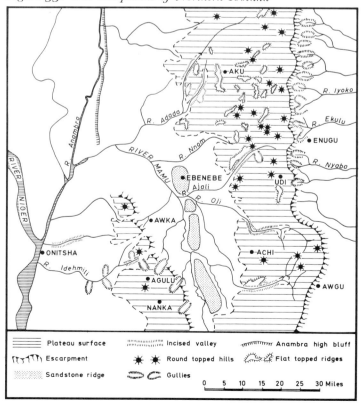

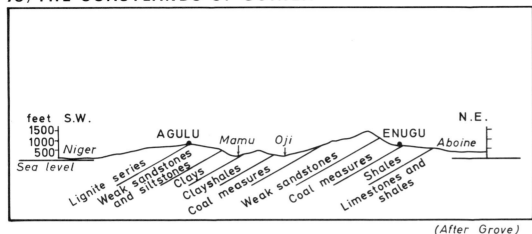

Figure 34. A West to East Cross-section across the Scarplands

(After Grove)

which are breached by open broad vales. In some areas, the hills are arranged in perfect rows which suggest that they are remnants of formerly continuous ridges which have since been broken up into hills. These landforms stand out clearly in the new 1:50,000 topographical sheets of the plateau area, and are of great geomorphological interest.

Many of the hills, especially those with flat tops as well as the ridges, are surmounted by cappings of hard concretional ironstone, which may be up to fifty feet thick. It has been suggested that the dome-shaped residuals have developed from flat-topped hills (Iloeje 1961), following the successful removal of the lateritic capping which tends to preserve the flat tops.

Around Maku, that is in the extreme southern portion, the plateau is heavily dissected by the headstreams of the Oji and Mamu Rivers. Farther north, the plateau surface carries numerous flat-bottomed dry valleys which usually separate the residual hills and ridges. The complete absence of surface drainage over most of this geomorphic unit is not surprising, in view of the great depth (up to 1,000 feet on the crest of the Enugu escarpment) of the highly porous and permeable falsebedded sandstones, which underlie the plateau surface.

The escarpment bordering the northern and eastern edges of the plateau is one of the most prominent relief features in Nigeria. The descent from the crest (about 1,400 feet) to the foot (about 900 feet) is very steep and almost vertical in some places, particularly along the section facing the Cross River plains. This section is also much indented and carved into a series of sharp-edged spurs projecting into the plains. In some places, these spurs have been breached by erosion and are now partially or totally isolated from the escarpment. Juju rock, which lies close to the police rifle range at Uwani, Enugu, is an excellent example of these outliers.

Near the villages of Ukehe, Ukana and Akwegbe, the scarp face is cut by large gaping gullies which occur mainly on the higher slopes of the escarpments. Lesser gullies are to be found along the headstreams of many rivers draining eastwards into the Cross River plains. Most of the gullies are about 300 feet deep and in most cases, such as at Ukehe and Nsudde, a spring issues at

the foot of the vertical backwall of the gully. The gully heads are generally semi-circular, and their walls, which are vertical, exhibit a most fascinating artistic design cut by storm waters. Alluvial fans and slumped earth rubble characterize the gully floors, which are usually dry except after a heavy rain storm.

The valleys of streams flowing eastwards into the Cross River are of great topographical interest. The upper courses of these streams, which issue at the head of the plateau gullies, flow over impervious shales and sandstones before plunging over the escarpment into the plains below. Along their short traverse of the plateau surface (a distance of three to eight miles) these streams develop a variety of valley forms, which correspond closely to the varied geological formations—hence the steep-sided gorge of the sandstones area, followed shortly by a mature, almost senile valley on the impervious shales. At the edge of the escarpment the streams cascade over the hard underlying sandstone and coal measures, where they acquire greater erosive power to cut another gorge-like reach over the scarp slope.

Apart from the Ebenebe-Umuduru sandstone ridge, the lowland area occupied by the Lower Mamu and the Upper Anambra Rivers is a featureless plain, which is heavily wooded in some areas. It is underlain by the Imo Clay Shales, and in the south it separates the Udi-Nsukka Plateau from the Awka-Orlu Uplands. The sandstone ridge is steep-sided, and breached at various points by water gaps. The rivers in this plain have extensive flood plains, which may remain swampy for a considerable part of the year.

West of the Mamu plain, the ground rises steeply to form the Awka-Orlu escarpment, which marks the eastern limit of another plateau surface within this region. As in the case of the Enugu escarpment, the face of this scarp slope is cut by many erosion gullies of which the most extensive are those at Agulu, Nanka and Ekwulobia. The surface of the Awka-Orlu Plateau is, however, quite different from that of the Udi-Nsukka Plateau for unlike the latter, it is almost completely devoid of hills or ridges. The general elevation is approximately the same, but it has a denser vegetation cover than the Udi-Nsukka Plateau. One of the most interesting relief features of the area is the Agulu lake, which was formed as a result of the damming of the Upper Idemili River by sand deposits eroded from gullies, which open into the Idemili valley near Adazi market. The lake is forty feet deep and covers about 300 acres.

CLIMATE AND VEGETATION

The total annual rainfall, as well as the length of the rainy season, decreases towards the north and north-east. Over most of the region, the rains begin in April and end in November, the rainiest month being September. The August break is not marked except in the south, where it may last for two weeks. The total rainfall in the northern part of the region is about fifty-four inches per annum (Ankpa), increasing to over seven inches in the south.

About ninety per cent of the rain falls between April and October, and the fact that the rain falls in sharp thunderstorms is of great significance to the development of sheet and gully erosion, which have already destroyed much land in parts of the region.

Mean annual temperatures rarely fall below 80° F. although it is generally cooler between June and November. The hottest months are February and March, the two preceding months being kept cooler by the harmattan.

The vegetation of the region has been so much modified by centuries of human occupation, that traces of the climatic climax are difficult to come by, even along the virtually inaccessible scarp slopes. Woody shrubs clothe the Mamu lowland, while the plateau and scarp surfaces are characterized by open-grass cover. The landscape around Udi is particularly devoid of trees, but northwards woodlands and oil palms reappear. The dense concentration of oil palm trees around Obukpa in Nsukka Division, but particularly in the area immediately south of the Igala Plateau, is striking.

SOILS AND SOIL EROSION

A wide range of parent materials, consisting largely of cretaceous and tertiary sediments, and the varied nature of the topography have combined to produce a variety of soils in the region. All the soils are known to be acidic in reaction and most of the crops grown are tolerant of acidity. One of the most prominent and most widespread soil groups consists of the Acid Sands, while Lateritic and Alluvial soils make up the two remaining groups.

The Acid Sands, which are derived from sandstones, occur on the plateau surfaces. They have a poorly developed profile and are structurally unstable, and therefore readily given to degradation and erosion. Intense leaching due to high rainfall and exposure of the surface, as a result of continued cultivation, results in increased acidity; but under forest cover, the acidity is reduced considerably in the upper horizon. Soil fertility in the Acid Sands depends mainly on the organic matter content of the surface layer, rather than on the chemical composition of the parent materials. Hence the rapid rate of soil impoverishment when the plant cover is removed.

Lateritic soils are found mainly in the Anambra drainage basin, including the Mamu Plains. Laterite also occurs on the plateau surfaces as well as on the tops of ridges and some hills. These soils develop in flat and gently sloping surfaces, where water movement is impeded, and in areas where the water table comes very close to the surface during the rainy season. On the hills and ridges as well as along the foot of escarpments, the laterites consist mainly of ferruginized sandstone, formed from the oxidation of ferrous compounds in seepage water; but at Udi and Maku, lateritic soils tend to be concretionary and vesicular.

Alluvial soils occur mainly along the major river valleys such as the Mamu and the Upper Anambra, as well as in the valleys of smaller streams draining into these rivers. Soil conditions in these valleys make it possible for crops to be planted much earlier than in the neighbouring upland farms. Alluvial soils are often set aside for the growing of yams and cocoyams.

The large concentration of population on the plateau areas, and the shortage of farmland in the area, have resulted in overworking of available soils. Sheet erosion by wind as well as by running water is common in the plateau areas around Udi, Nsudde and Agulu. It is less spectacular than gully erosion, but occurs over an extensive area. Areas affected by sheet erosion can be readily recognized by the fact that the roots of small tufts of grass are exposed as a result of the top soil between the tufts being washed or blown away.

A more spectacular and probably more destructive type of erosion plaguing the uplands and scarp slopes of this region is gully erosion. The character of the gullies has been described on page 78, but the destruction and problems posed by gully erosion have yet to be considered.

Soil erosion in the scarplands of south-eastern Nigeria is generally attributed to man's interference with nature's balance in the soil. Apart from overfarming and overgrazing the land, destructive methods of cultivation such as making ridges or lines of mounds along the slopes have initiated gullies which have engulfed vast areas of land. Footpaths leading to streams at the foot of scarp slopes

Plate 15. (a) Erosion at Agulu.

Plate 15. (b) Erosion at Agulu.

(as at Agulu), and the concentration of runoff in artificial drainage along newly made roads (as along the Awgu-Udi road), have sometimes led to the development of extensive gullies. In certain areas, however, soil erosion is induced by inherent structural and climatic conditions, the steep slopes of the escarpments and the violent nature of the rain storms being of great significance.

The loss of soil from the area exposed to erosion is only a part of the destructive work of soil erosion. Further down-slope, more soil is lost to sedimentation resulting from the depositing of the soils and debris brought down from the gullies.

THE HISTORY AND PROBLEMS OF SOIL CONSERVATION

Although the threat posed by gully erosion in parts of the region was recognized many years earlier, it was not until 1945 that a practical attempt was made to conserve the land and tackle the advancing gullies at Agulu. In that year, a soil conservation scheme, financed with funds provided from the Colonial Welfare and Development Fund, was set up at Agulu to check the growth of gullies and to serve as a demonstration area for anti-erosion organizations from other eroded areas. Villages close to the gully heads were evacuated and farmlands under the threat of advancing gullies, or found to be very much impoverished, were put out of cultivation.

Some evidence of the construction work directed at checking the gullies and reclaiming the land can still be seen in the Agulu village of Amaoji. These include circular soak-away pits or sumps (four feet in diameter and five feet deep), dug alongside footpaths to help reduce surface runoff, cashew trees and *acioa bateri* planted to reclaim the land and contour ridges. By 1950, the erosion control unit had carried out some work on 134 gullies, built 805 dams, 24 miles of contour ridges and 33 miles of path with 4,336 sumps. Large areas were planted with trees and villagers were instructed on how to check erosion. A sum of about £25,000 was spent during the first five years, after which there was little control.

Right from the start, the Agulu Soil Conservation Scheme was faced with many problems. There was the question of finding alternative plots for those whose farm-lands were put out of cultivation as a result of conservation regulations passed by the Native Authority. The view of the administration was that compensation, whether in cash or land, should be paid by the community. At the same time, dissatisfied ex-servicemen, who had just returned from the Second World War, insisted that it was the duty of the administration to reclaim and restore the land.

A large number of local people still see the gullies as the work of angry gods, and earlier attempts to enforce farming on the contour and the use of ridges instead of mounds, were not well received. New methods of land utilization involving crop rotations, planting cover crops and green manuring were also frowned upon. The gullies continue to extend and since 1964, the state Ministry of Agriculture has indicated the Government's intention to fight the gullies once more.

THE PROBLEMS OF RURAL WATER SUPPLY

In spite of high annual rainfall exceeding sixty-five inches over most of the region, the upland areas, which are underlain by highly permeable sandstones, suffer from inadequate supplies of water for domestic use. No perennial streams cross the areas underlain by falsebedded sandstones, and all over the plateau surfaces there is very little surface drainage. The few springs are far between and emerge at great depths along the foot of the escarpments. Water shortage is acute during the dry season, when many people are obliged to travel from three to seven miles on foot to fetch water.

During the rainy season, drinking water is obtained from the roofs of houses and the stems of coconut trees, while water for cooking comes from catch pits dug in front of most compounds. Water from these catch pits serves as drinking water when other sources of rain water have been used up. The pits serve as breeding grounds for frogs, snails and mosquitoes; and the water itself is contaminated by human excrement, and is known to be a major cause of intestinal diseases and guinea worm. As soon as the dry season sets in the pits dry up, and water becomes more difficult to obtain.

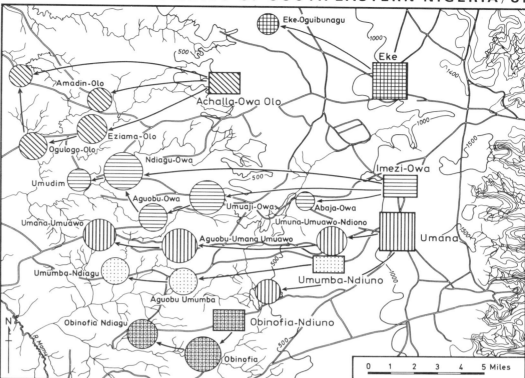

Figure 35. Westward Migration of Settlement in the Plateau Area North of Udi. Each parent village is enclosed in a rectangular frame, while other settlements in the group (identifiable by the shading pattern) are enclosed in circular frames

One of the traditional ways in which people have sought to combat water shortage is to store water in large earthen pots, which are then placed under dense tree groves which provide shade, and thereby reduce the rate of evaporation. Often, mosquitoes breed in the pots while the water turns greenish as a result of fungus growth. Trading in water has become an established profession in some villages, where water is sold in four-gallon kerosene tins at three to six pence per tin, depending on distance from the nearest water point. Underground water resources can be tapped by sinking deep boreholes; but few villages on the plateaux can afford the cost of such wells, since the water table on the Udi plateaux, for example, lies at a depth of 200–300 feet.

In areas blessed with perennial streams, access to the water may be hampered by the steepness of the valley slopes, and as pointed out earlier gullies have often been initiated by footpaths leading to the streams. Another problem arises from the fact that people wade into the streams to draw drinking water and to bathe as well as to wash clothes, with the result that the water used by villages further downstream becomes progressively more polluted. Many villages have now been provided with standing pipes from reservoirs fed from deep wells, but there is still a lot to be done.

THE DISTRIBUTION AND CHANGING PATTERN OF RURAL SETTLEMENTS

The greatest concentrations of population in the region are found on the plateaux, where the soils appear to be easier to cultivate than the heavier soils of the river flood-plains. The oldest settlements are located on the plateaux

which, in addition, provided easily defensible sites in the hills and ridges which occur all over the uplands. During the last fifty years, however, there has been a marked tendency for groups of people to break away from their parent villages to set up daughter settlements on the relatively sparsely settled lowlands, where crop yields are much better.

In the plateau area lying between Udi and Ukehe, the distribution of daughter settlements indicate an east to west movement of population towards the vast Mamu Lowlands (Figure 35), but nearer Nsukka migration has been primarily eastwards in the direction of the Cross River plains. Most daughter settlements started as temporary farm hamlets, which have since become permanent villages. The parent village is often easy to trace particularly in Nsukka area, where the name of the daughter settlement consists in attaching the suffix Agu (=farm) to that of the parent village. Thus Eha Ndiagu was founded by farmers from Eha Alumona, while Ibagwa-Agu and Nkpor-Agu were founded by migrants from Ibagwa and Nkpor respectively.

A similar arrangement of settlement is noticed in Awka Division, where the majority of present day settlement divides into two parts, usually Eziama and Ifite or with suffixes such as Enu (=on the hill) and Ani (=farm). In all such cases, Eziama, which literally means the true or real villages, refers to the parent village, which is generally located on the upland or Agba Enu zone of the Division; while the Ifite half, which is of more recent age, is always located on lower ground.

A few hill settlements persist in Nsukka area to remind one of the periods of insecurity when harassed villagers retreated to the hills for protection. At Aku, the contrast

Figure 36. An Aerial View of the Ozubulu Area showing the complete Dispersal of Settlement

between the congested hill village and the newer, but scattered settlement at the foot of the hill is striking.

Increasing population, which has resulted in extreme fragmentation and scarcity of farmland in the upland areas of Awka and Udi Divisions, has led to a complete scatter of compounds over the landscape of districts like Agulu, Ogidi and Ozubulu. Figure 36 gives a vivid impression of the cultural landscape of Ozubulu area. The main farmlands in such districts have been almost completely replaced by compoundlands which are cropped yearly. Each compound consists of one to ten houses and is completely surrounded by a wall of mud or concrete and the land around it is cropped with yams, maize and greens. The farmer therefore lives in the midst of his land, but the problem here is that the holding, which rarely exceeds half an acre, is too small to be economical.

THE HISTORY AND PROBLEMS OF RURAL–RURAL MIGRATIONS

The shortage of farmland is most acute in Awka and Udi Divisions, and for several decades farmers from these areas were content to migrate to lease farmlands in the Mamu and Anambra Lowlands, as well as along the Lower Niger valley. Short-term leases for one harvest period were common and rents were paid in kind and, later, in cash as well as in kind. In 1921 there was a misunderstanding between Awka migrants, who were new to Igbariam farmlands, and non-Awka migrants, who resented the influx of Awka people into Igbariam territory. Apparently non-Awka migrant farmers wanted to eject Awka tenant farmers, who were more industrious and were always willing to pay higher rents. A four-day raid on farms belonging to migrant tenant farmers from Awka resulted in the destruction of crops and other property for which the raiders were forced to pay a compensation of £7,000. Today, a great number of migrants from Awka go to distant farmlands in Asaba and Benin Divisions, while many others work as labourers in the plantations and timber concessions of the Benin Lowlands.

Villagers from the eastern upland areas of Udi and Nsukka migrate to farm in the Cross River plains; the largest concentration of migrant farmers being at Nike village-group territory, about five miles north-east of Enugu. These migrants farm not only for subsistence, but also to sell to the Enugu market, just as migrants to the

Uturu area of Ogwashi Uku in Asaba Division farm for the Onitsha food market.

Rural emigration is essentially selective in that the bulk of the migrants consist of young able-bodied men. There is no information on the number of migrants who are away from a given village at a particular time, but there is some indirect evidence to show that the figure is considerable. In 1955, for example, the Awka Divisional Council complained of decreasing revenue owing to the migration of men to distant farmlands, where they normally pay their tax and rates, and pointed out that such migrants usually leave their families behind at Awka, where the council is expected to provide some basic social services for them.

A permanent colonization of sparsely settled areas, through resettlement schemes, would seem to offer an alternative to the present system of farming such areas on a tenancy basis. This suggestion, however, raises a number of issues touching on the land.

THE ECONOMY OF THE FOOD DEFICIT AREAS OF AWKA AND ONITSHA

Farming is the most important occupation in all parts of the scarplands, but in the very densely settled parts of Awka and Onitsha Divisions, the local farmers do not produce enough food for subsistence. They have therefore had to depend on food imports from Onitsha urban market. Crops grown in these food deficit areas are the same as for other parts of Iboland, with yams, cassava and maize predominating. Farming methods and the farming calendar are also similar.

One of the main food items which are produced in such food deficit areas as Ogidi and Nnewi are fruits including oranges, avocado and African pears, pawpaw, bananas and plantains. These fruits are grown mainly on compoundlands, and are in continuous supply all through the year. Maize and vegetables such as pumpkins and 'bitter leaf' are also grown for sale to the urban markets of Awka and Onitsha. Housewives, who take these fruits to Onitsha, usually return with yams and other food items to supplement whatever their farms can produce.

An important fruit which has made it possible for dense populations to survive not only in the uplands of Awka, but in other parts of the Eastern States, is the oil palm. Unfortunately, there is very little effort to cultivate oil palms in these areas, where existing trees are already becoming old. A Government scheme for rehabilitating palm groves has been in existence for several years, but so far it has not made any appreciable impact in the villages.

Trading in foodstuffs and manufactured consumer goods contributes a significant addition to the family income. Women play an active part both in trading and in farming, but large-scale trade in palm produce and imported goods, as well as the bulk handling of trade in foodstuffs like yams and rice, is directed by men.

Education is regarded as a major investment, since a successful son is expected to send home, at regular intervals, some money for feeding his ageing parents and for paying the fees of younger relatives. Misguided attempts, by successful members of the community, to help younger ones have often resulted in shocking cases of nepotism and abuse of office by highly placed persons from these impoverished uplands.

Traditional crafts were formerly an important source of income to some families. At Awka, for example, the gild of blacksmiths produced such specialized goods as dane guns and farm implements. Pottery, basket making and wood carving are still important, but iron working has declined considerably following the importation of cheaper and better quality goods from abroad.

TERRACE AGRICULTURE

Before the pacification of this part of the country, the hill dwellers of Nsukka district, the Maku area and central Igalla, cultivated much of their food on terraces constructed along the slopes of these hills. Today, with the abandonment of most of these hill-top settlements, the terraced slopes are no longer in use except in a few areas such as Nkpologu, Aku and Maku. The remains of abandoned terraces are common in the areas near Ukehe and Nsukka.

The most extensive area of terrace cultivation in Nigeria today is found in the Maku district of Agwu Division. The area lies immediately northwest of Awgu and west of the main east-facing escarpment, but it is possible to observe the impressive terraced hills as the motorist approaches Agwu from Enugu. The view is particularly fascinating during the months of April to August, when crops are growing in the fields.

Maku people have been described as exceptionally efficient hill farmers, who work their land to the utmost by intensive terrace farming. The widths of the terrace platforms vary from five to ten yards, depending on the gradient of the hill-side and are protected by carefully constructed terrace walls which run along the contour. Soils in the area are reddish brown in colour, and contain abundant ferruginized rock fragments. In some farms, outcrops of horizontally-disposed beds of ironstone which

Plate 16. *Juju Rock. A laterite capped erosional survival fronting the Enugu escarpment.*

Plate 17. *Abandoned terraces at Nsukka.*

occur along the slopes are utilized as foundations for the terrace walls.

According to the 1961 Agricultural Sample Survey of Maku, the average number of terraced plots cultivated by each farmer is five, each plot being rarely more than 0·03 acre. One hundred and forty-five plots were surveyed, the largest single plot covering 0·32 acre and the smallest 0·01 acre. Crops grown on these terraced gardens include yams, cocoyams, maize and pumpkin.

CASHEW PLANTATIONS AND THE CASHEW INDUSTRY

The introduction of cashew trees (*Anacardium occidentale*) into the sandy grass plains of the Udi Plateau has provided

an area where oil palms, rubber and cocoa cannot do well with a substitute cash crop. The cashew tree is a native of South America, where it grows in the sandy areas of north-east Brazil, and once planted it does not require much care or attention. No manuring is required, although it responds to it, and the large amount of leaf fall from it, together with its ability to thrive on impoverished soils, is one of the factors which recommend its use in reclaiming those areas affected by sheet and gully erosion.

The cashew tree is a fast-growing and fast-maturing plant, which takes only three years from planting to the harvesting of the first fruits. Once it starts bearing, it continues to double its previous year's yield until the tenth year, after which it maintains a constant level of production for another twenty years.

Cashew trees provide a variety of products, but considerable capital is needed for installing the necessary processing equipment. The apples, usually called false fruits, are eaten, and in Brazil wine is made from the juice. The real fruit carries the kernel or cashew nut, which is protected by two layers of shell. Phenol, a compound of great commercial value, used as an antiseptic and disinfectant as well as in the preparation of plastics, dyes and drugs, is extracted from the shells, while gum can be obtained from the branches of the tree. At present, the most important product of the cashew in the country is the nut, which is roasted and distributed for eating.

There are at present three state-owned cashew plantations with a total acreage of 2,300 acres. The Ajali River Cashew Estate, which was opened in 1952, is by far the largest of the three (1,300 acres). It is the centre for processing fruits grown in the three estates as well as from private farmers; and since 1959, commercial piggery production, based on cashew nut waste, has been an important feature of the cashew industry. The other two plantations are the Oji River Cashew Estate and the Mbala Cashew Estate, each of which is about 500 acres in extent.

FARM SETTLEMENTS

Two of the twelve farm settlements planned by the former Eastern Nigeria Government are located in this region. One is located at Uzo-Uwani, in Nsukka Division, and the other at Igbariam, in Onitsha Division. At Igbariam, which is an area frequented by migrant tenant farmers from the uplands of Awka Division, many of these migrants had to be displaced from the land acquired for the 6,500-acre farm settlement. The settlement, which started in 1962, is designed to settle 400 educated farmers each of which is provided with nine acres of oil palm, five acres of citrus trees and two and a half acres of arable land to be ploughed with tractors. Each settler also has an additional half acre of land set aside for vegetables and poultry, and rice is grown by communal effort.

At Uzo-Uwani farm settlement the emphasis is not on tree crops but on swamp rice, which is grown under modern methods of irrigation. It is located on a suitable site in the Anambra Lowlands, where the terrain makes it possible for irrigation water to flow under gravity along the eleven-mile main canal and the distributary channels. Individual families in this 10,560-acre settlement will have about sixteen acres of land, ten of which are to be planted with rice. Onions are also planted as a cash crop, and each settler has the usual two and a half acres for food farm and half an acre of compoundland for house and garden.

The Government Farm Settlement Scheme hopes to attempt to reverse the trend of migration from rural to urban areas, to absorb some of the unemployed primary school leavers and to demonstrate to and educate the people in the possibilities of large-scale farming. It aims at increasing and maintaining the output of food and agricultural products by making rural areas more productive, through fuller use of sparsely populated land. These are laudable objectives, but the cost of settling each settler, which was initially estimated at £3,000 but later reduced to about £2,000, is very high; and in any case the number of school leavers to be absorbed is very insignificant. The failure of demonstration farms, set up by the Extension Division of the Ministry of Agriculture, to make an impact on local farming methods suggests that these settlements are not likely to have much influence on peasant farming in the various localities.

COAL MINING AT ENUGU

Nigeria is the only country in West Africa producing coal at present, and the coal field is located in the eastern part of the scarplands of south-eastern Nigeria. Mining is still confined to the Enugu district, where coal was first discovered in 1909, but the estimated reserves of 72 million tons in the area is much less than the 170 million tons reserves in the Northern Nigeria section of the coal field. The first coal mine in the Enugu area was the Udi mine, opened in 1915, but abandoned two years later when the Iva valley mine was opened to tap the same locality. Three other mines are now under production and these are the Okpara mine (1952), Ekulu mine (1956) and the Ribadu mine (1961).

Compared with the Jos Plateau tin industry, coal mining at Enugu started off very well, in that by 1916 a railway line for evacuating the coal to the port of export at Port Harcourt had been completed. Indeed the port of Port Harcourt was built originally as a coal port. The railway itself became the greatest customer of Enugu coal, which has until recently remained the main source of fuel for running the locomotives. Production during the early years was also stimulated as a result of acute shortage of coal throughout West Africa, owing to lack of shipping space during the 1914–18 War. In consequence, the output of 24,500 tons in 1916 rose to over 83,400 tons in the following year; considerable quantities being exported to Ghana and Sierra Leone. Readers may find these figures more meaningful if they realize that Britain's coal output in 1913 was 280 million tons. During the decade ending in 1960 the total output of Enugu coal averaged about 640,000 tons a year, but production has since declined for reasons which are given below.

The coal, which is of sub-bituminous grade, occurs in seams of which five have been identified (Figure 37). The thickest seam in the Enugu area is number three seam, which varies in thickness from four to six feet. Mining is still restricted to this seam whose favourable situation, together with the low dip, has made it possible to mine the coal from adits driven into the hill-side. Mining is by the pillar and stall method, and often no pit props are required since the roof of the seam is strong enough to stand up well for long periods without support. As may be expected, adit mining has resulted in a decline in productivity in the older workings, where the coal face has receded from the entrances, thereby increasing the

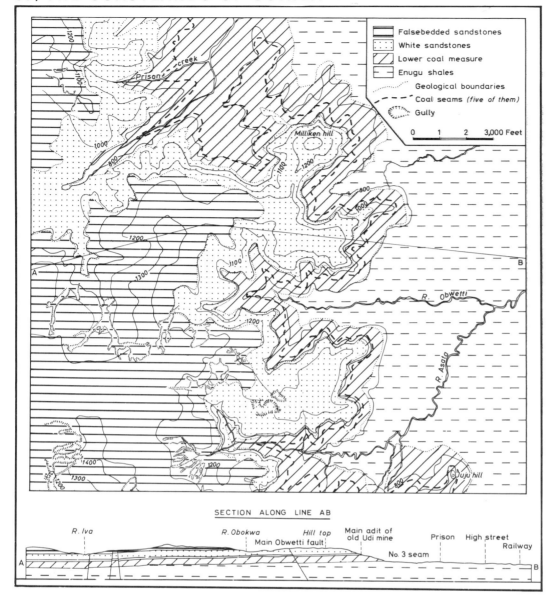

Figure 37. Geology of the Enugu Coalfield

hauling distance. At the same time, there have been increased labour costs featuring a considerable rise in wages.

Unlike tin and petroleum which is mined by private companies, Nigerian coal has always been mined under the direct supervision of a government department. Initially, the mines were administered by the Nigerian Railways, but later coal mining became the responsibility of a separate government department. In 1950, the Nigerian Coal Corporation, a federal government statutory corporation, was formed to take over the assets and liabilities of the previous operating department.

One of the main handicaps of the Nigerian coal industry, which has been running at a loss during the last twenty years, is the location of its mines. Heavy transport costs are involved in delivering the coal to consumers in Lagos and other parts of the country. Coal for use in Lagos and the Western State is railed to Port Harcourt, from where it is shipped to Lagos and railed again to destinations north of Lagos. Thus, while the pit-head price in

1960 was about 50 shillings per ton, the price per ton at Lagos and Ibadan was 110 shillings and 120 shillings respectively. This situation has contributed significantly to the recent tendency for users of coal to turn to other sources of power:

During the last ten years, the largest consumers of coal have been the Nigerian Railway Corporation, which takes about half the amount of coal produced in the country, the Electricity Corporation and the Nkalagu Cement Factory. The dieselization of the railways and the production of petroleum and gas have combined to lead to a substantial decline in the demand for coal. Nor is coal a popular domestic fuel in Nigeria. The main problem of the Nigerian coal industry today is where to find markets for the coal mined. At present the industry appears to survive simply because if it closes down the number of unemployed persons will go up. Yet there has been a series of retrenchments of miners since 1960 and this trend is likely to continue.

Nigerian coal is a non-coking variety and is therefore

Plate 18. A Part of Enugu. Residential houses in this city rarely exceed two stories.

Figure 38. The Growth of Enugu

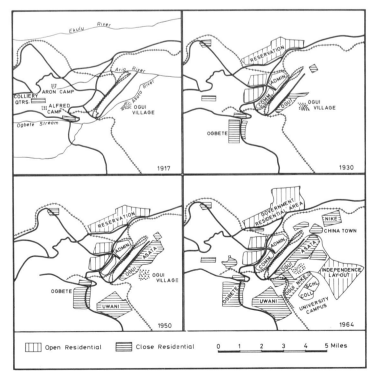

Plate 19. Teaching blocks at the Enugu Campus of the University of Nigeria.

unlikely to be in great demand when the proposed iron and steel industry comes into being. The establishment of a chemical industry (including fertilizers) based on coal as a raw material has been under consideration for some time, but it has not yet been confirmed whether such a project will be economical or not. Indeed, with the refining of crude petroleum for local consumption at Eleme, it appears that a future Nigerian chemical industry will be based on by-products of the oil industry rather than on Enugu coal.

Shortage of farmland on the plateau villages has acted as an incentive to villagers to migrate to work at the mines. The labour strength in 1963 was 3,200 and the average daily output for the year was 2,200 tons, based on mine working days. Miners work round the clock in three shifts for a five-day week of eight hours a day.

ENUGU TOWN

Enugu (143,000 in 1963), the administrative capital of the East Central State, owes its origin and early growth to coal mining and is still fondly referred to as 'coal city'. Before mining started in the area the only settlement on its site was the small Nike village of Ogui (Figure 38). In 1915, the mining camps together with the European colliery staff quarters was given the name of Enugu (= hilltop), although in actual fact the new settlement was located on the plains at the foot of the escarpment. There are many other Ibo villages with the name Enugu, and all of them are located on hills. Enugu is therefore one of the new towns of tropical Africa which have arisen as a result of contact with Europe. Its growth has been very rapid during the last twenty years, and today Enugu is not only an administrative and mining town but also an industrial and educational centre.

The growth of residential districts reflects the functional growth of the town. Ogbete or Coal Camp which is one of the oldest planned residential areas was built for miners, while China Town started in 1923 as a special residential area for African railway workers. Mining brought about the development of commercial activities to service the local population, and Ogui Town grew up to accommodate migrants attracted by new opportunities offered by the town. The European reservation, which is a feature of the British colonial empire in Africa and India, was built on the far northern side of the railway, and was separated from the African townships by a neutral zone, which was to provide an excellent site for the Enugu sports stadium.

Since the end of the Second World War, the growth of Enugu has been as a result of its position as the seat of the regional administration. Administration now employs more labour than the colliery, which was formerly the main employer of labour; and the newer residential areas of Asata, Uwani and Ogui-Nike have all grown up to provide accommodation for these workers.

The grandiose buildings at Independence layout, which were reserved for ministers of state, are a living testimony to the distorted sense of mission of the Nigerian politician whose exaggerated idea of his importance and corruption was one of the causes of the army revolt of January 1966. It is the latest development in residential district, and contains the ultra-modern Hotel Presidential.

Industrial development at Enugu is still in its infancy, largely because of the dominance of Port Harcourt, Aba and Onitsha in this sphere. The coal industry is on the decline and so is the pottery industry at Ekulu, following the development by government of a larger pottery establishment at Umuahia. There is a large furniture factory and a steel rolling mill at Emene.

Works consulted and suggestions for further reading:

1. Floyd, B. N., 'Soil Erosion and Deterioration in Eastern Nigeria' *Nigerian Geographical Journal* Vol. 8 pp. 33–43 1965

2. Floyd, B. N., 'Terrace Agriculture in Eastern Nigeria: The case of Maku' *Nigerian Geographical Journal* Vol. 7 pp. 33–44 1964

3. Grove, A. T., 'Land Use and Soil Conservation in parts of Onitsha and Owerri Provinces' *Geological Survey of Nigeria* No. 21 1951

4. Hair, P. E. H., 'Enugu: An Industrial and Urban Community in East Nigeria 1914–53' West African Institute of Social and Economic Research. Annual Conference Report, sociology section p. 143 1953

5. Iloeje, N. P., 'The Structure and Relief of the Nsukka-Okigwi Cuesta' *Nigerian Geographical Journal* Vol. 4 pp. 21–39 1961

6. Udo, R. K., 'Disintegration of Nucleated Settlement in Eastern Nigeria' *Geographical Review* No. 55 pp. 53–67 1965

7. Udo, R. K., 'The Migrant Tenant Farmer of Eastern Nigeria' *Africa* Vol. 34 pp. 326–39 1965

8. Wilson, R. C. & Bain, A. D. N., 'The Nigerian Coalfield: Section II. Parts of Onitsha and Owerri Provinces' *Geological Survey of Nigeria* No. 12 1928

9 The Cross River Basin

The main problem in defining this region is concerned with the boundary separating it from the scarplands. Many of the rivers flowing down the escarpment to join the Cross River rise on the eastern edge of the plateau, which is part of the scarplands. Also, both the existing collieries as well as Enugu town lie in the Cross River basin, although it is more convenient to discuss both along with the scarplands, which in effect include that part of the Cross River plains bordering the Enugu escarpment. It is now possible to see that river-basins do not necessarily make geographical regions.

Vast tracts of the region are very sparsely settled or virtually uninhabited. Much of it still constitutes a pioneer fringe offering great prospects for the expansion of plantation agriculture, farm settlements and timber exploitation. The isolation and lack of roads in parts of the region contrast markedly with the developed state of transportation in the northern and central parts of the palm belt. Other important aspects of the geography of the basin include the role of the Aro-Abam-Nike fraternity in transforming the cultural landscape during the second half of the nineteenth century, the rapid expansion of rice culture in the grass plains of Abakaliki, intra-regional movement of population and the expansion of commercial plantations. The decline of the Cross River waterway and that of the ancient port town of Calabar are also of considerable interest.

RELIEF AND DRAINAGE

Excepting the two highland areas of Oban and Obudu, which are a part of the ranges making up the Eastern Borderlands, the Cross River basin consists of a low-lying region which is called the Cross River plains. From the foot of the escarpment at Enugu, the plains stretch eastwards for 50 miles and cover about 200 miles in a north-south direction. The underlying rocks consist of shales and sandstones, and the land rises steadily northwards, from 200 feet in the south to over 500 feet in the north-west. Kitson attributes the origin of the plains, which are a product of sub-aerial erosion, to an ancient drainage system which he calls the Older Benue and which, according to him, flowed from the present Upper Benue, entering the sea at the mouth of the present Cross River. The headward erosion of streams draining from the plateau suggests that the present position of the escarpment marks the stage reached so far in the westward extension of the Cross River plains.

The present Cross River system is a rejuvenated network, the vast and seasonally flooded rice fields of Abakaliki and Afikpo representing traces of an older and more extensive flood plain. The valley of the main stream is flanked at intervals by steep scarps and isolated hills as at Adadama, but there are no interruptions in the waterway which is navigable all the year round, particularly along the lower reaches. Valley features of streams flowing over the Udi Plateau to join the Cross River have been described in the chapter on the scarplands, but sections lying between the escarpment and the Cross River itself present some interesting topographical features which deserve our attention. The sudden drop of streams from the plateau over the escarpment to the plains below, and the flat nature of the plains induce a sudden change in the character of the valley, such that the rivers become shallow and spread out in broad flat valleys. Marshes and temporary lakes are regular features along these rivers but further downstream, the rivers enter the Cross River with renewed cutting vigour.

THE DISSECTED HILL COUNTRY OF BENDE-AFIKPO DISTRICT

This area lies south of the line joining Okigwi to Afikpo, and drains into the Cross River through the Enyong Creek. A large number of small rivers flowing through very steep-sided valleys, carved out of a thick underlying layer of soft sandstone and forming definite dendritic systems, occur all over the district. So cut up is the landscape that the main roads, to avoid as many valleys as possible, follow the crest of the ridges which form local water sheds. The road from Umuahia to Uzuakoli traverses a representative part of this district and there are as many as twelve wooden bridges to be crossed in travelling through the distance of elven miles separating these two settlements. This is the home of the Eastern or Cross River Ibos, where the notorious head hunters of Abam Clan still live on hill sites. The grassy appearance of the hills, particularly at Ohafia and Nkporo, in a climatically forest environment emphasizes the extent to which man has tampered with the vegetation of the area.

The Enyong Creek which drains the district is a misfit, its headwaters having been captured by the Imo River at a point very close to Umuahia. Below Ikpe Ikot Nkon, the narrow course of the creek spreads out into an extensive swampy country, which is everywhere less than one hundred feet above sea level. Surface water is superabundant in this part of the district, where the slightest rise in the terrain forms the source of a stream. The streams are in many cases lost in the swamps, without direct access to the Enyong Creek; a situation which

Plate 20. The ascent to the Obudu Plateau. A state agency maintains a cattle ranch and hotel facilities for tourists.

reminds one of the scene around the shores of Lake Chad. Roads are few and difficult to build; the nine-mile Itu–Atan Onoyom road, which runs parallel to the Cross River, being essentially a causeway over these swamps. During the rainy season the few water-shunning settlements such as Nkana, Obot Etim and Obio Usiere are completely cut off by flood water and can only be reached by canoes. The menace of fierce, biting mosquitoes, for which Itu and Arochuku are notorious, adds to the difficulty of the local environment.

OBAN AND OBUDU UPLANDS

These highland areas, which are westward extensions of the Cameroon-Adamawa highlands, represent the oldest and highest land surfaces in the South-eastern State. The Oban hills area lies north of Calabar and consists of a mass of steep-sided hills interspersed with valleys and ravines. The hills, which are generally over 3,000 feet above sea level, consist of granite, gneisses and schists and are drained by swift streams characterized by small falls and rapids. Both highlands are covered with dense forest vegetation, excepting the village clearings and farms, which are often hidden away by trees. The top of the Obudu Plateau is, however, a grassland area with a scatter of light bush. Both uplands are rather isolated, sparsely peopled and relatively backward and undeveloped. The natural attribute of a cool climate and the absence of tsetse-flies on the Obudu Plateau have been exploited by establishing a holiday resort and a large cattle ranch on this highland area, but great difficulty and expense were encountered in opening the only road that winds up to the plateau.

RAINFALL, SEASONAL SWAMPS AND VEGETATION

The wettest parts of the Cross River basin, as may be expected, are in the south and east; the proximity of the former to the sea and the uplands in the latter area explain this phenomenon. A decrease from south to north is noticeable in the annual rainfall figures for Calabar (119 inches), Itu (106 inches) and Afikpo (79 inches), while an east-west decrease is obvious from the figures for Obudu (77 inches), Ogoja (73 inches), Enugu (71 inches). The fact that Abakaliki, which is in the central part of the region, has 83 inches of rain per annum suggests that other factors, other than mere position, play an important part in the rainfall distribution.

All over the basin, well over 83 per cent of the annual rainfall comes between May and October, during which time swamps arise along the rivers as well as in the flat interfluves of Afikpo and Abakaliki areas. The swamps, which are used as rice fields in Abakaliki, usually occur in small patches of rarely more than one acre and are caused by the deep layer of shale in the subsoil and by silt deposits which appear at flood times, making it difficult for water to drain away from the upper soil.

Abakaliki Province is very poorly served by perennial streams, and the problem of rural water supply is as acute here as in the scarplands and the palm belt. Settlements too are dispersed and each compound obtains its supply of water from rain water stored in large ponds dug out of the underlying impermeable shales. Often, water in these ponds does not last much longer than in the rice swamps. People wade into the ponds to fetch water for drinking and other domestic uses, and herds of cattle are commonly seen drinking from the same source. It is therefore understandable why there is a high incidence of guinea worm in Abakaliki.

Mangrove swamps characterize the Cross River estuary and the lower reaches of the Calabar and Kwa Rivers; and apart from the much farmed area around Calabar, the whole area enclosed by the Cross River and the Nigeria–Cameroons boundary consists of high forest, comparable in luxuriance with the forests of Benin and Ondo Provinces. It was this borderland region that Johnston described in 1888 as 'an utter wilderness of forest, uninhabited by man' and today the forest cover remains very dense and impenetrable, except where it has been cut down for establishing plantations of rubber, cocoa and oil palms. Many plants in this area have been associated with Central rather than West African species; the Cross River being considered as a major vegetation divide between West and Central Africa.

Another area of high forest occurs north of the Cross River bend and extends to the foothills of the Obudu Plateau, but the rest of the basin consists of secondary vegetation of grass and open woodland. In the dissected hill country around Uzuakoli and Item there are still extensive tracts of forests which have grown up on long fallows, but at Abiriba, Nkporo and Edda the vegetation becomes more open. Between Enugu and Abakaliki the vegetation consists of guinea savanna, with a conspicuous absence of the oil palm which dominates the secondary forest farther south. Small patches of forests are, however, common in the sparsely settled Nike territory immediately north of Enugu township.

About forty miles east of Abakaliki, the vegetation begins to change. Fan palms dominate the grassy plain which stretches for miles in the direction of the Obudu hills and southern Tivland.

PEOPLE AND TRADITIONS

The Cross River basin is inhabited by people of different ethnic groups, the most numerous being the Ibos, Ibibios and the Ekois of the borderlands. The dominant influence of Calabar is at once apparent, particularly along the Cross River valley, where the cultural influence of Calabar is still considerable. For several centuries, up to and including the first two decades of this century, the Cross River was the main connecting link between the region and the outside world. The slave traders, the missionaries and later, the political officers of the British, penetrated this part of the country by way of the Cross River. Today Efik language, which is spoken by the Calabar people, is understood by the inhabitants of both banks of the river up to Ikom. Even Cross River Ibos, such as the Ohafias, have until recently looked to Calabar for western education rather than to the neighbouring Ibo areas, the reason being that the headquarters and higher educational institutions of the Christian mission operating in their district were located at Calabar. Now that the slave trade has since been stopped, and the trade in palm produce largely diverted to Port Harcourt, the Cross River and its main tributary the Enyong Creek have become notorious highways for smuggling of goods, including alcohol, tobacco, drugs and cloth from the Equatorial Guinea island of Fernando Po. Calabar remains the base of this illegal trade which is dominated by Bende Ibos.

Two neighbouring Ibo sub-tribal groups, the Aros of Arochuku and the Abam people of East Bende, deserve particular mention here. We have already come across the Aros in connection with their colonies in the palm belt,

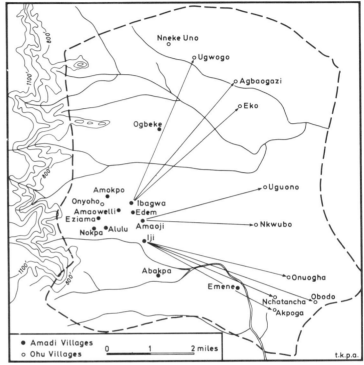

Figure 39. Amadi (freeborn) and Ohu (slave) Villages of Nike

but as pointed out in that context, the largest of these colonies exist in the Cross River basin. Arochuku itself consists of a number of small nucleated villages each of which colonized a particular section of what are now the Eastern States of Nigeria. Many writers have credited the Aros with greater intelligence than the average Ibo, largely because of their ability to organize successfully a bogus deity, the Long juju, through which they obtained much wealth, slaves and, in some measure, succeeded in making themselves feared wherever they lived. This notorious juju was destroyed in 1901 by the British.

Aro domination of vast areas of the Eastern States was made possible by their Abam mercenaries, who fought not so much because they were paid much cash, but largely because wars afforded each male Abam an opportunity of killing a man in order to become initiated into manhood. The Abams themselves live next to the Aros in a broken country which, like Arochuku, is drained by the Enyong creek system. Like the Aros, the Abam people live in compact villages with a peculiar arrangement of houses similar to that for Ohafia (Figure 41).

Another group of Ibos which featured prominently during the pre-colonial days were the Nike people of Enugu District, and it appears that they were a northern

Plate 21. Ibo settlement in the grassland area of Nkalagu.

Plate 22. A hanging bridge of branches and ropes at Afikpo.

agent of the Aros. Nike people were formidable fighters, who raided vast territories for slaves and ended up by acquiring more land than they could effectively occupy. Their defence strategy of establishing picket settlements of slaves at the periphery of their territory, while concentrating the settlements of freeborns at less assailable sites (see Figure 39), was no less ingenious than the Aro system of acquiring wealth.

Other tribal or sub-tribal groups which deserve mention here include the Ezza Ibo of Abakaliki who migrate to farm in various parts of the basin, including Nike territory, and the Okoyong people who occupy the territory north of Calabar. Like Nike, Okoyong has much unsettled land; but the people are of Ekoi descent, and live in small nucleated settlements in forest clearings.

FARMS AND TRADE COLONIES OF OLD CALABAR

Unlike other important slave ports along the Nigerian coast such as Bonny, Opobo Town and Badagry, Calabar maintained food farms in its immediate hinterland. These farms, which were often referred to as plantations, were worked by slaves; but their owners usually spent parts of the year on the farms, returning to the city for important festivities. Some of these farms were located as far afield as the Kwa River and beyond. Indeed during the slave revolts, following the preachings of Christian doctrine at Calabar, the farms acted not only as a hideout for runaway slaves, but some of them also became the stronghold from where the slaves organized a series of revolts against the ruling classes.[1] During one such revolt in 1851 the slaves are reported to have invaded Duke Town, ravaged its plantations and threatened to burn down the town.

Trading, rather than farming, was the main occupation of the indigenous Efik population of Calabar and, in order to facilitate this trade, the Efiks established a number of trading outposts along the Cross River and Kwa River valleys. Ikot Offiong, Itu and Nwaniba were large Efik colonies but in the Upper Cross River valley, each trading settlement had only a few Efik trade envoys. The epithet 'Efik trade empire' is sometimes used to describe the sphere of influence of Calabar merchants in pre-colonial days. It should be understood, however, that the Efiks were essentially middlemen in the slave and later the palm oil trade. They traded not by imposing terms, but often with the permission of the local river bank tribes.

THE GROWTH AND DECLINE OF CALABAR

Calabar is probably the oldest existing urban centre in the Eastern States, having been founded more than 300 years ago. It is located on the Calabar River and is forty-two miles from the open sea. During the days of the slave trade Calabar was an important port, its inhabitants acting as middlemen between the people of the hinterland and European traders off the coast. The location of Calabar was also an important factor in the prosperity of the town in the early days of the trade in palm oil. For several decades, Calabar served as the leading educational centre for what is today the Eastern States of Nigeria and was for a brief period (1901–6) the political capital of the British Protectorate of Southern Nigeria. But since the second decade of this century, the political and economic significance of its location have changed, and today Calabar has declined beyond recognition. Trading beaches which were formerly the scene of bustle and activity are now populated by abandoned warehouses.

The paradox of the decline of Calabar lies in the fact that it appears to be a by-product of the general economic development of the country. The opening of roads and railways has led to a decline in the use of waterways and a port like Calabar, which has no direct road or rail link to the main hinterland of the Eastern States, has suffered loss of trade. The establishment of Port Harcourt and the growth of that port has been the most decisive factor in bringing about the decline of trade at Calabar. Calabar is therefore a stranded depressed area, that is, an area which is depressed as a result of loss of locational advantage or through the deprivation of its hinterland. Like other stranded areas, it is characterized by pronounced un-

[1] Dike, K. O., *Trade and Politics in the Niger Delta* p. 156 London 1956

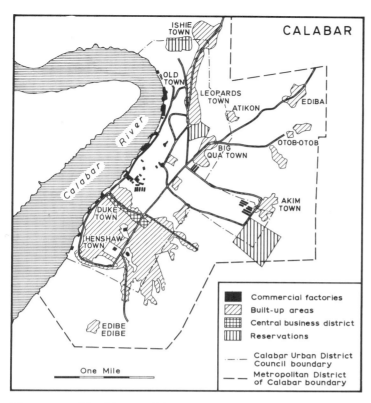

Figure 40. The Towns of Calabar

Figure 41. Ohafia—Old and New Settlement Types. The inset is an enlargement of the old traditional compound

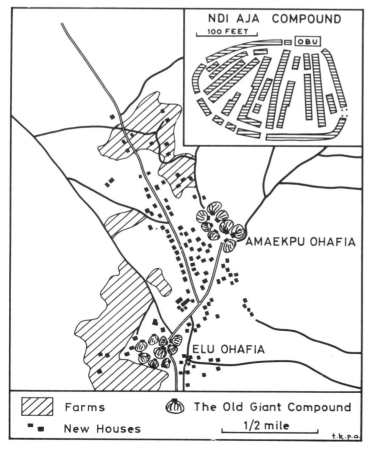

Plate 23. A street in Duke Town, Calabar.

employment leading to emigration, reduction of total income, reduced buying power and severe social problems.

Figure 40 shows the towns of Calabar. The built-up area has expanded at a very slow rate, but the situation may improve if the proposed plywood and other factories making use of products from the forests and plantations in the immediate hinterland are set up. Already, a cement factory is under production and the new highway now under construction will go a long way to opening up and extending the hinterland of the port of Calabar.

TRANSFORMATION OF RURAL SETTLEMENT

With the exception of a small part of Abakaliki Province, the region is characterized by compact settlements consisting of small hamlets and fairly large villages. In Ezzikwo area of Abakaliki on the other hand, there is an extreme case of dispersal of habitation, such that compounds are scattered about the landscape at intervals of one-eighth to one-quarter of a mile. It is in this area that attempts at village integration have been made since 1960. The need for integration was first felt during the 1950's, following a recurrence of robberies and crimes perpetrated by a local lodge, the Odozi Obodo Society, which constituted itself into an illegal court imposing heavy fines and capital punishment on many people brought before it. The local administration also advocated village integration as a means of developing the area, since it is neither practicable nor economical to provide pipe water or electricity to areas in which people live so scattered about. The first integration attempt at Abina village turned out to be very successful. This was early in 1962, and before the end of that year nineteen other village areas had made formal requests to the administration to inspect and approve sites which they had selected.

At the same time, there has been a growing tendency towards dispersal of settlement in other parts of the region. The break up of the large nucleated village in Ohafia (Figure 41) is a case in point. Here the younger generation prefers to build detached houses instead of living in the traditional giant compound.

LOCAL MIGRATIONS IN THE CROSS RIVER BASIN

For several decades, the sparsely settled areas of Nike territory, eastern Bende, Enyong and Okoyong as well as the old slave plantations of Calabar have been major centres of absorption of migrant tenant farmers from various parts of the Eastern States. The coal fields and urban area of Enugu, and lately the rice fields of Abakaliki, have also attracted population from various parts of the Cross River Basin, and so have the modern commercial plantations located in the immediate hinterland of Calabar.

Ezza migrants, who come from Abakaliki, appear to be the most widespread group of tenant farmers in the region. They are to be found all over the northern part of the Cross River plains where they have founded two large colonies, Ezzagu and Effum, in Ishielu local council area. Their other numerous farming outposts were prevented from growing into large colonies by early British administrators, who also built the Munshi Wall to prevent neighbouring Tivs of the Benue valley from expanding into parts of Abakaliki and Ogoja Provinces. These restrictions were imposed in order to check tribal clashes which were often caused by land disputes. The curious thing about the Ezzas is that their home district is also a centre of absorption for stranger farmers.

Ezza Ibos are considered to be the best yam farmers in the East Central State. Their constant migrations appear to be connected with the fact that the yam does best in newly cleared fallows, although Chapman attributes Ezza expansion to inherent land-grabbing tendencies, arising from reluctance to cultivate the same ground at regular intervals like other Ibos. It is not yet clear what impact rice expansion has had on the volume of Ezza migration, but it is reasonable to expect a decrease similar to that observed for the Ukuani District of Urhobo Division and Irun in Ekiti Division, following the introduction of rubber and cocoa respectively into these areas.

The short distance migration of strange farmers from Edda and Akaeze in Afikpo Divisions, into Uzuakoli and Bende territories, differs from Ezza migration in that it consists of a seasonal flow of farm labourers. Many of these labourers work for cash, while others receive in payment farm plots which they cultivate for themselves. Their movements in and out of Bende is made possible by the environmental difference between Afikpo and Bende. Afikpo is open grassland, while much of Bende is largely wooded. The Afikpo farmer therefore has no serious problem in preparing his land for farming. By late January, when the harmattan sun has scorched the

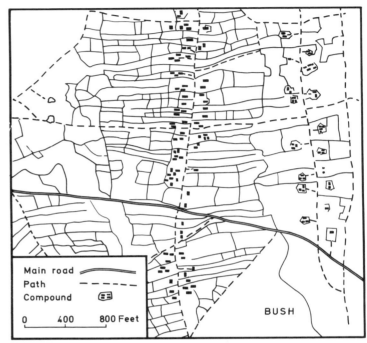

Figure 42. Ezza Ibo Settlement (near Abakaliki)

grass dry, the Afikpo farmer fires his plot without expending much labour in clearing the brush. This allows him time to travel to Bende area, where he hires himself out to clear the bush for those farmers who require additional hands. While the cleared patches at Bende are left to dry before firing, the Afikpo farmer returns home to hoe his farm, which is all planted by April, at which time he returns to Bende with his large hoe specially made for raising huge yam hills. After planting those who work for cash return home, while the rest remain to cultivate their own plots.

Another important area where numerous migrants are found is in the Cross River plains at Enyong, Okoyong and Calabar. At Enyong the main occupation of the migrants, who live in scattered farm huts, consists of harvesting and processing of palm fruits. Cassava is produced in large quantities by migrants to Okoyong and Calabar and is marketed in the form of garri, which is exported to the food-deficit areas west of the Cross River. Migrants to this area come mainly from Abak, Uruan, Ikot Ekpene and various parts of Iboland.

THE BAMENDA-CROSS RIVER-CALABAR SCHEME

An organized redistribution of population, through permanent colonization of virtually uninhabited land, would appear to offer a better alternative to the present system of farming such land on a tenancy basis. This was precisely what the Bamenda-Cross River-Calabar (B.C.C.) scheme set out to do. A settlement was established at Kwa Falls near Calabar and was designed to accommodate 200 families. Each settler was to be provided with seventeen acres of land, two acres for his house and compoundland, ten acres for food crops and five acres for oil palms. In addition, cash advances of up to sixty pounds were made to settlers to assist them to establish themselves.

A pilot scheme of 342 acres preceded the 5,870 acre main project. Clearing for the main scheme started in 1947, two years after eight settlers had already been on the pilot scheme; but as early as the following year, it was generally felt that the settlement side of the scheme had failed. In 1950 3,000 acres of the land already acquired was leased to the then Eastern Regional Production Development Board for development as a palm plantation, while the settlement scheme continued on the remaining acreage. It made very little progress and in March 1955, the scheme was finally abandoned.

There are some interesting similarities between the B.C.C. settlement scheme and the current farm settlement scheme. Both schemes involved the government in considerable expenditure and settlers were accordingly required to work under strict supervision so that the capital invested could be recovered at the shortest possible time. Initial clearing of the bush and planting of tree crops was done by hired labour, and in both cases settlers were provided with compoundlands for growing food. Recent farm settlements have, however, laid more emphasis on tree crops for export.

THE DEVELOPMENT OF COMMERCIAL PLANTATIONS

When the settlement aspect of the B.C.C. scheme was finally abandoned in 1955, the whole establishment at Kwa Falls was taken over as an oil palm plantation by the Eastern Nigeria Development Corporation (E.N.D.C.). The only other plantations which existed in the region before that date were the 4,000-acre Rubber Estate at Ikot Mbo and the 12,000-acre Calabar Oil Palm Estate both of which belong to Palmol Ltd., a subsidiary of the United Africa Co. Ltd.

Before 1950, the Nigerian Government was opposed to the plantation system and turned down several requests by foreign capitalists, who wanted to establish oil palm plantations in the country. Instead, the Government sought to expand local exports by encouraging peasant farmers to obtain and plant improved seedlings supplied from experimental stations of the Department of Agriculture. Later developments were to prove that though well-intentioned, the anti-plantation policy of the Government was not realistic. In 1951 therefore, when Nigerians took over agricultural policy from British administrators,

Table 12   PLANTATIONS IN THE CROSS RIVER BASIN

Estate	Date	Management	Acreage Acquired	Acreage Cultivated as at 1965
Ikot Mbo Rubber Estate	1907	Palmol	4,000	3,560
Calabar Oil Palm Estate	1937	Palmol	12,000	7,000
Kwa Falls (Oil Palm)	1947	State Govt.	6,000	5,000
Ikom Cocoa Estate	1953	State Govt.	2,049	1,069
Calaro Oil Palm Estate	1954	State Govt.	17,175	9,860
Ikang Banana Plantation	1954	Danish Co.	15,000	Abandoned in 1959
Oban Rubber Plantation	1955	State Govt.	12,000	7,172
Ikot Okpora Road (Rubber)	1959	Dunlop	20,000	15,000
Umahia Cocoa Estate	1959	State Govt.	3,750	2,758
Abia Cocoa Estate	1960	State Govt.	4,000	3,594
Arochuku Cocoa Estate	1960	State Govt.	2,580	2,494
Bendehe Ayuk (Cocoa Estate)	1961	State Govt.	2,406	2,221
Obubra Cocoa Estate	1962	State Govt.	5,000	2,023
Nko-Obubra Rubber Estate	1962	State Govt.	5,000	2,432
Amaeke Abam Rubber Estate	1962	State Govt.	5,000	2,716
Biakpan Rubber Estate	1962	State Govt.	6,206	2,300

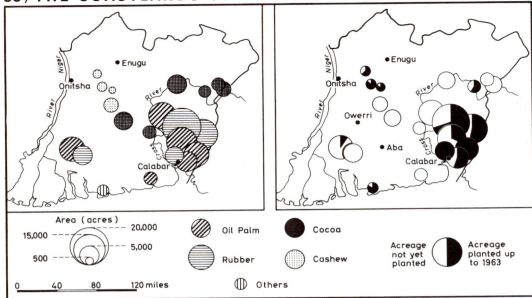

Area (acres)

15,000 - - - ⊘ - - - 20,000
500 - - - ⊘ - - - 5,000

0   40   80   120 miles

▨ Oil Palm   ● Cocoa
▤ Rubber   ⊡ Cashew

Acreage not yet planted ◖ Acreage planted up to 1963

▥ Others

Figure 43. Plantations in the Eastern States of Nigeria

there was a complete change in favour of the plantation system. The next ten years, the plantation decade, was to see the rapid development of plantation agriculture in the country but particularly in the sparsely inhabited district enclosed by the Cross River (Figure 43).

Almost all the plantations listed in Table 12 belong to State Development Corporations, which are financed almost exclusively from funds provided by the State Marketing Boards. Since these funds had been accumulated through the payment of prices to palm oil producers which were much lower than those the Marketing Board earned on the world markets, it was originally proposed that part of the surplus be used for developing the oil palm industry and for the benefit and prosperity of the producers and areas of production. The development of plantations in this region is a part fulfilment of this idea; but before 1966, by far the greater percentage of the funds was invested in prestige as well as industrial projects not located in the main palm oil producing areas.

The expansion of cocoa in the forest areas of Umuahia and Ikom Districts is directed at diversifying the economy of the Eastern States, and reminds us of the situation in the Western State, where plantations of oil palm rather than of cocoa have been established by Government agencies. Rubber production is expanding rapidly, the largest plantation being the 20,000-acre Dunlop Rubber Estate at Ikot Okpora road, where a sum of £4 million has already been invested.

Government support for, and encouragement of, plantation agriculture since 1950 stems from its belief that plantations will create employment opportunities in the rural areas, and thereby arrest the drift of population to the towns. It is doubtful if much has been accomplished in this direction; but the plantation appears to offer the most realistic approach to the problem of redistributing the rural population of the Eastern States. The plantation labourer can come from any part of the country, although local people will grumble if their chance of employment is diminished thereby. But no ugly incidents need occur, since the 'foreign' labourers have not come to colonise land belonging to other tribes. Past attempts at redistributing population have also confirmed that even though some people from the land-hungry areas of Iboland have spent almost all their working life outside their village of birth, such people have rejected outright the idea of being resettled permanently in a distant area. A labourer in a plantation can return to his birthplace on retirement, but not so the resettled farmer.

A ONE-THOUSAND-ACRE FARM AT OZU ABAM

The one-thousand-acre farm at Ozu Abam, which is owned by one Mr Ogbuagu, is a good example of what enterprising individuals can do to develop the economy of the very sparsely settled parts of the region. Mr Ogbuagu's farm is located near an all season laterite road and is within an hour's drive from Umuahia town, which provides an adequate market for the produce of his farm. In addition to existing wild palms cultivated palms have been planted, and fortunately a large stream flows through the farm, making it possible for a pioneer oil mill to be built directly on the farm.

Abam people and other Cross River Ibos live in closely nucleated villages, unlike the Abakaliki Ibos for example. There is therefore a considerable area of contiguous land capable of being developed as large commercial farms. The long cherished hope that the establishment of 'nucleus', or experimental, plantations in various parts of southern Nigeria will influence local people to adopt plantation methods may be said to have been fulfilled in this one-thousand-acre farm. Indeed, the readiness of the Government to grant this farmer a loan for erecting the oil mill is indicative of its appreciation of this farmer's business acumen.

Other crops grown on this large farm include cocoa and citrus. Food crops including yam and vegetables are also cultivated on a commercial basis while goats and poultry are also kept. The author spent two nights at this farm in 1962, during which time he was served with food (including meat) produced on the farm.

FOREST EXPLOITATION

Export of logs to Western Europe and of sawn timber to other parts of the Eastern States has become increasingly important in the economy of the forested parts of this region. Apart from the timber stands in village groves or farmlands, the area enclosed by the Cross River has some 320 square miles of reserved forests which are now being exploited under Government control. The current plan is to work the reserves on an eighty-year rotation, and this allows for the exploitation of at least four square miles of woodland per annum.

At present, the chief handicap facing timber extraction is the difficulty in transporting the logs in the absence of approach roads. Logs for export are floated in rafts to Calabar, while those for internal trade are sawn over pits dug in the forests. A few saw mills now exist at Calabar and Oron, and there is a proposal to establish a plywood mill at Calabar.

PROBLEMS OF TRANSPORTATION

Vast tracts of this region, but particularly the forest belt east of the Cross River, are inaccessible to motorised transport and herein lies the greatest problem confronting development in the region. The various plantations in the area have had to spend considerable sums opening up approach roads, and often the only transport found in the district belongs to these plantations, or to local government councils. Occasionally the stranded traveller will come across a mammy waggon chartered by food contractors from Enugu or Abakaliki for the purpose of evacuating yams, cocoyams, and other food items purchased in bush markets in Obubra, Yako, Bahumunu and other areas east of the Cross River.

There are Government-owned car ferries at Ikot Okpora, Ediba and Obubra, but the roads leading to them are often impassable during the rainy season. A new highway linking Calabar to Ikom is now under construction and is expected to open up much of this trans-Cross River District to commercial cropping.

THE INTRODUCTION AND EXPANSION OF RICE IN ABAKALIKI AREA

Before the Second World War most of the rice consumed in this part of Nigeria was imported, but following the imposition of war-time import restrictions the possibilities of growing rice in the rain fed seasonal swamps of Ogoja and Abakaliki Provinces were explored by the Government. Following on what was regarded as a very encouraging result from an experimental rice farm in 1942, rice cultivation was formally recommended in the following year. Since then, the acreage under rice has expanded so much that in some villages rice is now much more important than yam as a farm crop. In 1962, the acreage under rice in these two Provinces was estimated at about 60,000 acres.

The physical requirements of rice cultivation include level land, heavy fertile soil and an impervious subsoil, plenty of water and a temperature of over 70° F., conditions which are adequately met by the Abakaliki-Ogoja environment. But since the swamps of this area are not continuous, the rice fields themselves are also not continuous, and indeed there are some villages which do not grow rice because they have no swampy land. Economic factors favouring the rapid expansion of rice include the increasing need for cash to meet various social obligations as well as to pay school fees and taxes. The fact that this part of the region had no major cash crop, the oil palm and cocoa being grown on a very small scale in only a few villages, was an important factor in the ready acceptance of rice. Other factors include the fact that compared with yam farming for which the area is very well known, rice cultivation required little or no capital, except the land. The cost of seed yam for a one-acre farm in the area has, for example, been put at £30 as compared with £0·75 for rice seeds; and in addition, yam cultivation is more demanding of labour and time. Compared with yams, rice is easily stored and last, but not the least, the demand for land and labour by rice is not in conflict with that for yam, since rice is cultivated on land not suitable for other food crops, and since the crop is cultivated after yams have been planted.

It is also fortunate that there were no bad harvests in the first few years and that the price of rice kept on improving every year. In the case of the Sokoto Mechanized Rice Scheme, where considerable damage was done to the crop as a result of premature flooding in 1953, five years after swamp rice cultivation was introduced, there was a wide-spread reaction against the scheme and the acreage under rice fell in 1954 to a third of the previous year's figure (see page 95). The rice scheme near Oshogbo in western Nigeria, which was started in 1954, fared even worse as a result of crop failure owing to drought in 1957, after which rice growing in the area was completely abandoned.

Yam has been and is still the main crop grown in the Abakaliki area, and at present many families still concentrate on yam cultivation, using only hired labour to grow rice in the swamps on their land, while some even lease out their swamps to strange or migrant tenant farmers. But the desire of the Government is that more attention be paid to swamp rice, which Pierre Gourou considers to be the most suitable carbohydrate for tropical lands, since swamp rice gives a good yield, avoids the need for fallow and prevents soil erosion.[1] Yam farming is, however, still a matter of prestige and membership of some of the important secret societies is opened only to adult males with a specified minimum number of yams.

Educated people like school teachers and employees of local government councils played an important part in the expansion of rice culture by taking part in cultivating the crop, as well as in trying to persuade the people that the displacement of yam by rice will not enrage the god of yams. Migrant farmers have also done a lot to expand the acreage under rice. Such farmers rent land for only one cropping season, since land is not sold or given for long lease in the area.

Most families cultivating rice devote from two to seven acres to this crop. In general the indigenous population cultivate rice and yams while the migrant tenant farmers plant rice and cassava as the main crops. Only a few farmers manure their rice nurseries, but after planting the crop is never fertilized.

After harvest, many farmers store up part of their rice crop for a few months with the view to getting a better price than is obtainable at harvest time. A number of middlemen feature in the rice trade, some of whom take to

[1] Gourou, P., trans. by Laborde, E. D., *The Tropical World* p. 97 1955

rice marketing as a part-time job in addition to rice farming, just as rubber tappers in the Benin forests also operate as itinerant traders in rubber sheets. The paddy is parboiled in large discarded oil drums, after which the rice is milled, the main milling centres being Abakaliki and Afikpo. Almost all the mills are privately owned, although there are a few mobile mills owned by the Government Department of Agriculture.

Most of the rice produced in the region is sold in Nigeria. Increased circulation of money and spending on luxury goods, as well as investments in better housing, suggest that the Abakaliki rice farmer has never had it so good. There is, however, room for greater improvement in yield as well as in income. New complementary industries including the collecting and sale of wood for parboiling rice, rice parboiling itself, and the milling industry, have further improved the local economic situation by creating new employment opportunities.

Works consulted and suggestions for further reading:

1. Blanckenburg, P., Rice Farming in the Abakaliki Area (mimograph) NISER. Ibadan 1962
2. Dike, K. O., *Trade and Politics in the Niger Delta*. London 1956
3. Harding, H. J. M., 'The Bamenda Cross River Calabar Scheme' *Farm and Forest* 1952
4. Nzekwu, O., 'Uburu and the Salt Lake' *Nigeria Magazine* No. 56 pp. 84–96 1958
5. Udo, R. K., 'Sixty Years of Plantation Agriculture in Southern Nigeria' *Economic Geography* No. 41 pp. 356–68 1965
6. Udo, R. K., 'The Cross River District of Eastern Nigeria' *Journal of Tropical Geography* No. 20 pp. 65–72 1965
7. Udo, R. K., 'The Growth and Decline of Calabar' *Nigerian Geographical Journal* No. 10 pp. 91–106 1967

Part Two The Middle Belt

10 The Grass Plains of South-western Nigeria

This region is made up of Oyo and parts of Abeokuta Provinces, as well as parts of the ancient West African State of Borgu. The greater part of it lies in the Western State, where it constitutes the least developed part of that State. It is a problem area, much of it being virtually uninhabited and until the post-war years there was no substantial development of a cash economy. Environmental conditions preclude the propagation of any of the tree crops which have brought wealth and progress to the forest areas further south. Tobacco, rice and cotton are of growing importance as cash crops, but these are mostly produced for the Nigerian market. Another distinguishing feature of this region is the primitive state of its communications, and the still largely undeveloped economy which makes it comparable with the Cross River district, which is also a border region.

Apart from the general stagnation of the greater part of this region, there are various aspects of its environment, economy and demography which place it within the Middle Belt of Nigeria. These include its open undulating landscape which is studded with occasional inselbergs and other rock outcrops, the character of its subsistence economy which features the cultivation of grains like millet, maize and guinea corn and root crops like yams and cassava, as well as the sparse population of the region. Like many other parts of the Middle Belt, this region suffered a lot from Fulani raids during the nineteenth century, and today much of its settlement landscape is a product of inter- as well as intra-tribal warfare in pre-colonial days.

Environmental conditions suggest that there is great scope for developing agriculture, including cattle ranching. The main limitations to using land for agriculture include erosion hazard even on gentle slopes, laterite outcrops as well as iron pan which occur close to the surface, and rock outcrops, including inselbergs and quartzite ridges. Labour shortage is another problem confronting the expansion of cash cropping, which appears to be the sure way of arresting continued emigration to the towns and farms in the cocoa belt. Bariba labourers from Borgu are commonly found in the cocoa-growing areas of Abeokuta and Ibadan, and since such migrants are not averse to working on the land they are likely to stay behind to take advantage of opportunities offered in commercial farms established in their home districts.

GEOLOGY, LANDFORMS AND SOILS

With the exception of a small area near Meko in Abeokuta Province, the region is underlain by igneous and meta-morphic rocks of the Basement Complex. In the area south of Meko, the Basement Complex is overlain by sandstones of Tertiary formation. The soils developed on these parent materials are essentially different, but lateritic outcrops, representing the product of intense chemical weathering in a previous age, are common over both basement and sedimentary rocks.

The uniform aspect of the landscape is particularly striking because of the open character of the vegetation. Most of the area is characterized by slopes of two to six per cent. Numerous inselbergs and quartzite ridges are found in various parts of the region, where they dominate the landscape for long distances. Prominent inselbergs or groups of inselbergs which provided defence outposts in the past include the Ado rock at Ado Awaiye, Old Eruwa, Oke Iho, Oke Ile and Ilaji. The general level of the land increases northwards and north-eastwards from 200 feet in Ijale to 1,000 in the north; and everywhere inselbergs such as those at Igbeli (2,001 feet), Shaki (1,600 feet) and Igboho (1,660 feet) rise several hundred feet above the general surface of the land.

Rocks of the Basement Complex which occur in the region are mostly gneisses, granites and schists; the first two being associated with the domed inselbergs already discussed, while the schists are associated with quartzite ridges of the type found in Ilesha area of the cocoa belt. In areas like Iseyin, where these quartzite ridges predominate, the streams have steeper slopes but the steepest slopes occur, as may be expected, in the immediate vicinity of the ridges.

The Western State section of the region is drained by parallel north-south streams of which the Okpara, Ofiki, Oyan and Ogun are the main streams. Those parts of Northern Nigeria which may be included in this region drain into the Niger (Figure 44). Valley types vary considerably and include V-shaped valleys with broad floors, saucer-shaped valleys and real V-shaped valleys. Rock outcrops, laterite benches and laterite outcrops occur along the major breaks of slope as one approaches the valleys. Apart from the large valleys whose broad floors are given to periodic waterlogging during the later part of the rainy season, the whole region is well drained. The streams are fullest towards the end of the rainy season but become dry for most of the dry season, when even the main rivers may also dry up.

Variations in soil types are largely influenced by slope and parent material. Around Iseyin, where quartzite and schists associated with quartzites form the parent materials, the main soils consist of brown sandy loams overlying red-brown sandy clay; the red colour and the clay coming

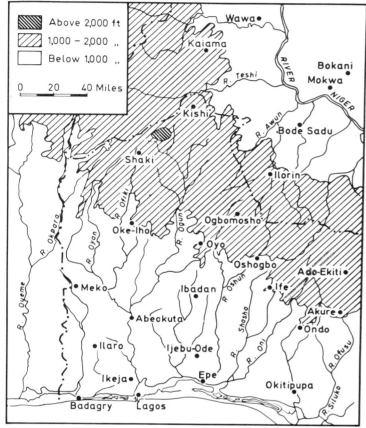

Figure 44. Relief and Drainage of South-Western Nigeria

from the breakdown of the schists. Quartzite and quartz stones are also prominent on the surface and indeed throughout the soil profiles. Concretionary ironstone is also common. In the Meko area where the parent material is sandstone, the soils vary from red-brown ironstone gravel soils with occasional gravel-free soils on the Meko Plateau to red-brown and clayey soils with abundant ironstone concretions and pan in the Meko Valley.[1]

The influence of topography on soil texture to produce a catenary sequence along valley slopes is as marked here as it is in the cocoa belt. Deep wash soils, which are usually sandy and free from ironstone gravel, are found in the lower slopes and in association with alluvial soils in the valley bottoms. On the hilltops and upper slopes the soils are shallower.

Land considered suitable for intensive cropping in the region include those areas having sandy clay loam soils, as well as areas having a concretionary layer which is not close enough to the surface to interfere with cultivation. A greater variety of land such as swamps and other poorly drained soils, inselbergs, quartzite ridges and other rock

outcrops as well as shallow soils with abundant ironstone gravel or pan close to the surface are considered not suitable for intensive cropping. Such land may, however, be used for grazing.

CLIMATE AND VEGETATION

There is very little variation in the climate of the region, which has a moderate rainfall of 45 inches at Meko in the south-west, increasing to 53 inches at Kishi in the north-east. The short dry season which lasts from three to ten weeks is well marked, and in certain years the long dry season is very severe. The rainy season varies considerably in length, in its intensity and reliability. Observations have shown that crops like maize, which have high-water requirements, can be adversely affected in years when the short dry season is pronounced. In order to avoid severe crop failures, the local farming calendar has been adapted to make for two growing periods, the first commencing with the early rains in March and the second in August, after the short dry season.

For most of the region, the rainy season, that is the period in which at least 2·5 inches of rain falls in a month, averages twenty-eight weeks. Temperature conditions remain virtually unchanged throughout the year, the mean annual temperature in the south being about 80° F., increasing to about 82° F. in the north. The relative humidity decreases slightly in the northerly parts where it averages about seventy-six per cent at 9 a.m. as compared with eighty-five in the south. There is however, the usual drop in relative humidity during the period of the harmattan, which in this grassland region lasts from November to March.

The region falls within the Guinea savanna vegetation belt, but there is considerable variation in floristic composition and structure even within short distances. Cultivation and burning are largely responsible for the great differences between the present-day biotic vegetation and the climatic climax. Available evidence confirms that much of these areas which are now uninhabited were once settled and cultivated. The vegetation in such areas does not therefore represent the natural climax, although it does give an idea of the ability of the vegetation to regenerate when left to itself.

Differences in the character and floristic composition of the vegetation are often due to micro-climate as well as to soil and drainage conditions which may restrict cultivation

[1] A more detailed description of the soils of the region is given in 'The Report on the Land Use Survey of the Oyo-Shaki Area, Western Nigeria' United Nations (FAO Land use Survey Team) Ibadan 1962

Plate 24. Rural Water Supply in Ilorin Province. Scenes like this are common all over rural Nigeria. Clothes are washed in the stream and dried nearby on the grass.

or modify the influence of fire. Poorly drained sites for example usually support fringing forests, since they are only cultivated occasionally and are rarely disturbed by fires. Shallow soils, which are not usually farmed because of poor yields and heavy soils, which are difficult to cultivate with primitive tools particularly during the dry season, usually carry dense forest vegetation with tall trees. As a rule, open savanna is characteristic of heavily farmed areas while savanna woodlands occur around settlement zones or in areas distant from human settlements. Forest outliers of mixed floristic composition, having a canopy exceeding eighty feet in height, are found on upland sites.

During the rainy season the grass is green and luxuriant, but coarse, reaching a height of five to eight feet. In the dry season it becomes brown and dry and it is at this time that bush fires are common. The fires usually leave vast areas completely bare and blackened but regeneration is rapid and starts even before the rains. This is indeed one reason for the seasonal firing of the bush by cattlemen, whose intention is to enhance the growth of fresh and succulent grass at a time when grazing is usually scarce.

POPULATION AND RURAL SETTLEMENTS

The native population of this region is made up of Yorubas and Baribas, the former predominating. In addition, there is a growing stranger population of Fulani cattlemen who usually settle in small villages close to Yoruba towns, where they sell their animal products. The sparse population of the region, vast areas of which are uninhabited, constitutes the greatest problem facing the development of its economy. Unfortunately, the isolation of the greater part of this region and the undeveloped state of its economy has tended to encourage emigration into the cocoa belt, thereby increasing the local manpower problem.

Considerable evidence exists to show that this grassland region was much more densely settled in the past. Indeed the main concentration of population in Yorubaland up to the beginning of the nineteenth century was in the grasslands of this region, rather than in the forests or the forest-savanna boundary as is the case today. The depopulation of the area followed a series of wars directed against the Yorubas by the Fulanis from the north and the people of Dahomey from the west. Eye witness accounts of the destruction perpetrated by the Fulanis have been left behind by early European explorers like Lander and Clapperton, who passed through several villages that had been destroyed by the Fulanis.[1] As late as 1950 it was still possible to identify the sites of many deserted villages in and around the Oyo forest reserve and today, only twelve of the fifty-five important settlements recorded by Clapperton during his tour through this part of Yorubaland can be identified. The havoc done by raids directed from Dahomey was equally disastrous, and today most of the border region remains uninhabited or sparsely populated.

Intra-tribal warfare amongst the Yorubas also led to the destruction of many more settlements and human lives during the nineteenth century. The destruction of Ijaiye by Ibadan forces in 1862 is a case in point. The population of Ijaiye in 1953 was 1,500 as compared with an estimate of 40,000 a hundred years earlier.[2] Amongst other things, these wars provided an increasing incentive for the local population to concentrate in large settlements. For defence purposes many settlements including

[1] Clapperton, H., *Journal of a Second Expedition into the interior of Africa* p. 33 London 1829
[2] Hinderer, D., *Church Missionary Intelligencer* p. 251 London 1851

Ado Awaiye, Oke Iho, Oke-Ile and Igana were located on hilltops. But few of these hill villages could withstand a long seige, largely because the settlements were necessarily small owing to limited building space on the hills. Hill villages destroyed between 1881 and 1890 when the Dahomeans organized four expeditions into the western part of the region included Ilaji, Aiyetoro, Oke-Ila and Igana.[1]

During the last thirty years many of these hill settlements have descended to the plains. A number of farm villages have also sprang up in the territories belonging to the larger towns of Oyo, Iseyin and Shaki, to provide accommodation during the farming season or the working week to farmers who are obliged to cultivate land which is more than six to ten miles from the town. In the case of Oyo town such distant farm villages have made it possible for farmers from Oyo to settle and cultivate cocoa in those parts of the town's farmland where soil and climatic conditions favour the growth of this important cash crop.[2]

FOOD CROP PRODUCTION

As in other parts of the Middle Belt climatic and ecological conditions permit the cultivation of root crops in the forest belt, and grain crops in the far north. The major root crop grown is yam while maize is the most important grain crop. Rice is of growing importance even amongst the people of Shaki district who eat very little rice. Other food crops of importance include guinea corn, cassava, cowpeas and millet. Cropping is on ridges and mounds, ridges being used for guinea corn, millet and groundnuts while yams are largely grown on mounds which may be very high in areas like valley bottoms where the soil is relatively damp. Yams may also be planted on ridges as is done in Oko District near Ogbomosho, where dried stalks of guinea corn are often used for staking yams.

Yam is the staple food particularly in the south and east, where many farmers plant between two and three acres of yams in one year. White yams (*Discorea rotundata*) are usually planted between December and January that is before the rains come while yellow and water yams (*Discorea cayensis* and *Discorea alata* respectively) which are more sensitive to draught conditions are planted much later. The relatively larger acreage of yams found in parts of Oyo and Ilorin Provinces helps to explain the large quantities of yams railed from stations between and including Oshogbo and Ilorin.

Small plots of groundnuts are usually planted for local consumption, but maize which is planted twice yearly, in April and in September, is much more important.

Cassava is planted after yams have been harvested and often takes more than a year to mature. Mixed cropping is the rule, and in many areas it is common to see a farm plot in which yams, maize, pumpkins, pepper and beans are grown at the same time.

Crop yields are not very high since local farmers do not use fertilisers. Experiments have, however, been carried out on the use of various mixed fertilisers on a number of crops including yams; and experimental plots may be found in many parts of the region. These experiments have confirmed that maize production can be doubled by the use of fertilisers, but there is the important question of whether or not the proceeds from sales of extra crops will be enough to offset the money invested on fertilisers. The system of guaranteed prices is one way of tackling such a problem.

THE DEVELOPMENT OF CASH CROPPING

The main cash crops grown in this region today are tobacco, cotton and rice; that is in addition to cassava and yams which have already been discussed. Much of the credit for the recent expansion of tobacco goes to the Nigerian Tobacco Co., which has done more for tobacco than the governments have done for any other crop. At present, the acreage under tobacco is controlled strictly by the requirements of the Company which has been obliged, on a number of occasions, to impose limitations on the acreage planted by farmers so as to prevent over production. For a rather poor region with few economic crops, such restrictions constitute a serious handicap.

Cotton production does not suffer from such limitations, since cotton has a large internal market and is also being exported. It is a crop for which the Government has shown great interest, and like tobacco it is grown in other parts of the country. Rice, which is a food crop, is considered here as a cash crop because in Shaki District the main reason for cultivating rice is to sell the crop for cash. Both upland and swamp rice are cultivated, but details about this and the other two cash crops are given under the sections dealing with each crop.

Two cash crops which have been introduced into the region since the early 1950's are cashew nuts and pineapples. At present they are produced by the Western Nigeria Development Corporation at their estates at

[1] Gleave, M. B., 'Hill Settlements and their Abandonment in Western Yorubaland' *Africa* Vol. 33 p. 349 1963
[2] Goddard, S., 'Town-Farm Relationships in Yorubaland: A Case study from Oyo' *Africa* Vol. 35 pp. 21–29 1965

Eruwa and Upper Ogun, although a few farmers also grow pineapples for sale in nearby urban markets. Cash crops which have been recommended for trial include beniseed, castor and sisal.

The expansion of cash cropping in the region appears to be the only way of bringing into the district the much needed labour force for developing its vast acreage of cultivable but uncultivated land. Already, tobacco and cotton are proving attractive and may, like rubber in Ukwuani District of the Niger Delta, lead to a decrease in emigration to the cocoa belt. Cash cropping is also likely to prove attractive to migrant tenant farmers, who have so far not been attracted to the sparsely settled areas of the grass plains of south-western Nigeria.

Table 13 CALENDAR OF FARMING ACTIVITIES IN OYO DIVISION

Month	*Agricultural Activity*
October November	Harvesting of guinea corn, and preparation of guinea corn plot for yam. Early yam planting.
December January February March	Yam planting continued. Harvesting of cotton, beans and cowpeas. Preparation of land for early maize and late yam planting.
April	Planting of early tobacco. Late planting of yam. Planting of early maize, okro and cowpeas.
May	Planting of guinea corn.
June	Weeding. Harvesting of early maize and early tobacco.
July	Harvesting of yams. Planting of late tobacco.
August	Preparation of land for late maize, beans and cowpeas, and guinea corn. Harvesting of early beans and cowpeas.
September	Planting of late maize, guinea corn and beans. Harvesting of late tobacco.

RICE PRODUCTION

Rice cultivation was introduced into the grassland areas of Abeokuta by early Christian missionaries as far back as the middle of the nineteenth century, and for many years before the Second World War the main source of rice in southern Nigeria was from this area. But Abeokuta rice is upland rice, unlike the rice grown in Shaki in northern Oyo Division. Thus while rice cultivation in Shaki has meant the cropping of riverine swamps, which were hitherto not farmed during the rains and were used

for occasional grazing in the dry season, the expansion of upland rice in Abeokuta has resulted in the displacement of both yams and cassava. Often farmers who cultivate rice in Abeokuta cannot afford the time and money to grow yams, and since yams appear to make greater labour demands the general tendency has been to grow rice and maize in the same plot in place of yams and maize which was the usual crop combination in the past. Rice milling is also considered less tedious than making garri from cassava, hence the growing preference of rice in place of cassava.

Rice was introduced into the Shaki experimental station in 1945 and six years later there were about ten farmers growing the BG 79 swamp variety in the district. Apart from ploughing all other aspects of cultivation was done by hand and were rather laborious, although yields were good, about 2,000 pounds per acre. Milling methods were crude, but things changed when, in 1953, the Western Nigeria Development Board took active part in rice culture in the area. In 1953, 500 acres were ploughed and 300 acres cultivated with rice. Forty per cent of the harvested crop was to go to the Board in return for the mechanized cultivation services of ploughing, discing and planting. In addition, the Board promised to buy the remaining sixty per cent from farmers who were willing to sell their share.

The main centres of rice cultivation were in the villages of Shaki, Aha, Ago Are, Ago Amodu, Ogburo and Sepeteri; but in most cases the fields were rather small and scattered for efficient tractor operation. For this and other reasons including poor yields obtained in 1953, the Board decided to discontinue with an arrangement which it felt would only lead to an increase in non-recoverable expenditure. In 1955 therefore the Shaki rice scheme was left in the hands of the Government Department of Agriculture, and since 1960 rice cultivation has been restricted to Shaki and the villages of Ago Amodu, Irawo, Tede and Aha.

In view of the poverty of this region, a great need exists for encouraging rice cultivation as a means of raising cash income. But there are many problems facing rice cultivation and these include low yields, diseases and labour shortage.

TOBACCO FARMING IN OYO PROVINCE

One of the main areas producing tobacco on a commercial basis is the grass plains of south-western Nigeria, where experimental work on the propagation of Bright Virginian variety started as far back as 1915. Good crops were obtained around Ilorin but curing presented a serious problem and only poor quality tobacco was produced. Attempts to encourage local farmers to cultivate the crop met with no success until 1933 when a pilot cigarette factory was established at Oshogbo. The British-American Tobacco Company, the parent body of the Nigerian Tobacco Company, played an important part in the early development of the crop. Seeds were distributed free, and later fertilizers and sprays were provided on long- and short-term credit.

Production of tobacco in this region was at first concentrated around Ogbomosho, where the rate of expansion was so great that by 1938 southern Nigeria was already producing 398,000 pounds as compared with 52,000 pounds in the north. Emphasis at this time was on air-cured tobacco which is cured in a similar way to tobacco grown in the Zaria and Sokoto districts, but in 1940 the Nigerian Tobacco Company began to produce flue-cured tobacco in north-western Oyo. Since flue curing requires much skill and capital the Company, which formerly undertook the curing of leaves bought from farmers, now encourages farmers to form co-operatives or small business companies for the purpose of processing the leaves. A complete barn site with four barns and ancillary buildings may cost up to £1,500, and the Company is always ready to lend money to co-operatives who are expected to repay it over a period of ten years.

The spread of tobacco in Oyo Division (Figure 45) has introduced a new outlook in the agricultural landscape. In place of the small scattered plots in which the peasant farmers grow a variety of crops at a time, tobacco is grown as the only crop in relatively large blocks comprising as much as sixty acres. Such a large acreage is made possible by the abundance of land in the region and mechanical aid made available to village co-operatives by the Nigerian Tobacco Company. The first crop is sown in nurseries in February and transplanted in April at the beginning of the rains. It is harvested in June and July when the second crop is also planted to be harvested in August and September. As in the case of maize the second crop is usually not as good as the first. Another important fact about tobacco cultivation in the region is that almost all field activities take place during the rainy season, which is also the season for food farming, thereby resulting in competition for labour between both. After harvest tobacco fields may revert to fallow or may be re-cultivated with foods crops.

Most tobacco is grown within a mile of barn sites, the distribution of which provides a good guide to delimiting the area in which the crop is grown. The location of the

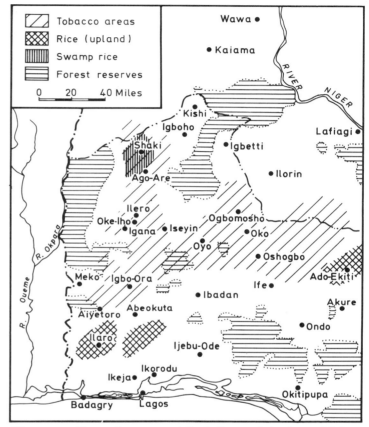

Figure 45. Forest Reserves and Cash Crops of the Grass Plains of South-Western Nigeria

barns themselves is influenced by the availability of motorable roads, since fuel for curing has to be transported to the barn sites.

RECENT DEVELOPMENTS IN COTTON GROWING

The local weaving industry, which is widespread in the region, has always depended on locally grown cotton; but the first era of cotton expansion in this region started during the second half of the nineteenth century, under the direction of the Abeokuta missionaries, who sought thereby to undermine the slave-centred cotton economy of the southern United States. The 1861 export figure of 0·2 million tons declined to an insignificant figure by the close of the century, but in 1903 interest in cotton growing was revived by the field agents of the British Cotton Growing Association. The main centres of production at this time were in the Ilugun and Ishan areas of Egba Division. Another period of decline followed the opening up, during the 1930's, of better favoured cotton areas in the Northern

States, where almost all the cotton in Nigeria is produced.

The present Government programme of large-scale production of cotton in the grasslands of south-western Nigeria has been prompted by the desire to provide a cash crop for this undeveloped region. Since 1962 an increasing acreage of cotton has been sown by peasant farmers receiving Government support in the form of advice on the methods of cropping and use of insecticides. Planting seeds of the Allen 26 J variety, which is highly recommended for this locality, are also distributed free to farmers while the Government undertakes to buy from the farmer all the seeds of this variety.

Experiments directed at improving cotton yield have established that in this region it is best to grow cotton on large flat-topped ridges. But since cotton is often planted after an early season crop of maize, tobacco and melons, this is only possible in areas where the other crops are grown on ridges. The crop requires weeding four to five weeks after sowing and a second weeding seven weeks later. According to the Ministry of Agriculture bulletins on cotton growing, the best time for sowing the Allen 26 J is during the first week in July, that is if the best yields are to be obtained.

As a cash crop cotton has a bright future in view of the rapidly expanding domestic market and the fact that the crop is also exported. But there are a number of problems facing cotton growing in the area. These include insect pests, poor yields on soils of low fertility and crop failures which may occur as a result of unreliable rainfall. Costs of fertilizers and insecticides have also tended to raise the nominal capital which a cotton farmer needs. And finally, like other cash crops in the region, cotton is faced with the problem of an inadequate supply of labour in the area.

FOREST RESERVES AND FOREST PLANTATIONS

No less than twenty-five per cent or 2,600 square miles of the region is under forest reserves which are administered by the Forestry Division of the Ministry of Agriculture and Natural Resources. At present the local population has no rights in the forest reserves and no agriculture or grazing is permitted, although people may collect firewood which is in short supply in various parts of the region. Unfortunately these reserves are generally exposed to the annual bush fires of the Nigerian savannalands, with the result that tree cover is sparse and mostly of poor size and form.

Although so much land has been put under forest reserves, there is as yet no sign of a shortage of farmland in any district. Rather, there are another 3,000 square miles of uninhabited land which at present lies as a buffer between the reserves and the cultivated areas. There is therefore sufficient farmland to permit long fallow periods of over eight years, while the buffer areas will meet the needs of an increased demand for farmland for several decades. Such buffer areas offer much scope for mechanized farming and make it unnecessary for anyone to interfere with the forest reserves.

The growing demand for firewood which is in short supply around the towns, and the need for good quality building poles, have led to the establishment of forest plantations in various parts of the region. In 1964 the Western Nigeria Forestry Department had about 1,000 acres of land under forest plantations in units of about 50 to 300 acres. These plantations, which consist mainly of teak with some *cassia siamea*, are chiefly in the vicinity of the main towns including Oyo, Iseyin, Oke Iho, Shaki and Ogbomosho. Private individuals and communities also own forest plantations and indeed, most of the plantations now managed by the Forestry Department were originally under private ownership. Existing private plantations vary in size from one acre to about twenty acres and include fuel plantations located close to tobacco barn sites.

With the exception of the forest plantation at Ode-Ogun which is being managed for timber, the rest are all managed on a coppice rotation of ten to twelve years for the production of fuel and poles. Annual yields vary from 50 cubic feet on the poorest sites at Shaki to 135 cubic feet on the best sites at Ejigbo. They supply the neighbouring towns with good building poles and most telegraph poles in the region are of teak.

CATTLE REARING AND GRAZING DEVELOPMENT

For an area which is covered by savanna with a dense and vigorous grass growth, the cattle population of about 40,000 heads is certainly small. The main reason for the small number of cattle which is owned by the Fulanis is the high incidence of animal diseases, particularly that borne by the tsetse fly. The stock farms at Fashola and Upper Ogun, run by the Western Nigeria Ministry of Agriculture and Natural Resources, demonstrate that trypanosomiasis can be controlled, particularly by using resistant breeds of cattle. At present, the cattle population is concentrated in the far north, and so far there is no attempt by the local Yorubas to keep cattle.

Primitive grazing methods and inherent rural conservatism are important factors which account for the low standard of living of the cattle Fulani. No cattle dogs are employed, and in the circumstance the number of herds handled by one man is low and so are the returns per man. There is no attempt at pasture management and cattle are usually kept past their prime and are generally sold in times of need, since the Fulani still count the number of cattle in one's herd as prestigeous.

Investigation on methods of control of stock diseases, and the establishment and management of improved pastures have already been carried out by the Western Nigeria Ministry of Agriculture. Mixed grass-legume pastures, which are the basis for grazing in most temperate regions, give much higher returns than local natural pastures and have been recommended as ideal for future grazing in this region. Fortunately mixed grass-legume pastures have been successfully established in the grass plains of south-western Nigeria. This success, which is rare in the tropics, has been attributed to the rainfall pattern in the region. It offers great possibilities for developing cattle rearing and mixed farming on a large scale. The problem, however, is that such pastures are expensive to establish. For this reason, what is required in the immediate future is careful management of natural pastures which have considerable value.

Problems of managing natural pastures by the Fulani, who have since adopted semi-nomadic or even settled life in such cattle-rearing areas as the Jos Plateau and parts of the Eastern Borderlands, include lack of funds to cover the cost of fencing and provision of water supplies, both of which are necessary for working out a carefully controlled rotational grazing. There is also the problem of competition for land with the indigenous farming population and one way of getting over this will be the integration of cattle and crop farming. Since some difficulty is envisaged in introducing mixed farming and since, for a given village territory the land area under cultivation at any time rarely exceeds twenty per cent, the following proposal has been made.[1] That for a given area, the land could be fenced into five paddocks one of which would be cultivated at one time while the remaining four are grazed by the cattle Fulani. After two years the first paddock will revert to fallow and a second paddock be selected for cultivation. Such a system will give considerable return from farmlands, since the cattle manure will more than make up for reduced fallow periods in certain areas.

This programme for managing natural pastures has been adopted with modifications in the Ilora farm settlement which is located in this region. It is proposed that each settler will be provided with six head of cattle in addition to pigs and poultry which he now keeps; but at present cattle in the settlement are managed centrally rather than by individual farmers. Towards the end of 1964 there were seven paddocks and two large cattle pens in this settlement which, at that time, had a cattle population of 218, consisting primarily of Ndama breeds which are reputed to be resistant to trypanosomiasis. The paddocks are fenced with barbed wire or bush hedges and field rotation is practised, although bush grazing is permitted occasionally.

The commercial cattle ranch established by the Western Nigeria Development Corporation at the Upper Ogun Cattle Estate is based on improved pastures. The high cost for clearing the land and preparing it mechanically for sown pasture and of fencing the paddocks with teak posts at about £120 a mile, as well as expense in providing water supplies, have so far slowed down the expansion of land under improved pastures. Considerable supplementary grazing from natural pastures using Fulani methods has therefore had to be adopted. Cattle breeding is an important feature of the Fashola livestock farm which is also managed by the same Regional Development Corporation.

CRAFT INDUSTRIES

In the nineteenth century, the mining and smelting of iron ore was centred within the triangle formed by Ibadan, Ogbomosho and Iseyin as apexes. The ore, which was obtained by open-cast mining, consisted of laterite which was smelted in kilns in which charcoal, palm-nut shells and green wood were used as fuel.[2] Smelting was organized as a family industry and the pig iron produced was in great demand for making farm implements and weapons of war. As in other parts of the western Sudan this all-important industry, which is the basis of all modern industry, has disappeared rather than becoming consolidated as was the case with the charcoal iron industry in Britain and Scandinavia. But the smiths who worked this iron still remain, depending for their raw materials on imported iron bars and scrap.

Oyo town and district specialize in carving calabashes for use in decorating houses, but the main use of the calabash in Yorubaland is as receptacles for sundry purposes. Other industries based on plant products include grass mats, the making of cloth looms and wood carving, including the carving of doors and building posts. But the most important and most widespread surviving traditional

[1] 'The Report on the Land Use Survey of the Oyo-Shaki Area, Western Nigeria' p. 37
[2] Ojo, G. J. A., *Yoruba Culture* pp. 96–7 London 1966

industry in this region is the textile industry. The main centres today are Iseyin, Oyo, Ilorin and Oshogbo. In the past all stages of the textile industry were carried out in the region, from growing the cotton to the making and dyeing of yarns and weaving. During the last thirty years the textile industry has tended to concentrate on dyeing adire cloths, the raw materials of which consist of imported bleached cotton shirting and locally grown indigo as dye. Imported yarns which are dyed locally, and imported dyes are also used in making rather heavy and expensive cloth for which Iseyin is renowned.

These industries are still carried out in the compounds of the entrepreneurs, who also supply much of the labour. They are essentially small-scale industries, but there is a growing tendency towards the establishment of small co-operatives for the production and marketing of these crafts.

Works consulted and suggestions for further reading:

1. Coppock, J. T., 'Tobacco growing in Nigeria' *Erdkunde* No. 19 pp. 297–306 1965
2. Forde, D., *The Yoruba-speaking peoples of South-western Nigeria* (Ethnographic Survey of Africa) London 1951
3. Gleave, M. B., 'Hill Settlements and their Abandonment in Western Yorubaland' *Africa* No. 33 p. 349 1963
4. Goddard, S., 'Town-farm Relationships in Yorubaland: A case study from Oyo' *Africa* No. 35 pp. 21–9 1965
5. Ojo, G. J. A., *Yoruba Culture* London 1966
6. United Nations F.A.O. Land Use Survey Team 'Report on the Land Use Survey of the Oyo-Shaki Area, Western Nigeria' Ibadan 1962
7. Anon, 'Nigerian Beef—The Story of a stock-rearing experiment' *Nigeria Magazine* No. 40 pp. 314–27 1953
8. Anon, 'Road to Shaki' *Nigeria Magazine* No. 42 pp. 150–77 1953

11 The Dissected Uplands of Afenmai, Ekiti and Western Kabba

One of the prominent highland areas in Nigeria is the dissected uplands generally referred to as the Kukuruku Hills. Like many other place names which appealed to the early British colonial administrators the word Kukuruku was a nickname given to the local inhabitants (of southern Kabba), who were alleged to utter a cry which sounded Ku-ku-ruku when they were fleeing from the Fulanis to their rocky retreat. This word is now considered derogatory by the people, who have since induced the government to change the name of the former administrative Division of Kukuruku to Afenmai. The region, however, covers parts of Ekiti and Owo Divisions as well as parts of western Kabba, that is in addition to Afenmai Division. The higher parts of these uplands form a major watershed between streams, draining southwards into the Bight of Benin and streams flowing northwards into the Lower Middle Niger valley. As the approximate southern limit of Fulani penetration, the political divide between the former northern and southern Nigeria passes through these uplands, which also constitute the meeting place of cultures brought together during the military encounters of the nineteenth century.

On a small-scale map, the physical landscape has a superficial resemblance to the highland area around Ilorin; but large-scale maps or field observations confirm that the eastern part of the Kukuruku Hills constitutes a distinct geographical region. The hills and ridges such as those found at Ososo and Semorika are bolder and at a younger stage of denudation than the isolated masses in the Ilorin area, which constitutes part of the grass plains of south-western Nigeria. Also, unlike the Ilorin area, which is inhabited by the Yorubas and a few Fulanis, the uplands of Afenmai, Ekiti and western Kabba are occupied by several small indigenous tribes including Igbiras, Aworo, Akoko, Ora and Yagba. Nupe political domination of vast areas during the closing years of the nineteenth century and recent population movements into the area are other factors which mark out this part of the highlands for a separate study.

LANDFORMS AND SOILS

The uplands of Afenmai and western Kabba are underlain by igneous and metamorphic rocks of the Basement Complex, which outcrop as massive ridges and rocky hills over a greater part of the region. The general elevation of the land is about 1,200 feet, but there are numerous peaks rising above 2,000 feet. In his study of erosion surfaces in western Kabba, Clayton (1958) recognized two major land surfaces in the region, stable land surfaces and erosional land surfaces. The stable land surfaces, which he subdivides into African lateritic plains and Niger lateritic plains, consist of level or undulating plateau surfaces at over 1,200 feet for the African lateritic plains and over 750 feet for the Niger lateritic plains. Both surfaces are characterized by smooth rounded inselbergs, which are particularly numerous west and north of Kabba town and west of Igarra town; while flat-topped hills and bold ridges dominate the eastern and central parts of Igarra District. All over the stable land surfaces ironstone is widespread, occurring as pisolitic gravel, broken blocks, or continuous sheets overlain by clayey material at depths varying from three to eighteen inches. These rich ore deposits formed the basis of the local charcoal iron industry which has since ceased to exist.

Around Okene, Ososo, Kabba and Omuo-Oke, amongst other places, extensive high-level erosion surfaces stand above the general level of the stable land surfaces. The general elevation of these rugged surfaces, which are characterized by steep-sided granite hills, is about 1,500 feet. Soils in these higher areas are usually shallow and stony, although patches of reddish clay occur at the foot of inselbergs. More extensive patches of clay feature in the lower lateritic tablelands, where a marked catena arrangement of lateritic clay on the upper slopes and fine-grained to sandy clay at the base is typical. Apart from providing the basis for the local pottery industry, these clay patches provide the main areas of fertile farmland and can easily be identified on air photographs, where they occur as a

Figure 46. The Uplands of Afenmai, Ekiti and Western Kabba

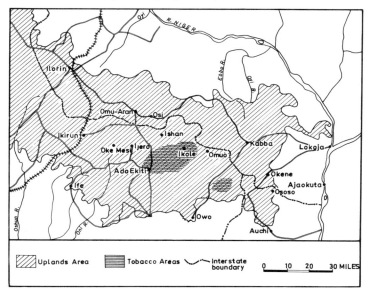

ring of heavy cultivation around the base of bold rock outcrops.

The widespread layer of ironstone found on the stable land surfaces is a product of intense chemical weathering and is not restricted to areas of basement rocks. Rather, rich ironstone of the same age also occurs on Mount Patti, near Lokoja, which represents an African lateritic plain developed on sedimentary rocks, but having the same summit level as the stable lateritic plain around Kabba town.

One of the main watersheds in Nigeria lies in this upland region, and separates streams draining northwards and eastwards into the Niger from those which drain directly into the sea. There are few large or perennial streams and all streams are incised, particularly where the stable surfaces give way to much lower land in the Niger valley in the north and east or the coastal plain in the south. Lack of water causes much hardship during the dry season, when temporary holes are dug along dry river beds for the purpose of obtaining water. Such water is usually contaminated and the incidence of guinea worm at this time of the year is high.

CLIMATE AND VEGETATION

Rainfall figures for Okene (49 inches) and Auchi (47 inches) give an idea of the annual total rainfall for the region. The double maxima regime, which features prominently in south-western Nigeria but decreases in intensity towards the north and east, is virtually unnoticeable in stations like Okene and Auchi. The rainy season begins in late March, but maximum precipitation occurs towards the end of the rainy season and is followed almost immediately by drought conditions. September is the wettest month with over eight inches of rain, but in November the region is already so dry that all parts receive less than one inch of rain. Tornadoes, which usually herald the coming and end of the rainy season, are rather destructive of crops and dwellings but crops suffer more as a result of delayed rains as well as from variability in the monthly rainfall, which for any given month may range between 70 and 130 per cent of the mean. In general, the percentage of variability from the mean increases when the rainfall becomes less, hence the high degree of variability during the planting season (February to April) and hence the adverse effects on crops.

The dry season, which lasts from November to early March, is usually a period of high temperatures (98° F. in the day) and intense heat. At this time of the year, farming activities come almost to a standstill, except in those parts of southern Kabba and western Afenmai where cocoa has been introduced during the last thirty years. The rivers and streams dry up and water for domestic use becomes very scarce. The cold harmattan from the northeast comes during the dry season, and usually has the effect of reducing the relative humidity from over eighty per cent during the rainy season to about sixty per cent. Its dryness, which derives from the fact that the wind blows over the vast and dry Sahara landmass, has some salutary effects on agriculture. Amongst other things it hastens the drying of cotton as well as guinea corn, the latter needing to be thoroughly dry if it is to keep well in storage.

Climatic and soil conditions favour the growth of dense savanna woodland but centuries of human interference and the persistent annual bush fires have reduced the natural vegetation to one of open savanna woodland. Tall grasses, often exceeding five feet in height, and trees with crooked and gnarled stems of about forty to fifty feet high predominate. Along the stream valleys the vegetation is of high forest type, and in the far eastern district of North Ibie in Afenmai Division cocoa farms are restricted to these wooded valleys.

ASPECTS OF THE POPULATION AND SETTLEMENT

The numerous small ethnic groups inhabiting this highland region were subjected, at various times before 1900, to a series of raids and invasions from the west and the north. The effects of these raids on the cultural landscape and changes brought about during the period of British administration are discussed in the next section. A considerable mixing of cultures occurs along the western and northern boundaries of Afenmai; Yoruba cultural influence being rather strong in the west, while the Igara groups of the north have adopted many Igbira customs. But Afenmai is inhabited by Edo-speaking people. In the whole region therefore three main cultural areas may be recognized. These are the Edo-speaking area dominated by Benin cultural influence, the Igbira area of Kabba with Okene as the main settlement, and the Yoruba cultural area in Kabba, northern Ekiti and eastern Owo Districts.

Afenmai Division, the inhabitants of which are grouped by ethnographers as Northern Edo is the melting pot of various cultures resulting from series of migrations from the north, west, east and south. For sometime it was a sort of no man's land bordered in the south by the once powerful kingdom of Benin, in the north by the Nupes, and in the west and east by the Yorubas and Igalas respectively. Today the people of Ivbiasakon claim Benin descent, while those of Akoko and Semorika moved in from the Yoruba west and the Igala east respectively.

Each linquistic group consists of a number of small tribal or sub-tribal groups usually referred to as clans, which are often named after the founders. The clan in turn is made up of a number of villages, each of which is divided into territorial segments called wards and inhabited by members of one or two closely related extended families. As in many other parts of the country therefore, the territorial organization of the wards, the villages and the clans reflects very closely the geneological pattern of the groups.

There are only a few large settlements in this region and these are Auchi, Igara, Okene and Kabba. In Afenmai about three-quarters of the population (204,200 in 1952) lived in villages with less than 4,000 inhabitants, but in Igara Division, where there are many larger villages, the ratio living in settlements of 4,000 to 10,000 persons is thirty per cent. With the exception of Igara town, which itself is made up of a string of villages, these large villages are essentially rural in character. Small nucleated villages are also common in the Igbira and Yoruba areas, where the population is also predominantly rural.

The influence of topography on settlement is considerable, particularly in the rugged parts of Igara Division, where settlements and farmlands are confined to narrow strips of land separating the granite hills. Hill settlements are still common, while some settlements are located at the foot of the hills. As a rule, settlements tend to avoid the main river valleys, including that of the Osse and Ebba Rivers. Today, the most important factor influencing the location of settlement is the road, but in the past the first consideration was that of security and protection from surprise raids.

Forested patches in the Ijumu-Arin District of Kabba in northern Ekiti, including Irun, as well as in western Afenmai have encouraged the introduction of such cash crops as cocoa, coffee and kolanuts. Since many of these forested lands are far away from the main villages, farmers have had to establish distant farm hamlets similar to those in the main cocoa belt. Many of these hamlets are still temporary settlements being occupied during the farming season; but in others, some people have taken up permanent residence. The town-farm relationship is the same as in the main cocoa belt.

A few pockets with fairly high population densities occur in parts of Igara Division and around Okene, where

there are about 400 persons per square mile. But since the people tend to concentrate in small nucleated settlements, there are considerable areas of uninhabited land. The most sparsely settled parts of the region are along the boundary zone between Igara and Igbira, north of Okene and that part of Ekiti lying north of the road from Omuo to Ishan.

Igbira migration into the non-Igbira districts of the region is one of the main features of recent population changes in the uplands of Afenmai and western Kabba. The Igbiras are very hardworking and migrate into Irun, Afenmai and Igara territories mainly as farm labourers who specialize in making yam heaps. In Auchi District Igbiras settle as self-employed yam cultivators who produce for sale in the neighbouring urban markets. Their settlements are usually located near the main motor roads so as to facilitate the ready transportation of yams to the consuming centres. Field enquiries in September 1966 revealed that in Afenmai no Igbira farmer is permitted to plant perennial crops like cocoa, and that in the more remote part of the Division the annual rent paid by these migrant tenant farmers was ten shillings per man.

Other migrants into the region include the Isokos of eastern Urhobo and Hausas. The former settle in scattered farmhuts and their main occupation is tapping palm wine or harvesting palm fruits and processing them for oil, while the Hausas who are particularly numerous in Irun have been attracted there by the local kolanut economy. Many people, especially the men, from Afenmai and Kabba people also migrate to work as labourers in the cocoa belt and rubber districts of western and midwestern Nigeria.

The population is made up of Moslems, Christians and pagans whose religion consists of ancestor worship. Shrines dedicated to the founders of settlements as well as the mythical ancestor of the particular group are found in most villages, and even those inhabitants who have since descended to the plains still go to worship occasionally at the pagan shrines on the hills. The Yorubas of Kabba worship the same gods as their kinsmen in the forest belt. Nupe domination was accompanied by the imposition of Islam while Christianity was introduced by British missionaries. The progress made by these new religions during the last fifty to a hundred years may be assessed from the fact that in 1952, forty-seven per cent of the total number of households in Igbira Division and twelve per cent in Kabba Division were Moslems, while Christian households made up fourteen per cent and sixty-two per cent of the total households in Igbira and Kabba respectively.

THE HILL VILLAGES AND TOWNS

The cultural landscape of the uplands of Afenmai and western Kabba is largely a product of nineteenth century Yoruba and Nupe raids and of British rule during the first half of the twentieth century. The period of Yoruba and Nupe raids saw an advance in the frontier of settlement as people retreated to inaccessible hill-tops for protection, while the period of British rule was marked by the descent of some settlement from the hills to the plains. As in the Jos Plateau, the Eastern Borderlands and at Idanre, some of these refugee settlements have survived almost intact but the indication is that they will be completely abandoned within the next generation or two.

Considering the Middle Belt as a whole, this upland region suffered most from slave raids carried out by Yorubas and Binis from the south and Nupes from the north. In the northern Edo areas of Igara and Afenmai Yoruba raids appear to have preceded Nupe domination of the area which was completed in the second half of the nineteenth century. Both aggressors wrought much damage on the population and economy, the Yorubas being remembered for raiding, burning of houses and carrying off slaves and livestock. But, unlike the Yorubas, the Nupes appeared to have been interested in territorial expansion. Villages which submitted straight away to the Nupes were spared, but they were obliged to pay heavy tribute in slaves and to encourage the spread of Islam. Many more villages were deserted as their inhabitants fled to the tops of the nearest rocky hills, while others were destroyed in the course of fighting.

In order to strengthen their fortifications, the hill-top villages were made practically impregnable by pouring palm oil over the smooth steep rock surfaces and thereby rendering them very slippery. In addition these hill villages were surrounded with one or two walls, while poisoned pegs were neatly concealed at the bottom of pits dug along the various approach paths. But in spite of these precautions only a few of these hill outposts managed to hold their independence until the 1890's when Nupe domination came to an end following the coming of the Royal Niger Company.

After the formal establishment of British rule, there was a notable retreat in the frontiers of settlement as many scattered communities started to re-group themselves in their old sites on the plains or on new sites. But some villages remained on the hills and refused to move to the plains even when persuaded to do so by the local administrative officer. It was the view of the British administrative officer that the inaccessibility of such villages as Semorika, Ososo and Ogbe created administrative difficulties and

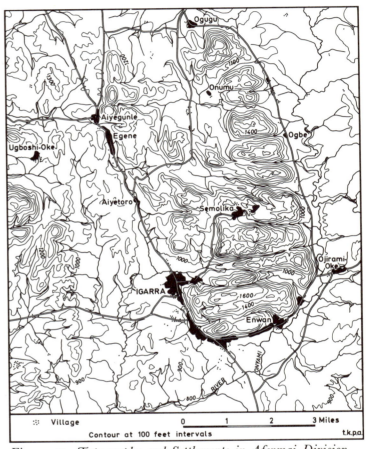

Figure 47. Topography and Settlements in Afenmai Division

when the inhabitants refused to descend to the plains the administration proceeded to burn their houses.

The descent to the plains continues and in several cases a settlement consists of a hill and a plain component. The case of Semorika is illustrated in Figure 47, and is reminiscent of such hill settlements as Idanre and Aku near Nsukka as well as several hill settlements in the Eastern Borderlands. Down on the plains, the road has proved to be an important factor influencing the arrangement of dwellings, hence the growth of several street villages in Afenmai Divisions.

FARMING PRACTICES

The crops produced in this region are as varied as its ethnic composition. Yams and cassava are the main food crops but maize and guinea corn are also important. Other crops include peas, beans, groundnuts and garden vegetables. Tree crops which are essentially cash crops are equally varied although none is produced on a large scale. The oil palm is probably the most widespread but kola, cocoa and the locust bean are also grown.

Farming is essentially a man's work, although women often cultivate crops like beans and groundnuts. Farming practices as well as the size of farms is largely determined by the extent of cultivable land and the distance of such land from the village. Usually, the interfluves, but particularly the hill-tops, where the villages are located, are rugged and stony and the soils are lateritic and difficult to work. Where cultivable soils, including riverine deposits along the larger river valleys, are very distant from the settlement, the men have been obliged to establish farm hamlets where they spend the working week or the whole farming season. In the small clan area of north Ibie in Afenmai Division there were about twenty farm hamlets in 1965, located at distances of over seven miles from the parent village. The same number of farm hamlets were counted in the Ijumu-Arin District of Kabba during the same year.

Although it is generally true to say that the emphasis on grains—guinea corn and maize—increases toward the north, the main factor determining the importance of any crop or crop combination in a particular village area is the soil. Yams and cocoyams predominate in the wet fields or *Akuro* as the Yorubas of Kabba call the heavy alluvial soils in the floodplains of the main rivers. Farms located on non-riverine areas with lighter, but not necessarily less fertile soils are usually referred to as dry fields or *Ofe*. Both root crops and grains are grown on such land.

Hill slopes were also cultivated in the past, but the local groups had no idea of terrace agriculture, unlike the Biroms of the Jos Plateau or the Ibos of Maku in Awgu Division. Their hill farms were therefore given to much soil erosion and had to be abandoned. In many areas, the hill slopes still consist of bare hard rock surfaces which cannot support any form of vegetation.

The preparation of farmland consists of the usual method of bush clearing and burning of the brush after one week. Mounds rather than ridges are then prepared, fields on the riverine floodplain featuring much larger mounds than those of the better drained, dry fields. In most of western Kabba, as well as in the less rocky parts of Afenmai, farmland is plentiful and both the local people and migrant farmers produce a considerable quantity of yams for internal exchange. Igbira migrants in Afenmai are particularly noted for selling out almost all their yam crop at harvest to food traders from Onitsha and school contractors, while the south-western part of the region exports yams and other foodstuffs to the main cocoa belt.

This region can thus be looked upon as a food surplus area, except that it is always hit by a hunger period lasting between March and May. The hunger period here arises from a lack of adequate storage facilities, unlike parts of the densely settled areas of the East Central State, where the hunger period is caused by the fact that the farmer does not produce enough to feed his family all through the year.

Production for export is almost entirely restricted to palm produce, although yam can properly be regarded as an important cash crop. Cotton growing is of long-standing importance. The crop is grown in small farms and is used largely for the local cloth-weaving industry at Okene and Ososo. Large-scale production of cotton, which started in the Western State in 1966, has not yet been extended to every part of this upland region.

POTTERY IN AFENMAI

Pottery[1] is an important traditional craft, particularly in those parts of Afenmai where farmland is very restricted as a result of rugged topography. Clay, which is abundant at the foot of some outcrops or along stream valleys, provides the raw material for this industry which is dominated by the womenfolk. Pottery has been practised for many generations, and now that clay supplies close to the villages have been exhausted the women often have to travel up to four miles to obtain clay. The labour and time spent in carrying clay from such distant clay fields can be avoided by adopting the Ekiti Yoruba method of setting up the potteries directly on clay fields which are located far away from settlements. Like the distant farm hamlets, some of these Ekiti potteries are known to have grown into permanent settlements.

Although some of the pot makers might have heard of the potter's wheel, this mechanical device has not yet been introduced into any part of rural Nigeria. Pots in Afenmai are therefore still moulded by hand, and the skill of the local pot makers is evidenced by the marked uniformity in the shape of pots of any given variety. Often as many as four to six pots are started at a time, each pot being built up gradually as the woman moves from one pot to another to add some lumps of clay. Loss sustained during the firing process depends largely on the quality of the clay and the care in ensuring that the pots are dry before firing. For poor-quality clay the loss rate may be as high as two for every three pots.

Some degree of specialization is noticeable in certain

[1] This account is based on B. A. Oshiekpekhai's essay on 'Pottery in Afenmai Division' Dept. of Geography University of Ibadan 1964

villages, but in general each pot-making village and indeed each pot maker produces pots for various purposes. The products include large pots for storing water or farm products such as beans, rice and groundnuts, smaller pots for carrying water from the stream, water coolers, cooking pots with covers and flattish pots for serving food as well as miniature pots used in offering sacrifices. Long tobacco pipes are also made. There are no fixed prices for these pots but the average market price for large storage pots is between three and five shillings, while pots for fetching water cost about a shilling and sixpence.

One of the greatest problems confronting the local pottery industry is that of poor transportation in the district. The roads are too hilly to permit transportation by bicycles and so the women are obliged to trek long distances with headloads of pots to the main village markets, some of which are as much as ten miles from the pot-making villages. When going to long distance markets, the women set out very early in the morning so as to arrive in the evening when the pots are sold.

Difficult conditions of working the clay pits during the rains have been largely responsible for the seasonal nature of the industry. Early morning rains may not stop in time for the women to get to distant clay pits, and in cases where they brave the rain, the slippery nature of the ground around the pits makes it difficult for them to obtain the clay. Poor weather conditions also create problems in drying the pots. There is, therefore, a sudden drop in production during the rainy season. Fortunately, the demand for pots is not great at this time of the year, as compared with the dry season, when water shortage creates a demand for water storage pots as well as pots for fetching water from streams. The dry season is also the harvest season, hence the great demand for pots used in storing groundnuts, rice, maize and beans. The mass production of pots during the dry season is therefore matched by a high demand for the products.

Finally, the appearance in local markets of cheap enamel and plastic wares, now made in Nigeria, is proving a real threat to the survival of the local pottery industry. Enamel plates are displacing local pots and it is becoming more fashionable to carry water in enamel or plastic buckets. The greater costs of these more durable wares will, however, permit the survival of the local pottery industry at least for some time.

OTHER CRAFT INDUSTRIES

Cloth weaving is an important craft at Ososo and Okene. At Ososo the yarn for weaving is still spun locally from cotton grown in the area. Weaving here is done by the women. Okene specializes in silk weaving which is based on imported yarn. It is significant that silk weaving at Okene started in the royal compound of the Atta of Igbirra and that the senior wife of the Atta even tried to breed silk worms but encountered much difficulty in feeding them. The loom used is the broad, upright loom usually used to weave cotton yarns or even raffia mats in Nigeria.

Ososo produces a special type of mat which commands a good price in other parts of the country. The method of production is unusual and the finished product of excellent quality. The mat is woven in grass in strips about five inches wide, after which the strips are sewn together to produce a soft, flexible and hard-wearing mat. This craft is almost exclusively left in the hands of men who are too old to do any other type of work.

TRANSPORTATION AND TRADE

There are a few federal roads in the region, but in recent years the regional governments have opened many roads to lorry traffic while the villagers, through communal effort, have also enlarged some footpaths for use by bicycle and in some cases by cars. But in the more rugged districts, transportation is still very primitive and the few roads are not well looked after. Logs put across a valley serve as bridges, and motorable roads may be closed throughout the rainy season because bridges along them have been washed away or worn out. Villages in these hilly areas remain rather isolated and their inhabitants are obliged, like the potters of North Ibie, to walk distances of over seven miles to the nearest large market.

A close relationship exists between the size of the rural population of a given district and the road density in the district. The areas on the western Nigeria side of the Ekiti-Kabba border for example are better served by roads, a contrast which is reinforced by the fact that a few yards after the boundary the tar-surfaced road from Ikare gives way to a laterite-surfaced road leading to Okene.

A long-standing trade in raw cotton as well as in locally made and imported textiles exists between the various parts of the region, and in so far as this trade is concerned, the various regional boundaries exist only on the map. Postwar improvements of roads and growth in lorry traffic has brought about some changes in the pattern and organization of this trade, although it is still dominated by the womenfolk. In pre-war years the trade in imported consumer goods, of which the most important item was European-manufactured cloth, was controlled by the Ekiti women, who bought their wares from the Lagos area.

Their retail trade sphere included parts of Kabba and west Igara. Many of the consumer goods now distributed in the area come from Onitsha market, where goods are much cheaper than at Lagos or Ibadan. Warri is also an important supplier of imported cloth to Igara, Ekiti and Afenmai.

Locally woven cotton cloth is also an important item of internal exchange amongst the various groups in the region. All facets of the industry, ginning, spinning, dyeing and weaving, are dominated by the women who also control the distribution of the finished product. Igbira women, who accompany their husbands to Ekiti or Afenmai, often spend their time weaving rather than helping their husbands in the farms. The increase in the number of Igbiras in Irun and other Ekiti towns, as well as in the Akoko Edo districts of Benin Province, has created a greater demand for raw cotton than these localities can supply; hence the development of trade in raw cotton between Kabba and these other areas. It is usual for women to carry loads of locally made, as well as imported, cloth into the village markets and to return with a cargo of raw cotton, which is much cheaper in those villages not located near the main roads.

OKENE TOWN

Okene is one of the hill towns which have now descended to the plains. The original hill town consisted of five quarters bearing the names of the five sons of the first chief of the town. A few of the poorer inhabitants still live on the hill.

The new town in the valleys consists of a group of settlements spread along the approach roads to the community centre, where the palace of the Atta, court offices, the dispensary and mosque are located. As at Idanre the topography of the new town has induced a ribbon development along roads passing through the narrow valleys in which the dwellings are built. Its population of 60,560 in 1963 is predominantly Igbirra. The town is now provided with pipe-borne water, and in view of the difficulty in obtaining water in the former settlements it appears that the supply of piped water played an important part in inducing the most conservative Igbirras to descend from the hills.

Works consulted and suggestions for further reading:

1. Bradbury, R. E., *The Benin Kingdom and Edo-speaking peoples of South-western Nigeria* (Ethnographic Survey of Africa) London 1957
2. Clayton, W. D., 'Erosion Surfaces in Kabba Province, Nigeria' *Journal of West African Science Association* No. 4 pp. 147–9 1958
3. MacRow, D. W., 'Change in the Hills' *Nigeria Magazine* No. 45 pp. 21–59 1954
4. Oshiekpekhai, B. A., 'Pottery in Afenmai Division' unpublished B.A. dissertation. Department of Geography, University of Ibadan 1964

12 The Middle Niger Region

This region is made up of parts of the provinces of Ilorin, Niger and western Kabba as well as Yauri Emirate in Sokoto Province. It is a vast area inhabited by numerous small pagan tribes, the larger ones of which include the Kamberis, Nupes, Gungawas and Igbirras. Contact between the groups is minimal, to the extent that along the Upper Middle Niger valley the Gungawas practise skilful irrigated agriculture while neighbouring groups like the Lopawa and Larawa, living only a few miles away, appear to be completely ignorant of the principles and importance of irrigation in an environment such as theirs. Yet there are no major physical barriers to communications as exist, for instance, along the Nigeria-Cameroons borderlands. In addition to the varied ethnic composition of its population, the region is very sparsely settled and produces very little for export. Some of the most backward indigenous people in the country are to be found in this region which has, in recent years, become the scene of large-scale capital intensive development projects featuring the Niger Agricultural Project at Mokwa, the Bacita Sugar Estate, the paper factory at Jebba and the multimillion pound Kainji Dam Project.

Fulani domination, which was restricted to only a part of the Benue valley, was extended over the entire Middle Niger region and may be considered as a factor which gives some semblance of regional unity to the region. It resulted in a large-scale depopulation of vast areas, particularly in Kontagora and Borgu districts where extensive areas are still uninhabited. This is a region with vast stretches of empty land awaiting settlement and development, but climatic conditions preclude plantations based on the main tree crops of the forest belt. Skilled labour and in many cases unskilled labour for working large-scale development projects have been in short supply in the past.

THE NIGER VALLEY AND WATERWAY

The dominant topographical feature of this region is the valley of the Niger which consists of two distinct sections— the Upper Middle Niger valley, which follows a north–south direction from Yelwa to Jebba, and the Lower Middle Niger valley, which extends eastwards from Jebba to Lokoja. Between Yelwa and Jebba the valley is cut through crystalline rocks of the Basement Complex and is characterized by several rapids, which impede easy navigation, while the Basement rocks protrude in many places through the sand fill of the river bed to form rocky islands. The Lower Middle Niger valley on the other hand is cut through sedimentary rocks and, like the Benue valley, it is free from rapids and falls.

At Yelwa the Niger flows through a wide trough with an extensive flood plain, but south of this town low hills close in and the channel becomes obstructed by several rapids up to Agwarra, where it bifurcates into two channels enclosing Foge Island. The western channel is navigable while the eastern channel is obstructed by rocks and rapids. Foge Island, which is about twenty miles long and measures eleven miles at its widest point, is part of the Niger flood plain and will be completely submerged by the Kainji Lake. At Bussa, where the channels join again, the channel of the Niger is very rocky and so is the surrounding flood plain. The inhabitants of Bussa and other settlements along the rocky valley between Bussa and Jebba are therefore obliged to travel long distances away from the river to find suitable farmland.

About thirty miles from Jebba, just below Awuru, the Niger valley narrows into a gorge which becomes rather narrow at Jebba, where it is bounded by vertical walls of quartzite. Several islands, including the Juju Rock, can be seen from either of the railway bridges crossing the north and south channels at Jebba. The character of the valley changes below Jebba. Its width is much greater and extensive swampy plains occur along both banks. The extent of these fadamas can be seen at Bacita where advantage has been taken of the rich soils, as well as the adequate supply of groundwater in the dry season, for growing sugar cane under irrigation. Throughout this section of its course (Jebba to Lokoja) the Niger flows through its own alluvium, its channel being confined by rather straight banks which support a savanna vegetation of grass and scattered trees. Patches of strong red-clay occur along the banks of the Lower Middle Niger and are easily recognized from the fact that they support a dense vegetation of low forests.

Physically Jebba is the head of navigation of the Niger waterway, but extreme fluctuations in water levels constitute a major handicap to vessels plying beyond Lokoja. Between Jebba and Lokoja vessels can carry full loads for only October and part of November when the annual peak level due to local rains is reached.

RELIEF AND DRAINAGE OF THE COUNTRY BORDERING THE NIGER VALLEY

Away from the Niger flood plains the land rises on both sides to form upland areas, most of which consist of gently undulating country. The Nupe territorial area is characterized by a low-level non-lateritic plain of about 400 feet above sea level in the north, while the southern upland consists of a more varied surface which include the Agbaja

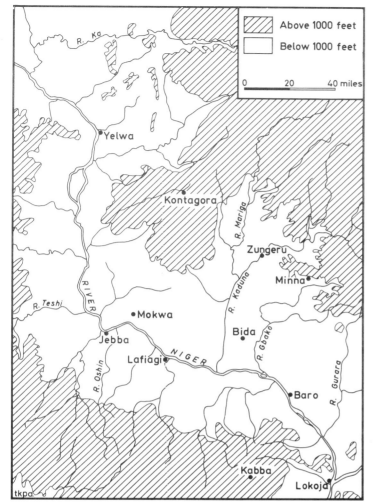

Figure 48. Relief and Drainage of the Middle Niger Region

Plateau and a highly dissected hill country. The north bank uplands are drained by north–south rivers of which the most important are the Kaduna, which meets the Niger at Pategi, the Jatau and the Gurara Rivers. These rivers provide important highways for local trade as well as fish, and in recent years their extensive fadamas have provided suitable land for irrigated rice fields.

The upland area lying east of the Ilorin–Jebba railway, but south of the Niger flood plain, is drained by shorter streams which flow south–north but have delayed junctions with the Niger. It is a low-level non-lateritic plain developed on sedimentary rocks, and so is the Agbaja Plateau which, like Mount Patti, is capped with thick layers of ironstone. Thin soils characterize these laterized areas but in the non-lateritic plain, the soils which are reddish-brown have a deep profile. North-west of the Agbaja Plateau, Basement rocks outcrop close to the Niger plains, giving rise to a dissected hilly country lying north of the line joining Agbaja to Akutukpa.

In Kontagora and Yauri Emirates, as well as in Borgu Division, the general elevation of the uplands is much higher, being well over 900 feet above sea level. Prominent hills occur to the east and north of Yelwa, and until recently some of them provided settlement sites for refugee pagan people fleeing from Fulani raiders. The Kontagora

section is drained by west-flowing streams whose open valleys are usually marked out by dense riparian woodland. Often no bridges are built across such valleys, but rather a cement patch at the bottom of a valley constitutes a sort of 'level crossing of rivers' which the motorists will soon discover to be a common feature along minor roads in the northern states.

CLIMATE, VEGETATION AND SOILS

The mean annual rainfall for Yelwa (40 inches), Bussa (40 inches), Mokwa (42·6 inches), Kontagora (46·6 inches) and Bida (48·5 inches) give a general impression of the spatial variation in the total annual rainfall. There is a general decrease from east to west, the length of the dry season being longer in the Upper Middle Niger valley than in the section below Jebba. The length of the dry season may vary considerably in such stations as Kontagora and Yelwa, but high variability in the monthly total rainfall is characteristic of the entire region. The types of rainfall regime confirm the view that the Middle Belt, of which the Middle Niger region is a part, is a zone of transition between the forested south and the Sudan savanna. Taking the mean for several years, stations like Mokwa show a double maxima in June and September, while Yelwa and Kontagora have a single peak in August, that of Bida being in September. A detailed analysis of rainfall figures for individual stations show the situation to be more complicated and more transitional in character. Between 1943 and 1962, for example, Yelwa had eleven years with single maximum, five years with double maxima and four years without any notable maximum period.

Extreme variation in the total rainfall for July and August is a general characteristic of the rainfall regime in this region. At Bida, for instance, where the mean monthly rainfall for July and August is 8·1 and 8·2 inches respectively, there was a fall of 0·85 inches in July 1958 as compared with 12·35 inches in July 1961. The corresponding figure for August was 11·25 inches for 1958 and 2·2 inches for 1961. A rainfall pattern such as this may prove disastrous to the rice crop of the Bida District, since it may result in a temporary drying up of swamps in which the rice is grown. The onset of the rains is also variable and often leads to late planting of food crops.

The occurrence of extensive swamps during the rainy season is an important factor in the expansion of rice culture in parts of the region. Flood water from the lower Kaduna valley often extends far inland, converting large areas into swamps. Several villages become isolated and can only be reached by canoes; a situation very similar

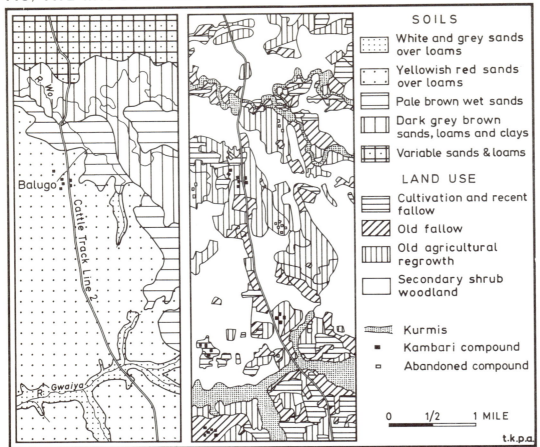

SOILS

White and grey sands over loams

Yellowish red sands over loams

Pale brown wet sands

Dark grey brown sands, loams and clays

Variable sands & loams

LAND USE

Cultivation and recent fallow

Old fallow

Old agricultural regrowth

Secondary shrub woodland

Kurmis

Kambari compound

Abandoned compound

0   1/2   1 MILE

t.k.p.a.

Figure 49. Soils and Land Use in the Kainji Lake Basin

to that found along floodplains of the Enyong creek near its junction with the Cross River at Itu.

March and April are the hottest months of the year. High day temperatures persist all through the year, the mean maximum temperatures being 85° F.; but there is a general cooling effect during the rainy season months of June, July and August.

The vegetation of this region, like its climate, is transitional and consists of open savanna woodland with a greater density of trees in the south. Marked differences which occur at close intervals both in the floristic composition and the open character of the vegetation are often caused by variations in soil types, topography, groundwater situation and human interference. The fadamas of the larger rivers support open savanna with occasional trees, but the valleys of the smaller and seasonal streams are covered with dense riparian woodlands or gallery forests. In Bida, Lafiagi-Pategi and further east, trees like the raffia palm, the oil palm and kola nuts grow wild in such forests and it is in such wooded parts of Nupe territory that the Northern Government proposed to start kola nut plantations with the view to reducing the heavy dependence of the north on kola grown in western Nigeria. In the more densely settled areas these riparian forests have been cleared for farming owing to the fact that in most parts of the region, but particularly in Kontagora and Borgu, suitable farmland is largely restricted to the valleys.

During the early dry season when the vegetation is usually burnt, the ground becomes barren and blackened. Several trees are destroyed in the annual fires while others merely loose their leaves but survive with partly burnt trunks. But no sooner is the bush fired than the grass begins to sprout, and in a few weeks the ground is covered with green grass. Some of the trees also come into new leaf before the rains begin. Rank grass and trees in full canopy dominate the landscape throughout the rainy season—a remarkable contrast with the barrenness of the dry season.

Parent material as well as topographical position are the main factors influencing the character of soils in the region. Soils developed on the Nupe sandstones are usually different from those of the Basement Complex. The flattish interfluves separating the numerous shallow valleys of the basement rocks areas are usually covered with deep gravelly loam with a reddish unmottled upper horizon. Middle slope soils on this geological formation feature gravelly and heavily-mottled brown-coloured soils, while the lower slope soils are often better drained and are invariably mottled red. Fine grained to coarse sands are common along the river valleys, and in the fadamas the soils are usually hard when dry. Lateritic ironstone is common everywhere except on the alluvium of the river flood plains.

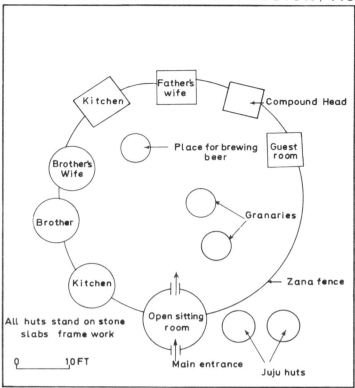

Figure 50. Ground Plan of a Gungawa Compound near Yelwa

TRIBAL DISTRIBUTION, POPULATION AND SETTLEMENT

The people of the Middle Niger region fall into three major groups, namely the riverine tribes such as the Gungawas, Lopawa and Nupes, the upland tribes like the Kamberi, Gwaris and Yorubas and finally the Hausa-Fulani group. It is possible to identify the nuclei of the Nupes and Yorubas, but most of the other tribes are found scattered over very wide areas. The resulting pattern of the distribution of tribal groups is one in which some districts consist of a thoroughly mixed population, instead of the usual arrangement whereby each tribal group settles in a clearly defined contiguous territorial area. This multiplicity of tribal communities within parts of the region has come about as a result of migration of people from different directions during the last one hundred years. Hausas and Shangawas for example came into the Kainji lake basin from the north, during the early years of the Fulani conquest, while the Kamberi came from the eastern borders of Kontagora Emirate.

Gungawas constitute one of the main riverine groups and are concentrated on the banks and islands of the River Niger between Gebbi (above Yelwa) and Bussa. On the fertile flood plains at Yelwa, where a large number of Gungawas have settled, many of them practise irrigated agriculture, the main crop grown under this system being onions. They live in huts grouped into large compounds (Figure 50).

Below Jebba the Niger valley is inhabited largely by Nupes whose main city is Bida. The Nupe population appears to be declining, a fact which has been attributed to endemic and widespread diseases as well as high infant mortality, although one has to be wary of population figures in parts of rural Nigeria. The Nupes live in large villages, most of which have daughter settlements which consist of small farm hamlets called *tunga* and are usually located within a radius of six to seven miles of the parent village. The relationship between these *tungas* and the main village is similar to that between the town and the farm in the Yoruba cocoa belt. The *tungas* of a village may be made up partly of stranger settlements of immigrants into Nupe territory, but *tungas* are often founded by villagers in search of better or more farmland and may be abandoned if harvests are poor or if the site proves unhealthy. The *tunga* is rarely permanent as compared with the main village. It is essentially a rural farm outpost, and according to Baldwin the *tunga* has no social life of its own. 'It possesses no market, no independent political organization . . . and celebrates its feasts and ceremonies with the mother village.'[1]

Many Yorubas, Hausas and Fulanis settled permanently in Nupe territory. The Fulanis are particularly numerous east of the Kaduna River, where they established permanent settlements after subjugating the Nupes more than a hundred years ago. These Fulanis have since been absorbed by the Nupe population, whose language they have adopted and with whom they intermarried. Their concentration east of the Kaduna River accounts for the higher density of population in this part of Bida Emirate, where some districts have well over seventy persons per square mile.

The Kamberis who are essentially upland dwellers are the most widespread group and are found in Kotonkoro District, Kontagora Emirate, Bussa, Agwarra and Wawa Districts of Bussa Emirate and Borgu Division. They live in small scattered hamlets often located in remote, inaccessible countryside. According to Gunn, Kamberis formerly lived in large towns in Yauri territory, which included much of present day Kontagora Emirate; but were forced to retire in small numbers into the bush, following the destruction of lives and settlements during Fulani military operations in the area during the 1850's.

Like the rest of the Middle Belt of Nigeria, the Middle Niger region is very sparsely settled, vast areas in Borgu and Kontagora being uninhabited. Documentary evidence, which consists of eye witness accounts of atrocities and destruction observed by early explorers and missionaries, confirms that the sparse population is largely a product of nineteenth century Fulani raids and wanton destruction of life and property. Large-scale development schemes such as the ill-fated mechanized agricultural project at

[1] Baldwin, K. D. S., *The Niger Agricultural Project* p. 31 London 1957

Mokwa, the Kontagora resettlement scheme and the Bacita sugar plantation have had no problems in obtaining extensive land in the region. But the problem of recruiting even unskilled labour in a sparsely populated area such as this has been gigantic.

During the dry season which lasts from November to April, several Nupe farmers migrate to work as labourers in the cocoa farms of western Nigeria. Such migrations usually take place after the crops have been harvested and migrants usually return home with sufficient money for tax or for bride price. A number of them invest their earnings in petty trading. The expansion of dry season farming through irrigation is likely to restrict this seasonal migration. In areas like Badeggi and Katcha, where farmers are already producing dry season crops of vegetables, with emphasis on onions under shaduf irrigation, seasonal migrations of farmers rarely take place.

SOME ASPECTS OF AGRICULTURAL LAND USE

The first important fact about farming in this region is that farmland is abundant, and so every member of any village community can farm as much land as he requires to maintain his family. Consequently, the traditional land tenure system in which control over land is exercised by the village head has survived intact, unlike some other parts of the country where pressure on farmland has led to individual land holding. For the same reason, strangers and immigrants who wish to settle in any village are readily accepted and allocated farmland by the village head. Rights over land is therefore usufructary but, contrary to popular conception, such rights do not cease immediately the land reverts to fallow, rather it continues for several years except in the case where the last occupier no longer wishes to farm the land.

Farm sizes are large by Nigerian standards, the limiting factor being the number of working adults per family or the amount of labour the farmer can employ. Some farmers possess only one composite farm, but although this may appear to be the sensible thing to do, most farmers prefer to farm different fields in order to counter the risk of crop failure which is quite common. Amongst the Kamberis who are reputed to be the most energetic farmers in this region, each adult male cultivates between four and eight acres every year. The lowest acreage per man is recorded in the Nupe area, where adult males rarely cultivate more than three acres per year. Another fact about farm sizes is that fadama farms and fields along streams are much smaller than fields on the uplands which are generally less fertile. In the

neighbourhood of settlements fadama farms measure about 0.1 to 0.3 acres, but larger units are common in areas which are distant from the village.

Guinea corn is the most important crop in the Middle Niger region and covers up to ninety per cent of the land cultivated by Kamberi farmers. It is the main staple food in Kontagora and Borgu as well as the raw material for beer, which the Kamberis and other pagan groups consume in large quantities. It is usually intercropped with millet and cowpeas. Yam is important amongst the Nupes and Yorubas of the lower Middle Niger region, where considerable surplus is produced for export to urban centres like Minna, Zaria and Kaduna.

Rice cultivation has expanded rapidly during the last fifteen years, as shown in the case of Bida Emirate which is reviewed below. Unlike other crops, it is grown continuously on the same field every year, although in some areas the land may be left fallow for one year after five years continuous cropping. In the lowlying fadamas of Yauri Emirate the average rice acreage cultivated by a farmer varies from two to five acres, and as a rule the size of rice plots on fadamas is much greater than that for any other fadama crop.

The main cash crops of the Northern States, namely

Figure 51. Land Use along the Niger Valley at Yelwa and Bussa

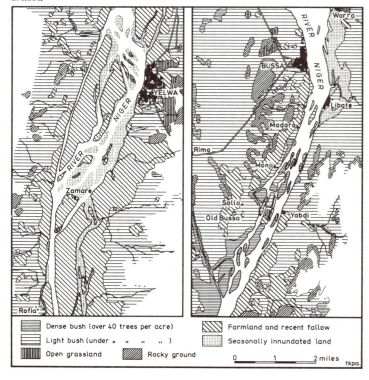

groundnuts, cotton and tobacco are grown throughout the region, but not on a large scale. Cotton is an important crop in parts of Yauri Emirate, but attempts to cultivate groundnuts on a commercial basis have met with total failure. Kola was introduced into the riverine districts of Bida, Lafiagi, Pategi and Kwara during the late 1950's but the crop is not yet popular because it takes as long as seven years after planting to come into bearing. In addition many young trees are lost annually through neglect and bush fires, hence the move to encourage farmers to cultivate the crop close to their compounds.

GROUP FARMING AMONGST THE NUPES

Group farming is an aspect of traditional food farming which was once common all over Nigeria and is still practised, albeit with considerable modifications, in various parts of the country. It is a system of farm-labour supply which makes it possible for a farmer to cultivate a larger acreage than he would normally be able to do if he depended strictly on family labour. Members of the same age-group from a particular village would decide to form a farming group, which worked in turns for each member. There is another arrangement, the Nupe type, in which a number of households combine to pool their labour together to farm as a group. The growing independence of young men and the commercialization of agriculture as well as the growing need to work for cash, rather than for a day's food and wine, has led to the replacement, in some areas, of group farming by paid labour. Amongst the Nupe, the change is not yet complete.

Nupe farming groups are organized on lineage basis and usually consists of a number of households which are members of the same extended family. The produce of the farm is controlled by the head of the group, who is often the oldest member of the group. Members' needs for tax money and bride price, as well as food for their families are usually met from the general pool. Group members may also cultivate individual plots, and this is the rule rather than the exception; but they can only do this during their spare time. For this reason such individual plots rarely exceed one acre.

Whatever may be said in favour of the Nupe type group farming, which was also very common amongst the Ibibios of south-eastern Nigeria, it is a system in which the younger men tend to be economically dependent on the elder ones. It works out well where land is plentiful and where communal tenure is still the rule. This is probably the reason why it still survives in Nupe territory. But the size of the groups is declining, and so is the size of farmland cultivated by the group. The decline follows a pattern similar to that of the disintegration of nucleated settlement in parts of south-eastern Nigeria, and the final stage will be one in which each individual cultivates his land with the help of his wife or wives and children. This stage has been reached in several parts of the country where farmers are now resorting to wage labour.

RICE PRODUCTION IN THE BIDA-LAFIAGI-PATEGI AREA

It was as far back as 1904 that Lord Lugard drew attention to the potentialities for swamp rice in the swamps along the Niger and Kaduna fadamas, and today these swamps constitute one of the major rice-producing areas in Nigeria. Since the rainfall is so unreliable rice farmers in this region have come to appreciate the need to conserve water in preparation for any emergency. Irrigation canals carrying water to the rice fields have in consequence been constructed along the fadamas of the Niger, Kaduna and Gbako Rivers. In areas where the flood plains are very extensive, the main irrigation channels are constructed by communal labour while individual farmers are responsible for digging the smaller channels leading to their rice plots. But the level of technology of the local people is still rather modest and so the acreage they can cultivate under their system of water control is very limited. Often their channels get damaged by floods because they are not well protected. A number of pilot irrigation schemes have therefore been organized by the Regional Ministry of Agriculture, with a view to opening up a greater area to irrigation.

Of an estimated 200,000 acres of land in the Kaduna-Gbako Plain of Bida Emirate which could be developed by irrigation, only 7,000 acres have so far been developed under the direction of the Ministry of Agriculture. This 7,000 acres is made up of six pilot schemes of which the largest are the Edozhigi, Tungan Kawo and the Badegi Rice Schemes (Figure 52). In each of these projects the land is laid out in several one-acre plots, which may be rented by any farmer from the Emirate on payment of a water rate of twenty-two shillings per acre. But in spite of an assured and controlled supply of water to rice fields in addition to the benefit of skilled supervision, management and advice made available by the Extension Division of the Ministry of Agriculture, only a few farmers have taken advantage of the Government sponsored irrigation schemes. One reason for this is that many of them are reluctant to pay the water rate. Indeed, a large number of those now cultivating plots in these areas do not

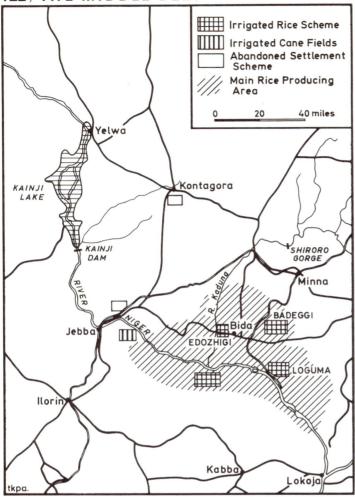

Figure 52. Recent Development Projects in the Middle Niger Region

themselves pay the water rate, but work as share croppers for town dwellers who have invested in the plots.

Mechanized cultivation of rice has been introduced and farmers may have their land ploughed at the rate of ninety shillings per acre of fadama land, or thirty-two shillings per acre of upland farms. This amount is payable after harvests, but the farmers consider it to be too high. Nearly every farmer plants the recommended BG 79 variety which is first planted in nurseries in June, and transplanted into the fields as from late July. The main implement for planting and for weeding is the universal hoe. Harvesting starts in October and often continues till early January. After threshing, which is done by women, the greater proportion of the harvest is sold to middlemen, the staple food of the local people being guinea corn rather than rice.

THE KONTAGORA LAND SETTLEMENT SCHEME

This land settlement scheme, which was started in 1949 by the Kontagora Native Authority, was one of a series of land settlement schemes established in various parts of tropical Africa during the years immediately following the end of the Second World War. Several of these schemes like that at Kontagora involved large capital investments, some were rather modest from the onset while others consisted of small-scale pilot projects. Only a few have survived till today and the Kontagora scheme is one of those which failed. But like the equally ill-fated Mokwa scheme nearby, which is reviewed below, it provided some lessons which though expensive, may yet prove useful in guiding future land settlement schemes.

The aim of the Kontagora scheme was to open up the virtually uninhabited parts of the Emirate, which had been laid waste a hundred years earlier by the savagery of over-zealous Fulani warriors. Unlike the Shendam Resettlement Scheme in the Benue valley (see page 144), in which the Authority decided on doing the absolute minimum for the settlers, the Kontagora scheme emphasized heavy capitalization so as to make possible rapid results and high profits, which would in turn make it possible for the settler to pay back his initial debt within a few years. It aimed at establishing fifteen settlements with twenty farmers in each by 1954. Each farmer was to be allocated thirty-five acres, half of which would be fallow while the use of plough and cattle would enable him to till the rest at a time. Emphasis was to be on mixed farming in which the main arable crops were to be groundnuts and guinea corn. At the start the cost per settler was put at £250, made up of money for purchasing livestock and equipment as well as the cost of clearing the land. In addition, about £9,000 was given to the planning authority for the provision of facilities like a dispensary, a market and central mixed farming depot for storing and maintenance of equipment.

The first hamlet, which consisted of Hausa farmers, was established in 1949 and was followed in 1950 by two hamlets of Kamberi farmers. In 1955, there were as many as 220 settlers but before the end of that year it was apparent that there was a great deal of dissatisfaction amongst the settlers, many of whom were tired of the system and wished to be allowed to withdraw. An exodus of settlers took place early in the following year, after the Settlement Authority had indicated that those who wanted to go could do so, provided they undertook to settle outstanding debts. In April 1956 only ninety-five settlers were left, and three months later the advisory board decided that since the benefits of the scheme to the settlers and the native administration did not justify the cost of operation, the scheme should be wound up.[1] More farmers left after the decision was made known to them, while a few who decided to stay on voluntarily handed in their ploughs, cattle and other equipment to the native administration and resorted to hoe cultivation.

THE NIGER AGRICULTURAL PROJECT AT MOKWA

The aim of this project which was launched in 1949 was the production, on a large scale, of groundnuts for export and guinea corn for local consumption, through the settlement of peasant farmers on the uninhabited parts of Niger Province in northern Nigeria. It was hoped that the project would also serve as a means of demonstrating better farming methods. It was a capital intensive enterprise in which emphasis was on mechanization. Strict control of the activities of the farmers was necessary for the efficient and economic operation of the project, but as in the case of the Kontagora scheme the settlers resented what they considered to be regimentation.

Clearing started in 1949 and by 1954 about 9,600 acres of bush had been cleared and 163 families settled. Each settler was to cultivate twenty-four acres, as compared with an average of about two-and-a-half acres per adult male in the Nupe villages. This turned out to be impossible because machines could only be used for clearing, ploughing and ridging but not for weeding. To make matters worse, casual wage labour was not available in this most sparsely settled part of Nigeria. The introduction of a share-cropping arrangement, under which the settler was to keep a third of the harvest while the remaining two-thirds went to the management, served as a further disincentive to hard work. Once the initial enthusiasm started to fade out there was nothing to induce the settlers to remain, since there was ample land back in their native villages to which they could return and cultivate in the traditional way. But this fact needs no emphasis in view of the experience of the Bamenda-Calabar-Cross River Resettlement Scheme, in which settlers from areas where farm land is scarce also backed out of the Scheme.

In spite of the high hopes expressed in the 1950 annual report of the Colonial Development Corporation, which together with the Nigerian Government formed the Niger Agricultural Project Limited, that the project was most satisfactory from every point of view, political, social and economic, it soon became clear that all was not well. As early as 1951 several settlers at the first village of Ndayako were already slack in doing their farmwork and in March 1952 a check revealed that only twenty-one out of seventy-eight farmers were in residence at Ndayako. The others had deserted their farms to cultivate other plots under traditional methods, and in that year the company had to take over about 290 acres of groundnuts fields for direct cultivation when the settlers failed to cultivate their allotments. In 1953 the Colonial Development Corporation withdrew formally

from the project, and the following year the company was liquidated. The project had failed.[2] Today Mokwa is no more than an experimental farm run by the Northern Nigeria Ministry of Agriculture.

COMMERCIAL SUGAR PRODUCTION AT BACITA

Nigeria's first commercial sugar factory which is located at Bacita near Jebba came into production in 1964. Its present capacity is about 30,000 tons of refined sugar per annum, but plans are afoot to double this figure by 1972. In 1963, however, the country consumed over 78,000 tons of sugar; hence the proposal to establish other sugar factories at Bida in this region as well as in the Anambra and Ofada areas of the East Central State and the Western State respectively.

The sugar manufactured at Bacita comes from the sugar-cane which is not a new crop in Nigeria. Rather, the crop has been grown on the fadamas of northern Nigeria for several decades. It is grown in fields which rarely exceed two acres and almost all of it is consumed by chewing the raw cane, excepting in the Zaria district where the production of brown sugar has been an

[1] See the Second Annual Report of the Northern Regional Development Board 1956/7 p. 14 Kaduna
[2] A detailed history of the Mokwa Agricultural Project is available in *The Niger Agricultural Project* by K. D. S. Balwin London 1957

Plate 25. Tending irrigated sugar cane at the Bacita Estate.

Plate 26. (a) River Niger at Rofia ferry point.

Plate 26. (b) Village of Shangunu.

important rural industry since the First World War (see page 163).

Although farmers in the immediate vicinity of the factory are being encouraged to grow cane for the refinery, it has never been the intention of the factory to rely on cane from such a source. A factory relying on peasant cane production, if it were to be feasible, would have been located in Zaria. But various considerations including transport cost and problems of phased growing ruled out an arrangement which might not have fared much better than the pioneer oil mill scheme in the oil palm belt. The factory, therefore, depends on cane from a 6,500-acre estate on which it is built.

The crop is grown under irrigation, water being supplied from the Niger River. For the first three miles, the water flows by gravity along a 143-feet wide and 32-feet deep canal at the end of which is a pumphouse with three electrically driven pumps, which raise the water to such a level that it can be distributed to the cane fields by gravity flow.

At Bacita, sugar-cane is planted between mid-November and April, while harvesting lasts from the end of November to May. There is therefore a great demand for labour between November and May after which the greater percentage of labourers are laid off. Although the estate is located in a very sparsely settled area, it does not experience difficulty in recruiting unskilled labour. Indeed the influx of job seekers to Bacita in 1964 was such that the Regional Government's instruction that Northerners should be given preference was rigidly applied. The fact that much of the period, November to May, is an off-season in the agricultural calendar of the Sudan may account for this availability of sufficient hands to work on the estate.

Sugar produced at Bacita is sold in bulk to breweries, soft-drinks factories and to the Tate and Lyle cubing factory at Ilorin where it is cubed and marketed. By-products of the refinery include bagasse which is the fibrous residue left after the cane has been crushed, and molasses which is the thick viscous scum left behind after the refining process. It is estimated that for each ton of refined sugar, one ton of dry bagasse and thirty gallons of molasses are produced. Currently the bagasse is used as a fuel but if,

and when, oil is used for firing the boilers the bagasse will provide an important source of raw material for the nearby paper factory at Jebba. Plans are in hand for the manufacture of rum, gin and industrial alcohol from the molasses which can also be made into excellent cattle feed.

THE NIGER DAMS PROJECT

The Niger Dams Project is the latest and most capitalized of the series of development projects which have been launched in the Middle Niger region since the end of the Second World War. It is a multi-purpose river development project which provides for the building of two major dams at Kainji on the Niger and at Shiroro Gorge on the Kaduna River as well as a subsidiary dam at Jebba. The first stage of the project, which consists of building a dam at Kainji (630 miles from the sea) with a power station of four 70 M.W. generating units initially, is nearing completion. Amongst other things this dam will provide full flood control in the Niger valley as far downstream as the Kaduna River confluence, and partial flood control from the Kaduna confluence to the Benue confluence at Lokoja. The significance of this fact is that the control of flooding of the fadamas will permit the expansion of agriculture on these fertile alluvial flood plains. A 500 square mile man-made lake will be created behind the Kainji dam and is expected to provide water for irrigation and will also serve as a major fishing ground, with an estimated catch of 10,000 tons per annum. The dam will also provide an alternative bridge across the Niger and thereby reduce the present congestion at the Jebba railway bridge, which is also used by road vehicles and cattle. Navigation through the dam will be made possible by a system of locks, while the regulation of the flow of the Niger below the dam site will considerably extend the existing shipping season.

When the demand for power increases, the installed capacity of the dam will be raised to 980 M.W. The planning authority calculates that this power potential will not be exhausted before 1980 and considers that work on the Jebba dam will not start till 1982. The Jebba Dam, which will be the second phase of the project, will add another 500 M.W. to the installed capacity and will provide a second bridge at Jebba as well as navigation control up to Lokoja. The third stage of the project will be the hydro-electric power scheme at Shiroro Gorge and when completed the total installed capacity of the Niger Dams will be 1,730 M.W.

It is possible to foresee drastic modifications in the over-all scheme as a result of the large crude-oil and natural gas reserves in the Niger Delta. Already natural gas is being used to generate electricity at Afam Power Station near Port Harcourt. The loss of the Eastern States markets which constitute one of the major electricity consuming zones in the country will result in a considerable drop in the demand for power from Kainji. This will have wide implications for a project which depends for its economic viability on the rapid growth in the demand for electricity. The £87·6 million Kainji hydro-electric power station, which is only the first stage of the project was completed in December 1968 and commissioned on February 15th, 1969.

Plate 27. The Kainji Dam.

Figure 53. The Kainji Resettlement Scheme. A shows the Pre-Settlement Villages while B shows the Resettlement Villages

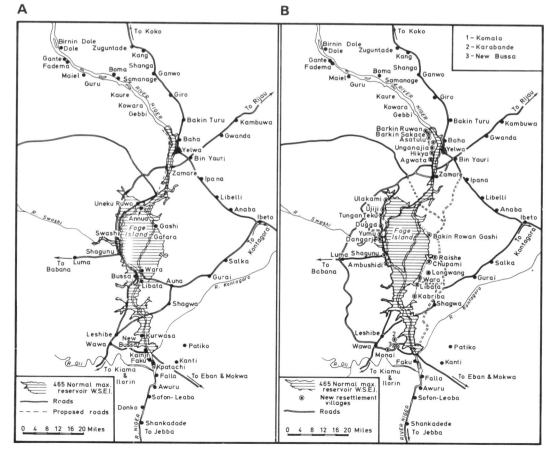

Plate 28. The Town of Old Bussa.

Plate 29. New Bussa.

THE KAINJI RESETTLEMENT SCHEME

The Kainji Lake, which will cover about 500 square miles, will drown several riverine settlements in the emirates of Bussa, Kontagora and Yauri. It will involve the resettlement of about 50,000 people of several ethnic groups including the Bussawa, the Lopawa, the Laru, the Gungawa and the Kamberi. In addition, vast areas of very fertile alluvial land will be submerged by the lake and alternative land will have to be provided for the resettled peasants whose interests deserve considerable attention, since the purpose of building the dam is to improve the general living standard of the country, including those of the peasants who have had to be evacuated.

Experience in other parts of tropical Africa including Ghana has shown that the best way of compensating displaced peasants is to help them to resettle on new sites. All the resettlement sites in the Kainji Lake Basin were selected in 1965 and the town of New Bussa, which is located near the dam site at a distance of about thirty miles from Bussa, was completed in the middle of 1966. This was the first town in Nigeria to be completely built up and supplied with basic amenities like water and light before the people moved in. It is well laid out and neatly built, but its problem is how the inhabitants will obtain a living. Unlike Bussa, this new town is several miles away from the Niger and yet the people are primarily fishing folks. The soils around New Bussa are also considered to be rather poor for farming and the spectre of a ghost town hangs over this settlement.

About half of the built-up area of Yelwa town will be submerged and will have to be rebuilt. The new village sites and roads are shown in Figure 53B. One practical problem in resettling the various ethnic groups has been that of keeping such water-conscious people as the Gungawas, who practise irrigation, and the main fishing groups close to the shores. Where their land has been completely submerged, this has necessitated a two-stage resettlement. Upland groups like the Kamberri have first had to be moved further inland so as to create room at the shores of the lake for the riverine folks.

Resettlement schemes often provide opportunities for introducing innovations aimed at improving agriculture and the rural economy in general. The need for such improvements is particularly felt in the case of resettlement connected with water development projects where they are regarded as part of the overall compensation for displaced peasants.

Works consulted and suggestions for further reading:

1. Angulu, U. A., 'Paddy Rice Cultivation in Bida Emirate' Unpublished manuscript Dept. of Geography, University of Ibadan
2. Baldwin, K. D. S., *The Niger Agricultural Project* London 1957
3. Federal Government Publication *Proposals for Dams on the Niger and Kaduna Rivers* Lagos 1960
4. Oguntoyinbo, J. S., 'Agroclimatic Problems and Commercial Cane Sugar Industry in Nigeria' *Nigerian Geographical Journal* Vol. 8 pp. 83–98 1965
5. Ojo, G. J. A., 'The Changing Patterns of Traditional Group Farming in Ekiti, North Eastern Yoruba Country' *Nigerian Geographical Journal* Vol. 6 p. 31 1963
6. Nadel, S. F., *A Black Byzantium: The Kingdom of Nupe in Nig[...]a* (Oxford Studies in African Affairs) London 195[...]
7. The Land Capability Survey Prepared for the Niger Dams Resettlement Authority. Soil Survey Bulletin No. 26. Institute for Agricultural Research Samaru 1964

13 The Jos Plateau

The Jos Plateau of Nigeria is one of those restricted areas of tropical Africa, where the systematic exploitation of its resources by modern methods has created an 'economic island', surrounded by vast areas with a poorly developed exchange economy. It is also a geological island of volcanic formation, and both its varied landforms and its tin-based economy are closely associated with the various phases of volcanic activity in the area. During the Fulani conquest of the surrounding plains in the early nineteenth century, the hills and steep slopes of the plateau provided adequate defence strongholds to which the indigenous pagan population retreated. It was the difficulty which the plateau country presented to mounted Fulani horsemen that saved the local pagans from political domination by the Fulanis, and this explains why the British arrived to find that this part of northern Nigeria was inhabited by small independent pagan groups, which were not organized into large states. At the beginning of this century therefore the Jos Plateau was also a cultural island surrounded by Fulani-dominated societies, in which Islam was imposed as the state religion. But during the past fifty years tin mining and the associated influx of stranger elements to the mines have brought about remarkable changes in the economy and aspects of the local society. Tin-mining landscapes, such as that shown in Figure 58, demonstrate clearly the transformation which has also taken place in the physical landscape of certain districts during this period.

GEOLOGICAL HISTORY AND CHARACTERISTIC LANDFORMS

The Jos Plateau is probably the most striking morphological feature in Nigeria. It is an erosion relic, which covers an area of about 3,000 square miles, at a general level of about 4,200 feet above sea level and is surrounded by high plains with altitudes ranging from 2,000 to 3,000 feet above sea level (Figure 54). Apart from the southern margin which is both very steep and rather regular in outline, the plateau is bordered by an irregular margin with gentle slopes. The highest surface of the plateau occurs in the surroundings of Ngell and Bukuru, from where the headwaters of rivers flowing into Lake Chad, the Niger, the Benue and the Gongola radiate approximately north, west, south and east respectively. The Ngell-Bukuru neighbourhood therefore constitutes the hydrological centre of Nigeria. This watershed presents a rather interesting aspect in that there are no striking relief features like high ridges or rocky mountains which feature at water divides. Rather the picture presented is one of an undulating, swampy plain diversified by a few broken ridges and low granitic

inselbergs. These headwaters have, however, carved out narrow rocky valleys on the plateau surface and their descent to the surrounding plains is marked by picturesque waterfalls and narrow gorges, which are fast cutting back into the plateau itself.

This region has a unique but simple geological history, and it is necessary to grasp the main events of this history if we are to interpret correctly the various landforms that are to be found on the surface of the plateau. Two of the three hill types that occur on the plateau are closely associated with two distinct phases of volcanic activity in the area. Details of this history have also been important in helping to locate the major concentrations of tin deposits in the area. It is known, for example, that some of the most important tin deposits are to be found at the bottom of pre-Fluvio-Volcanic river valleys, where they were re-concentrated and subsequently buried by lavas of the Fluvio-Volcanic series; and not at the primary sources where the tin occurs as stock works or small veins in the Younger Granite.

In pre-cretaceous times the area now occupied by the Jos Plateau consisted of rocks of the Basement Complex, Archean gneisses and schists of igneous and metamorphic

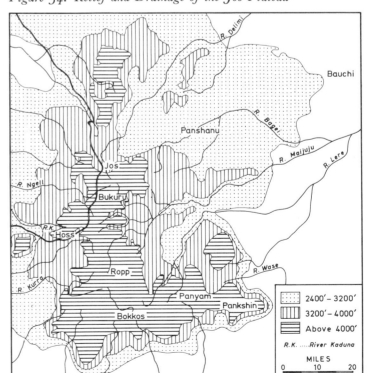

Figure 54. Relief and Drainage of the Jos Plateau

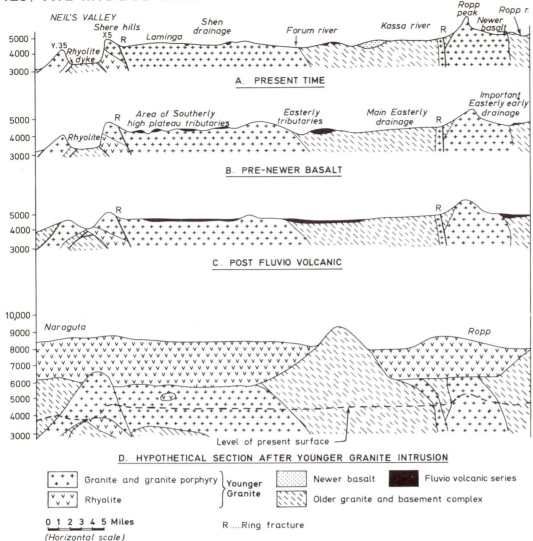

Figure 55. Geological History of the Jos Plateau

origin, which outcrop over a large part of northern Nigeria. Sometimes in the early cretaceous times a new phase of volcanic activity occurred, resulting in an extensive invasion of the Basement rocks by rhyolites of the Younger Granite series, accompanied and followed by the intrusion of porphyries of the same series. The geology of the region at this time was of the general form shown in Figure 55D; and it was at this stage that tin veins and stockworks were intruded. The land surface was then reduced in elevation during a long period of erosion, which removed over two thousand feet of rock and produced a fairly level surface drained by sluggish rivers which deposited sediments over wide areas. It was during this period that much tin-bearing rock was eroded and the cassiterite deposited in the valleys. During the mid-tertiary period more volcanic activity occurred, giving rise to great floods of basalt which flowed down existing river valleys and buried the alluvial tin gravels. This series which consists of a lower or fluvial part of sands, grits and variegated clays and an upper or volcanic layer of basalt is called the Fluvio-Volcanic series. The position occupied by the series at that time is shown in Figure 55C.

It resulted in a considerable reduction of the local relief. The estimated thickness of the succession of sands, clays and basalts which comprise the series is 200 to 300 feet and this suggests that all but the highest elevations on the plateau surface were submerged.

The post-volcanic basalt surface was then exposed to a long period of erosion and intense chemical weathering, when the basalt was deeply dissected and decomposed to clay, while leached-out iron oxides were redeposited as bands of ironstone or laterites. This post-Fluvio-Volcanic erosion cycle appears to have been preceded by localized uplift, hence the development of more rapid streams in place of the sluggish rivers of pre-Fluvio-Volcanic times. The level of the land surface was reduced as much as 500 feet in some localities, and in many parts of the plateau all that is left of this basalt surface is a large number of flat-topped laterite-capped hills. It is this hard capping of indurated ironstone that explains the character and the ability of these hills to withstand rapid denudation.

During the period extending from late tertiary to recent times there was another phase of volcanic eruption in which extensive flows of basalts—the New Basalts—filled

large areas of the post-Fluvio-Volcanic river valleys. These recently extinct volcanic cones form the third type of hill masses on the plateau and the more recent ones are preserved in a perfectly good state at Panyam, Vom and Miango. The craters of these volcanoes are equally well preserved and some of them contain water while a large number have since been breached but, as at Panyam, the former lake level is clearly marked in the crater.

The lower courses of post-Fluvio-Volcanic river valleys were blocked by lava from this last phase of volcanic activity and many of the original streams were forced to take new courses. The implications of this for tin mining include the necessity to reconstruct the courses of these old valleys, along which alluvial tinstone was reconcentrated.

Investigations over the years have confirmed that the major concentrations of alluvial tin within modern valleys are greatly influenced by the river gradient; the major deposits occurring where the gradients average between twenty-five to seventy-five feet per mile. Gradients greater than this tend to prevent the deposition of tin, while lesser gradients make for very slow movement of sand and thereby inhibits effective concentration of tin.

Plate 30. Gurara Falls. The Jos Plateau abound in waterfalls some of which have been harnessed to provide power for the local tin mining industry.

Plate 31. Rocky landscape on the Jos Plateau.

The result is that the amount of sand present is so high that it is not economical to work such tin deposits.

CLIMATE, VEGETATION AND SOILS

The climate is much more pleasant than that of the surrounding plains, and Jos town has come to be regarded as a holiday and health resort for European nationals working in Nigeria. The most significant factor in this respect is certainly the comparatively low relative humidity, which is less than twenty-five per cent between November and March, that is during the dry season when the dessicating harmattan blows. The weather at this time of the year is very windy and dry, and may become rather trying to Nigerians from the coastal areas. The open nature of the plateau reinforces the wind speed, while the dry and bare ground provides considerable dust particles which intensifies the hazy character of the harmattan.

As a result of the high elevation of the plateau average annual temperatures are lower than in the surrounding plains, as well as in places like Enugu and Lagos which are much further south and nearer to the sea. The average temperatures at Jos for example are 8° F. lower than at Lagos. Rainfall figures for the plateau also show the effect of local relief, the mean annual rainfall of fifty inches for Jos being considerably higher than that of the neighbouring plains.

Of more importance to mining and agriculture is the seasonal distribution of the rainfall. About ninety per cent of the rain falls in the six months between April and October, the wettest months being July and August. The rain comes in thunderstorms of high intensity, particularly at the beginning and towards the end of the rainy season. The distribution of the rainfall during any single storm is usually very irregular. Grove has recorded that during one storm in September 3·5 inches were recorded at Jos Airport in four hours, while the gauge at Shen, six miles away, registered 1·8 inches and that at Sabon Gida only 0·8 inches. This characteristic is however not peculiar to Jos, but is also common in places like Ibadan where similar irregularities have occurred within the city.

The present day vegetation of the plateau is largely a product of centuries of destructive exploitation of the original woodland, which is now replaced by open grasslands. Considerable destruction of woodland occurred in early times when there was great demand for charcoal by the local iron industry, which was based on the smelting of lateritic iron ore. But it was in the early part of this century that the clearance of woodland was intensified,

partly to meet the demands of the tin industry and the large influx of immigrants attracted by the industry, and partly as a result of the retreat of the frontiers of settlement from the hills to the plains, following the pacification of the area. In the centre of Jos Division, that is in the districts of Kuru, Gyel and Kwon, where almost every tree has been felled, the vegetation consists only of grass except near some villages where thick hedges of cactus (*Euphorbia Kamerunica*) have been planted around the household farms or compoundlands. Small groves of *Male* and *Atilis* (*Canarium*) are also found around some villages but the main farmlands are completely devoid of trees, and so are the flat-topped lateritic hills. Fringing woodlands and bamboo thickets may still be found along the valleys of the more isolated streams, and these relics of vegetation confirm the existence in the past of a vegetation of extensive savanna woodland.

Trees planted around many homesteads, as well as natural regeneration in the Naraguta Forest Reserve and scattered 'plantations' marked in the new 1:50,000 sheets of this region, illustrate that the plateau can still support dense woodland vegetation. This is fortunate in view of the acute shortage of fuel which has resulted in the use of dried cow dung as fuel, thus depriving the soil of farmyard manure. The need for large fuel plantations has been recognized, but such plantations will have to compete for land with grazing and farmland. This explains why the few existing wood plantations are restricted to hill areas like Forum Hills and Kuru Hills, which are not suitable for cultivation. Fuel plantations have also been established on soils destroyed by soil erosion.

Imperata grass (speargrass) predominates in new fallows, but may be partially replaced by *Pennisetum pedicallatum* (*kasuwa*) and *Hyparrhenia spp.* (*yama*). If the land remains uncultivated for many years, the cover which eventually emerges is a fire climax which consists of tall savanna grasses in which *Hyparrhenia*, *Andropogon gayanus* and *Heteropogon* predominate. These grasses come up at the end of the dry season and have remarkable powers of re-growth after the annual bush-burning. They provide excellent fodder when young and are also used for thatching.

In many parts of the Jos Plateau the soils are closely related to the topography as well as to the parent material of which a wide range exists. Climate is also an important factor in the formation of older soils which occur in fairly level areas. The marked dry season and the open nature of the landscape provide suitable conditions for the development of lateritic soils which are very common on the plateau surface.

Skeletal soils occur at the foot of rocky hills or along

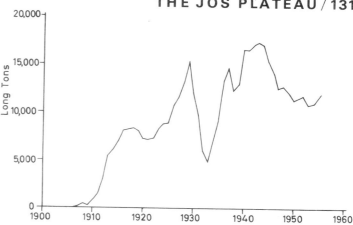

Figure 56. Tin Production in the Jos Plateau up to 1955

narrow river valleys and represent the earliest stage in soil formation from materials weathered from granite, schists and gneisses. The most widespread type is developed on detritus from granitic rocks and is commonly found in the Jos-Bukuru Hills as well as in the Hoss-Vom Hills and in the area south of Pankshin. At the surface, this reddish-grey and rather shallow soil is composed of coarse sand but the clay and silt content increases with depth. In spite of their shallow depth and coarseness, skeletal soils are heavily cultivated, largely because they occur at the site of pagan settlements which are usually built close to rock outcrops, which serve as shelter from winds and provide firm foundation for huts.

Skeletal soils derived from schists and gneisses are more restricted in occurrence, but they are less coarse and more fertile than those derived from granite. This is confirmed by the fact that they have produced good crops for three to four years without being manured or fallowed. All skeletal soils have the advantage of being well drained, except where the rock is close to the surface.

At a lower level and on gentler and less rocky slopes skeletal soils give way to colluvial soils which may be coarse or fine in texture, although the most coarse colluvial soil is finer textured than skeletal soils. Fine colluvial soil predominates in the chief mining areas including Bukuru and Barakin Ladi as well as in the wider river valleys. Colluvial soils are generally not well-drained and are given to sheet erosion, particularly near the streams, where the gentle slopes have been bared by overgrazing. The subsoil is clayey and hardens on exposure to form concretionary soil. Numerous gullies have developed along footpaths over these soils.

Soils derived from the Newer Basalts vary considerably according to the depth and rate of weathering. They are dark, reddish-brown or chocolate in colour and are well drained. In most areas including Panyam, Vom and Miango, these volcanic soils are heavily farmed and rarely lie fallow. Poorly drained basalt soils occur in certain tracts and although they are also fertile, high ridges are necessary if good crops of *acha* and *dauro* are to be obtained.

Sandy-loams which may be red or reddish-brown in colour predominate in areas of the Basement Complex. They are very deep soils and are suitable for guinea corn, beans and sweet potatoes.

TIN MINING ON THE JOS PLATEAU

The mining and smelting of tin, like the smelting of iron by primitive methods were known to the people of the Jos Plateau and surrounding districts long before the British occupation of Nigeria. Indeed, the search for the source of tin in 1902 by the Mining Department of the Niger Company started after some European merchants had seen Hausa traders trading in tin metal at Ibi on the Benue. The tin found with these traders came from local furnaces constructed and operated by Hausa smelters at Liruien Delma and Liruien Kano. The molten tin was cast in small moulds, made of damp ashes pressed around a number of straws set parallel to each other. Rods of tin produced from this process were usually fourteen inches long, with diameters varying from 0·04 to 0·08 of an inch and were traded in bundles of one hundred which cost about one shilling and three-pence.[1]

In 1904 the occurrence of workable deposits of tin on the plateau was proved and mining started almost immediately. Production was restricted since mining was carried on by hand, but the greatest problem facing the industry during its first decade was that access to the deposits was made very difficult by the pagan peoples of the plateau area. The tin was carried as head-loads to Loko, a port on the Benue River. It took about twelve days to travel the distance of 200 miles between the mines and the port, where tin was loaded into barges to be taken to Forcados for shipment to Liverpool. The cost of transporting tin to the coast in this way was twenty-nine pounds ten shillings a ton and as much as thirty-five days was required to deliver the tin to Forcados. Transportation improved considerably with the opening in 1911 of the Baro rail route and became much better with the opening of a direct line from the minefield to Port Harcourt, the port of export. The outlet of Nigerian tin has since changed from the delta ports of Forcados and Burutu to Port Harcourt and Lagos.[2]

Figure 56 shows the progress in the annual production of tin since 1905. The major fluctuations indicated in the graph reflect events outside Nigeria. The effect of the depression of the early 1930s is reflected in the sharp fall in production just as the sudden rise in production during the war years (1939–45) coincides with a period when Nigerian

[1] Anon. 'Tin Mining in Nigeria' *Nigeria Trade Journal* Vol. II No. 2 pp. 20–3 1954
[2] Ogundana, B., 'Changing Port Outlets of Nigeria's Export Commodities' *Nigerian Geographical Journal* Vol. 9 p. 37 1966

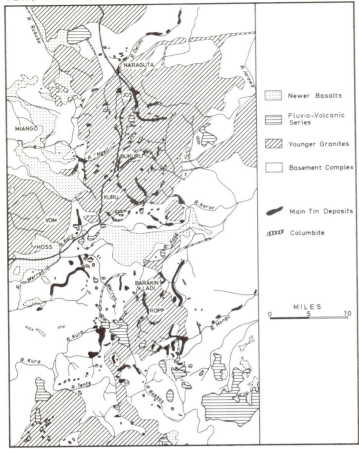

Figure 57. Geology and Minerals of the Plateau Tinfields

Figure 58. A Tin Mining Landscape around Bukuru

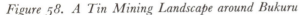

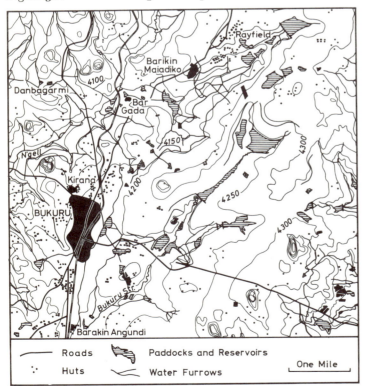

tin was placed at a premium as a result of the loss to the Western powers of the tin resources of Malaya. Some of the factors which explain the steady decrease in production since the end of the war include greater competition by other producers, higher production costs, in spite of the relatively cheap wages and the fact that post-war exploitation has been planned as against rapid working of easily worked deposits which featured during the war years.

Most of the tin and the columbite deposits which occur with it are alluvial deposits which are found in small, locally mineralized zones in the Younger Granite formation (Figure 57). Some of the deposits are in or near existing river beds, and others, which are away from existing water courses, lie in previous river beds which have been overlaid with lava flow. The extraction of the tin which occurs here as a heavy dark-coloured sand is carried out in two stages. The first stage involves earth moving in order to get at the tin, which is washed in water and allowed to settle out, while the second stage is that of concentrating the ores to 'shipping grade' which contains up to seventy-two per cent pure tin.

The tin is worked mainly by the open-cast, hand-paddocking method, but the use of hydro-turbine gravel pumps and heavy draglines is also important. Factors affecting the choice of method include capital, the nature and size of the deposits, availability of water, the cost of labour and accessibility to power lines. In the past tributing, a form of free-lance mining in which independent labourers work for a company and are paid by results, was common. The company built the camp in which the tributors lived and provided a number of salaried supervisory staff to watch the operations. But tributors tended to work the richer parts of the ground, leaving low-grade ground not only unworked, but covered with waste dumps. In this way, many small leases were abandoned after the extraction of much less ore than could have been obtained by systematic working. Today, most of the tin is recovered by mechanical methods powered by electricity generated from local hydro-electric power stations.

Figure 58 shows a tin-mining landscape near Bukuru, the most striking features of which consist of the system of artificial drainage made up of paddocks and water furrows. Dams built to conserve water in reservoirs as well as paddocks excavated in the course of mining, provide sufficient water to enable mining to be carried out even during the dry season. These paddocks and reservoirs, which are also used for watering stock and for irrigation as well as for rearing fish, have converted this part of the Jos Plateau into a 'Lake District'. The other man-made features of the landscape are the large mounds of mining dumps of overburden excavated from the mines. After many years, some grass may grow on these mounds and when this happens, they give the impression of being erosional survivals. Some of these mounds may disappear in future if the government policy governing re-soiling of disturbed land is carried out. This policy stipulates that a mining company shall, when required to do so, remove and stack the top soil and after mining, fill up, level and drain open-cast excavations; and that the government will be responsible for the care of the top-soil while stacked and for its subsequent replacement.

At this point it is proper to examine briefly the claim that tin mining has deprived many indigenous people of farmland, and that it has contributed directly and indirectly to the menace of soil erosion on the plateau. The position today is that no more than fifty square miles (out of the total area of about 3,000 square miles) of the plateau has been affected by mining. Since mining in certain areas is carried out in land which is of little value to the local farmers, the actual extent of land lost to agricultural use is much less. It is true, however, that in some localities, tin mining has led to a decline in soil fertility and has tended to increase susceptibility to soil erosion. At the same time, employment of the local people as labourers in the mines has helped to relieve pressure of population in very densely populated areas.

A tin-smelting plant with two furnaces, each capable of smelting twenty tons of tin per day, has been in operation since January 1962, and the bulk of the metal is now exported in its pure form. Production figures have showed considerable fluctuation during the last fifteen years. In 1952 and 1953, the total export of tin was 11,164 tons and 11,942 tons respectively, valued at £8·46 million and £8·55 million. Ten years later in 1963 the quantity exported was only 9,830 tons valued at £9 million and a year later it had increased by 7·6 per cent to 10,577 tons while the value went up by thirty-nine per cent to £12·5 million. One fact which emerges from this array of figures is that the price of tin has been rising in recent years. But this has not always been the case during the fifteen-year period under consideration. In February 1951, for instance the world price for tin reached the unprecedented height of £1,600 a ton but dropped to £600 per ton in July and August 1953. The average price in 1965 was about £1,368 per ton.

Apart from direct revenue benefits from rents on mining land, fees for licenses and royalties, the country benefits from tin mining in many other ways. It offers employment opportunities to both skilled and unskilled labour, while the government also benefits indirectly from the earnings of the railway which transports the tin to the port of export.

Reserve estimates suggest that at the present rate of production, the life of the minefield will expire about 1980. It is, however, possible that, as in the past, improved methods of mining may extend the expected life.

BY-PRODUCTS OF THE TIN-MINING INDUSTRY

Columbite, the ore of niobium, is the chief by-product of the tin-mining industry and is found associated with tin in the alluvial deposits and also within certain pegmatites. The mineral also occurs in the Younger Granites as a primary constituent, when it is usually associated with varying proportions of the tantalum-bearing mineral, tantalite.

Niobium, which is produced from columbite, is a rare element with high resistance to corrosion, and is used as a carbide stabilizer in the preparation of stainless steel for manufacturing gas turbines. Nigeria produces over ninety-five per cent of the world's present total output. Before the war, the mineral was an unwanted by-product of tin and was left on the waste dumps of the tin mines. War-time demand led to a peak output of 1,000 tons in 1944, and when in 1953 columbite prices rose to £3,000 per ton (at a time when the price of tin was only £600 per ton) the waste dumps were worked for columbite. In 1954 and 1955 about 3,000 tons of columbite valued at £5 million were exported. Since then, the price has been on the decline, and in 1961 the value of the 1,800 tons exported was £1·2 million. A few companies are now working primarily for columbite, the remaining ore being obtained as a by-product of tin mining.

Another by-product of the tin-mining industry is zircon, a mineral used in the manufacture of refractory materials. In the last few years between 1,000 and 1,500 tons of this mineral have been separated every year. Thorium concentrates, consisting of the minerals thorite, monazite and radioactive zircon are also being separated as by-products of the tin- and columbite-mining industries. The present-day demand for thorium is rather limited but it is envisaged that the mineral may eventually form an important source of atomic energy.

Other by-products have been recovered from tin and columbite mining on the Jos Plateau but the last to claim our attention is tantalite, which is another rare mineral. In the Jos Plateau it occurs in pegmatite veins. Peak production was in the war years, when twelve tons were produced in 1944 and thirteen tons in 1945. Production in recent years has rarely exceeded two tons. All the ore goes to the United States where it is used for manufacturing electrodes, tantalum carbide for tools and in the production of special steels for making surgical and dental instruments.

EFFECTS OF MINING ON THE POPULATION

The most important effect of mining on the local population has been the influx of Nigerian strangers—Ibos, Hausas and Yorubas—to the plateau. There is also a large concentration of European population. It is these strangers, both Nigerian and foreign, who make up the urban population of the two plateau towns of Jos and Bukuru, while neighbouring suburban market centres such as Fusan Hausawa are populated largely by Hausa traders.

Many of the Nigerian strangers work on the mines, while a large number are also engaged in providing various services for the African as well as expatriate mining population. Imported consumer goods are distributed in retail stores and in the open markets through the agency of this secondary population, who also handle the trade in foodstuffs like yams and garri, which are in great demand by Ibo and Yoruba migrants. During the 1952 census forty-four per cent of the population of Jos Division was made up of stranger elements. The sex ratio of 1,094 males to 1,000 females confirms the migrant character of the population of the division.

Over one-third of the Nigerian strangers were Hausa traders and mine-workers. We may recall here that straw tin was first found in the hands of Hausa traders at Ibi, and today these traders handle the bulk of the illegal trade in tin. The large size of a population with a relatively high earning-power has created a growing market for Fulani cattle milk and milk products. This is one reason for the recent increase of Fulani cattlemen on this fly-free high plain. At the same time, the dependence of Nigerian strangers on locally produced food is minimal, since much of the food that they consume is imported from the forest belt and from other parts of northern Nigeria. The large increase of population on the plateau cannot therefore be said to have aggravated the pressure on farmland, except that soil impoverishment and soil erosion induced by overgrazing have rendered some land unsuitable for cropping.

The view that tin mining has not greatly affected the pagan's occupational structure is no longer tenable. Amongst other things, the new condition of things has brought down many pagans from their hill outposts to the plains. Many of them provide unskilled labour in the mines, though the response of the local farmer to increased market opportunities, created by the increase in the secondary population, has been slow. Indeed the economies of certain local communities have become so dependent on the mines that considerable problems will be created when mining comes to an end. It has also been suggested that the pagan peasant appears to be better off on his farm than if he were to work continuously in the mines. This view is, however, based on the analysis of questionable data, and tends to ignore the fact that the mine-worker, whose farm is being looked after by his wife or a relative, will still be much better off than the full-time farmer.

FARMING IN THE JOS PLATEAU

Farming methods adopted by the pagan[1] population of this region have undergone remarkable changes during the last fifty years. In the pre-colonial period and during the early part of this century, many pagans lived on hills, the slopes of which were cultivated. With rather primitive instruments, these pagans were able to construct and maintain terraces on the hill slopes so as to prevent soil erosion. These terraces were cultivated very intensively, a practice made possible by the use of household manure. This was a remarkable adaptation to their environment. But in recent years the pagans have abandoned the hills to farm on the plains, where they adopt the wasteful method of shifting cultivation, since there is more farmland on the plains.

The farming economy of the pagans is based on the collective cultivation, by a number of households, of such staple grain crops as acha (*Digitaria excelsis*) and millet, and root crops such as yams and cocoyams which are planted in more humid tracts, especially along the stream banks. The traditional staple and the most widely cultivated crop is acha or hungry rice of which there are several varieties. In parts of the plateau such as the area around the craters of Panyam, where extensive tracts of rich soil occur, guinea corn, maize and millet replace acha as the main crops. Green vegetables, including beans are cultivated in compound gardens.

Crops which have been introduced in recent years include cassava, potatoes and lettuce, the last two of which are in response to the needs of the urban population of Jos and Bukuru. These two centres have always had a large European population which provides a steady market for potatoes, but it was during the war years when potato supplies from abroad were erratic that potato cultivation on the plateau started on a considerable scale. Today both the indigenous pagans as well as Hausas and settled Fulanis are being encouraged to cultivate potatoes,

---

[1] The term 'pagan' is used to describe Nigerians whose religion is not Christianity or Islam.

which are also in demand by the Europeanized African population of the southern towns.

Traditionally, farming is organized and directed by the head of each compound. Much of the land cultivated in any one year is directly under the control of the compound head, who also takes charge of the common granary. Members of the household also have small plots allocated to them personally, but they are all entitled to rations from the central barn when their individual supplies are exhausted. Supplies of grain for making beer, which is a favourite drink amongst the plateau pagans, also come from the central granary. In recent years, this system of farming, which tends to make the younger generation economically dependent on the heads of compounds, has undergone drastic changes in some areas. Communal land tenure is being replaced by individual ownership and buying and leasing of land is now commonplace. Earning from the tin mines is certainly responsible for the present economic independence of the younger generation and the consequent break-down of the collective farming system.

The tendency to build isolated huts in distant farmlands is a recent development, which has been made possible by the rapid replacement of communal land tenure systems by that of individual land-holding. This develop-

Plate 32. Cactus lined footpath near Kuru. In parts of the Jos Plateau the cactus is used as a fence around compounds, and is planted along field boundaries.

Plate 33. Weathered Inselbergs at Kuru. Jos Plateau.

ment deserves encouragement since it enables the farmer to live on his farm, thereby reducing the time wasted in travelling to the farm, as well as making available household manure for the land.

Farmland in such areas as Gyel, Zawan and Vom is considered inadequate to meet local farming needs. A land use survey carried out in 1943 revealed that in the territory of Gyel village one-fifth of the land was rocky or barren and that about six per cent had been rendered unfit for cultivation by mining. Most of the remaining land was cultivable but being of low fertility required a long fallow period. Increasing population and the consequent rise in the demand for farmland had, however, led to much reduced fallows and soil impoverishment. This is one reason why the pagans of Vom, Gyel and other districts have been obliged to rent land from neighbouring villages on the plateau or to descend to cultivate the lower plains of the Benue valley.

The present situation in which the population of this region depends largely on foodstuffs coming in from other parts of the country is undesirable and could create considerable problems of food-shortage if mining suddenly comes to an end. Indeed the situation in October 1966, when, as a result of the killing of Ibos and the evacuation of about 10,000 surviving Ibos to eastern Nigeria, the economy of Jos came to a sudden halt, is a pointer in this direction. The owners of lorries carrying food, as well as the distributors and many potential consumers left with the refugees; hence the sudden shortage in the supply of essential foodstuff. For such reasons, there is a great need to increase food production on the plateau. The fact that the plateau does not produce export crops emphasizes the importance of increased food production, since tin mining will certainly come to an end sooner or later.

THE CATTLE-OWNING FULANI OF THE JOS PLATEAU

The Jos Plateau is said to provide the finest grazing in northern Nigeria. It is free from tsetse infestation, it has adequate water supplies and there are vast areas of good pastures. This region has therefore proved very attractive to the ubiquitous Fulani pastoralists. But Fulani penetration into the plateau dates from the establishment of British rule because the pagan tribes of this region had still not been subjugated when the British arrived. At first the Fulani cattle herders came for only a part of the year, the dry season, but over the years an increasing number of Fulanis have decided to remain permanently on the plateau.

Official thinking is in support of encouraging the sedenterization of the Fulanis in the hope that such settlers could be profitably used to initiate schemes of mixed farming in the region. Amongst other things, mixed farming on a large scale will go a long way to increasing food production on the plateau, while the sedenterization of the Fulanis will also ensure a regular supply of milk to the Vom creamery. At present, this factory is obliged to close down for a part of the year, when some of the cattle migrate to distant grazing areas.

The traditional attitude of the local pagan population has always remained one of apprehensive hostility to the Fulanis, who raided them for slaves in the past. Many pagan farmers have suffered loss of crops as a result of the tramplings of Fulani cattle, and naturally, they resent this.

Remarkable changes have, however, taken place in recent years. In order to cater adequately for the increasing number of cattle on the plateau and to arrest soil impoverishment, serious thought has been given to establishing a close liaison between the pagans and the Fulanis. One proposal, which has since been tried, has been the establishment of co-operative farming groups amongst the pagans who, in a field rotation agreed with the Fulanis, arrange to farm the kraal sites which the Fulanis have used. But this arrangement is only seen as a step to an eventual integration of arable and stock farming under the same individual.

Another significant change is that many Fulanis have settled down to cultivate the land. Apart from supplying milk to the urban population and the Vom creamery, these settled Fulanis now grow crops of millet and guinea corn for their domestic use. They have also been encouraged, along with the pagans and Hausa settlers, to grow potatoes as a cash crop to be sold in Jos and other main towns in the country.

THE DEVELOPMENT AND PROBLEMS OF THE PLATEAU DAIRY INDUSTRY

Like many other industrial enterprises in the developing countries of the world, the plateau dairy industry[1] started as an emergency measure to provide fresh butter locally at a time when supplies would be held up by the Second World War. Before this time the only commercial outlet for surplus milk produced by the Fulani cattle-rearers consisted of daily sales of milk to the local population, and the sale of clarified butter fat (ghee) to commercial

[1] Based on 'The Dairy Industry in Plateau Province' *Nigeria Trade Journal* Vol. VIII No. 1 pp. 6–9

firms who, in 1938, exported 1,400 tons of clarified butter fat to Britain. But during the war years, the shipping difficulties which prevented the import of fresh butter, also prevented the export of clarified butter fat, thus denying the Fulani a useful outlet for their surplus milk. The new dairy scheme benefited from this development in that it was ensured an adequate supply of milk, while the Fulanis welcomed the alternative outlet which the industry provided for their surplus. But there were many difficulties in organizing the collection of this surplus.

The dairy scheme was initiated by officers of the Veterinary Department who made it a success right from the start. Production at the end of the first year was 36,760 pounds of butter, and the opening of another centre at Miango, that is in addition to the main centre at Vom, raised production during the second year to 168,000 pounds. In 1942 350,000 pounds of butter were produced in addition to 13,000 pounds of cheese and several tons of clarified butter fat for cooking. This initial success encouraged the building of a second factory at Kumbul in Pankshin Division. In the late 1950's these two factories were pulled down and replaced by a new factory equipped with modern machinery, a development made possible by the transfer of the enterprise to the Northern Regional Development Corporation. In addition to butter and cheese, dried skimmed milk is also produced for distribution, through the Ministry of Health, to children whose diet is deficient in protein. The production of dried milk started in 1958 and was made possible by a joint effort of the Northern Nigeria Government and UNICEF to tackle the increasing number of cases of *Kwashiorkor*, a disease caused by malnutrition, in northern Nigeria.

Some of the early problems of the industry have since been overcome, but others have still to be solved, while new ones have arisen. One of the earliest difficulties was that the milk supplied was rarely fresh because even though the local climate is relatively cool, the milk turns sour readily. The common practice of adding impure water to milk before sales also detracted much from the quality of the produce. Considerable difficulty was also caused by seasonal variation in the supply of milk arising from the fact that the Fulanis have different grazing areas for the wet season and the dry season. The present practice, whereby the factory gets its supply of cream from contractors, has gone a long way to solving these earlier problems. Today the main problem facing the plateau dairy industry is how to compete with imported butter, which is of better quality.

Works consulted and suggestions for further reading:

1. Grove, A. T., 'Land Use and Soil Conservation on the Jos Plateau' *Geological Survey of Nigeria* No. 22 Kaduna 1952
2. Hodder, B. W., 'Tin Mining on the Jos Plateau of Nigeria' *Economic Geography* No. 35 pp. 109–22 1959
3. Pugh, J. C., 'The Volcanoes of Nigeria' *Nigerian Geographical Journal* No. 2 pp. 26–36 1958
4. Sassoon, H., 'Birom Smithing' *Nigeria Magazine* No. 74 pp. 25–31 1962
5. Anon. 'The Dairy Industry in Plateau Province' *Nigeria Trade Journal* No. 8 pp. 6–9 1960
6. Anon. 'Tin Mining in Nigeria' *Nigeria Trade Journal* No. 2 pp. 20–3 1954

14 The Benue Valley

Unlike other major African rivers including the Niger River, the Benue flows through a valley which is free from rapids and waterfalls. The river owes this uniqueness to the fact that throughout its 500 miles below Yola, it flows through sedimentary rocks. Navigation is therefore possible throughout its course in Nigeria except in the dry season, when the water level is so low that its sandy beds are exposed at long intervals. Occasionally, the occurence of rocky banks (Figure 59) gives rise to sharp bends which hamper easy navigation.

In a study of the Benue drainage basin, published about ten years ago under the misleading title of 'The Benue Valley', A. T. Grove recognized four physiographic divisions within the basin. One of these divisions was designated the Valley Floor Plains and is considered here to be the only part of the Benue basin which can properly be referred to as the Benue valley. So defined, the Benue valley covers an area of over 22,000 square miles in Nigeria,[1] and is made up of two physiographic divisions, the river and its flood plains, and the lowland areas which lie above flood levels.

THE BENUE AND ITS FLOOD PLAINS

The Benue, which rises from the Adamawa Highlands in the western Cameroons, is the largest tributary of the Niger which it meets at Lokoja. It enters Nigeria a few miles east of Yola, after meandering through a vast but sparsely cultivated flood plain which opens out from a width of two miles at Garua to six miles at the Faro confluence. Below this confluence, the river enters Nigeria and passes through the Wuro Boki Village Flats, where the channel bifurcates into shallow crossings. At Dasin Hausa, where sandstone rocks on the south side of the river approach the Bagele Hills, the flood plain narrows to 4,000 feet, a narrowing which has already been surveyed and selected as a site for the proposed Yola Dam. Cultivation in this part of the valley is almost restricted to the south side, since the Bagele Hills, which continue right to the north bank, are still wooded.

Sandbanks, straight high-water shores and a few meandering channels with islands characterize the forty-mile stretch between Yola and Numan. Numerous fishing villages built on natural ridges rising above high-water level populate this grass covered flood plain. In some areas, the villages are built on high water-free sites constructed by the people, who through building new huts on the ruins of older dwellings often succeed, after a few generations, in raising a former marshy site above floodwater level. The Ndom villages near Numan are good examples of such settlements.

The Gongola, which is the main tributary of the Benue

[1] The total area drained by the Benue is 130,000 square miles, of which 90,000 are within Nigeria.

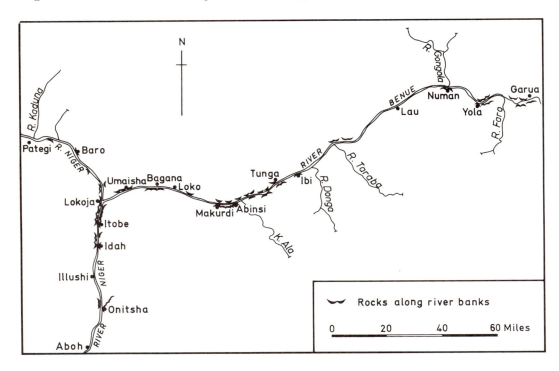

Figure 59. Rocks along the Benue and Lower Niger Valley

from the north, joins the river opposite the town of Numan which is built on a high ground overlooking the left bank of the Benue. The stretch between Numan and Lau has fairly straight banks, particularly on the north bank which is closely followed by a natural levee, along which run footpaths linking such riverine settlements as Yumburu, Kabawa and Jen. North of this levee, occurs an extensive flood plain with many lakes, some of which dry up during the dry season. The river bed itself is plagued by rapidly-changing shoals which are difficult to cross. Along this stretch the fishing villages are rarely permanent because of the instability of the river channel which may shift to such an extent that a fishing settlement, formerly located near the river, may be left at a distance of up to a mile from the new channel. Whole settlements have also been destroyed by bank erosion, but such villages as Jen have maintained their sites for over one hundred years, in spite of the fact that the river bed has since shifted a considerable distance away from the settlement.

Lau may be regarded as the end of the upper reaches of the Benue, which is characterized by sudden rises and falls in the river level. Below Lau the effect of the inter-mittent rainfall is less pronounced, being evened out by the storage capacity of the river and flood plains, and by the increasing number of tributaries which rise from well watered highland areas. It is below this town that the Benue is fed by three of its largest tributaries—the Taraba, Donga and Katsina Ala. The river changes considerably between Lau and Amar. Its channel becomes deeper and the Benue Plain, which is rather narrow at Lau, opens out as the Great Plain of Muri in the heart of which stands the village of Amar. The tree density increases so much that near Amar the trees provide an effective screen between the river and its flood plains. Ibi is also situated in the heart of the Muri Plain, the northern part of which is given over to extensive flooding during the rainy season.

Between Ibi and Makurdi the volcanic tract near Abinsi provides one of the most picturesque reaches of the Benue. Here the worn and weathered cones and banks of lava rise above the wooded plains. Below the volcanic tract, the river is bounded on both sides by low wooded banks which give way, at intervals, to broken plains

Figure 60. Sections across the Benue Valley

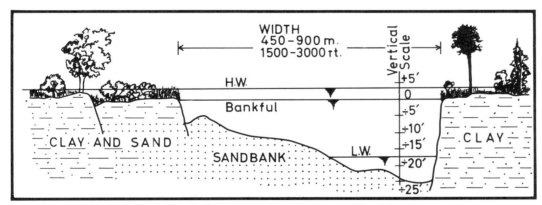

THE BENUE BETWEEN LAU AND AMAR

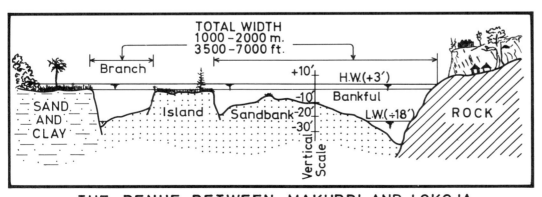

THE BENUE BETWEEN MAKURDI AND LOKOJA

Plate 34. The Benue bridge and waterway at Makurdi.

projecting inland for considerable distances. At Makurdi sandstone hills close in on both sides of the river, which is here forced into a 2,200-feet bed over which the only bridge across the Benue is built. The Makurdi defile is considered to be the only possible dam site on the Benue, apart from Das in Hausa. Apart from the alluvial swamps near Loko, the remaining part of the lower Benue is flanked at intervals by discontinuous hill ranges. Below Umaisha the great alluvial plain, which marks the confluence of the Niger and Benue, opens out, and before reaching Mozum, the scarp slope of Mount Patti, which overlooks the confluence, comes into full view.

All the tributaries of the Benue enter the river unobtrusively. Often, they appear like branches of the Benue flowing round large islands and joining the main river some distance downstream. The Taraba, for instance, forms a fluviatile delta where it enters the Benue with two secondary channels flowing into the Benue, at points two miles and nine miles below the confluence of the main channel and the Benue. Excepting the Gongola, all the larger tributaries of the river rise south of the Benue Valley, and most of them are shallow rivers with numerous islands and sandbanks. Only a few of them are navigable.

THE HIGH PLAINS OF THE BENUE TROUGH

The term high plains is applied to those parts of the Benue lowlands lying above flood level, but below the 1,000 foot contour line. Unlike the flood plains which are alluvial, the high plains are erosional and are cut in

sedimentary formations. The most extensive of these plains is the Great Plain of Muri (Figure 61) which covers most of Muri Emirate. In the west, that is in the region of the Shemankar River, the Muri Plain is dull and consists of extensive swamps along the fadamas, but away from river channels savanna woodland predominates. Settlement here is concentrated near the large rivers and the salt springs; while vast areas which lack water in the dry season are sparsely settled and rarely cultivated, being given over to tsetse flies. Further east the Muri Plain consists of undulating sandy lowlands whose monotony is broken here and there by hills developed on tough sandstones. The Dalli Hills, which occur very close to the Taraba River, are examples of hills developed on sedimentary rocks. The southern part of the Muri Plain between Wukari and Jalingo presents a similar aspect and similar problems to human settlement as the northern part. This part is peopled largely by the Jukuns and the Fulanis, but as in the north a combination of swampy conditions during the rains and lack of water during the dry season has led to the concentration of villages alongside the main river valleys.

East of the Donga Valley the south Muri Plain is developed on sedimentary as well as on crystalline rocks. There is, however, no topographical change marking the geological boundary. The only distinguishing feature between areas developed on different geological formations appears to be in the hill forms found in the various areas. Hills found in the sedimentary areas are flat-topped as a result of lateritic capping, while the erosional

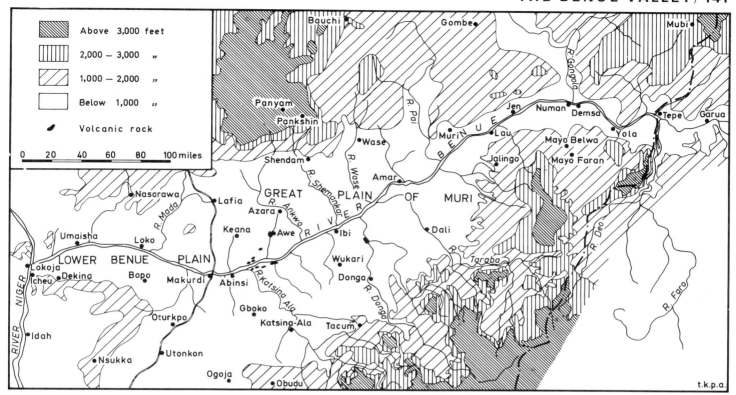

Figure 61. Relief and Drainage of the Benue Basin

survivals forming the hills of the crystalline areas appear to be dome-shaped.

The lower Benue Plain is less extensive but more varied in aspect than the Great Muri Plain. West of the Okwa River, it consists of a dissected sandstone plateau which continues westwards to the banks of the Niger and beyond. Numerous flat-topped hills abound. Between the Okwa and the Modu Rivers the hills give way to an undulating sandy grass plain which is heavily wooded along the river courses. Further east the plain opens out in a northerly direction until it reaches the Ankwe River, beyond which lies the Great Plain of Muri. A deep cover of sandy drift overlies this eastern part of the Lower Benue Plain, whose surface is often broken by ridges of rock. Around the salt-making village of Awe occur a number of worn volcanic cones. A large part of this eastern section is still heavily forested except where local population pressure has led to widespread deforestation, particularly south of the river.

POPULATION AND SETTLEMENT TYPES

Excepting the southern part of Tivland, which has a fairly dense population of about 500 persons per square mile, the Benue Valley is very sparsely settled, vast areas such as the central part of the Great Muri Plain being virtually uninhabited. Outside Tivland settlements are few and far between, and consist of small compact villages located near the main streams draining into the Benue. The Tivs live in scattered homesteads, although nucleated villages were the rule in the past when Tiv settlements were fortified with strong mud walls or pallisades and ditches. East of Lau the number of villages increases amongst the hills which close in on both sides of the river. Hill settlements still exist although many of the hill sites, with their terraced gardens, have since been abandoned for more accessible and productive sites on the plains.

It is usual to explain the sparse population of the Middle Belt, of which the Benue Valley forms a part, by reference to extensive slave raids during the eighteenth and nineteenth centuries. But slave raiding does not offer an adequate explanation for the whole of the Benue Valley. Rather there are large tracts of the plains where there is no indication that the indigenous population has even been larger than it was at the time of the British occupation in 1907. Examples of such areas include northern Tivland and Adamawa west of Jalingo where settlement has always been restricted as a result of swampy conditions during the rains, lack of water in the dry season and the ravages of the tsetse fly. Yet these empty lands are very fertile, particularly along the fadamas or river flood plains, which are well cultivated in the vicinity of the few settlements. Distance from settlement rather than availability of suitable farmland sets the limit of cultivation in much of the Benue Valley.

In Yola District and the neighbouring parts of Adamawa the explanation for the sparse population is largely historical, and is linked up with the Fulani conquest of this part of the Benue Valley. Under Mallam

Modibó Adama, after whom Adamawa is named, the Fulanis carried out a local jihad in the Upper Benue Valley, when many of the indigenous pagan people inhabiting the open flat and fertile plains of the area were raided for slaves by Fulani horsemen. Many of those who escaped were obliged to retire to the nearby hills, hence the greater number of people in the more rugged country-side where the hillslopes as well as the intervening plains are still cultivated. This historical fact is still reflected in the present-day domestic politics of the Benue Valley where the Tivs, who were never conquered by the Fulanis, have proved rather rebellious to the Fulani-inspired feudal administration of northern Nigeria.

At this stage it is possible to see that the population of the Benue Valley consists of two large cultural groups—the indigenous pagan people who form by far the largest population, and the Fulani/Hausa group who are Mohammedan by faith, and are relatively newcomers to the region. The most important pagan tribe is the Tiv, who form the single largest pagan tribe in northern Nigeria and who numbered about 700,000 in 1953. It is believed that they migrated into the middle Benue Valley from the highlands south-east of their present territory, and although their main concentration is south of the Benue Valley, they have since spread out to occupy the northern plains.

The rapid expansion of the Tivs in all directions is one of the most notable features of this tribal group. The Munshi Wall built about 1912 by the Colonial administration was designed to restrict the southward expansion of the Tivs and thereby prevent boundary disputes with other neighbouring groups. That such restriction was not effective is indicated by the fact that the Tivs not only 'climbed over the wall', but also migrated in other directions. The main reason for this migratory habit is, according to the Tivs, the search for new or more farmland.

The other pagan tribes include the Jukun of the south Muri Plain, as well as the Idoma and the Bassa of the Lower Benue Plain. Like the Tivs these are settled agricultural people. The Fulanis are found in the Upper Benue Valley where they form the ruling group, Adamawa being the far eastern limit of Fulani domination of the Sudan. As in the Middle Niger Valley they are found living side by side with the local pagan groups, some of which still go about without any type of clothing. There are also a significant number of Hausa and Ibo settlers. Indeed, as far back as 1899, Moseley attributed much of the economic development of the Benue Valley to Hausa traders, who at that time outnumbered the indigenous population in certain settlements. In this connection it may be recalled that British penetration of Tivland followed the massacre of seventy-six Hausa traders during a fight between the Hausas and the Jukuns, in which the latter called in Tiv assistance.

Tiv compounds and that of most other tribal groups in this region consist of the usual round mud-walled huts with conical roofs of thatch. The sleeping huts are generally raised on short stilts to keep out water. Each compound, which consists of a group of sleeping huts, reception huts and granaries of members of one extended family, is referred to by the name of its headman.

The growth of satelite settlements is a recent and wide-spread development in the food surplus district of southern Idoma. With the growing emphasis on cash crops of which swamp rice, yam and soya beans are the most important, it has become necessary to cultivate larger acreages. This has led to the cultivation of lands which are very distant from the nucleated villages of the local people. Hence the need to establish farm huts where farmers spend most of the farming season, at which time many of the villages are partly deserted.

CASH CROP AND FOOD PRODUCTION IN THE BENUE VALLEY

In the Middle and Lower Benue valley ecological conditions permit the inhabitants to take part in both the grained-based economy of the north and the root-based economy of the south. Thus there are three important staple crops, yams (July and August), guinea corn (December) and bulrush millet (May and June) whose harvest months are shown in brackets. The Tivs are the most industrious farmers in the whole region, although their method of farming is wasteful and destructive of trees and soil. In addition to the three staple crops, the Tivs grow maize, rice, sweet potatoes, beans, cocoyams, cassava and groundnuts. Beniseed and cotton are grown all over Tivland (Figure 62).

As in other parts of the country, there are two classes of farmland, the compoundland or kitchen gardens where vegetables are grown, and the main or distant farmland. Compoundlands are cropped every year, while a simple three year rotation is practised on the main farmland. This rotational system may be tabulated as follows:—

First Year: Yams (*Dioscorea*) and vegetables (or cotton as a pure stand)
Second Year: Bulrush millet (*Pennisetum*) and guinea corn (*Sorghum*)
Third Year: Beniseed (*Sesamum indicum*)

The minor crops listed above, including okro and water melon, are usually grown as intercrops although pure stands of each are also common.

Bush clearing amongst the Tivs consists of pulling up grasses which are left on the ground to dry. There is no bush firing here during the first year of the rotation, since the dry grass is used for 'capping' yam heaps. Other crops grown on the same plot with yams, or separately on neighbouring plots, are usually cultivated on ridges. It is estimated that forty per cent of the farm work is done by males who expend half of this labour on preparing land for yams.[1] The rest of the work of weeding and cultivation of other crops is mainly done by the women, while the men go out hunting.

In the densely settled southern districts, the fallow period varies from two to seven years, the average being four, as compared with ten to fifteen years of fallow in sparsely populated areas of Tivland and the Benue valley in general. In villages where land shortage is acute crops such as groundnuts, cassava and sweet potatoes are planted on fallow land. Hence the great decline in soil fertility in southern Tivland, where the light sandy soils are as acidic as the acid sands of the East Central State. Since this is a tsetse-ridden country the use of domestic livestock for the production of pen manure or the adoption of a mixed farming system has not been given serious consideration. Rather, attempts have been made to encourage permanent cultivation through the inclusion of quick-growing leguminous green manures, such as *Macune utilis*, in the local rotation.

An organized resettlement of the population on the lines of the Shendam Scheme discussed below appears to be the obvious alternative to solving the problems of soil deterioration and impoverishment in southern Tivland. Fortunately, there is sufficient land within the Tiv tribal area so that the thorny question of Tivs colonizing the land belonging to other tribes will not arise.

In the Upper Benue valley, where the northern grain economy predominates, millet and guinea corn are the main crops. Groundnuts, sweet potatoes and maize are also widely cultivated. Both the cotton plant and indigo for dyeing cotton have been grown for many centuries, and in the middle of the nineteenth century locally made strips of cotton cloth were a standard medium of exchange in most of Adamawa and Bornu. This part of the Benue valley is rather remote and lacks a substantial money crop. It is an area where cotton and groundnuts can be expanded as cash crops.

As a food surplus area the Middle and Lower Benue valley is an important agricultural region in Nigeria.

Yams produced here are railed to Kano, Onitsha and other urban centres in the Northern and Eastern States for distribution. Cassava in the form of garri, millet and rice are other important foodcrops produced for internal exchange. The rapid expansion of rice, particularly amongst the Tivs and the people of Idoma Division, is impressive, for even though these people do not eat much rice they expend much energy in reclaiming stream beds and swamps for cultivating rice.

Cotton is of growing importance in this part of the Benue valley but beniseed, which is almost restricted to Tivland, is the most important export crop from the Benue valley. As an important source of edible oil beniseed is to the Tiv what the oil palm is to the people of southern Nigeria or the groundnut to the Hausa, and it has been cultivated in this part of the Benue valley for a long time. The rapid expansion of the acreage under beniseed was brought about by the need to obtain money for tax and the fact that the crop was in demand outside Nigeria for use in manufacturing margarine, cooking fats and confectionery. The fact that the Government Department of Agriculture advised the people to adopt beniseed in place of cotton is also an important factor in the expansion of this crop.

A comparatively new cash crop, whose production is at present concentrated in the Benue valley, is soya beans. In Tivland the expansion of soya beans has resulted in a decline of the acreage under beniseed, even though the two crops cannot be said to be competing directly for land or even labour in the area. Normally soya beans are cultivated on newly cleared fallow between the months of July and August, while beniseed is cultivated in April and on land which is about to revert to fallow. The growing seasons are therefore different and so is the class of farmland. But the fact that a good farmer can earn enough by working normal hours on his beniseed and soya bean farms has made it undesirable for him to work overtime planting beniseed in April, as he used to do when that was the only cash crop. Hence the present decline in the area under beniseed.

The presence of migrant farmers from the East Central State in parts of the food surplus areas of the Benue valley deserves mention. These stranger farmers are largely Ezzas from Abakaliki Division and are to be found cultivating yams and rice in Idoma Division. Many of them go as labourers who specialize in making yam mounds. It is interesting to observe that the Tivs, who are as mobile as the Ezzas with whom they share a common boundary, do

[1] Briggs, G. W. G., 'Soil Deterioration in the Southern Districts of Tiv Division, Benue Province' *Farm and Forest* Vol. 2 pp. 8–12 1941

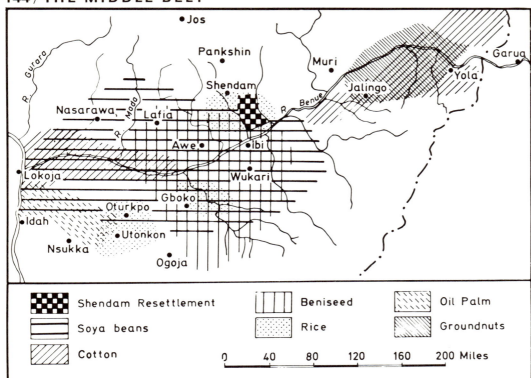

Figure 62. The Benue Basin—Cash Crops and the Shendam Resettlement area

not encourage migrant tenant farmers in their land.

THE SHENDAM AGRICULTURAL DEVELOPMENT AND RESETTLEMENT SCHEME

The purpose of the Shendam Scheme, which had 8,500 settlers in 1960, is to control the downhill migration of pagan farmers from the southern slopes of the Jos Plateau into the fertile but virtually uninhabited plain lying between the Shemankar and Wase Rivers. Like other resettlement schemes the Shendam Scheme also seeks to improve the material welfare of these pagan farmers by teaching them better farming methods and by introducing cash crops.

To many of the pagans the descent to the plain was no more than a recolonization of their former territory which they had been forced to abandon while fleeing from Fulani horsemen, who raided and conquered the lowlands of Shendam Division in the early years of the nineteenth century.[1] But this movement into the plains was not organized. Rather, by abandoning the intensive form of farming in which small terraced gardens on the foothills were put under permanent cultivation, and reverting to the wasteful practice of shifting cultivation, the people succeeded in destroying, within a few decades, considerable tracts of woodland in the area. The Shendam Scheme was therefore launched to control this migration and to resettle the people with a view to improving their earning power.

The Scheme is directed by the Shendam Native Authority and consists of the establishment of groups of villages to which migrants are directed. Each village has its own grazing land and communal forest area, on the

basis of forty acres per family. In addition, each family is allocated twenty acres of farmland, a third of which is to be used for food crops and two-thirds for cash crops. Cropping is based on a system of rotation and manuring prescribed by the local agricultural officer. Apart from a grant of £750 from the Colonial Welfare and Development Fund the whole cost of the Pilot Scheme, started in 1948, was borne by the Shendam Native Authority, which also voted over £8,000 towards the cost of the whole project. The pilot scheme centred around the first resettlement village of Sabon Gida, which was initially peopled by fifty settlers. Sabon Gida was a success and was followed by another village, Mabudi, in 1949. The following year two other villages, Dorawa and Mahanga, were built and by the end of 1950 no less than 174 families had been resettled. This expansion was made possible by a grant of £13,000 from the Northern Regional Production Development Board.[2] More settlements have since been established and the scheme can be said to be successful even if the progress is not spectacular.

The Scheme's policy of doing the absolute minimum for the settlers has much to recommend it in view of the fact that the Scheme has had to depend largely on the energy, self-help and initiative shown by the settlers. Roads and water supplies were provided as well as food during the first dry season. Enthusiasm at the new settlements is reported to have been much higher than at Sabon Gida, to the extent that in the first season each settler had cleared enough land to grow sufficient food to carry his

[1] Fremantle, J. M., *Gazetteer of Muri Province* pp. 43–7 (up to December 1919)
[2] Anon. 'Operation Resettlement' *Nigerian Marketing Board Journal* Vol. I No. 2 pp. 40–52 1952

family throughout the year. The cost of providing subsistence for the first year dropped, in consequence, from £20 for Sabon Gida to fifty shillings for Mabudi settlers. In all the settlements the settlers had to clear the land and build their houses. This explains why the first village of Sabon Gida was established at a cost of only £2,000 cash.

Forty head of cattle were introduced into the pilot settlement at Sabon Gida in the hope that animal husbandry would be incorporated into the farming system. The prevalence of the tsetse fly has, however, presented a considerable problem for this aspect of the scheme. The situation is still under study and there is therefore no mixed farming at present.

Plate 35. The Adamawa Gudale breed of Fulani cattle.

Plate 36. Fulani Milk Maids in Yola district of the upper Benue valley.

CATTLE IN THE BENUE VALLEY

The cattle population of the Benue drainage basin during the rains is put at one-and-a-half million head, but the number of cattle found in the Benue valley even during the dry season is much less than this figure. The large number of cattle in the basin is concentrated on the fly-free highlands of the Jos Plateau and the uplands of the eastern borderlands. The Benue valley itself is infested with tsetse flies all through the year, to the extent that about a third of all sleeping-sickness cases reported in Nigeria are from Benue Province.

During the dry season cattle from the uplands are driven to the plains of the Benue valley, where grazing is available (Figure 63). At this time the tsetse are closely confined to the vicinity of streams, but since water is hard to get in parts of the plains the cattle have to go to the streams where the flies are concentrated. As in other parts of the country this pest has proved a serious setback to animal husbandry in the Benue valley and various methods have been employed to exterminate it. One of such methods is the clearing of riverine thickets and other woodlands, but the main point against this method is the sparse population of vast areas, since the cleared bush easily reverts to dense bush after a few years unless the cleared area is effectively occupied. An alternative method is to use insecticides, but this is expensive.

Other factors which combine to restrict the area suitable for dry-season grazing include poverty of grazing in many areas, lack of water over considerable stretches and diseases other than trypanosomiasis. The increasing demand for farmland by settled cultivators also places some restriction on areas available for dry-season grazing. There is therefore a great need to control not only the spread of hill pagans to the plains, as is being done in the Shendam Scheme, but also to extend such control to the Tivs, who

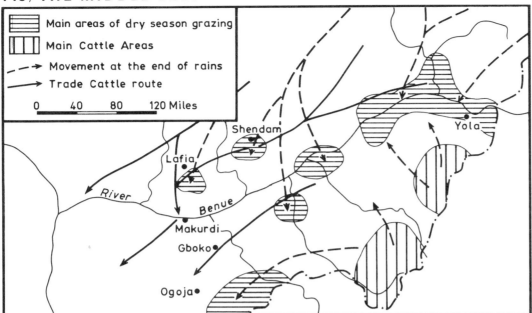

Main areas of dry season grazing
Main Cattle Areas
Movement at the end of rains
Trade Cattle route

0   40   80   120 Miles

Shendam
Yola
Lafia
River
Benue
Makurdi
Gboko
Ogoja

Figure 63. The Benue Basin—Main Dry Season Grazing Areas

are always on the move in search of new additional farm-land. The problem here is that the cattle belong to the nomadic Fulani and not to the local pagan people. Measures seeking to restrict their farming activities for the sake of creating grazing for Fulani cattle will certainly meet with strong opposition, particularly in those areas which successfully resisted Fulani domination in pre-colonial days.

The reported increase in recent years of the number of cattle kept in the Benue valley[1] confirms that the ravages of the tsetse-fly can be brought under control by extending the area under effective occupation by the local popula-tion. Formerly cattle-rearing in the Benue valley was restricted to the Fulani-dominated areas around Yola and Numan, but since the early 1950s an increasing number of cattle have been kept, even during the rainy season, in the Benue valley administrative divisions of Lafia, Wukari and Lowland. This change is made possible by the progressive recession of the tsetse-fly belt consequent on the clearing of woodland and the elimination of game, following the expansion of the area under cultivation. As people descend from the hills to settle and cultivate the plains the area under forests is reduced, while the area for safe grazing increases.

SALT MINING AND OTHER MINERALS IN THE BENUE VALLEY

Salt has been worked in the Benue valley for a long time and was an important item of inter-tribal trade in pre-colonial and early colonial days. The two salt-bearing districts of the region are shown in Figure 64. In the western district, the main surviving producing centres are Awe, Keana and Akiri, while those of the less-important eastern district are Bomanda and Jenoe. Both districts are believed to be detached synclinal areas formed by localized folding, and the brine springs of Awe, Azara and Bomanda

have been associated with anticlinal axes along which the salt-bearing beds within the synclines approach the sur-face. In both districts the salt occurs as weak brine within the upper layers of the Muri Sandstones and the method of extraction has remained unchanged over the years.

The Benue salt industry is run by the womenfolk who are responsible not only for extracting but also for market-ing the salt. It is a seasonal industry which is largely con-fined to the three months of the year when the ground is dry enough to permit large-scale production. At this time of the year (the dry season), many women whose salt plots are far from their villages migrate to settle in camps located near the salt pits. The method of extraction is simple, the first step consisting of sprinkling salt water from local springs on bare soil. A thin deposit of salt is left behind when the water dries up and this is scraped off and placed in filters which consist of clay waterpots with holes in the bottom. More salt water from the spring is poured over the heap in the filter and the salt is obtained in crystalline form after the solution has been boiled over a wood fire. The salt pits are flooded during the rains when the plains are inundated. Production then ceases and the women return to their villages. The only contribution of the men is in draining the pits of rain water before the next production season begins. In the past the pits were drained by using pots and calabashes to scoop out the water, but today small hand-pumps are used.

Like many other indigenous industries in the country, the Benue salt industry suffered a serious setback with the establishment of British rule in Nigeria. The displace-ment of locally produced salt by better-quality European salt is almost complete, and today the demand for Benue salt is restricted to the few who still prefer the flavour of local salt to the imported stuff. There was a short-lived boom during the war years when salt had to be rationed. Since the reserves are very limited and the brine from these

[1] Grove, A. T., *The Benue Valley* Kaduna 1957

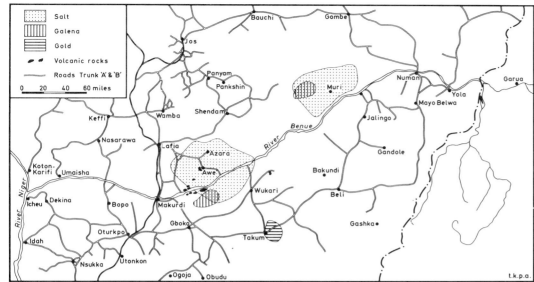

Figure 64. The Benue Basin— Minerals and Communications

districts is considered to be too weak to permit exploitation on modern lines, it is very unlikely that the salt works will be highly developed except perhaps during a national emergency.

Small quantities of tinstone have been found in the western slopes of the Shebsi Hills in Muri Emirate and on the eastern slopes of the Vere Hills in Yola Emirate. But by definition these deposits occur outside the Benue valley and so far none of them has been exploited. Our consideration of other minerals will therefore be restricted to galena, which is mined and used as a cosmetic by the local people who also trade it to other neighbouring tribes for the same use. Small pockets of silver also occur within the veinstuff of this mineral.

Galena deposits in the Benue valley are closely associated with salt deposits in that both minerals occur in close proximity or even within the same locality. The problems of mining are also similar to the extent that during the rains, and for some time after, the pits are full of water and are therefore unworkable. As in the case of the salt works, operations are restricted to only three months of the year, but in this case the pits fill up even during the dry season as a result of percolation from the sides and bottom. Miners are known to spend a good part of the day emptying the water accumulated during the night before actual mining starts. The danger of the sides falling in limits the size of the pits while tunnels constructed into the side of the pits are very short since the people have no idea of the use of props. The result is a wasteful extraction of the deposits.

Idoma Division of the Benue valley is one of the few areas where iron was smelted in the country until the industry was forced to close down by the importation of cheap iron from Europe. The centre of this indigenous iron works was in the hills north of Bogo, where numerous kilns for smelting local iron ore were still to be found in 1935. Iron from Idoma was used for making farm implements and other articles, including weapons.

THE BENUE WATERWAY

The Benue made a great impression on its early explorers, who saw it as a great waterway which could open much of the eastern part of the central Sudan to European influence and trade. Partly as a result of the primitive state of their vessels, and partly because there was very limited contact and trade between the various tribal groups, the people of the Benue valley made very little use of this waterway before the beginning of this century. But it was through the Benue waterway that the early European traders penetrated the eastern part of this country, and today the produce of the Benue valley reaches the Benin ports by way of the Benue waterway.

The point was made earlier that the Benue is navigable throughout its course in Nigeria, provided there is sufficient depth of water. Unfortunately navigation is good only at the height of the wet season, being difficult at the beginning and end of the wet season, and impossible during the dry season. Lack of water constitutes the main source of shipping troubles. The flats of the Upper Benue restrict the available depth of water and may cause groundings. To prevent any groundings river pilots often make an orientation trip by canoe during low water. During the Benue season which commences in June the river traffic to and from Lokoja is directed by such pilots, although local guides are also required to guide navigation through particularly bad stretches.

Above Lau the length of the shipping season is very short owing to the deficiency of the discharges during the greater part of the year. Two months after the shipping season has commenced there is a marked drop in the discharges of the upper reaches. During this August drop ships are frequently delayed, since the depth over crossings is as little as five to eight feet. Another steep fall occurs in October when ships must have cleared the river. Since it is difficult to predict the exact time of this fall, most of the ships leave the Benue well before the sudden drop in water

Plate 37. The Ferry crossing at Jimeta and Fulani milk girls waiting to cross.

level, thereby shortening the navigable season considerably. But there are occasions when ships do not manage to leave in time, in which case they are locked up until next year's flood which may take another eight months.

The programme for improving the navigability of the river consists of improving the river bed and the water levels and regulating the discharges from the Benue and its distributaries. The river bed is to be improved by dredging reputably bad crossings. It is estimated that if this is done yearly in May, that is a month before the opening of the Benue season, it will be possible to start the season ten to fifteen days earlier and that this may result in a five per cent increase of the fleet capacity during the Benue season. The regulation of the river bed to prevent the danger of shifting channels and of bank erosion is also considered as a means of improving the river bed. Improvements of water levels and the regulation of discharges will require the construction of dams in the upper reaches of the Benue. Two dams, one at Lagdo which is forty miles above Garua, and another near Yola, have already been proposed. The Lagdo dam, estimated to cost £6 million, would overcome the present unpredictable August fall which renders navigation uncertain during the shipping season. It will also extend the shipping season at Garua from one-and-a-half to three months. The Yola dam is considered necessary to check the vagaries of the Faro tributary which is the main cause of trouble arising from irregular flow. The Yola dam, estimated at £14 million, will double the length of the present shipping period for Yola and Numan and quadruple that of Garua. The delta ports will therefore be guaranteed a more continuous flow of traffic since vessels will operate for longer periods.

Most of the vessels operating on the Benue are owned by foreign trading companies: the United Africa Company (U.A.C.), John Holts and the French trading firm of Compagnie Française de l'Afrique Occidentale (C.F.A.O.) being the main ones. Total river transport fluctuates with good or bad river seasons as well as with good and bad

harvests. Charges per ton/mile are classified for various types of goods, but in general freight rates are above the average for other Nigerian river transports, owing to the short period of navigation and the unpredictability of the water levels. Freight rates per ton/mile vary between a penny and sixpence, the average being a little below threepence.

Another category of fleets using the river is the government fleet whose history dates to the establishment of British rule, when the only means of transport into this part of the country was provided by the Benue River. These fleets are used for official duties by such government departments as the Inland Waterways and the Medical Department. They are never used for commercial purposes. The third category of fleets is made up of vessels of a size intermediate between the barges owned by the commercial companies and the African-owned canoes. These vessels are now produced at the Makurdi Boatyard.

The main river ports along the Benue are Makurdi, Ibi, Numan, Yola and Garua, the last of which lies outside Nigeria and is 610 miles from the confluence at Lokoja. Port terminal facilities are poor and there is no adequate provision for quick handling of goods. In many cases there are no landing stages, and in all cases the handling of goods is not mechanized.

Works consulted and suggestions for further reading:
1. Armstrong, R. G., 'Igala and Idoma Speaking Peoples' in *Peoples of the Niger-Benue Confluence* (Ethnographic Survey of Africa) Ed. by D. Forde pp. 77–152 London 1955
2. Bohannan, P. 'The Migration and Expansion of the Tiv' *Africa* No. 24 pp. 2–16 1954
3. Bohannan, P. and Laura, *The Tiv of Central Nigeria* (Ethnographic Survey of Africa) London 1953
4. Briggs, G. W. G., 'Soil Deterioration in the Southern District of Tiv Division' *Farm and Forest* No. 2 1941
5. Cratchley, C. R. & Jones, G. P., *An Interpretation of the geology and gravity anomalies of the Benue Valley, Nigeria* (Geophysical Paper No. 1) London 1965
6. Grove, A. T., *The Benue Valley* Kaduna 1957
7. NEDECO *River Studies and Recommendations on Improvement of Niger and Benue* Amsterdam 1959
8. Nzekwu, O., 'Keana Salt Camp' *Nigeria Magazine* No. 83 pp. 262–78 1964

15 Bauchi and the Gongola Basin

About half the length of the new 400-mile Bornu Railway extension passes through this composite region which is made up of the Bauchi High Plains, the broken hill country of Gombe and the dissected basalt-capped Biu Plateau. According to the rather optimistic review of revenue potential made in 1960, much of the traffic which the railway is expected to generate in order to pay its way will come from this region. Indeed, one of the final points made in support of this railway extension was that in spite of the increasing importance of road traffic in the region, existing transport facilities, including the Benue waterway, were incapable of meeting the increasing exportable surplus produce in the locality. Yet, like other parts of the Middle Belt, the Gongola Basin is very sparsely settled and experience elsewhere has confirmed that a new highway or railroad is not likely to make much impact in a virtually uninhabited district. It is yet too early to make definite statements on the economic situation of the new railway which reached Maiduguri in 1964, but annual returns up to the end of 1966 show that both the passenger and goods traffic are much below the projected figures.

This region is made up of the administrative divisions of Bauchi, Gombe and Biu and may be considered as a wide cultural gap between the Jos Plateau in the west and the Mandarra Mountains in the east, excepting that the Biu Plateau itself also stands out as a cultural island. In general the plains, the most extensive stretches of which occur in Bauchi, are occupied by a mixed population of Hausas, Fulanis and pagan groups whom the Fulanis raided for slaves, while the uplands are still settled by some pagan groups who fled thither in order to escape mounted Fulani raiders.

GEOLOGICAL HISTORY AND RELIEF FEATURES

Geologically, the region consists of an ancient crystalline basement which outcrops in the west as well as along the eastern border, but is overlain in the central and Biu districts by sedimentary and volcanic rocks respectively. The crystalline basement comprises the remnants of highly metamorphosed sedimentary rocks which are considered to be the oldest rocks in the region. It was in the process of a Lower Palaezoic regional metamorphism, during which the Older Granites were intruded into the sedimentary rocks, that the latter were transformed into granite and migmatite.

The Bima Sandstone, consisting of continental grits, sandstones and clays, was laid down in the southern part of the Chad Basin which was one of the two major local depositional basins of the Upper Cretaceous era; the second one being the Benue Basin. This formation varies in thickness from 300 to 10,000 feet, and in this region it consists wholly of continental deposits although Marine shales are found in the Benue Basin. Its deposition was followed by a widespread but shallow marine transgression affecting the lower Gongola valley by way of the Benue. In the Benue valley and further south the marine conditions were restored much earlier, to permit the deposition in late Cretaceous times of the Gombe Sandstone which consists of sandstones, siltstones, shales and ironstone. The great anticlinal structures, which are very marked in Cretaceous rocks, were formed during the deposition of the Gombe Sandstone which is comparatively much less strongly folded.

A period of subaerial erosion followed, during which parts of the Cretaceous sequence were removed; but during the early Tertiary, sedimentation started again. The Kerri Kerri Formation, which is another continental sequence of flat-lying grits, sandstones and clays, was deposited at this time. This formation dips gently to the north and north-east below the Chad Formation and is about 650 feet thick. It rests unconformably upon the folded Cretaceous rocks and its surface, which is not folded, is overlain by laterite. In the Daura Hills and near Damagun the lateritic capping which exceeds five feet has given rise to flat-topped hills similar to those on the Nsukka Plateau. Along the escarpment at Kadi, where the laterite is exposed, it measures fifteen feet in thickness while a borehole sunk near Potiskum proved that the laterite layer which lay beneath a soil profile of five feet was twenty-seven feet thick.

The Biu Plateau which covers about 2,000 square miles of the eastern part of this region was formed during the period of late Tertiary and Quaternary volcanic activity in the area. It was built up by extensive basaltic flows resulting from this volcanic activity. Proven thickness of the basalt rarely exceeds 100 feet although it is thought that the basalt may be as thick as 800 feet in some parts. A number of well-preserved volcanic cones built of basaltic agglomorate, ash, lavas and tuffs form prominent relief features in the northern part of the Biu Plateau. Most of these volcanic vents have well-defined craters with breached rims and steep conical sides, similar to the vents of almost identical age which appear at Panyam on the Jos Plateau.

Largely owing to its varied geological composition, the region provides a great variety of topographical forms featuring low, swampy plains, rugged hills of granite and sandstone, volcanic plugs and plateaux developed on sedimentary and volcanic rocks. Prominent hill features

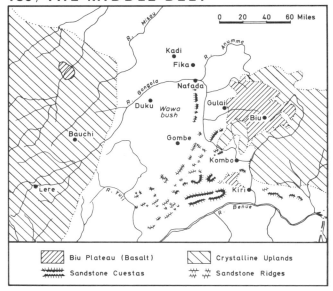

Figure 65. The Gongola Basin—Relief and Landforms

appear on almost every geological formation, those of the crystalline basement rocks consisting of isolated rocky hills and low ranges which are common in the area around Bauchi town. In areas of sedimentary rocks the most impressive hill features are formed by the Bima Sandstone, the strong structural trends of which are closely reflected in the linear and elliptical hill patterns found on this surface. But the commonest landforms of areas underlain by the Bima Sandstone are cuestas, which often dominate the landscape for hundreds of square miles, as in the case of the Bima ranges and the Wade Hills (Figure 65). Then there are the hills which are associated with the numerous volcanic plugs and cones in the Biu Plateau.

The so-called Kerri Kerri Plateau, which is developed on sedimentary rocks, unlike the better-known Biu Plateau which is formed of volcanic rocks, is not higher than the Bauchi Plain in the west. It consists of a highly dissected inclined plain, marked by a broken escarpment in the south. Flat-topped laterite-capped hills flank the deep, narrow valleys which have been cut by rivers draining into the lower Gongola. The higher plateau of Biu is equally dissected and in both cases the term plateau should be applied with reservations.

DRAINAGE CHARACTERISTICS

The Gongola River, which is the largest right-bank tributary of the Benue, is the most important river in the region. Its upper course as well as most of its tributaries are seasonal streams but it is possible to obtain water along these valleys during the dry season by digging within a few feet of the river bed. August and September are the months when the rivers are full, the rate of rise and fall being very rapid. Numerous examples of superimposed streams and of complete as well as incipient river captures have been identified and are discussed in this section.

In various parts of the Gongola valley, and along some

of its tributaries, the course of the rivers appear to be completely independent of the surface structure. This unusual situation has come about as a result of the fact that the original surface rocks, Tertiary sediments and basalt flows in this case, on which the rivers cut their valleys initially, have been completely removed. At the same time, the rivers maintain their course on the newly exposed strata and are therefore said to be superimposed. An excellent example of superimposition along the Gongola occurs at Kombo where the river has cut a gap through a ridge of steeply dipping, indurated sandstone. Several east-flowing tributaries between Nafada and Gombe also show evidence of superimposition.

The capture of the upper Gongola, which formerly flowed into Lake Chad, but now drains into the upper Benue, is one of the most recent developments in the drainage of the region. It is one of the most readily recognized cases of river capture in Nigeria and appears to have taken place in the vicinity of Ngalda, where the Gongola abruptly changes its course from east to south. The former course extended north-eastwards across the Mutive Plain in the direction of Lake Chad. A number of minor captures of rivers formerly flowing into Lake Chad through the Komadagu Gana have been identified in the Potiskum-Damaturu area, where several dry wind gaps abound. One of these minor captures involves the Gungeru River, which flows northwards to within four miles of Murba, where it swings sharply south to join the Gongola system, its former course being marked by the broad dry valley at Murba. As a result of these captures streams flowing north to join the Gana River occupy broad, shallow, misfit valleys and contain running water only after a heavy rainstorm. Finally, like most captures in West Africa, the piracy effect of the lower Gongola has robbed the Chad Basin of its scarce water resources.

CLIMATE, VEGETATION AND SOILS

The rainfall decreases from about 43 inches at Bauchi in the west to about 35 inches in the north and east. The sudden drop in the annual rainfall total, from over 56 inches for Jos to a little below 43 inches for Bauchi, is largely due to the fact that Jos, which is on a higher elevation, has more rainfall than other stations along its latitude, and that Bauchi lies on the leeward side of the Jos Plateau. Another example of a localized upland effect on rainfall occurs on the Biu Plateau which records an annual rainfall of about 40 inches as compared with 35 inches for the surrounding plains.

Most of the rain falls between June and September,

although the rainy season actually begins in May. There is little information on the rainfall intensities but heavy falls of over three inches in one hour may occur occasionally. Early afternoon and night thunderstorms are common and the peak month is in August when places in southern Nigeria are experiencing the short dry season. As in other parts of the country, the maximum daily temperature decreases slightly during the rainy season while the relative humidity increases. At Bauchi the hottest month is April, that is just before the rains set in. Maximum shade temperatures of about 104° F have been recorded at Bauchi during April, while the relative humidity, which is about ninety-four per cent in August, drops to less than ten per cent during the harmattan.

Open savanna woodland, with trees of up to twenty feet high and more, is dominant over extensive areas. The trees usually occur singly or in small groups, the space between being occupied by a herb layer of non-woody species including grasses. In addition to this herb layer which is locally dominant, a shrub layer of woody species up to ten feet high may be present. In the Bauchi Plains human interference through cultivation, grazing and burning has reduced the vegetation of many places to Acacia shrub. But dense savanna woodland is common in the virtually uninhabited Duguli area of Bauchi where such grassland animals as lions, giraffes and chimpanzees abound.

Soil types vary not only from one geological province to another, but also according to the slope of the land and location along or far from a river valley. On the Bauchi Plains laterite is common on higher sites, while more productive soils occur along the narrow flood plains which provide farmland for cultivating cotton and maize. The footslopes of some outcrops have been laid out in terraces for cultivation. Concretionary ironstone also occurs on the basalt plateau of Biu which has more fertile soils than the Bauchi Plains. The problem in the Biu Plateau area is the lack of extensive good farmland owing to great dissection of the high relief of this area. The dark-brown gravelly soils which occur on most of the steeper slopes are terraced with low stone walls. Guinea corn and groundnuts are the main crops of these terraces, while swamp rice is grown in the heavier dark-brown soils of the valley floors.

Soils developed on the Kerri Kerri Formation are generally coarse, loose and reddish-brown in colour. The occurrence of concretionary ironstone on this formation has already been noted. These laterite patches often occur on the surface or at a shallow depth. They support good crops of millet, guinea corn, beans and groundnuts, but the fertility of these soils is largely due to the use of cattle manure.

RURAL WATER SUPPLIES

In view of the short duration of the rainy season (May to September), and the seasonal character of most of the streams, water supply is a major problem for some villages. The dry season is a period of acute shortage of water but the water situation varies with the various geological provinces. On the Bauchi Plains water can be obtained from wells sunk in areas of deeply weathered rocks, but apart from the fact that such areas are few and far between, supplies from them are not very reliable. Water supplies are also poor on the Biu Plateau which is heavily dissected by numerous streams most of which contain no water during the dry season. This is a major handicap not only to cropping but also to recent attempts at sedentarization of the cattle Fulani.

It is in the area covered by rocks of the Kerri Kerri Formation that the problem of rural water supplies appears to be most acute. At the beginning of the dry season, when surface water supplies have failed, vast stretches of low-lying areas assume an arid aspect. As in other parts of the region the water situation here has retarded agricultural expansion and has made it impossible for cattle to stay long enough in localities where good grazing is available during the early part of the dry season. The situation is worsened by the fact that in the permeable sandstones of the Kerri Kerri Formation the water table often lies at depths of up to 600 feet, thereby making open wells impracticable. This is the case in the waterless plateau of Wawa and the arid plains of Gombe. But where the water table is relatively shallow, as at Potiskum and Kafarati, very high yields have been obtained from wells sunk in the Kerri Kerri Formation. In addition, clay lenses within this formation sometimes give rise to perched acquifers, which are particularly important in areas where the ground water is too deep to be reached by wells. Such a perched acquifer at a depth of 150 feet provides water for the village of Kadi where the permanent water table lies at a depth of 600 feet. The problem with perched acquifers is that water supplies from them may not last for many years. Relatively shallow wells in the Wawa Bush area of Gombe Division, which were probably sustained by perched bodies of water have, for instance, dried up and have failed to produce any water even after being considerably deepened.

In the past water tanks excavated in the ground were constructed in waterless areas underlain by the Kerri Kerri Formation to catch storm-water running along shallow depressions and store it for use during the dry season. These tanks, which are locally referred to as *tabkis*, were usually excavated by slave labour, but today *tabkis* in the Wawa Bush are dug by a large mechanized team. The *tabkis*, some of which exceed fifteen feet in depth, are usually excavated where clay outcrops so as to form a watertight floor. It is these *tabkis* that have permitted settlement in some areas previously restricted to nomads and wet season cultivation. As a device for preserving water in relatively dry districts the *tabki* is not peculiar to the Gongola Basin, but is common in Abak Ifia near Ikot Ekpene where water is stored in clay pits dug under thick forest vegetation which helps to reduce the rate of evaporation (see page 68). Elsewhere, the bulk of the rural population depends on wells and shallow seepages for water during the dry season. Concrete-lined wells, provided by local government authorities or as part of the rural water supply improvement scheme of the regional government are now common, but a number of villages still depend on unlined wells and seepage pits. Supplies from unlined wells are, however, rather precarious and often as polluted as water from the *tabkis*.

POPULATION AND SETTLEMENT

Pagans[1] constitute the bulk of the population of the region, much of which was a major source region for slaves. Bauchi, which in Hausa means slavery, was founded initially as a Hausa slave collecting centre in the middle of a pagan country. Like other Hausa colonies such as Lere and Gombe, Bauchi was built on the plains where the pagans were readily subjugated. Many of these plain pagans have since adopted Islam and are clothed, unlike their counterparts in the hills bordering the Jos Plateau and along the eastern borderlands. The plain pagans live in small villages located at or near the base of hills, as well as in walled towns in the open plains.

During the early part of this century it was usual to distinguish two other groups of pagans in Bauchi, and these were the hill pagans and the mounted pagans. Both groups may be regarded as a product of the Fulani Jihad. Many communities of hill pagans maintained their independence from Fulani rule until the coming of the British and some of them are still to be found living in small hamlets located on inaccessible hill-tops. The Burra of the Biu Plateau are an example of hill pagans who still live in compounds scattered all over the rugged landscape of the area. In addition to farming, which is very much restricted in such hilly areas, these pagans are stock breeders; dwarf cattle, horses and donkeys being the more common domestic animals. The mounted pagan differed from other groups in that like the Fulanis they fought on horseback. The relatively high number of horses in the region is therefore a long-standing feature dating to pre-British days. A number of small independent states survived in the neighbourhood of Bauchi Emirate and may be regarded as a testimony to the determination and ability of the local pagans and Hausas to resist the imposition of Fulani rule.

Hausas, consisting largely of migrants from Kano and Zaria are found particularly in the west and north of Bauchi Emirate, where they live in small communities amongst the settled Fulani. Outside the main urban centres many of these Hausas are itinerant traders, and in the towns they provide much of the retail services which until 1966 was dominated by Ibo and Yoruba traders. Like the Kanuri who have migrated to occupy the eastern parts of Bauchi Emirate, the Hausas intermarry with the settled Fulani and as in other parts of the Northern States, Hausa, which the pagans speak as a second language, is the lingua franca.

The Fulanis are scattered all over the region, partly because they form the ruling group in all towns and villages of importance, and partly as a result of their seasonal wandering with the cattle in search for dry-season grazing and water. In the past the cattle Fulani, many of whom are still pagans, employed some slaves to cultivate their farms. Today they depend largely on grain grown by settled cultivators. The settled Fulani are particularly numerous in the Gombe area where they live in small villages. Their main occupation is farming, but they also keep cattle.

The Gongola Basin is one of the very sparsely settled parts of Nigeria. There are only a few districts where the population density exceeds 200 persons per square mile and these include the area south-west of Bauchi town, Tangale-Waja and southern Biu Districts; all of which are independent pagan strongholds. The historical factor in the distribution of population is thereby implied particularly since the more sparsely inhabited areas with less than 250 persons per square mile are mainly located on the plains and lowland areas. In this regard, the contrast between the sparsely settled Ningi area which borders on Kano Emirate and the south-west of Bauchi town is striking. The latter area is situated near the foothills of the Jos Plateau and has a relatively large concentration of villages. Availability of rural water supplies however appears to be the decisive factor in the location

---

[1] The term 'pagan' is used to describe Nigerians whose religion is not Christianity or Islam.

Plate 38. Cattle grazing on farmland from which grains have recently been harvested. Cattle droppings usually constitute the only form of manure applied on such land.

of human settlement, and hence in the distribution of population. The Duku-Wawa area which is very sparsely settled because of its deficiency of water is a case in point. In this area, perched acquifers, which provided a reasonable supply of water in the past, have dried out and permanent settlement is made possible only by the construction of water tanks or of tabkis in clay depressions.

Large settlements are few and include the district administrative headquarters of Bauchi, Gombe and Biu. Bauchi is also a provincial headquarters. The small walled village, which is rather common in the Zaria District, is scarce in the Bauchi area but farm hamlets are numerous.

ASPECTS OF THE AGRICULTURAL ECONOMY

Various aspects of the agricultural economy including farming practices, field sizes and the crops grown are similar to those obtaining in other parts of the Northern States. The average size of holdings for example exceeds four acres in Bauchi Province while crops grown include guinea corn, millet, cassava and groundnuts. The region is relatively very poor and is not a major exporter of any crop although the main agricultural exports of the Northern States do very well in the area. Considerable changes are however taking place, and there is now a growing emphasis on production for cash rather than for household consumption.

Guinea corn followed by millet are the dominant crops in Bauchi Province but cassava and beans are also widely cultivated as foodcrops. With regard to export crops, groundnuts are far more important than cotton, al-

though the situation may change in the near future. At present the acreage under cotton is expanding but, as in other parts of the Northern States, the cotton acreage fluctuates from year to year, being largely influenced by the availability of seed groundnut. In years when a part of the seed groundnut has been consumed owing to bad harvests in the previous year, farmers usually devote more acreage to cotton, the seeds of which are provided free by the Marketing Board.

The largest concentration of livestock south of latitude 11° N. occurs in the Gongola Basin. In 1962 Bauchi Province had a cattle population of 460,000, a figure which was only exceeded by those for the more northerly Provinces of Sokoto, Kano and Bornu. Yet almost every part of the region is infested with tsetse flies. The main concentration of cattle are on the Biu Plateau and in the upper Gongola district. Other domestic animals include goats, sheep, horses and donkeys, the last two of which are still used for transporting men and goods.

A review of Government development projects since 1950 confirms that the region has been a neglected area in so far as agricultural development is concerned. Neither the mechanized agricultural projects of the Middle Niger region nor the resettlement schemes of Sokoto and Benue Provinces have been tried in the Gongola Basin. The isolation of the region before the opening of the new Bornu railway must have contributed to this neglect. Attempts to increase agricultural production in the areas now served by this railway will probably invite more Government attention and investment in the general development of parts of the region. Already a soil survey of several thousand square miles of land on both sides of

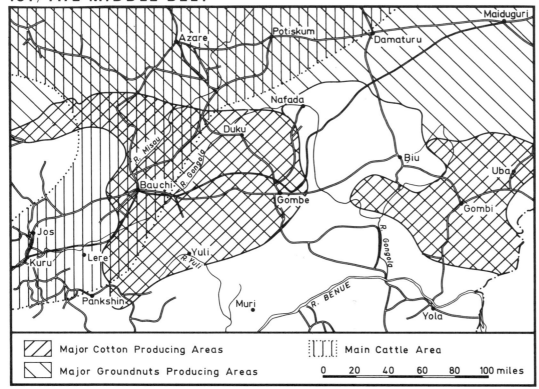

Major Cotton Producing Areas

Major Groundnuts Producing Areas

Main Cattle Area

0   20   40   60   80   100 miles

Figure 66. Cattle and Cash Crop Areas of the Gongola Basin

the railroad from Gombe to Maiduguri has been completed.

DEVELOPMENT OF ROAD AND RAIL TRANSPORTATION

The new Bornu railway extension from Kuru, near Jos, through Bauchi, Tafawa Balewa and Gombe to Maiduguri passes through the central part of the region. Before this railroad was opened, the region was served by roads along which surplus agricultural products were sent to the nearest railhead at Jos or to the nearest river port on the Benue. Apart from the Bauchi–Gombe and the Bauchi–Maiduguri roads the quality of roads are rather poor, and most of them are impassable during the rainy season. The point has repeatedly been made that instead of investing over £20 million on building a new railway, the Government should have developed access roads as well as improved navigability on the Benue. These are valid points, but they were considered at length before a final decision was made that a railway was more suitable. Views expressed regarding the suggestions to improve the Benue and develop roads in preference to building a railway are presented in this section.

Apart from the navigational problems presented by the Benue, that river is usable for limited periods particularly beyond Makurdi. Yola is reached from July to October and Makurdi from June to November but unfortunately, even this short period of navigability does not synchronize with the harvest periods for export crops produced in the Gongola drainage basin. The marketing of groundnuts which are harvested from September to October begins in November, while the selling of cotton starts in December.

The distance by road from central and northern Bauchi to the Benue was also considered to be so great that freight was unlikely to be attracted on a large scale to the Benue ports. Hence the conclusion that the River Benue, even with improved navigability was unlikely to play an important part in the economic development of Bauchi and the Gongola Basin, excepting perhaps those areas in the south which are not far from that waterway.

Road transportation in Nigeria is supplied mainly by individuals rather than by large companies and this was a major point which the pro-railway group harped upon. Apart from privately owned lorries belonging to Onitsha traders, road transportation in the Gongola Basin was supplied mainly by the United Africa Company, who maintained a fleet of lorries for evacuating their produce to the Benue ports and for distributing imported merchandise. But the advocates of the railway extension considered such facilities woefully inadequate to meet the needs of this vast region. They argued that road transportation could only function effectively if an organization, with efficiency and effectiveness equal to that of a railway, could be set up, but they contended that such an organization would operate at a great cost to the country.

A few practical questions arise now that the railway has been built. The traffic survey carried out before the railway was built was based on a forty mile produce corridor, which was considered to be the effective area which the railways will serve. Feeder roads are still to be built and the case made against road transport by the pro-railway school will still apply to these roads unless the railway undertakes to operate the vehicles on them. How realistic are the high hopes of the railway on the revenue potential of the extension as far as the Gongola Basin is

Plate 39. *The railway station at Bauchi. Bauchi lies on the new 400 miles rail extension to Maiduguri.*

concerned? In a sparsely settled area such as this it appears that the case for the railway extension was overstated. Approach roads must be good and exportable surplus considerable before the drawing power, as well as the influence of the new railway, will lead to rapid developments along the forty-mile corridor.

Estimates in 1960 of exportable surplus covered a wide range of products including groundnuts, cotton, grains, beans, rice, onions, maize and cassava. But it was only possible to have an idea of increases in crop output over the years in respect of groundnuts and cotton. No figures were available for foodcrops and it appears that the estimated surpluses were rather too high. It may take several years before the initial estimated quantities can be produced, but no one should expect the new rail extension to perform wonders.

Plate 40. *A homestead in one of the village resettlements in Bauchi Province.*

Works consulted and suggestions for further reading:

1. Carter, J. D., *et al.*, 'The Geology of parts of Adamawa, Bauchi and Bornu Provinces in North-eastern Nigeria' *Geological Survey of Nigeria* No. 30 1963
2. Davis, J. A., 'Biu' *Nigeria Magazine* No. 45 pp. 75–92 1954
3. Falconer, T. D., *The Geology and Geography of Northern Nigeria* London 1911
4. Grove, A. T., *The Benue Valley* Kaduna 1957
5. Ramsay, D. M. & de Leeuw, P. N., 'An Analysis of the Nigerian Savanna, I The survey area and the vegetation developed over Binia sandstone' *Journal of Ecology* No. 52 pp. 233–54 1964
6. Ramsay, D. M. & de Leeuw, P. N., 'An Analysis of the Nigerian Savanna, III The vegetation of the middle Gongola Region by soil parent materials' *Journal of Ecology* No. 53 pp. 643–60 1965
7. Appendix C of *Bauchi–Bornu Railway Extension: Review of Revenue Potential 1960* Lagos 1960

16 The Central High Plains of Northern Nigeria

Along with the Jos Plateau, the central high plains of northern Nigeria, which are made up of Zaria Province and parts of Minna and Nasarawa Districts, form the heartland of Nigeria. Most of the streams draining that part of the country lying north of the Niger-Benue trough rise from these two regions which, like the Middle Niger region, constitute the melting pot of numerous tribal groups. The central highplains is a region of contrasts, of open flat valley sections alternating with gorge sections as in the case of the Kaduna River, of large walled ancient cities like Zaria thriving side by side with new towns like Kaduna capital city; a region where skin-clad or naked pagans still trade side by side with heavily-clad Hausas, and where Muslim rulers govern subjects who are still predominantly pagan, particularly in the south. The human contrasts are brought out more clearly by considering the changing economy of the Zaria Hausa and that of a pagan group of the Gwari tribe.

Recent archeological evidence indicates that Nok culture which was first uncovered in the Jos Plateau was widespread in this region. Nok culture flourished from about the fifth century before the birth of Christ to A.D. 200 and the people who inhabited this region at that time appeared to have been settled agriculturists who kept cattle. Terracotta figures which are ranked as considerable works of art and are considered to be of a high technical standard have been found in places like Abuja and in several parts of the Jos Plateau. Evidence found along with these figurines, some of which were elaborately decorated with necklaces and bracelets, suggest that the people knew how to work iron.

The ancient history of the region is still to be reconstructed but fortunately we have a fuller picture of its more recent history which is tied up with the foundation of the Hausa states, the infiltration of Mohammedanism, the Fulani conquest and the establishment of British rule. Zaria, which was the southernmost of the Hausa states, remained, for a long time, the chief source of slaves for the caravan terminal markets of Katsina and Kano, and during the Fulani conquest the southern part of the region suffered from large-scale depopulation. British rule brought the railways and roads as well as the establishment of new towns and the growth of existing ones. But compared with the Jos Plateau or the Kano region, this region has not shown any signs of rapid development over the years. Apart from cotton and groundnut in the Zaria district, it does not produce much for export. The railways have neither attracted population nor stimulated production. Rather, with the exception of the urban centres of Kaduna, Zaria and Minna, the region remains sparsely populated and largely undeveloped.

LANDFORMS AND DRAINAGE

This region consists of a peneplain developed on pre-Cambrian rocks of variable composition, the Older Granite, schists and quartzites predominating in the triangular area enclosed by lines joining the towns of Minna, Zaria and Bin Gwari. Smooth low ranges characterize the schists but the most conspicuous relief features, which consist of isolated or massed inselbergs, are associated with the Older Granite.

The highest parts are in the north around Zaria (over 2,700 feet), and in the neighbourhood of the Jos Plateau (over 3,500 feet); the general slope of the land being in a westerly and south-westerly direction (Figure 67). Apart from a few small streams like the Gurara and Mada Rivers, which drain directly into the Niger and Benue respectively, the entire region is drained by the Kaduna River which is a major tributary of the Niger. The dominance of the Kaduna River system is so great that this region, which also contains the former northern Nigeria capital of Kaduna territory, can be properly designated the Upper Kaduna Basin.

Unlike most rivers in this part of the country, the Kaduna is a perennial stream although it is subject to great seasonal fluctuations in level. Its long profile consists of numerous valley steps with steep gradients separated by stretches with low gradients. It is along some of the more important of these valley steps that the river has cut such deep gorges as the two-mile ravine in granite at Shiroro and the six-mile gorge through schists at Guria. The direction of flow of the Kaduna River above Kaduna capital city and of the Galma tributary above Zaria indicate clearly that these headwaters formerly flowed into the Rima valley, but have since been captured by streams flowing into the Lower Kaduna valley.

In the dry season, the smaller rivers have little or no water in them but they are usually in flood during the rainy season when the surrounding countryside is converted into fresh-water swamps. These seasonally flooded lands are highly prized as valuable agricultural land and, as in other parts of the Northern States, are cropped with tobacco, onions, sugar-cane and rice.

CLIMATE, VEGETATION AND SOILS

The rainfall is heavier in the south and east but decreases northwards towards Zaria and westwards in the direction of Kontagora. The high annual rainfall of 61 inches for

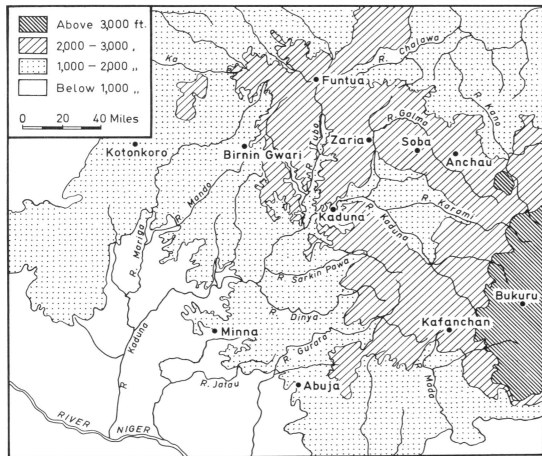

Figure 67. The Relief and Drainage of the North Central High Plains

Kafanchan in the eastern part of the region may be readily explained by the relief effect of the neighbouring slopes of the Jos Plateau but it may not appear so easy to explain why the more northerly town of Minna with 53 inches of rain per annum should have more rain than Bida with 48·5 inches. Bida is of course in the Niger trough, which has a rain-shadow effect, whereas Minna lies directly on the slopes overlooking the lowlands of the Middle Niger, and is therefore exposed to the full force of rain-bearing winds. At Kaduna the annual rainfall is 51 inches, decreasing to about 42 in the Zaria District.

Throughout the region there is only a single rainfall peak which comes in August or September. The rainy season is much longer in the south and east, where it begins in April and ends in October. In the northern part, which corresponds with the Zaria District, the rainfall regime is similar to that of the Kano region and like Kano, both Zaria and Samaru have a rainy season which lasts from mid-May to September. According to Smith the inhabitants of this northern part of the central high plain distinguish four seasons as follows:

Bazara: the hot dry season of the harmattan, from mid-February to mid-May.

Damina: the rainy season, from mid-May to the third week in August.

Kaka: the harvest season, from the third week in August to the third week in November.

Rani: the cool dry season of the harmattan, from the third week in November until mid-February.

The harmattan which blows for four to five months in this region, as compared with two or three weeks in the coastal areas, is as important in the lives of the people as is the onset, duration and vagary nature of the rainfall. It begins to blow during the month of November, and is associated with cold dry winds and dust storms. The spread of cerebro-spinal meningitis, which usually begins towards the end of November, reaches its peak in March and subsides in May, has been attributed to the character and duration of the harmattan.

This region lies in the northern sub-zone of the Guinea savanna vegetation. In the south and east, where the rainfall is heavier and in areas not subjected to much firing, savanna woodland with trees of about twenty to forty feet high predominate. Trees such as the shea butter (*Butyraspemum parkii*), tamarind (*Tamarindus indica*), locust bean and the rubber climber (*Landolphia heudelotii*) are common in the more wooded parts. In the drier district around and north of Zaria the vegetation consists of low orchard bush with a scatter of shade trees like the baobab, silk-cotton and shea butter. Deleb palms are common along river valleys which are readily identified by the dense growth of woodland made possible by favourable soil conditions along such valleys.

Away from the river valleys the main types of soil are the red lateritic soils (*jan kasa*) of northern Zaria and the heavier and more fertile blackish soils (*bakin kasa*) which occur farther south. The lateritic soils are shallow, of low or medium fertility and are suited to crops like groundnuts and millet but not cotton which is grown on the deep and fine-textured black soils. Apart from these two major soil groups, the Hausas of Zaria distinguish several other soil types which on analysis at Samaru research station have been found to be very similar in granular composition.

SLEEPING SICKNESS AND THE ANCHAU SETTLEMENT SCHEME

In Nigeria[1] sleeping sickness, which is almost confined to the Northern States, is particularly severe in the central high plains and also in the Lower Benue valley. Observations in these areas, which are very sparsely settled, confirm the view that a certain minimum human population is required to control the fly and make habitation possible. Once the population is as low as twelve persons per square mile in a rural area with few streams, or about seventy per square mile in an area with several streams, tsetse infestation becomes so severe as to make the area uninhabitable.[2]

A medical survey of the Anchau District of Zaria Province in 1934 showed that about a third of the population of about 50,000 had sleeping sickness and that in some hamlets, as many as fifty per cent of the people were infected. The report of a reconnaisance survey carried out the following year stated that the population of the district was so scattered that anti-tsetse measures would be impracticable. It recommended that people be concentrated into smaller areas, which could be kept tsetse free by clearing neighbouring strips of riverine vegetation, and that a series of such concentrated settlements be so arranged as to form a great tsetse-free corridor (Figure 68) linking the districts of Ikara, Anchau, Kudara and north-eastern Lere. A minimum population density of seventy persons per square mile was considered necessary to keep down regrowth in the cleared streams.

Resettlement within the corridor measuring about seventy miles long, with an average width of ten miles, started in October 1937. It consisted of the amalgamation of a number of hamlets to form villages which were established on well-drained sites, located at considerable distances from swamps. The original idea was to lay out a series of twelve-acre farms with an eighty-yard water frontage, the farms extending up the slope for about half a mile. Such an arrangement of parallel farms was advocated for two reasons. In the first place each farmer would have a range of soils suitable for crops as varied as yams and groundnuts as well as his own piece of grazing and secondly each farmer would be held responsible for the regular slashing of the eighty-yard riverine woodland fronting his holding. But this idea was later abandoned

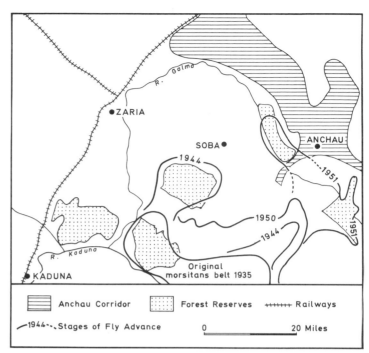

Figure 68. The Anchau Tsetse Eradication Scheme

partly because of the winding nature of the streams and partly because the arrangement was in conflict with local ideas of land holding.

Each settlement was provided with a cement-lined well which was usually located at the centre of the village and surrounded by a fenced grass lawn. The provision of clean well water served the dual purpose of restricting the incidence of guinea worm and of decreasing the man-fly contact which came about because most hamlets drew their water and did their washing in tsetse-infested streams. In addition to the declared aim of tsetse eradication in the area, the Anchau Settlement Scheme has also been concerned with general economic development featuring the introduction of mixed farming, pig-keeping amongst the non-Moslems and the planting of fruit trees, including pawpaw, orange trees, guava and mangoes.

The spread of the tsetse-fly since the 1940's, particularly the *G. morsitans*, which is considered to be the most serious vector of animal trypanosomiasis in the Zaria District, has been a source of concern to the Tsetse Control and Eradication Service. In 1951 this species threatened to invade the Anchau corridor but was checked and since then various eradication schemes have been started all over this region. These include the Zonkwa scheme (1958) near Kafanchan and the Ririwai scheme (1959), which is located eighty miles east of Zaria. The need to destroy some woodland in order to restrict tsetse infestation has often resulted in a clash between the Tsetse Control Service and the Forestry Department. Firewood plantations near villages and patches of *doka* woodland preserved on heavily eroded areas have been known to become infested with fly and

[1] This account is based on T. A. M. Nash's 'The Anchau Settlement Scheme' *Farm and Forest* Vol. 2 pp. 76–82 1941
[2] Harrison Church, R., *West Africa* p. 164 Longmans 1957

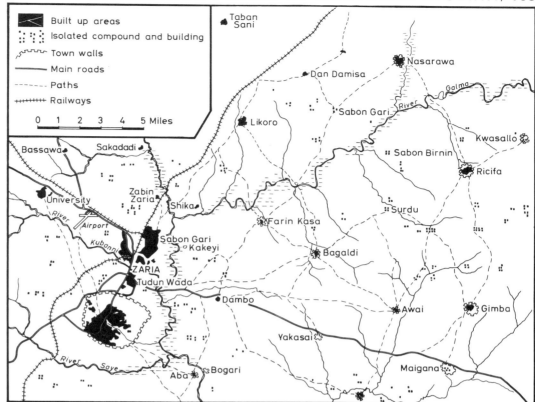

Figure 69. Settlement Types in the Zaria District

have in consequence been declared a source of danger to man and animal.

POPULATION AND SETTLEMENT TYPES

Hausas constitute the indigenous and dominant population of the northern part of Zaria Province but the rest of the region is peopled by numerous pagan tribes, Zaria Emirate having as many as thirty of such small ethnic groups. The Gwaris, who live in western Zaria Province and the Minna District of Niger Province, are one of the most prominent of the non-Hausa indigenes of the region and are known to have suffered much from Fulani raids. But although many Gwari districts were depopulated, these people were able to resist complete Fulani domination up to the time of British occupation.

The Fulanis are not very numerous but are by far the most widespread tribal group in the region. As in many other parts of northern Nigeria three types of Fulanis may be distinguished. These are the Bororo or cattle Fulani, who are nomads and cannot be regarded as very ardent Moslems, the Agwai who are semi-nomadic cattle keepers, and the town Fulani who are the truly settled Fulani and who form the ruling class of most of the emirates of northern Nigeria. In the Zaria District, the semi-nomads or Agwai Fulani are usually employed to tend the cattle of the often wealthier town Fulani. Their state of semi-nomadism is essentially transitional and is one through which many a settled Fulani has passed through.

Extensive slave raiding in the past has left its imprint in the sparse population of the area as well as in the cultural landscape, the Zaria area having the largest number of walled villages in Nigeria. In most areas the population density is less than a hundred persons per square mile, and in Gwari tribal area there are some districts with less than thirty persons per square mile.

Naturally the Fulanis, whose position as rulers was entrenched under the policy of indirect rule adopted by the colonial administration of Nigeria, feel superior to the other groups, including the Hausas. It is also natural that these groups have long resented the Fulani, whose era of absolute rule appears to be on the way out as a result of the chain of reforms following the Nigerian political crisis which started in 1966.

A study of the new 1:100,000 topographical map of the Zaria District reveals that there are three main types of settlement in this part of the central high plains (Figure 69). This is also true of other parts of the region and the three types of settlements are the small hamlets and scattered farmsteads, the old walled villages and the large cities such as Zaria, Kaduna and Minna. The hamlets usually consist of a few compounds, while the isolated farmstead is usually a compound of one or more huts. Unlike the old villages, these hamlets are not walled round, although most of the compounds are screened with fences of mats. In parts of Zaria District some of the old walled village sites have since been abandoned or are populated by a few huts only, while a number of scattered huts occupy what was formerly the farmland of the village.

Plate 41. The Zaria campus of the Ahmadu Bello University.

The walled village, like the walled city, was clearly a product of the unsettled social condition of the pre-colonial period. Many of them were located on hill sites, and terrace cultivation amongst the Kamuku people of Minna District dates from this period. The Gwari village of Kuta was also built on a hill and surrounded by a wall, five and a half miles in circumference, while Birnin Gwari was sheltered in a thick growth of a *kurmi* or forest island. The rapid disintegration of village settlements amongst the pagan groups indicates clearly that nucleation in this area was induced by the state of social insecurity. The few large villages which have never been walled are certainly more recent than the walled villages.

Urban settlements include the ancient walled city of Zaria and the twentieth-century railway junction towns of Kaduna, Minna and Kafanchan. Zaria and Kaduna presents two contrasting examples of old and new in urban development. A few aspects of their urban landscape, including the residential districts and their retail structures, are reviewed below.

THE CITY AND TOWNSHIP OF ZARIA

The walled city of Zaria is one of the oldest urban centres in Nigeria. It was founded in the fourteenth century and

remained for several centuries an important political rival of Kano. Today Zaria is the capital of Zaria Emirate and the most important centre for higher education in the Northern States of Nigeria. Numerous Islamic schools exist within the old-walled city while modern institutions including the Ahmadu Bello University and the Institute for Agricultural Research and Special Services are located at Samaru, about seven miles from the city.

As in the case of Kano, the walled city is almost exclusively occupied by the local Hausa and Fulani population while Nigerian strangers, foreigners and the various institutions including schools and hospitals occupy the residential areas of Tudun Wada and Sabon Gari which are creations of the colonial period. Much of the open space enclosed within the city walls is still to be built up, a situation which is similar to that of Kano and Katsina.

Zaria is one of the few industrial towns in the northern part of Nigeria. The seventeen-acre Nigerian Tobacco Company's factory, which employs about 350 African staff, produces approximately eighty million cigarettes of various brands every month. In addition, Zaria has a large cotton ginnery, a £300,000 cosmetic factory and a bicycle assembly plant. The Zaria Oil Mills Ltd., which handle about 170 tons of guinea corn and 4,500 tons of groundnuts yearly, makes guinea corn and groundnut cakes and flour for local consumption. Zaria's industries are therefore largely based on the processing of locally grown agricultural products.

Zaria is within easy reach of Lagos, Kano and Kaduna by road, rail or air. The Zaria–Kano road is one of the best motorways in the country, while the airport has a unique location which is midway between the town and city of Zaria and the educational suburb of Samaru.

KADUNA

Kaduna (which means the place of the crocodiles) is unique amongst Nigeria's towns. Like Enugu, the capital of the former Eastern Nigeria, it is a new town founded during the second decade of British rule in Nigeria, but unlike Enugu and Jos which are mining towns, Kaduna is essentially an administrative town. Its establishment in 1917 brought to an end a protracted search for a suitable administrative capital for northern Nigeria. The first capital was Lokoja (1899–1901), followed by Jebba (1901––2) and Zungeru (1902–17). But Zungeru was excessively hot and infested with mosquitoes and so, on the recommendation of Lord Lugard, Kaduna was built at mile 570 on the Lagos–Kano railway, at a point where the railway crosses the Kaduna River. Ten years later, its importance as a railway town was increased when Kaduna became a major rail junction and Nigeria's biggest passenger exchange point where trains from Kano, Kaura Namoda, Port Harcourt and Lagos met on the evenings of Tuesday, Thursday and Saturday.

In recommending the site of Kaduna, Lugard expressed the view that the climate was invigorating, the soil good and adapted for vegetable and flower gardens and the water supply pure and inexhaustible. He also made the point that the site was within fifty miles of the great trade centre of Zaria. As with other towns in British colonial territories, a segregated African quarter grew up between the Government residential and administrative area and the new rail junction south of the Kaduna River. A 400-yard open space separated the African town from the administrative town in the north and the railway town in the south. In 1919 the population of Kaduna was 3,000 but by 1952 it had risen to 45,000 and ten years later it was almost 150,000. Post-war increase in the population has been largely due to the influx of job seekers to this new town which is now second only to Kano in commercial and industrial importance.

As the administrative capital of the former Northern Region of Nigeria, Kaduna still has a large population of civil servants, a great majority of the remainder depending

Plate 42. Hamdala Hotel, Kaduna.

for a living on various forms of services which they provide for this administrative group. The 1967 political reforms in the country are bound to change Kaduna from an administrative to an industrial town since a large number of the civil servants will be deployed and transferred to the various state capitals, leaving only a small proportion at Kaduna which is the capital of the North Central State.

Kaduna is an important military training centre for recruits and officers of the Nigerian army as well as of the police force and the air force. Nigeria's only ordnance factory which manufactures ammunition and other military equipment is located at Kaduna. There are several large textile factories such as Kaduna Textiles Ltd., which has an annual production potential of 46 million yards of grey baft in ten-yard pieces, Arewa Textile Ltd. and Norspin Ltd., which in addition to producing yarn for handweavers also makes the canvas for Dunlop motor and bicycle tyres. Nigeria Breweries Ltd., makers of Star Beer and soft drinks, has its northern factory at Kaduna.

The ultra-modern Hamdala Hotel at Kaduna is one of the best and most expensive hotels in the country. Recreational facilities include the one million pound olympic-style Ahmadu Bello Stadium opened in 1964 and the Kaduna Club. Like all the former regional capitals, Kaduna has two radio stations and a Television House.

THE ECONOMY OF THE HAUSA POPULATION

Although Hausa is spoken as a second language amongst the pagan groups, the main concentration of Hausas in this region is in the northern part of Zaria Province, particularly around Zaria city. Permanent Hausa settlements are common in the pagan districts of Gwari and Abuja, but the account given below is based on the situation in northern Zaria, where the economy is similar to that of the Hausa in Kano and Katsina. In the pagan areas to the west and south of this region, the economy is much more typical of the Middle Belt in that it features the cultivation of grains and root crops, the use of ridges and mounds and the farming of large acreages, exceeding three acres. In the past, there was a considerable economic link between the Hausa-Fulani on the one hand and the pagans on the other. The latter acted as slaves supplying farm labour for the Hausa-Fulani who are now obliged to till their own farms, although those who can afford it still employ paid labour provided by pagan migrants as well as local Hausas.

Compared with the other two main tribal groups in Nigeria, the Ibos and the Yorubas, the Hausas lead a rather simple life and appear to be more fatalistic and less money conscious. The rich amongst them attach more importance to making the pilgrimage to Mecca than to expensive houses, cars and dresses which are the signs of success amongst the more sophisticated southerners. But it will be absurd to attribute Hausa simplicity to their religion. It is however true that their religion has until recently kept them behind in the acquisition of Western education. Hence the fact that in spite of their long history of trade, industry and administration, the control of various essential services including retail trade and the organs of administration has been in the hands of Ibos, Yorubas and expatriates from Britain and the Middle East. Hausa itinerant traders are found all over the towns of southern Nigeria, but the general impression of the Hausas in Hausaland is that they live on farming supplemented by craft products. Unlike the Ibos or the Yorubas, they carry on little trade except perhaps the distribution of kolanuts. Closer acquaintance with the Hausa economic system however reveals a more complicated situation in which the categories of specialization include farming, craft, trade and wage labour.

With the possible exception of the numerically insignificant but growing elite in urban centres, almost all the Hausas in Hausaland farm to some extent. In most cases the same farmer produces crops for subsistence as well as for internal exchange and for export. The short duration of the rainy season, which lasts just over four months during which food for the coming year must be grown, makes farming a part-time occupation even for those who would rather wish to be classified as full-time farmers. By December, all the foodcrops have been harvested and farming activity is restricted to the monthly picking of cotton until March. During this period, men who have no fadama plots find little to do, and therefore engage in craft production. The great uncertainties of food farming in the region are also an important factor which leads men to practise such subsidiary occupation as craft production, hunting and working for wages.

In rural areas, therefore, craft production which is usually carried on with farming is a part-time occupation. The situation is different in Zaria and other towns where full-time craftsmen abound largely because they tend to receive greater returns from their crafts than is possible in rural areas. Both in the towns and rural areas, craft production is usually carried on by individuals or families.

Two types of *kodago* (i.e. labour for wages) are recognized. The first is the wet season *kodago* which is carried on near the labourer's home, so that he can devote some time to cultivating his own farm. The intensity of farmwork during this season is so great that farmers who decide to work for wages at this time of the year usually do so at the expense of their own farms. For this reason, Zaria depends largely on migrant pagans for *kodago* labour, since local farmers will take to working for cash on other people's farm only when they are in dire need of cash. Dry season *kodago* is limited to fadama farming or unskilled manual labour in the towns. It is usually associated with the seasonal migrations of farmers to work in other parts of the country at this time of the year; a practice referred to locally as *cin rani* (= eating off the dry season, i.e. practising one's occupation away from home during which time one's grain is not eaten but left in the granary).

The work performed by clerks, messengers, policemen and many others employed by the local councils or state government, is regarded as a craft by the Hausas; and so we are left with trading as the remaining major occupation of the people. Local trade between urban centres and the surrounding rural areas may be distinguished from long-distance trade of which the most important is that with southern Nigeria. In both cases the trade includes the exchange of such goods as natron, expensive embroidered cloths, pepper from other parts of northern Nigeria, kola nuts, palm oil and manufactured goods which are produced in or imported through southern Nigeria.

Zaria and Kaduna are the main urban centres in the Hausa-dominated areas of this region and serve as collecting points for produce like groundnuts, cotton, sheanuts and hides and skins, which are destined for the export market. These urban areas are also major wholesale and retail trade centres supplying manufactured goods, natron, kola-nuts and palm oil to the rural districts. In return for these and other services including education, the rural areas supply grains, root-crops, beans and vegetables to the urban centres. Donkeys and road transport are of great importance in the conduct of local exchange between town and countryside, while the road and railway dominate the long-distance trade between

Plate 43. A Market Scene in Kaduna. Traders who have got no space in covered stalls stay in the open where they use grass mats to shield themselves from the scorching sun.

the region and southern Nigeria. Trade goods exported from the Zaria District to the towns of the forest belt include cattle, perfumes, onions, locally-made cloth and leather goods, beans and groundnuts. Cattle traders usually have agents resident in towns like Ibadan, Lagos and Enugu and it is these agents who actually arrange the sales of cattle to the butchers. Proceeds from cattle sold in western Nigeria are usually invested in purchasing kola-nuts as well as manufactured goods for despatch to Zaria.

Retail trade in kola-nuts is probably one of the most profitable enterprises in the region and indeed all over Hausaland. It is a long-standing trade and today, as in the days of Henry Barth's travels (1850–4), there is no hamlet, however small or remote, in which kola-nut is not in constant use. The distributive trade in kola-nuts can well be compared with the sale of cooked food in Yoruba towns and villages. But while the food retail trade in Yorubaland is controlled by women, the retail trade in kola at Zaria is dominated by men who usually receive their nuts on credit in much the same way as the butchers in southern Nigeria obtain cattle on credit. These retailers then employ young boys to hawk the nuts in the markets, motor parks or from compound to compound.

THE PRODUCTION OF BROWN SUGAR AND GINGER IN ZARIA PROVINCE

In Nigeria the sugar-cane grown on peasant farms is used for chewing, excepting in the Zaria area where the production of brown sugar by local peasants is of long-standing importance. According to Irvine the Church Missionary Society in Zaria produced and sold in 1918 soft molasses sugar and sticky brown sugar crystals which are known in commerce as demerara sugar.[1] The cane is crushed in simple mills operated by manual labour or by machines. Both the number of crushers imported into Zaria and the tonnage of brown sugar produced showed a steady increase between 1945 and 1953, but since then the high price obtainable for chewing cane and the growing competition of refined sugar has led to a decline in the production of brown sugar. The production of commercial sugar at Bacita is likely to reduce further the demand for peasant-produced brown sugar, which may die a natural death when Bacita and other factories now proposed are able to meet the country's sugar needs.

The ginger industry in the southern part of Zaria Province has been described as the most specialized type of export production in the pagan areas of the Middle Belt. Ginger which is used as a spice, particularly in confectionery such as ginger cakes and in the manufacture of ginger ale and ginger beer, is a native of tropical Asia and was introduced into this region as a result of several attempts by the Administration to develop export production in the area. Amongst other things, the Department of Agriculture undertook seed selection and the development of curing techniques suited to local conditions.

Ginger thrives best on light well-drained soils with

[1] Irvine, F. R., *A Textbook of West African Agriculture* p. 279 London 1934

plenty of manure, but in the Zaria area, where the farmers do not use much manure, the crop is usually grown in wooded valleys where leaf fall provides organic matter. The seed, which consists of short pieces of rhizome from the previous year's crop, is planted on ridges in late April or May, after which the farmer gives very little attention to the crop. The real labour-demanding part of the industry is in preparing the harvested crop for the market. This involves peeling the rhizomes, washing them in about six changes of water before drying them in the sun; the processes of washing and drying being repeated until the desired colour is obtained. Amongst the pagans of Zaria Province, much of this tedious work is done by the women, and fortunately this curing process takes place during the harmattan which aids in drying and bleaching the ginger.

The largest pre-war shipment of ginger from Nigeria was in 1935 when 342 tons, representing eight per cent of the world output in that year was exported. After that year production declined owing to a fall in world prices and the greater emphasis on cotton and groundnut cultivation in the area. The situation today is that, as a result of better prospects since the 1963–4 season, the crop is now marketed by the Northern Nigeria Marketing Board. In that season the Board exported 3,650 tons of the crop.[1]

TOBACCO PRODUCTION IN THE ZARIA AREA

The oldest established area of commercial tobacco production in the Northern States is the Zaria area which, until 1948, was indeed the only area producing commercial cigarette tobacco in this part of the country. About sixty per cent of the crop raised in this area is still grown during the rainy season on the uplands, in contrast to the situation in Sokoto Province, where the bulk of the crop is raised on the fadamas as a dry season crop. This situation explains why tobacco competes for land and labour with foodcrops in the Zaria area. As an upland crop, tobacco is usually preceded by an early crop of millet. It is often sown on the same piece of land for two or three years after which the plot is left fallow and a new one cultivated.

Rain-fed tobacco in the Zaria area is planted out from nurseries in August and harvested in October and November. The crop which is air-cured is then hung up to dry in temporary curing barns called *rumfas*, where it is left until the months of April or May, when the rising humidity of the first rains makes it possible to handle the leaves again. Crops grown in this area are sent to the

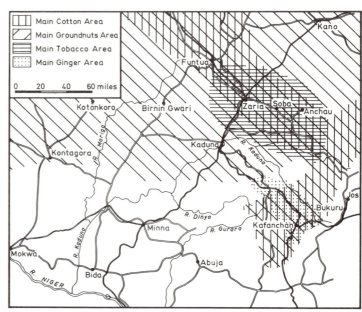

Figure 70. The Cash Crop Areas of the North Central High Plains

Nigerian Tobacco Company's factory at Zaria which manufactures cigarettes and cigars.

ASPECTS OF THE ECONOMY OF THE PAGAN POPULATION

The pagan population of this region is concentrated in the southern half which has more rainfall and where the terrain is often more rugged as in Abuja and parts of Minna. This area is even less suitable for cattle than the Zaria District, and although it is relatively well served by rail and road transportation it produces very little for export as compared with the Zaria District. The most widespread of the pagan people inhabiting the region are the Gwaris, who are concentrated in Minna Division and to a lesser extent in Abuja and Nassara Divisions. This section presents a general account of Gwari economy which is based on farming, hunting, pottery and weaving, the last two of which are dominated by the women.

Gwari territory is particularly sparsely populated and farmland is plentiful. There is however no unoccupied land in the sense that all land is owned by one village or another. Once a piece of land is granted to a man it cannot be alienated, not even when it reverts to fallow, unless the man gives an indication to the village head that he no longer intends to use the land. Farming

[1] Annual Report of the Department of Agriculture, Northern Nigeria 1963/4 p. 26

practice varies from district to district. The use of manure, for instance, is not very common amongst the Gwari of Abuja, who farm one plot for only three years after which it is left fallow. In Minna District, on the other hand, a two-year rotation of crops, in which guinea corn and millet is grown in the first year, and cotton, groundnuts or tamba in the second year, as well as the use of animal manure, makes it possible for a piece of land to be cropped for up to ten years before it is left fallow.

In Abuja as well as in Minna, increasing demand for farmland has led to the cultivation of plots which may be located at a distance of up to five miles from the town or village. This has given rise to the building of farm huts where the farmer spends the whole day, returning only at night. In some cases, the farmer may spend the night or even weeks in such distant farms.

The collective or group-labour service which was very common in the past is still practised today. By this system a farmer who finds that the work in his farm is too much for his family may call on others to help. Payment for such services is usually in the form of food and beer provided by the owner of the farm. In the past, a chief could also call out the entire labour force of the village to work on his farm; but as in other parts of the country, this practice is not common today.

Guinea corn, much of which is used for brewing beer, is still the main crop and is interplanted with millet and beans. Maize and hungry-rice are the other grains grown on upland farms while swamp rice is of growing importance in the marshy land along the Kaduna River. Various varieties of yams are also cultivated and cassava, which was once disliked by some Gwari groups, is still regarded as food for times of famine. Almost every farmer grows some tobacco which is consumed locally. Large-scale production of tobacco for cash is a possible development if only the Nigerian Tobacco Company will extend its sphere of operation to this part of the country. A surer way of developing the pagan areas appears to be the expansion of food crop production with a view to exporting surplus food to other parts of the country.

Although Gwari women take part in farming, their main occupation is pottery and weaving. In the small Gwari town of Kwali for example, most of the women are potters who produce a wide variety of pots, the most remarkable of which are the giant wide-necked water-storage pot with a capacity of twenty to thirty gallons. Vertical looms are used for weaving broad multi-colour cloths. Dyeing of locally-spun thread or of imported white cloth as well as of raffia used for making bags is also an important subsidiary occupation. Usually the indigo is

cultivated by men who sell it to their wives or other women.

The Gwaris keep large herds of goats and fowls but pigs and sheep are less numerous. Hunting is an important source of meat since domestic animals are rarely killed, except on festive occasions. Gwari territory is also an important dry season grazing ground for Fulani cattle. Guinea fowls abound in the bush in the wild state, although some are kept. Thousands of guinea fowl eggs are railed to southern Nigeria every year during the rains (May to September) which is the breeding season for wild guinea fowls.

Trade in imported goods is not as developed as in the Zaria District and the kola-nut does not appear to be the indispensable item of food that it is amongst the Hausa population. In general the pagans have less cash to spend, largely because of the absence of a substantial cash crop. Foodstuffs and craft products are the main trade goods to be seen in the village markets which are held every four days. Donkeys are in common use as a means of transport to the market and farms, but the most popular form of transportation is human porterage, in which people carry loads on shoulders rather than on their heads.

Works consulted and suggestions for further reading:

1. Cohen, A., 'The Social Organisation of Credit in West African Cattle Market' *Africa* Vol. 35 pp. 8–19 1965
2. Coppock, J. T., 'Tobacco growing in Nigeria' *Erdkunde* No. 19 pp. 297–306 1965
3. Crowder, M., *The Story of Nigeria* London 1962
4. Glover, P. E., *The Tsetse Problem in Northern Nigeria* especially chapter 7 Nairobi 1961
5. Jones, G. I., 'The Beef Cattle Trade in Nigeria' *Africa* No. 16 pp. 29–38 1946
6. Prothero, R. M., 'Land Use of Soba, Zaria Province, Northern Nigeria' *Economic Geography* No. 33 pp. 72–86 1957
7. Russ, W., 'The Geology of Parts of Niger, Zaria and Sokoto Provinces' *Geological Survey of Nigeria* No. 27 Lagos 1957
8. Smith, M. G., *The Economy of Hausa Communities of Zaria* Colonial Office London 1955
9. Temple, O., *Notes on the Tribes, Provinces, Emirates and States of the Northern Provinces of Nigeria* Lagos 1922

Part Three The Nigerian Sudan and the Eastern Borderlands

17 Sokoto and the Rima Basin

With the exception of Yauri Emirate and those parts of Gwandu Emirate which occupy both banks of the Niger, Sokoto Province lies within, and can be said to constitute, the Rima drainage basin. It has an area of 36,000 square miles while that of the Rima basin is 35,000 square miles. Apart from the Maradi tributary whose middle course traverses the neighbouring country of Niger Republic, the entire Rima system is contained within Nigeria. The Rima and its tributaries constitute the major physical feature of the region, but in an almost semi-arid area the Rima system is more than a feature of the landscape. As the main source of water for man, beast and plant, the Rima and its affluents are an important factor in the location of economic activity as well as in the distribution of population and settlements. For this reason, aspects of the hydrology of the basin are considered in detail.

Administratively the region consists of the two most senior emirates of Sokoto and Gwandu, which were initially ruled respectively by the son and brother of Usman dan Fodio, the leader of the Jihad which ended in the Fulani conquest of much of northern Nigeria, as well as the smaller emirates of Argungu and Zuru. It is in this historical connection that Sokoto is best known to the people of the Sudan and indeed to the outside world. The

Fulani rising started within the region and most of the fiercest battles were fought here, but the most important fact to Nigerian Moslems is that Dan Fodio, 'the Commander of the Faithful' died and was buried in Sokoto, which has now become a place of pilgrimage. Fulani political domination is still intact, owing to the British system of indirect rule, in which the feudal aristocracy was encouraged as an instrument of administration. Today the emirs and their courts still have much power, and at the present pace of educational development it will take several years to see through any significant reforms.

THE GEOLOGY AND PHYSICAL LANDSCAPE

Two major geological regions may be recognized—a region of pre-Cambrian rocks in the south-east and a region of young sedimentary rocks in the north and west (Figure 71). All the main tributaries of the Rima rise from the region of pre-Cambrian rocks, which is characterized by broken plains from which rise steep-sided granitic, gneiss and quartzite inselbergs. Extensive belts of phyllites occur along the Ka River between Bakwium and Anka as well as in the east of Maradi. The phyllites are soft, fine-grained and dark-coloured rocks, which have been largely

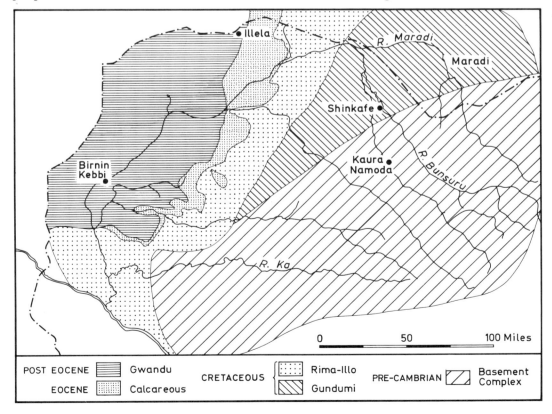

POST EOCENE	Gwandu
EOCENE	Calcareous
CRETACEOUS	Rima-Illo
	Gundumi
PRE-CAMBRIAN	Basement Complex

Figure 71. The Geology of the Rima Basin

invaded by a series of igneous intrusions which give rise to some of the numerous inselbergs. Apart from areas where recent erosion has removed the surface covering, the plains are covered by sandy drifts which are predominantly of local derivation.

The region of pre-Cambrian rocks is dissected by numerous shallow valleys, which form the drainage channels of streams flowing into the upper reaches of the Rima tributaries. The badland topography, which features in this region, is a result of the rapid headward erosion of the streams which in turn is caused by the rapid and high rate of surface run-off. Conditions which encourage this rapid run-off include the broken nature of the landscape which creates considerable slopes, the low permeability of the rocks and the character of the rainfall which comes as short sharp thunderstorms.

In the sedimentary region the character of the landscape depends very much on the underlying rock, except in areas where a thick mantle of drift has concealed many minor irregularities to produce a rather monotonous aspect. There are two major rock groupings in this region, an older Cretaceous series known as the Gundumi and Rima-Illo series and the younger series of Eocene and post-Eocene age known as the Calcareous and Gwandu groups. The former series, which lies immediately west of the pre-Cambrian region, are soft and easily eroded resulting in a rather flat landscape, with a wide shallow valley. The area underlain by the Eocene and post-Eocene series covers the western and northern part of Sokoto Province and consists of a plateau of sandstone, capped by an extremely resistant layer of lateritic ironstone, which produces flat-topped hills whenever the surface is broken by recent river erosion. The Sokoto River, for instance, flows through a broad flat-bottomed trench-like valley between two steep and worn escarpments, which lead up to the plateau on either side. The cliffs bordering the river valleys in this part of the sedimentary region rarely reach 200 feet in height, but may be very rugged as at Goronjo. In the north and north-east of Sokoto, the relative relief of the dissected sandstone plateau has been considerably reduced by accumulations of blown sand which covers the floors of the smaller valleys.

All the tributaries of the Rima rise from the pre-Cambrian region and flow in rather restricted and narrow valleys until they pass into the area of the younger sedimentary groups, where they develop broad valleys with extensive flood plains. The large quantities of sediment deposited in the lower reaches of these tributaries result from the sudden change in gradient, the reduction of velocity and loss of energy as the rivers enter the region of open broad valleys. During the floods the rivers spread out over the vast flood plains which they traverse as slow-moving shallow sheets of water in contrast to the fast streams in the upper reaches. As a result of the extensive deposit of sands in the sedimentary part of the valleys, river beds tend to be higher than the surrounding valley floor which becomes more liable to flooding. The reported increase in flood heights over the years may be attributed to the deterioration of the beds of these rivers, as a result of excessive aggradation. Increase of surface run-off owing to deforestation and cultivation is a contributory factor but the question of climatic change does not appear to arise, since available evidence indicates that climatic conditions have remained stable since Roman times. In any case if climatic change were a factor, drier conditions would be expected.

Increasing flood heights along the Rima valley have resulted in the retreat of settlement from the valley to the plateau. A Forestry Department survey in 1937 noted that as a result of such forced retreat of the settlement frontier, the inhabitants of towns situated on the edge of the Rima plain, where formerly they grew excellent crops of guinea corn, have been forced to leave their farms and migrate to the less fertile land on the sandstone plateau. One of the Rima flood plain towns which has had to be rebuilt is Maradi in the Niger Republic. The new town, with its broad unsurfaced streets radiating from a central place in a pattern which reminds one of the Etoile in Paris, dates from 1945, and is located on a raised platform overlooking the ruins of the old settlement. Further evidence of the increasing height of the Rima floodwaters is provided by the extensive damage in 1961 to the irrigation and drainage works of the Wurno Irrigation Scheme which was caused by unusually high floods.

Owing to the extensive spread of available water along the flat valleys of the area of younger sedimentary rocks, but particularly along the Lower Rima valley, much of the discharge of the Rima system is lost by evaporation and seepage. This explains why the Rima contributes very little to the flow of the Niger. Indeed, according to Major Burdon, the Rima had no channel connection with the Niger in 1903 as a result of the deterioration of the lower Rima channel by excessive aggradation. Rather the whole mass of the water was lost in the marsh of the lower Rima and the present channel to the Niger is said to have been cut by the British administration.[1] The silting of the river bed is also responsible for the deterioration of the harbour of Birnin Kebbi, which was once an important riverside market town.

[1] Burdon, J. A., 'In discussion after paper by G. S. Elliot on "The Anglo-French Niger-Chad boundary" ' *Geographical Journal* No. 24 p. 520 1904

CLIMATE, VEGETATION AND SOILS

As in other parts of the tropics, rainfall is the most important or rather critical element of climate in so far as agriculture is concerned. Unlike temperature conditions, which remain uniform all through the year except for the difference between day and night, the rainfall shows a marked seasonal variation. Average annual rainfall ranges from 43·9 inches at Funtua in the extreme south-east to 28·9 inches at Sokoto. The rainfall is concentrated in a short wet season, which extends from mid-May to mid-September. The dry season therefore lasts for more than seven months, being particularly dry from November to March or April, when no drop of rain may fall. The character of the rainfall, which comes in short intense showers, is also important when considering the amount of run-off, as well as gully erosion on the plateau areas of the basin, and the rate of sedimentation of the water channels. In Gusau much of the rain occurs as daily falls exceeding one inch, and this is rather intense for this part of the country.

The harmattan persists from November to March, during which time normal vegetative growth ceases. Temperatures remain very high in the day, but as a result of rapid radiation due to cloudless skies the nights are very cold. Coming as it does from the desert, this wind is not only dry but also dust-laden, such that stationary objects are quickly covered by dust while visibility is greatly impaired by a haze of dust particles. Bodily discomfort at this season is considerable, and one can well imagine the plight of the local peasant walking barefoot on the hard lateritic surfaces of the Sokoto-Goronjo area.

The question of climatic change, which has already been referred to in passing, deserves more comments at this stage. It was in 1935 that Stebbing first postulated the idea that the climate of the area immediately south of the Sahara, that is including the Rima Basin, was becoming drier and that desert conditions were spreading southward. His postulate of the 'encroaching Sahara' was based on observations made during a hurried tour of parts of the southern Sahara, rather than on long-term climatic and hydrological data. In rejecting this postulate, Brynmor Jones (1938) argued that if dessication had actually occurred, it would not be difficult to find evidence of it in the field. Such evidence would include signs of sand encroachment, declining rainfall, a lowering of the water table and southward retreat of the frontier of settlement and cultivation. A Forestry Commission, set up jointly by the French and British Governments in 1937 to investigate this problem, did not find any such evidence. The results

of many other investigations on this topic have been adequately reviewed by Bovill (1958) who concludes that the climate of this region, and other neighbouring districts south of the Sahara, has not changed significantly since Roman times.

Under natural conditions, as in the forest reserves, the vegetation is that of a typical Sudan savanna which consists of an almost continuous grass cover and thick tree cover. The trees, which average twenty-five to fifty feet in height, are a mixture of fine-leaved thorny trees and of broad-leaved species of the Guinea savanna. The Dum Palm (*Hyphaene thebaica*) and the Baobab (*Adansonia digitate*) are common, particularly in the north. Both trees, together with the locust bean, shea butter tree (*Butyrospermum parkii*), *Acacia albida* and Kapok (*Bomba costatum*) are of considerable economic importance to the people, and are consequently protected in much the same way as villagers in southern Nigeria protect such fruit trees as the oil palm and the African pear which grow on their farmlands. In the very densely settled parts of this region as around Sokoto only a very impoverished secondary vegetation survives. Both the surface and the rugged slopes of the lateritic-capped sandstone plateaux of the Sokoto-Goronjo area are virtually devoid of vegetation in the dry season, when the red-skinned Sokoto goats, which roam these rugged slopes, go through a hunger period similar to that which the human population experiences.

Soil profiles in this region show a rather sandy topsoil and a clayey subsoil in which concretions are common. Once the vegetative cover is removed through over-cultivation, overgrazing and periodic firing, the topsoils are readily washed off by rainwater. Gully erosion is common along the slopes of cliffs bordering the river valleys, and it has been observed that gullies in such areas cut back very rapidly. The areas bordering the rivers are the most densely settled due to the need to establish settlements near water sources, and the fact that the increasing height of floodwaters in the basin has resulted in a retreat of settlements from the flood plains to the edge of the plateau surfaces. Footpaths leading from these settlements to the streams have often provided initial flow channels which have developed into large gullies. Examples of such gullies abound along the laterite road from Wurno to Goronjo. Gullies have also been known to originate at the downward end of furrows in fields where ridging is along the slope, rather than along the contours.

The soils which occur along the extensive fadamas or seasonally flooded river valleys differ from the general description given above. In the first place they provide more fertile farmlands except where the drainage is very poor, in which case only swamp rice can be cultivated. Secondly the fadamas are very close to sources of water for dry-season irrigation, their major handicaps being the erratic nature of the flood height which may destroy crops and habitations. Recent irrigation and drainage schemes in the Rima Basin include the 4,500 acre Wurno Scheme, the 1,950-acre Kwarre Scheme and the 7,000-acre Bunza Fadama Scheme, all of which are designed to control soil water in order to facilitate maximum exploitation of the fadama soils.

TRADITIONAL AGRICULTURE AND ANIMAL HUSBANDRY

Farming in the Rima basin is dominated by a grain economy based on the cultivation of millets, guinea corn, upland rice and maize for food as well as money crops like cotton, groundnuts and tobacco. Millet is by far the most widely cultivated grain and is often inter-cropped with guinea corn. In the drier parts of the north and north-west a quick-maturing variety of bulrush millet (or *gero* in Hausa), which takes about three months to ripen, is grown. The plant grows to a height of six feet and produces a rod-like concentration of grains which form the staple food of the people. Different varieties of guinea corn or *sorghum* are also cultivated. These include grass sorghum and sweet sorghum, both of which are grown for fodder, as well as grain sorghum which produces grains for human food, while the bran and leaves from the mature plants are fed to animals. The stems of guinea corn are as much as twelve feet long and are used for fencing, mats, thatch and fuel.

Maize and upland rice are grown where conditions are less dry as in the south and south-east. Groundnuts were formerly grown for local consumption, but are now featuring as an important export crop marketed through at least twenty-five gazetted central places. Indigenous varieties of rice have been cultivated in the Rima Basin for centuries and imported varieties, which are now more widely cultivated, were introduced in the recent past. Small gardens of tobacco and sugar-cane which are found in the fadamas are also a long-standing feature in the traditional agriculture of this region.

Field size and field systems are typical of other Hausa districts in the Northern States. Outside the administrative districts of Sokoto, Hama Ali, Dingyadi, Gumbi and Bodinga where land hunger has led to permanent cultivation or resulted in reduced fallow periods, farmland can be said to be abundant for local needs, and individual households of a man and two or three wives usually cultivate as

much as four to eight acres. In the more arid and infertile sandy areas the average acreage cultivated by each household is as high as nine acres. As in other parts of the country, household farms rarely occur in one continuous stretch. The two-fold division of farmland into compound-lands and distant farmland is very much a part of the local agricultural system as is the case in southern Nigeria. Compoundlands are cultivated every year, and the establishment of permanent cultivation around Sokoto and the neighbouring districts can properly be regarded as resulting from the encroachment of compoundlands on distant farmland consequent on increasing demand for cultivable land.

The curious thing about traditional farming in this region, as in other parts of the Sudan, is that in spite of the much larger acreages cultivated by each household, few of such households produce more food than they need. Yields per acre fluctuate from year to year, being largely influenced by climatic and soil conditions. Crop failures may be caused by delayed rains, except in areas near enough to water channels for water to be obtained for watering crops. The use of household manure is restricted to compoundlands where yields are also better. Demonstration farms of the extension division of the Regional Ministry of Agriculture confirm that with improved cultivation technique and the use of fertilizers the yield per acre can be greatly increased.

A broad ethnic specialization is obvious in the two main economic activities of the Rima Basin, in that farming is dominated by the Hausa population, while cattle rearing is largely in the hands of the Fulanis. Many Hausa peasants also own cattle, just as a large number of Fulanis have abandoned their traditional nomadic life to become sedentary cultivators. Yet there is very little integration of crop farming and cattle rearing, except that guinea corn stalks and by-products of groundnuts and millet are fed to cattle during the dry months (November to April). In addition, cattle pens (*zaribas*) are sometimes sited on land intended for cultivation, so that such land may benefit from droppings from the penned animals.

The dominant type of cattle in Sokoto Province are called the Bokoloji, the Sokoto-Gudali or simply the Sokoto cattle. They are medium-sized deep-bodied animals but are bigger and heavier than the White Fulani. The Sokoto-Gudali are considered to be less resistant to trypanosomiasis than the White Fulani, and this explains why the local Fulanis do not go south with their cattle, but wander about the province in search of dry-season grazing. Observations at Shika Stock Farm reveal that Sokoto cattle show good adaptability to fattening on

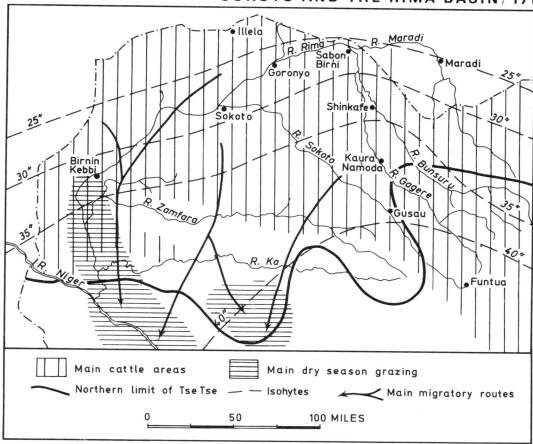

Figure 72. The Rima Basin—Rainfall Distribution, Main Cattle Areas and Cattle Routes

Plate 44. Shepherds tending rams and sheep in Sokoto Province. Overgrazing has exposed vast areas of this province to sheet erosion.

grassland. They weigh about 1,100 to 1,450 pounds at five to six years when they are ready for slaughter and are considered to be very good beef cattle. Sokoto cattle are also used for producing milk, the surplus of which is disposed of by Fulani women who use the proceeds to obtain such household requirements as corn, rice and salt. These cattle are also used for draft purposes, and in this respect they are considered to be very reliable although rather slow.

Large numbers of the Sokoto red goat, a small short-legged animal, are found not in the backyard as in the forest belt, but wandering about the fields in search of food. These hardy small animals are well-known for their red skins—the famous Moroccan leather which has featured in the trans-Saharan trade for many centuries. The goats provide the main source of meat since the people rarely kill their cattle for food. Their skins are used for making various articles including water containers, belts, mats and sandals. Sheep are also reared and are in great demand for Moslem religious festivals and other social celebrations. The donkey is, however, the commonest domestic animal in this region, as indeed in the whole of the Sudan. Like goats and sheep, donkeys are left to wander about the village and fend for themselves. Many families keep at least a donkey which is used mainly for transporting various items such as grain, firewood, cotton and groundnuts as well as human beings. Horses and camels are also kept.

POST-WAR DEVELOPMENTS IN AGRICULTURAL PRODUCTION

Sokoto Province cannot be considered as a major exporter of any agricultural produce in the way that Kano Emirate is identified with groundnuts or the Benin forests with rubber. It exports cattle to southern Nigeria, but it is not a food-surplus region. Efforts to develop agriculture in recent years have therefore been concerned with the expansion of food crops and export crops. The exercise so far consists of expanding the acreage under existing crops which have since been integrated into the local farming calendar. No new crops have been introduced from outside the country except that improved varieties of crops like cotton, rice and tobacco have been imported with the view of raising the quality of local produce.

The production of groundnuts for export, as indicated by the tonnage purchased at various buying stations, is concentrated in the eastern part of Sokoto Province, particularly in the region of the Funtua–Kaura Namoda railway. Since climatic and soil conditions in the region are generally suitable for groundnuts, and since the crop is not restricted to irrigated areas, accessibility to markets appears to be the dominant factor influencing the rate of expansion of groundnut cultivation. The pattern of cotton production is broadly similar to that of groundnuts, except that in the case of cotton, production is not merely concentrated but restricted to the eastern part of the province. An extensive potential cotton-producing area lying between the Lower Rima valley and the Dahomey boundary is yet to be developed. Further observations on the expansion of these two crops will feature when dealing with the main cotton and groundnut belts. At present we shall examine two schemes in agricultural production development, which have brought about considerable changes in the rural economy of the affected areas. These are the Sokoto Mechanized Rice Scheme and the Agangara Fulani Settlement Scheme. The rapid expansion of tobacco cultivation in this region is also reviewed.

THE SOKOTO MECHANIZED RICE SCHEME

Swamp rice has been cultivated in the Rima Basin for a very long time, but production was in small fields which were worked with the hoe. The Sokoto Mechanized Rice Scheme, which was started in 1948, aimed at large-scale expansion of rice production with the help of heavy machinery. In view of the scattered nature of fields in this area, the scheme necessitated the consolidation of holdings under some form of group farming. In this respect the Sokoto Rice Scheme is basically different from the Shemankar Mechanized Rice Scheme in the Benue valley, which involved the opening up for settlement of a hitherto empty area. In the Sokoto Scheme local farmers were obliged to pool their land together for ploughing, after which it was subsequently redistributed. Each farmer was charged a ploughing fee of thirty-five shillings per acre, although the actual ploughing costs often exceeded forty shillings per acre.

The first few years of the scheme were beset with many problems, one of which was the natural suspicion or cautious reception of change by rural folks. When, however, the people came to realize that a properly weeded ploughed field produced as much as a thirty per cent increase in yields compared with land cultivated with hoes, the problem which the scheme had to contend with was that of meeting the large demand made by farmers to have their lands ploughed. Thus in 1953 mechanical troubles and lack of spare parts for the heavy caterpillar D.7 tractors used for the scheme made it impossible to plough the whole 27,000 acres for which requests had been received. In this year, the farming season started badly with heavy rains which came a fortnight too early and caused considerable damage as a result of premature flooding. This early rain coincided with Ramadan, and by the time the fast was over the fields were invaded by so much grass that most farmers were deterred from undertaking their normal cultivation. This unfavourable start to the season produced a widespread reaction against the scheme so that the demand for ploughing fell to 9,000 acres in 1954.

Expansion of mechanized rice cultivation in this region has meant an encroachment on Fulani pastures, which reminds one of the proverbial conflicting demands for land between the settled cultivator and pastoral nomads in grassland areas. In the case of the Sokoto Rice Scheme a compromise has been arrived at to preserve as much of the pastures as possible.

THE AGANGARA FULANI SETTLEMENT SCHEME

Like the Sokoto Rice Scheme, the Agangara Scheme, which was initiated in 1951, was made possible by funds provided by the Northern Nigeria Production Development Board. The scheme was directed by the Sokoto Native Authority and had as its main objective the bringing of nomad Fulani cattle owners into the local economy, teaching them the value of quality in animals and providing a supply of cattle to Hausa mixed farmers in the district. To ensure that water was made available throughout the dry season, a masonry dam was built in 1951 at a cost of £1,000. Three hundred and fifty cattle were watered there until the end of April 1952, when lack of sufficient grazing drove the herds south. But the local grazing was sufficient to anchor these cattle for five months longer than usual, and clearly, this was made possible by the fact that water had been made available through the scheme.

A second dam was completed in 1953 and is located two miles from the first. This second dam is considered to be nearer the greatest local concentration of cattle, but the problem now is that of preserving grazing within the area. Bush fires started by local hunters during the dry season have been minimized by clearing fire traces. Those who are expected to benefit from the scheme are at present being supplied with free groundnut cake, cotton seed and salt, as an inducement to settle down. The plan is to get the people to realize the benefits of these concentrates, after which a charge will be made for any quantities supplied to them.

TOBACCO GROWING IN THE RIMA BASIN

Tobacco, like rice, is not a new crop in Nigeria but has featured as a minor crop in many parts of the country. Before the introduction of imported varieties of Virginian tobacco for cigarette manufacture, small plots of local tobacco existed in most villages in the Nigerian Sudan. The leaf was used for snuff, for chewing, for pipe smoking and for making 'bookies' or hand-made cigarettes, while the flowers were used for staining the teeth. In the past the crop was grown mainly as a wet season crop on upland areas, but today it is also grown as a dry season crop along river valleys, including those of the Sokoto, Rima and Zamfara Rivers. Large-scale production for cigarette

making started in this region in 1948, under the supervision of the Nigerian Tobacco Company, to which goes much of the credit for the expansion of tobacco culture in Nigeria.

Owing to the drier climate of the Sudan and the inadequacy of fuel supplies the tobacco grown in this region is air-cured. It is grown in small irregular plots, but since these plots are concentrated in the fadamas, the general impression is that of a large continuous tobacco plantation. This is particularly so in the Goronjo-Shinkafe area, where it is common to find continuous blocks of about 400 acres made up of numerous plots belonging to different persons. Around Goronjo and along the Sokoto River valley, some mechanical cultivation of land for tobacco is undertaken before the floods. This is usually carried out by the Nigerian Tobacco Company, which also maintains large nurseries on high ground overlooking the fadamas. The crop is grown under basin irrigation except in small patches in Gwandu town, where controlled irrigation using well water is practised.

One remarkable thing about the expansion of tobacco culture in Sokoto Province and indeed in the whole country is that it has been brought about through the initiative of a commercial firm, with a little help from the

Figure 73. Aspects of the Agricultural Economy of the Rima Basin

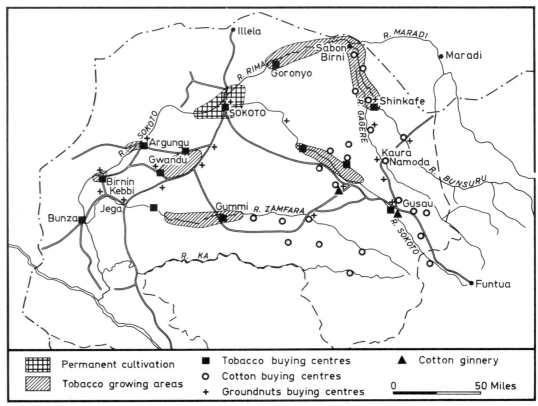

Agricultural Department but without any reliance on funds from the Marketing Boards. The success of this crop has been attributed to the foresight of the Nigerian Tobacco Company in making available to growers advice, supervision and both long- and short-term credit on a far more generous scale than government departments have been able to provide for other crops. So far, all tobacco grown in the Rima Basin is manufactured outside the region; but a cigarette factory at Sokoto has been proposed, and if built may lead to a considerable increase in tobacco growing in the area. Fortunately production is capable of expansion, although there is some competition from other crops and land uses for these fertile fadamas. In the Shinkafe area for instance certain fadamas, otherwise suitable for tobacco growing, are set aside for grazing by the nomadic Fulani.

DISTRIBUTION AND MOVEMENTS OF POPULATION

In 1952 there were 2·68 million people in Sokoto Province and this worked out at an average of seventy-three persons per square mile. For practical purposes, however, this later figure is virtually useless since it masks such gaps as exist between administrative districts with about twenty persons per square mile and those with well over 400. Besides, as much as twenty per cent of the land area is under forest cover and therefore virtually uninhabited. The highest densities occur in and around Sokoto town in the so-called Home Districts,[1] where the average density is about 400 persons per square mile; a concentration which reflects the focal influence of the capital of Sokoto Emirate and spiritual capital of Moslem Nigeria.

Gwadabawa District, which extends northwards from the Home Districts to the frontier with Niger Republic, has a medium density of over 200 persons per square mile. This appears to be rather high, considering the limitations imposed on farming by climate and soils. The concentration is recent when compared with that of the Home Districts and is attributed largely to immigration from Niger Republic. This influx of farmers from the southern part of Niger has occurred without attracting much attention because of the fact that the same ethnic groups occupy both sides of the border. Harvest failures further north and the provision of wells in the Nigerian side of the boundary are some of the reasons which have induced this influx of settled cultivators from Niger. Attempts so far made by the Sokoto N.A. to arrest this movement of population have not been' very successful.

Another area where the population density exceeds 200

persons per square mile is around Kaura Namoda which is the north-western rail-head. The high density here is partly responsible for, and is partly explained by, the fact that more cotton and groundnuts are produced around the Gusau-Kaura Namoda area than in any other part of Sokoto Province. Elsewhere in the region, the population density falls below 100 per square mile except along the valleys of the Rima, Bunsuru, Gagere and Sokoto Rivers where the density ranges from 100 to 200 per square mile.

The most important environmental factor influencing the distribution of population is the availability of potable water during the dry season. As a result of the scarcity of water in the dry season, certain villages in the Tangaza District were formerly occupied during the wet season only, the population being obliged to migrate in the dry season when their shallow wells dry up. Scarcity of water during the dry season also explains the concentration of population in lands adjacent to the main river valleys. According to Prothero, between seventy-five and eighty per cent of the total population of this region live in or near river valleys, and all the towns in Sokoto Province with a population of over 5,000 are located on or near river valleys. Many of these rivers dry up during the dry season, but at this time water can still be obtained at no great depth in the river beds. Away from the river valleys, artesian water occurs in the sedimentary rocks of north-western Sokoto Province and is being developed. New deep wells have been provided in various districts, and this has made it possible for permanent settlement to survive in the northern parts of Tangaza District. In the case of the waterless and virtually uninhabited Gunduni Bush area, the provision of an assured water supply in the 'early 1930's did not have any marked influence in attracting permanent settlement.

Apart from the availability of potable water, the pattern of population distribution in Sokoto Province is largely a product of the nineteenth century wars between the Fulanis and the former Hausa rulers of these districts. Many districts, which were formerly densely populated, were deserted and destroyed in the course of these wars. Marked concentrations of people featured in the vicinity of large fortified settlements, with powerful armies capable of protecting the immediate surrounding rural areas. In the Zamfara valley, most of the towns had double walls, one of earth and an outer wall formed by a dense border of woodland which made attack by mounted horsemen very difficult.

[1] The Home Districts consists of the administrative districts of Sokoto, Hama Ali, Acida, Gumbi, Dingyadi, Bondiga, Durbawa and Sifawa.

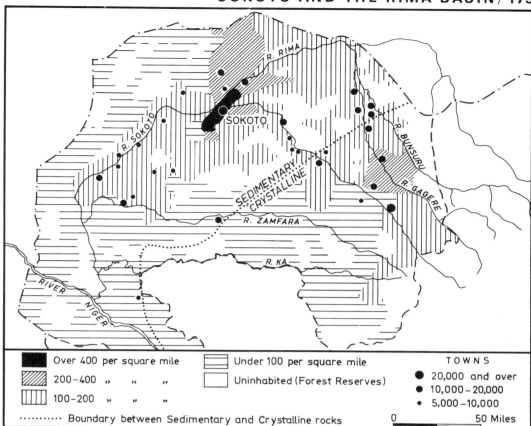

*Figure 74. Population Density
of the Rima Basin based on the
1952 Census (after Prothero)*

Immigration from neighbouring Niger Republic is only one aspect of population movements in Sokoto Province. Of greater importance, in so far as the number involved is concerned, is the seasonal migration of farmers and labourers from various parts of Sokoto to the main towns of northern Nigeria, to Ghana and to the cocoa belt of western Nigeria. Local migrations, involving the movements of farmers from the central and northern parts of Gwadabawa and Gada Districts to the fertile valley of the Rima in Gorongo and Wurno Districts, may be distinguished from long-distance migrations to other parts of Nigeria and West Africa. Those who travel long distances are mainly labourers who work for wages with which to pay their tax and support their families; the migrants being largely, if not entirely, male in composition. Important causes of this migratory movement include a progressive decrease in productivity over the years, poor harvests and excessive flooding leading to the destruction of crops and settlements.

A survey of labour migration during the dry season of 1952–3, that is from mid-October to the beginning of March, revealed that more than forty per cent of the adult males were away from the northern medium density zone, and that the figure for the home districts was nearer fifty per cent. According to this survey, most of the migrants from the northern districts went to the Upper Zamfara valley, which is now an important producing area for cotton and groundnuts. The southward migration of farm labourers from these northern districts is very similar to that of Afikpo farm-hands who migrate to work in Bende

Division (see page 94). In both cases the migrants are in a position to harvest early crops in their home districts before moving south to earn ready cash as farm labourers.

The timing of the seasonal migration from the northern district is such that the area cannot be said to have been deprived of its effective labour force by this movement. On the other hand, such migrants bring back some cash while their absence also reduces the demand on locally grown food. It is probable that in future many of the migrants from the densely settled areas will be absorbed locally in the Zamfara valley, which has vast possibilities for development as an export crop region.

COTTAGE AND FACTORY INDUSTRY

The pattern and location of traditional manufactures are those of a pre-industrial society. Local raw materials are used and there is a marked orientation towards the source of supply of raw materials. There is a considerable degree of local specialization in various crafts. Wurno and Moriki Districts, for instance, are noted for their weavers; Danga is noted for pottery; while the inhabitants of Dingyadi and Bodinga specialize in making reed and grass mats and hats.

Sokoto Town is well known for its leather work. In the past the region exported large quantities of the so-called Moroccan leather to the Mediterranean world. Moroccan leather, which comes from the skin of the red Sokoto goat, is still an important item of external trade. Professional leather workers abound in Sokoto Town, where each manufacturer operates within his compound. The main

Plate 45. The annual fishing festival at Argungu.

articles of manufacture are sandals, leather bags for women and poofs for the sitting-room. The leather workers use skins from almost every animal reared in the region. The top of a poof bought by the author from a local craftsman in 1965 was made of cow leather, the bottom of camel leather, while the sides were of sheepskin.

The only factory industry today is the large cement factory, located two miles south-west of Sokoto Town.

TRANSPORT AND TRADE

Transportation in the Rima Basin is still undeveloped compared with the situation in most of southern Nigeria or the Jos Plateau. Apart from the Zaria–Sokoto road and the road from Sokoto to Bodinga, which are amongst the best roads in the country, there are no tarmac roads in the region. A few so-called all-season roads surfaced with laterite exist, but considerable tracts of these are hardly passable during the rains. Dry-season roads are completely closed to motorized vehicles during the rainy season, at which time the local people resort to their pre-British transport system which relies essentially on the use of animals like the donkey, camel and horse. A vivid impression of the means and volume of traffic may be had by visiting Goronjo market during the wet season. One or two lorries come in along the laterite road from Sokoto and Wurno and are loaded with men, bags of kola and other merchandise. From Gada District come men carrying their farm produce as well as large calabashes with which they ferry themselves across the river, in much the same way as they did in the days of Henry Barth. Those from Sobon Birni and neighbouring villages come on horses or camels, but by far the greater number are seen riding on donkeys or walking along with heavily loaded and tired-looking donkeys. The eastern part of the province is served by the Zaria–Kaura Namoda rail extension and is by far the most developed export crop region in the whole province.

As a result of its central location between the Timbuctoo-Jenne region in the west and the Kano-Bornu region in the east, much of the west-east trade in cloth, natron, leather goods and kola-nuts has always passed through the Rima Basin. It was the transit trade in kola and slaves that brought great prosperity to the caravan town of Jega, which in the early nineteenth century was described as second only to Kano as an important commercial centre in Hausaland. The location of Jega at the head of perennial navigation on the Zamfara, and the fact that it could be reached by animal transport, were other factors which increased the market area of Jega, but its rise to prominence came after the Fulanis had sacked Birinin Kebbi in 1805. Like Kano, Jega is located on the twelfth parallel, but while Kano owed its prosperity more to the skill and industry of its craftsmen, Jega depended merely on its geographical situation. Hence its decline following the change in the significance of its location. Other towns on the caravan route from the forests of Guinea to the central Sudan were Gwandu and Sokoto.

Apart from slaves, cloth, natron and kola which came from outside the region, local products such as cloth and leather works also featured in the internal trade of the Sudan as well as in the trans-Saharan trade. Mention has already been made of the famous Moroccan leather which was the trade name of the goatskin from Sokoto. Today, Sokoto Province still carries out considerable trade with the forest region in the south. Large lorries carrying bags of kola and imported consumer goods go up to Sokoto every day from Lagos, Shagamu and Ibadan. As a return cargo these vehicles carry bags of onions, rice and other grains as well as local manufactures, while Sokoto cattle are exported to the south on hoof or by rail. Sokoto Town is a major distributing centre for kola and other merchandise from the south.

Works consulted and suggestions for further reading:

1. Bovill, E. W., *The Gold Trade of the Moors* Oxford University Press 1958
2. Glover, P. E., *The Tsetse problem in Northern Nigeria* Nairobi 1960
3. Jones, B., 'Dessication and the West African Colonies' *Geographical Journal* No. 91 pp. 401–22 1938
4. Ledger, D. C., 'Recent Hydrological Changes in the Rima Basin, Northern Nigeria' *Geographical Journal* No. 127 pp. 477–86 1961
5. Metteden, A. K., 'Cattle Trail' *Nigeria Magazine* No. 70 pp. 252–65 1961
6. Northern Nigeria Government *The Industrial Potentialities of Northern Nigeria* Kaduna 1963
7. Prothero, R. M., *Migrant Labour from Sokoto Province, Northern Nigeria* Kaduna 1958
8. Stebbing, E. P., 'The encroaching Sahara' *Geographical Journal* No. 85 pp. 506–24 1935

18 The Kano Region

The distinguishing features of the human geography of this open country of northern Hausaland include the great concentration of rural population around Kano and Katsina, the intensity of farming within and around these two ancient walled cities and the dominant position of groundnuts in the rural economy. This is the core region of Hausaland and is certainly the most developed and prosperous region of the Sudan. It contains two of the ancient 'ports' of the Sahara, Kano and Katsina which, together with Timbuctoo and Kukawa, served as the southern termini of the trans-Sahara routes to the Maghreb. The commercial importance of these cities derived from their location, but in addition to its advantageous position Kano had a rich agricultural and industrial hinterland. Today all these 'ports', with the exception of Kano, have lost their locational advantage and have since become stranded areas. But Kano continues to grow and in recent years modern factory industries have reinforced its economic base. Its 'port' functions have been increased by the fact that it is an international airport and a major railway station and its traditional industries have received a new lease of life following the greater demand for its product from the Nigerian elite and from thousands of foreign travellers passing through or visiting this city every year.

THE ORIGIN AND GROWTH OF KANO CITY

The precise date of the founding of Kano city is not known but evidence based on the Kano chronicle indicates that the original settlement was a small iron-smelting village at the foot of Dalla hill, and that the settlement was founded before the closing years of the eleventh century A.D. The walled city was built early in the twelfth century and the walls were not completed until A.D. 1150.

For many centuries Kano remained an industrial workshop, producing a variety of wares which were shipped to the Maghreb and Timbuctoo from Katsina, then the major port of the central caravan route. Its importance as a great commercial centre started in the fifteenth century, when it featured prominently as a distributing centre for kola from the forests of modern Ghana. The camel had been introduced about this time from the Sahara, thus improving trans-Saharan trade. The next four centuries were a period of fluctuating fortunes for Kano, a period in which Kano became a vassal state of Songhai and later of Bornu.

The real turning point in the growth of Kano came with the Fulani Jihad, which swept across Western Hausaland in the early years of the nineteenth century. Katsina resisted the Jihad and was subdued after a long siege. The southern terminus of the Ghadames-Air caravan route was transferred to Kano, while Katsina was completely by-passed by the route which went direct to Kano from Zinder. From this time, Kano replaced Katsina as the chief market of Hausaland and fifty years later Henry Barth was able to describe Kano as the commercial metropolis of the western Sudan. Barth estimated its population at 30,000 but added that this figure was more than doubled during the dry season, when the conditions of approach roads permitted an influx of traders. The population has always remained predominantly Hausa, but as a great commercial centre Kano also has a large number of foreigners.

In pre-British days the major items of trade exported from Kano were leatherwork, locally made cotton cloth and iron goods. It served as a collecting and distributing centre for such goods as natron from Lake Chad, kola from the forests of Guinea and slaves. European goods coming in by way of the Mediterranean included sword blades, copper, French silk, beads, sugar and what Barth referred to as Manchester goods. Firearms were much sought after but were in short supply.

THE TOWNSCAPE OF THE ANCIENT CITY

The visitor to Kano city who has read the journals of such explorers as Clapperton and Henry Barth will find that the townscape of the walled city has undergone little or no change during the last century and a half. The present writer had this impression in 1965 after driving through and viewing Kano city from the Dalla and Dutsi Hills. One main reason for this conservatism in the landscape is that developments in residential and industrial housing during the last sixty years have taken place outside the city walls, while housetypes and building materials used within the old city have remained virtually unchanged.

Remains of the fifteen-mile-long clay wall which encircled the irregular oval-shaped city can still be seen. Much of the open and unbuilt-up area within the walls is still used as farmland but the number of borrow pits from which came the mud for building houses has increased. Many of these pits cover several acres and may exceed ten feet in depth; they contain water for several months, during which they support a dense growth of water plants which present a rather pleasant greenish effect. But as a dumping ground for refuse and a breeding place for mosquitoes the pits constitute a major source of pollution and disease.

Most of the houses in the old city are still of clay and

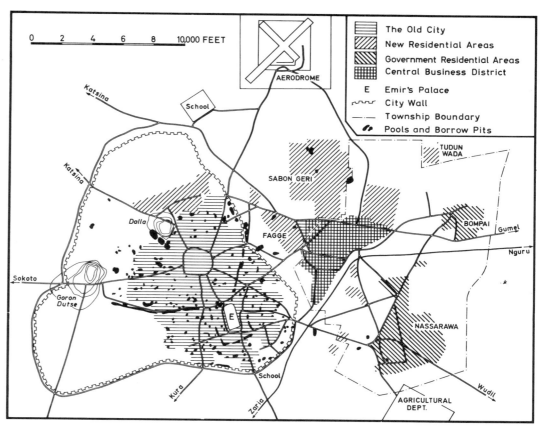

Figure 75. The City and Suburbs of Kano

are square in form. The roofs, which are flat, are also of mud. Each compound enclosure also contains several small round huts, which are roofed with the stalks of corn and thatched with long grass. The Emir's palace covers a large space in the heart of the old city, but the main mosque is probably the most imposing building within the walls of ancient Kano. Apart from the peaks of the Dalla and Dutsi Hills which dominate the landscape of the old city, the minarets of this magnificent mosque provide the most advantageous point for viewing the city.

Another common feature of the cultural landscape of old Kano is the dyepits, some of which are as old as the city. The pits are used for dyeing both leather and cloth, two products which have featured in the commerce of Kano for several centuries.

MODERN KANO
Population 295,430 in 1963

During the last sixty years, the commercial importance of Kano has increased enormously following the extension of the railway to the city in 1912 and the building of all-season roads from Kano to various parts of the country. Kano is also the second international airport in Nigeria, after Lagos.

The growth of residential districts as well as shopping and industrial areas has taken place outside the city walls. Kano is an embodiment of ancient and modern culture, the former being carefully preserved within the walls while the new residential areas with their well laid out streets, their playing grounds, modern houses and amusement centres compare favourably with such new towns as Port Harcourt, Enugu and Kaduna. Sabon Gari,

or new town, houses the stranger elements from other parts of Nigeria, while Nassarawa town is the high-class residential area formerly known as the European reservation. The two towns are separated by the central business district where the main open-air market is located.

Bompai is the industrial estate of Kano and the growth of factory industry has been phenomenal during the last ten years. The food and drinks industry processes local raw materials, the corned beef factory (1955) and the groundnut oil milling-factory being amongst the older industries. Over 120 head of cattle are slaughtered daily to supply the corned beef factory and the subsidiary Jollof rice factory. Soft drinks prepared and bottled at Kano include Fanta, Pepsi-Cola, tonic water and soda water.

Kano's traditional industries, including leather works and cotton textiles, which brought her fame and prosperity in the past, have now moved to the factory. The leather factory established in 1962 supplies part of the raw materials for the leather shoe factory which makes sandals, police boots and leather belts. Rubber for this factory as well as for the plastic shoe factory comes from midwestern Nigeria. There are two large textile mills each of which produces about 45,000 yards of cloth every week. Another traditional industry which has moved to the factory is the manufacture of perfumes which are in great demand by Sudanese people. Other industries in Kano include soap-making and the manufacture of enamel ware.

Just as the ancient residential quarters exist side by side with the modern ones, the traditional cottage industries continue apparently undisturbed by the factories. The indication is that they will continue to survive for some

Plate 46. The Kano central Mosque.

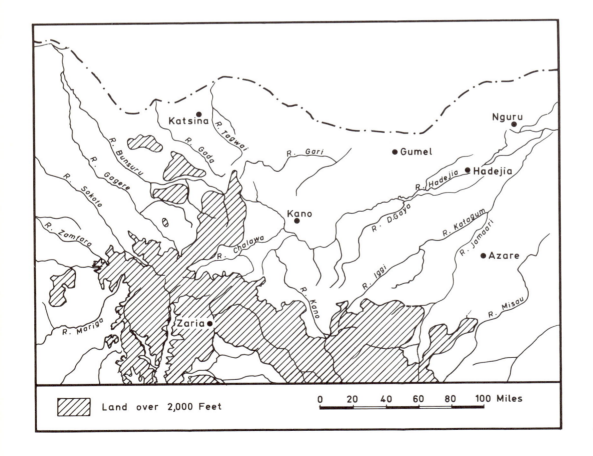

Figure 76. The Relief and Drainage of the Kano Region

time, particularly since their products are cheaper and since the wants of the people are still rather simple.

KATSINA
Population 90,540 in 1963

The decline of Katsina, formerly the southern terminus of the Ghadames-Air caravan route, has been referred to in connection with the growth of Kano. Its fate is very similar to that of Calabar which has declined following the loss of locational advantage to Port Harcourt. But the decline of Katsina is absolute while that of Calabar is relative.

As with Kano, much of the space within the city walls is still not built up but is used for farming and grazing. But unlike Kano, the few Nigerian stranger inhabitants resident in Katsina live within the city walls. Even the proposed modern residential area which has already been laid out in plots is to be accommodated within the city walls, now in ruins. There is however a small government residential area which was built outside the city to house officers of the colonial administration.

GEOLOGY, LAND FORMS AND SOILS OF THE KANO REGION

The Kano region, which in the main consists of Kano and Katsina Provinces, is underlain by crystalline rocks of the Basement Complex, except in the north and eastern part of Katsina Province and the eastern part of Kano Province, where cretaceous sediments overlap the crystalline rocks. In most areas the solid rock is covered by several feet of weathered materials or sandy drifts which have been accumulated under drier climatic conditions. In the south and along stream valleys there are numerous outcrops of the Basement rocks. Most of the region consists of gently undulating plains, particularly in the areas of sedimentary rocks, but in the Kano District there are a number of laterite-capped hills such as the Dalla and Dutsi Hill of Kano city. Such inselbergs usually stand up to heights of about 100 feet above the surrounding country which lies between 1,000 and 2,000 feet above sea level.

Lateritic ironstone is widespread and occurs both on the sedimentary and crystalline areas. Except where it has been exposed by wind or water erosion, the ironstone which in many cases consists of indurated weathered rock is buried beneath a thick layer of soil. It is usually exposed along the watersheds and in overgrazed patches.

Broad and shallow valleys are typical of the crystalline

areas and the river beds are usually choked with sand. There is a great seasonal fluctuation in the volume of water carried by the streams, most of which dry up completely during the dry season. The character of the valleys gives rise to extensive fadamas (flood plains) which are cultivated with vegetables during the dry season.

Weathered rock and sandy drift constitute the two main soil-forming parent materials, but differentiation in soil types depends largely on the catena arrangement. On the interfluves and upper slopes of undulating districts the soils are of red-brown to orange colour and consist of sandy clay loam overlying lateritic ironstone. These soils are cultivated even in areas where the ironstone is only a few inches beneath the surface. In the fadamas or seasonally flooded valley floors, heavier grey alluvial soils with a high clay content occur.

Accelerated soil erosion by wind and running water has laid bare certain tracts in the densely settled areas of the region. Wind erosion is particularly serious towards the end of the dry season, when the storms preceding the onset of the rains blow off much soil. Young seedlings have been known to be replanted. Gully erosion is most serious along valley sides where the slopes create favourable conditions for easy run-off. Footpaths leading to the streams and cultivation furrows have also initiated gullies which tend to cut back rather rapidly by sapping away the weathered rock materials.

CLIMATE, VEGETATION AND WATER SUPPLIES

Two factors, the latitudinal position of the Kano region and its interior location away from the sea, determine its climate which is hot and dry for most of the year. Maximum day temperatures of about 100° F. are common and the minimum temperature is about 55° F. Plant growth is therefore possible all through the year as far as the temperature is concerned but the rainfall, which is often unreliable, constitutes a serious problem.

The first rains come early in May and cropping follows almost at once. This is a most critical period in the farming calendar because if it does not rain again within the next week then the seeds are wasted and the crop must be resown. There have been occasions when the second showers have been delayed for more than three weeks, and in bad years sowing may be repeated three or four times. One effect of the irregular nature of the early rains is that in some years there is much demand for labour during the sowing season, since groundnuts, guinea corn, beans and sweet potatoes all have to be planted within a period of four to six weeks.

August is the wettest month, when an average rainfall of twelve inches is recorded for Kano and over ten inches for Katsina. In 1945, which was a particularly rainy year, Kano had over eighteen inches of rain in August and so did Katsina. The intensity of the rainfall between July and August is responsible for the fact that in such a dry area as this, crops are frequently lost as a result of too much rain. At this time of the year slight depressions and gently sloping areas with heavy soils become waterlogged and are therefore left uncultivated. The high intensity of the rainfall also encourages gully erosion.

The dry season begins in October. This is the season of the desicating harmattan which is very severe in this region. Grasses wither, trees shed their leaves while water courses dry up, the entire landscape appearing like a desert. Bush fires are common and dust storms blow away sandy soils from the sun-baked fields. Cold and rather uncomfortable nights are characteristic of this season.

Water for domestic use as well as for watering animals is in short supply during the dry season. Groundwater supplies are therefore of great importance, particularly since the rivers dry up during this time of the year. The main source of water is from wells, some of which are as old as the ancient cities of Kano and Katsina. Areas underlain by sedimentary rocks provide enough underground water for the basic needs of the population and stock in such areas, but the situation is less satisfactory in the crystalline areas. In parts of western Katsina where the drift is shallow, the underground water sources are inadequate to support permanent settlement.

Early explorers to Kano noted that the trade in water for domestic use was an important source of income for women. Today, a number of wells have been added to the older ones. Many of these new wells are lined with concrete, and like the older wells they have a walled top designed to prevent surface water from draining into them. But many villagers still make use of water trapped in open pits dug in the compounds, hence the large number of cases of guinea worm infection.

This region lies within the Sudan zone, but its vegetation has been completely modified as a result of several centuries of human occupation featuring bush clearing and burning for cultivation and hunting, as well as cattle grazing. In the closely settled areas around Kano and Katsina natural bush vegetation is almost completely absent, but several trees have been planted for shade and fruit. Such cultivated trees include *Acacia albida*, *Tamarrind indica* and *Butyrospermum parkii*. A considerable growth of natural vegetation occurs in areas which are remote from human settlement or which are marginal or uncultivable, but even in such areas grazing and bush fires restrict mature woodland to a few spots including the forest reserves, while scrub communities persist over most of the landscape.

Compared with the Guinea savanna, the vegetation here consists of shorter and more feathery grass. The number of thorny plants, usually a species of *Acacia*, is greater and the leaves of trees often smaller. *Acacias* which have varied coloured barks are particularly numerous in low-lying sites, including seasonally flooded ground along river valleys. Another important species of the Sudan zone is the Dum Palm (*Hyphaene thebaica*) which occurs singly or in dense groves. Galary forests or riparian woodland featuring a dense tangle of climbers persist along river valleys in areas remote from human settlement.

POPULATION AND SETTLEMENT TYPES

The population is predominantly Hausa but there is a considerable number of Fulanis and strangers from other parts of Nigeria. In the past, the Hausas were usually identified as settled cultivators in contrast with the nomadic Fulani, but today such a distinction can no longer be accepted because many Fulanis have since settled down as farmers.

In an area which has seen many periods of unrest, the tendency was for people to flock to surroundings where they were sure of protection from attack. This is one reason why the Kano District in particular has had a large concentration of population for many centuries. Recent developments in industries and agriculture have created employment opportunities for seasonal labour in the farms as well as skilled and semi-skilled labour in the city of Kano. In addition the Kano District has always been a rich agricultural district, and the fact that much of it is cropped permanently makes it possible for the high population density of over 500 persons per square mile to survive. This is the so-called Kano close-settled zone which consists of a near circular area of radius thirty miles from Kano city.

Two types of rural settlements may be recognized. These are dispersed compounds, and old nucleated villages. Dispersed compounds which may consist of a few huts or several huts and granaries are found scattered about the landscape. They are usually enclosed by a fence with a single entrance. The population of the compound varies from one or two persons to over thirty persons for the large extended family compounds. Around Kano city the dispersed compounds which remind one of parts of Iboland are of considerable age and appear to have been made possible by the fact that for a long time

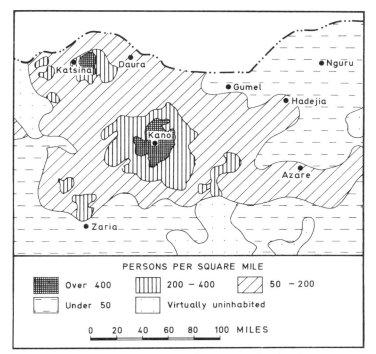

Figure 77. Population Density of the Kano Region based on the 1952 Census

Hausa rulers and later the Fulani Emirs were able to maintain peace in the Kano area.

The old nucleated settlements with over one hundred persons are walled, and remind one of the traditional settlement in an area where defence was a major consideration in the past. Formerly, each settlement had some cultivable land within its walls and was more of a miniature Sudanese town. Today, there has been an overspill of compounds beyond the walls, and available land within or between the compounds is usually cropped.

AGRICULTURAL LAND USE

Apart from settlements and uncultivatable rock surface or areas rendered useless for agriculture by erosion, the following categories of land use may be recognized. These are fadama farms, upland farms, forest reserves and natural grazings. Seasonally flooded river valleys or fadamas are much sought after for cultivation during the dry season when water from the stream bed is used to irrigate crops. The fadamas therefore make it possible for farmers to raise crops at a season when climatic conditions make it impossible to grow crops on the upland farms. Fadama plots are usually much smaller than plots on the upland farms and are rarely over a quarter of an acre. Onions, pepper and sugar cane are the most common crops grown on fadamas, but in the vicinity of Kano city fadamas are usually cropped with market garden vegetables meant for the Kano market or for export to other towns. Maize, rice and sweet potatoes are also grown in these areas which in the past were used not for farming, but as dry season common grazing land.

Fadama agriculture is essentially an off-season occupation. Moreover, plots are so small in size that, in spite

of higher yield per unit area, no farmer can raise enough food on such land. Farmers who cultivate these fadamas are therefore also engaged in cultivating upland farms which are, in essence, the principal farms. Around Kano and Katsina, upland farms are cropped permanently, a practice made possible by the careful application of manure on the land. Elsewhere, bush fallowing is the rule. Millet, guinea corn, groundnuts, beans and cotton are the dominant crops. Farm holdings here are much larger in size, varying from a little below three acres to over twenty acres.

Uncultivated land in this region is made up of forest reserves and grazing land. As in other parts of the country, no one is allowed to live within the forest reserves although grazing is allowed. Fulani cattlemen therefore build their huts close to the edge of the reserves which provide extensive wet-season grazing at a time when farms are being made in other areas. After harvests, however, cattle may be grazed on farmland when they feed on crop residues.

Kano Emirate has a few small forest reserves but the main Katsina Reserve covers an extensive area. Little or no timber is produced and distance from centres of population preclude the reserves from being useful as sources of firewood. Village or individually owned tree plantations, which are now common in the grassland areas of Oyo Province, appear to be necessary if the problem of firewood shortage is to be effectively tackled.

Natural grazing, like cultivated land, may be located in a fadama or on an upland area. Excessive pressure on available grazing land has resulted in severe degradation, and in some upland areas the grass cover is rather poor.

FARMING ACTIVITIES

The skilful system of intensive land use practised in the Kano close-farmed zone and around Katsina has been made possible by the use of various forms of manure. These include droppings from animals like goats, sheep and donkeys kept by the farmers themselves as well as household waste. Kano city has a large animal population which supplies manure to the surrounding farming villages. Human waste from the city is also occasionally used as manure; and between January and June, but particularly in March, donkeys loaded with manure going from the city to the farms are commonly seen along the main highways as well as the bush paths. The manure is usually applied by distributing it along the furrows between the ridges of the previous year after which the furrows are filled up with soil. In general, the intensity of application of manure decreases with increasing distance from Kano city or Katsina and around Ungogo village, which is five miles north of Kano city, it is estimated that manure application averages two tons per acre.

Farmlands are not as difficult to prepare as in the forest belt since bush clearing is unnecessary before firing the bush. This is one reason why large acreages of about five to eight acres are common. The typical farm in the close settled zones of Kano and Katsina is, however, smaller, being about three acres, while larger farms of about twenty acres may be seen in the more sparsely settled districts.

Guinea corn and millet are the first crops and are usually sown in late May or early June. Groundnuts follow in June and cowpeas in July. These are the main food crops of the Kano region although groundnuts are also an export crop. Generally guinea corn is the dominant grain crop in the south, but in the drier north millet becomes more widespread. Intercropping is common, millet and guinea corn being invariably grown on the same plot. Groundnuts may be intercropped with these grains but it is not uncommon to see the crop growing all alone.

Cassava is grown mainly as a food reserve for use during the period extending from the end of the dry season to the next harvest. Tobacco, indigo and onions are also grown for sale. The main activities during the growing season consist of weeding and repairing of ridges.

Millet is the first crop to be harvested and this is done in September, after which the farm presents a rather open appearance in which scattered stalks of guinea corn dominate the fields. November is another busy month in the farming calendar when guinea corn, cowpeas and groundnuts are harvested.

LIVESTOCK AND MIXED FARMING

The Kano region has the largest concentration of cattle in the country and we have already noticed their contribution to farming by way of providing manure, which permits permanent cultivation around the two cities of Kano and Katsina. Nearly all the cattle belong to the Fulani, who are obliged to migrate south during the dry season in search of water and grazing. Some settled Hausa and Fulani farmers also keep cattle, but apart from a small number which they fatten on crop residues before selling for slaughter, their cattle are generally entrusted to the nomadic Fulani who take care of them in return for some grains.

The dominant cattle breed in the region is the White Fulani which is comparatively a fair milk producer. They are also used for meat, for work as pack animals and for ploughing. The White Fulani is considered an excellent work animal and has been selected for the various government-assisted mixed farming units in northern Nigeria.

Most farmers keep goats, sheep and donkeys. Goats supply meat and skins for leatherwork and are often the property of the women. The main use of the donkey is as a means of transport to markets where cash crops are sold. Donkeys may be hired to transport other goods, including produce from the farms.

In northern Nigeria mixed farming means the keeping of cattle by farmers for the prime purpose of supplying manure for their fields. In some cases farmers use the animals for ploughing while others fatten cattle for beef. Farmers who own no cattle usually arrange for the nomadic Fulani to kraal on their farmlands in exchange for grains, but this method is inadequate for manuring large farms.

Government policy has been to encourage mixed farming with the view to maintaining soil fertility and encouraging the sedentarization of the Fulani. The system was formally started in 1928 by the Department of Agriculture, and by 1960 there were over 12,000 mixed farmers, about eighty per cent of which were in the Kano region. The main problems raised by mixed farming in such closely settled areas as the Kano District and the environs of Katsina city are the provision of food for the cattle. In such areas village grazing lands are usually overgrazed and degraded.

GROUNDNUT PRODUCTION IN THE KANO REGION

The Nigerian groundnut belt lies almost wholly within the Kano region where the crop was formerly grown for subsistence. Commercial production started in 1912 when the railway from Lagos was extended to Kano. The rate of expansion of the crop since then has been phenomenal, and since 1961 groundnuts have topped the export list as the most important agricultural export (by value) from Nigeria (Table 11). More and more areas are being brought under the crop and in the central parts of Kano Province cotton has largely been displaced by groundnuts. It is estimated that about one million acres of land came under groundnuts between 1911 and 1937, and it is remarkable that as with cocoa in western Nigeria the expansion of groundnuts in the Kano region has been carried out by the local peasants.

Today, Nigeria is the largest exporter of groundnuts in the world, export tonnage having increased from less than 200 tons in 1911 to about 650,000 tons in 1963, and about 970,000 tons in 1966 (Table 14). Another 200,000 tons was estimated to have been consumed locally in the same year. In terms of cash returns groundnut exports in 1963 were valued at £46 million, but its economic importance increases when it is realized that for several years groundnuts have provided about a quarter of the tonnage carried by the Nigerian railway.

Table 14 GROUNDNUT PURCHASES IN NORTHERN NIGERIA 1960/1 TO 1965/6

CROP YEAR	KANO AREA	OTHER AREAS	TOTAL (*long tons*)
1960/1	592,841	26,210	619,051
1961/2	676,160	9,359	685,519
1962/3	871,524	—	871,524
1963/4	786,727	—	786,727
1964/5	679,000	—	679,000
1965/6	977,000	—	977,000

SOURCE: *Marketing Board Statistics*

The groundnut (*Arachis Hypogea*), which is also called peanut or monkey nut, is a leguminous plant which thrives best on light, well-drained sandy soils. An annual rainfall of twenty-five to thirty-five inches, concentrated in the six months of the growing season, is ideal but the crop can be grown under drier or wetter conditions. Two main varieties are grown in the country: the creeping, bushy species spreading over the ridges and the bunched or upright type which sometimes grows to a height of eighteen inches. The Kano region specializes in the creeping type. The nuts are planted on flat-topped ridges about two-and-a-half feet apart and nine to twelve inches high. Planting takes place from April to June after which the nuts receive very little attention until the harvest time which begins in August and goes on till November.

Harvesting consists of pulling out the plants by hand and hoeing the ridges to recover nuts left behind in the earth. The nuts are then picked and dried in the sun after which they may be shelled or sold unshelled. Nuts meant for export are usually shelled and the work of decorticating and winnowing is done by the women, who use wooden mortar and pestle to beat out the shells, which are then winnowed off in open calabashes.

There is great scope for further expansion of groundnut cultivation in the region, particularly in the sparsely settled areas, since the farmers' inability to prepare and plant a larger acreage is the limiting factor in such areas. A case can be made for mechanization as a means of overcoming the labour problem. The Extension Division of the Regional Ministry of Agriculture is also carrying out a series of campaigns, including the establishment of demonstration plots directed at improving yields per acre.

MARKETING AND PROBLEMS OF EVACUATING GROUNDNUTS

The groundnut season, which is gazetted every year, begins early in November and goes on till March, the peak marketing month being December. Like cocoa and palm produce, the crop is marketed through a marketing board which in this case is the Northern Nigeria Marketing Board. Amongst other things the marketing board arranges for the orderly marketing of groundnuts by purchase through licensed buying agents, by bulk sale and by stabilizing the price paid to the producer.

Many grades of middle-men are involved in the marketing process which begins with the producer himself. The farmer carries his groundnuts in jute or leather bags which are loaded on to a donkey, an ox or a camel, for delivery to the nearest buying station which belongs to one of the sub-middle-men. Often there is a central marketing point with as many as a dozen sub-middle-men, each with his scales for weighing produce brought by the farmers. The scene presented at such buying stations is similar to that at any lorry park in any of the major Nigerian towns. But instead of touts struggling to persuade passengers to travel by a particular lorry, we have touts meeting producers on the road and trying to persuade them to deal with particular middle-men.

As in the case of cocoa in western Nigeria or rubber in the Benin Lowlands, there are a number of itinerant middle-men who buy the crop and undertake to process it before sale. In the Kano region such middle-men go from farm to farm with three or four donkeys which they use in transporting whatever crop they are able to buy.

Middle-men and sub-middle-men usually pay cash to the producer. Where a producer is already indebted to the middle-men for money lent during the growing season, and this is a common practice, such money is deducted before payment. An increasing number of middle-men also keep stores where they sell cloth, salt, soap and other consumer goods which they sell to the producers. All middle-men deliver their goods finally to one of the licensed buying agents who see to the delivery of the produce to the great groundnut pyramids outside Kano city. A pyramid may contain about 9,000 bags of groundnuts weighing approximately 750 tons. All pyramids are covered with tarpaulins awaiting evacuation to the ports of export.

Plate 47. Groundnut pyramids at Kano. An increasing amount of groundnuts is now evacuated by road.

Plate 48. Donkey transport near Zaria. The donkey is the most widespread beast of burden in the grasslands of Nigeria.

The ever increasing number of groundnut pyramids, which have become a feature of the cultural landscape of Kano, emphasizes the problem of transporting the crop to the ports of export. Transport facilities have not always been able to cope with the task of evacuating the crop. There is usually a carry-over of stock from one year to another and this results in major storage commitments and heavy storage costs. Accounting and stock checking is made more complicated; and much capital which could have been realized, had all the previous season's crop been evacuated, is locked up and cannot be used for purchasing new stocks; hence the necessity to use the reserves of the Marketing Board. In March 1954 for example, the Board had about £15 million tied up in stocks consisting of the 1953/4 crops. The situation improved greatly during the next ten years, as a result of an increase in the tonnage evacuated by road, but became much worse in 1966,

following the withdrawal of 160 railway workers from various parts of the Northern States.

Groundnuts from the Kano region are evacuated primarily by rail to Lagos and Port Harcourt; but roads are of increasing importance, and the combined rail and river route through Baro to Burutu and Warri is also used for evacuating groundnuts from Kano. The limiting factor in the case of the Baro route is the seasonal navigability of the Niger.

Lack of locomotives has been the main factor limiting the tonnage carried by the Nigeria railway which also has to provide cargo space for yams, beans and other food items destined for the south. Many more engines have been purchased in recent years, hence the rapid growth in the tonnage handled by the railway.

THE EXPANSION OF COTTON PRODUCTION

The main cotton belt of Nigeria lies in the western part of the Kano region where it overlaps with the groundnut belt, Katsina Province being by far the largest producer of cotton in the country. Outside Katsina the cotton belt extends north-westward into Sokoto Province and south-eastward into Zaria Province. The crop does best in well-drained loam or clay-loam soils. A rainfall of thirty-five to fifty inches per annum, but which is concentrated during the growing period, is considered adequate; although cotton is also grown in drier and wetter areas.

Cotton has been grown in this region for several centuries, although the basis of the present cotton industry is an imported strain, the 'Allen' cotton, introduced into Nigeria from Uganda in 1912. Seed breeding at Zaria has resulted in better-yielding varieties, the Allen 26C and the Allen 26J, which are now grown all over the region as well as in other parts of the country. The rapid spread of these improved varieties has been made possible by the fact that there is strict control in the distribution of cotton seeds to peasant farmers. Farmers sell their entire crop, seed and lint, to the ginneries from where they are provided with free seeds for cultivation. By this method the Department of Agriculture has succeeded in disseminating scientifically-bred seeds to most farmers.

Cotton, like the groundnut, is grown in small peasant farms and often the two crops are grown by the same farmer. There is, however, little actual competition between cotton and groundnuts since the former is more suited to heavier soils while groundnuts do best in light sandy soils. Soils, and to some extent climatic conditions, are therefore the main factors in the displacement of cotton by groundnuts in the Kano Emirate. The rapid expansion of cotton derives largely from the fact that it is planted in late July,[1] that is after the foodcrops as well as the groundnut would have been planted. Harvesting, which begins in December, also comes after both the groundnut crop and foodcrops have been harvested. Cotton therefore fits in very well into the local farming calendar.

Increased production in recent years has been attributed to increased planting and the adoption of higher yielding varieties but not to any increase in output per acre. Artificial fertilizers, which have been shown to increase yield considerably, are not used on a large scale, since few farmers can afford to buy the fertilizers. The habit of intercropping cotton with foodcrops is also responsible for poor yields since cotton cannot stand competition with other plants. The average yield per acre is estimated at 80 to 150 pounds of cotton lint, which is very low when compared with 521 and 273 pounds per acre for Egypt and America respectively.

In 1965 the total acreage under cotton in the country was estimated at about one million as compared with a quarter of that figure twenty years earlier. Greater emphasis on cotton in the Kano region is likely to lead to a situation similar to that of the cocoa belt, where food has to be imported. This situation may come about if the local farmers are taken in by the persistent claims of the Ministry of Agriculture that cotton is best cultivated in the first week of July if the farmer is to get the maximum yield possible. Such a change will upset the farming calendar, in that cotton will then be planted at the same time as food crops, thereby bringing about competition for labour. In such a case, several farmers may neglect to grow sufficient food so as to grow more cotton, although

[1] The Ministry of Agriculture recommends that cotton should be planted in the first week in July.

this need not be the situation if the farmer can afford to employ paid labour.

The marketing of cotton is also controlled by the Northern Nigeria Marketing Board and the marketing processes involved are similar to those of marketing groundnuts. In 1963, Nigeria exported 40,400 tons of raw cotton and 65,500 tons of cotton seed valued at £9·6 million and £1·4 million respectively. The following year, the amount of raw cotton exported dropped suddenly to 25,000 tons. This drop may be accounted for partly by the poorer crop in the 1963/4 season and partly by the increasing demand for raw cotton by local textile factories at Kaduna, Kano, Aba, Asaba and Ikeja.

Works consulted and suggestions for further reading:
1. Denham, D., Clapperton, H. & Oudney, W., *Narrative of Travels and Discoveries in Northern and Central Africa* London 1826
2. Grove, A. T., *Land and Population in Katsina Province* Kaduna 1952
3. Grove, A. T., 'Population and Agriculture in Northern Nigeria' in Barbour, K. M. & Prothero, R. M. (eds) *Essays on African Population* London 1961
4. McDonnell, G., 'The Dynamics of Geographic Change: the case of Kano' *Annals of the Association of American Geographers* No. 54 pp. 355–71 1964
5. Mortimore, M. J. & Wilson, J., *Land and People in the Kano Close-settled Zone* Department of Geography, Ahmadu Bello University, Occasional Papers No. 1 1964
6. Niven, C. R., 'Kano in 1933' *Geographical Journal* No. 82 p. 336 1933
7. Anon. 'Moving the Groundnuts from the North' *Nigeria Trade Journal* No. 2 pp. 10–12 1954

19 Bornu and the Chad Depression

As a major physical unit in the Central Sudan the Chad Depression is a geographical region, the western part of which constitutes the territorial area of the ancient Sudanese Empire of Bornu.[1] Schultze is therefore correct in asserting that Bornu is a political rather than a geographical entity.[2] In a regional study of Nigeria, however, Bornu can properly be considered as a geographical as well as a political unit. As one of the powerful states of the Chad Basin its boundaries extended eastwards to Lake Chad and its affluent the Shari, but during the partition of the continent, much of the eastern territory went to the German sphere of influence as part of the Cameroons, while the western part which was incorporated in British Nigeria retained its name of Bornu. In the south, its boundary is still marked by the rugged hills extending eastwards from the Middle Gongola valley to the Mandara Mountains. The northern and western boundaries are less well-defined and have undergone numerous alterations as a result of disputes with nieghbouring tribesmen.

Historically, Bornu has more in common with such states of the Chad Depression as Kanem, Bagirmi and Waday than with the rest of northern Nigeria. Indeed, Bornu was formerly a province of the Kanem Empire and it was from Kanem that the ruling tribe in Bornu, that is the Kanuris, invaded and subdued the former inhabitants who have since adopted the Kanuri language. With the decline of the Kanem Empire Bornu gradually extended its authority over the neighbouring districts, and in the early years of the eighteenth century it had become the dominant power in the Lake Chad Basin. When later the state of Bornu was attacked and almost subdued by the eastward advancing Fulanis, it was Mohamed-el-Kanemi, a Sheikh of Kanem descent, who helped Bornu to maintain its independence. Hence the significant fact that Bornu is one of the few states of the Central Sudan which successfully resisted Fulani domination in the nineteenth century.

Bornu is recognized as the oldest Moslem state in this part of Africa and its inhabitants are known to have been followers of the Prophet several centuries before the Fulani jihad.[3] Attempts by the Fulani to subdue this Moslem state clearly confirm the view that the jihad was very much a political campaign, at least in its later stages. Initially the Fulanis made considerable inroads into Bornu but were finally routed by el Kanemi, and as late as the 1850's Bornu is reported to have openly assisted Hausa patriots who were fighting against Fulani domination.

The open nature of her vast land boundary has always constituted the greatest defence problem of Bornu, since in this open grass countryside mounted horsemen as well as foot soldiers could strike from any direction, that is without marching along established communication arteries. Bornu has therefore suffered many invasions in the course of its history. In 1846, for example, the neighbouring state of Waday successfully invaded Bornu and destroyed the capital city of Kukawa, and again in the closing years of that century Rabeh invaded and subdued much of Bornu.

These invasions as well as the expeditions which Bornu carried out against the pagan groups of the Mandara Mountains had considerable effects on the population and the economy of the region. Many of the indigenous tribal groups were almost completely destroyed or absorbed by the Kanuris, who are the most numerous people and ruling group in Bornu. Some of the original groups still survive in difficult environments such as those occupied by the pagan groups in South Bornu. As a result of repeated raids by mounted horsemen from Bornu these pagan groups were forced to seek refuge on the hills, where many of them still reside, although they now descend to cultivate the plains at the foot of the hills.

Detailed information about the state of the economy during some of these wars is available in the journals of various travellers through Bornu in the early part of the nineteenth century. In 1851 for instance the borderlands between Bornu and the Hausa state of Kano were described by Barth as flourishing and populous, but three years later they had been reduced to a state of ruins and misery as a result of local warfare. In the Dikwa Emirate of Bornu, Barth observed that cotton fields were so neglected that many of them were overgrown with rank grass and bushes while fertile vales capable of yielding good crops of cotton were left uncultivated. Elsewhere, food farms were left derelict after their owners had been carried away as slaves or killed in the wars. It is not surprising therefore that severe and prolonged famines featured during these periods of unrest.

THE PHYSICAL LANDSCAPE AND DRAINAGE CHARACTERISTICS

Bornu consists of a vast open plain developed on young sedimentary rocks of the Chad Formation which consists mainly of clays with some sand horizon and gravels. The

---

[1] The Chad Basin occupies about 6,000 square miles of the Central Sudan, one-tenth of which lies in Nigeria
[2] Schultze, A., *The Sultanate of Bornu* p. 40 London 1913
[3] Bornu was converted to Islam in the eleventh century while the Hausa states were converted five centuries later

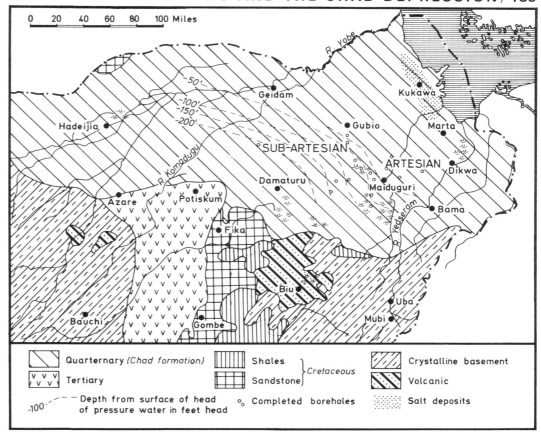

Figure 78. The Geology and Drainage of the Chad Basin

sediments, which are unfolded, dip gently towards Lake Chad, so that in Central Bornu well-borings show these clays to be over 200 feet in thickness. The whole formation is overlain by sandy drifts, which may be up to 300 feet thick in Central Bornu and under which concretionery ironstone is formed, as is the case around Kukawa. In the north-east the sands are rounded and appear to be of aeolian origin, while deposits in other parts are angular and of drifted fluviatile origin. In many places the clays become very dark as a result of the accumulation of organic matter and are then referred to as *firki*, the so-called black cotton soil. Where exposed at the surface the clays become plastic and saturated with water during the rainy season, when it is converted into swamps from which emerge numerous small streams, only a few of which actually reach Lake Chad. In the dry season the *firki* dries up and the swamps give way to a hard and brittle surface with numerous cracks. Water is scarce at this time except in isolated spots which are still covered with water. But the water table is still close to the surface, hence the numerous shallow water ponds which are dug along dry stream beds to provide water for man and beast.

The uniform aspect of the open landscape is striking, particularly during the rainy season, when vast areas in the Yedseram valley and the immediate neighbourhood of Lake Chad are flooded. The roads to Kukawa and Dikwa are bordered by stretches of *firki* swamps alternating with patches of slightly higher ground. Dune formations occur in Central Bornu and along the Bornu and Kanem shores of the lake. These dunes are associated with the numerous sandy islands which occur along the Kanem end of the lake and it is thought that they were formed during a period of desiccation which preceded the formation of the lake. These ancient dunes, together with the sandy drifts, support an abundant growth of trees, while the *firki* surface is relatively bare of vegetation, particularly in the dry season, when the grass is burnt.

The average elevation of the basin is 1,000 feet above sea level, the lake level being 800 feet above sea level. Owing to the nature of the terrain which appears to have no slope down to the lake, and the character of the *firki* soil which extends for many miles around the southern and south-western sides of the lake, few of the rivers flowing towards Lake Chad actually reach the lake. Rather, such rivers as the Yedseram and the Alo disappear into *firki* swamps at considerable distances away from the lake.

In Nigeria, the most important river draining into Lake Chad (considering its length and volume of water) is the River Yo or the Komadugu-Yobe. Its course is marked by an alternation of well-defined valleys carrying a single stream, and open swampy flood plains (*firki*), with many stream channels. Fifty miles from Lake Chad the Yobe virtually disappears and only a trickle reaches the lake. It contains no running water during the greater part of the year and consists only of a few large and many smaller pools during the end of the dry season. Normal flow begins about July, and by November its flat valley is completely flooded and can no longer be forded till the end of January. In so far as defence is concerned, the

Yobe is virtually ineffective as a natural barrier since it is fordable for about three-quarters of the year. Other rivers such as the Bunga, which flows past Jos town as the Delimi, reach Lake Chad in flood once in a generation.

Although the drainage basin of the Shari lies outside Nigeria, this river deserves mention here since it is by far the most important feeder of Lake Chad. It is estimated that about two-thirds of the volume of water discharged into the lake comes from this river and it is therefore not surprising that the rise and fall in the level of the lake is determined by the regime of this river. The Shari rises outside the Sudan, in the damp region farther south, from where it conveys a large volume of water into the drier north. In this respect, the Shari can properly be compared with the Nile, and the fact that it is the only affluent of Lake Chad which contains flowing water all through the year is thereby explained. The dominating position of the Shari in feeding the lake is obvious from the fact that at the end of December, that is in the heart of the dry season, when all the other affluents are at their lowest level and when the majority of the Nigerian affluents are already dried up, the lake is actually rising because of the large quantity of water it receives from the Shari at this time. The bed of the Shari is however not always full, being lowest at the end of the dry season while its highest water comes in October.

Lake Chad itself is a vast expanse of shallow water with three-quarters of its shores lying outside Nigeria. The actual area under water varies from 4,000 to 10,000 square miles according to the season of the year, being most extensive between the middle of December and the end of January. Its depth is only thirteen to nineteen feet, which means that it is the shallowest lake of its size in the world; but during the low water season, the depth of water is much less. At this time numerous mud and sandbanks emerge, the banks being overgrown with tall grasses and papyrus.

It is generally believed that the lake was much more extensive in the past and there is considerable evidence to show that it is still diminishing.[1] In the early 1920's Baga Ngelwa was a large lake shore market, but in the 1930's the market had ceased to exist since the water had become too shallow to allow the approach of canoes. Apart from the loss of water due to evaporation, the reason for the retreat of the lake is not yet understood. It is possible that loss of water due to evaporation is greater than the water provided by local rainfall and discharges from the affluents. The suggestion that this decline might be caused by loss of water through a subterranean outlet into the bed of the Bahr-el-Ghazal has since been discredited. The lake, however, loses much water to an upper subterranean reservoir which is tapped by shallow wells in the towns surrounding the lake.

The floor of Lake Chad and the soil of the surrounding shore-lands contain thick deposits of potash which forms one of the chief products of the lake, the other one being fish. For centuries this salt has been mined in the lake area, and during the days of Henry Barth it featured as an important item of trade in the central Sudan. Under the trade name of natron, potash was in great demand for a variety of uses. It passed for table salt in areas where salt was scarce or at times when the salt caravans from Bilma were not forthcoming. Today, as in the past, it is used for feeding cattle and horses, in the dyeing of cloth and leather and in the preparation of snuff from tobacco. Kano and Kukawa were the principal natron markets, and today there is still a considerable trade in this commodity. Its presence in the lake belt explains the saltiness of water in certain parts of Lake Chad.

ARTESIAN AND OTHER WATER RESOURCES IN THE CHAD BASIN[2]

Much of the Chad Basin is fertile and contains a large cattle population but cultivation is limited by the short duration of the rains, when no more than twenty-five inches fall in a year. During the rains water is plentiful, supplies coming from the rain and the rivers which are full at this time of the year. In the dry season, when cattle are forced to migrate in search of water, some water may be obtained from the bed of rivers like the Alo and the Yobe which, at this time of the year, consist of disconnected pools. Outside the river valleys shallow wells sunk through the sandy drifts to the level of the underlying clay beds also yield water which is from a subterranean reservoir lying above the main artesian reservoir of the basin, but below the level of Lake Chad. This reservoir is thought to receive its water partly from local rains and partly from the lake. The main artesian reserve of the area is, however, independent of Lake Chad and is therefore unlikely to be affected by the possible drying up of Lake Chad, which may occur if the imminent capture of the Logone-Shari by the Benue is not prevented.

The presence of an artesian reservoir in the Bornu region has been known for many decades, and it is fortunate that over much of the area physical conditions are

[1] Migeod, F. W. H., *Through Nigeria to Lake Chad* pp. 189–204 London 1924
[2] Geological Survey Department 'Pressure Water in the Chad Basin' *Nigeria Trade Journal* Vol. 7 pp. 147–50 1959

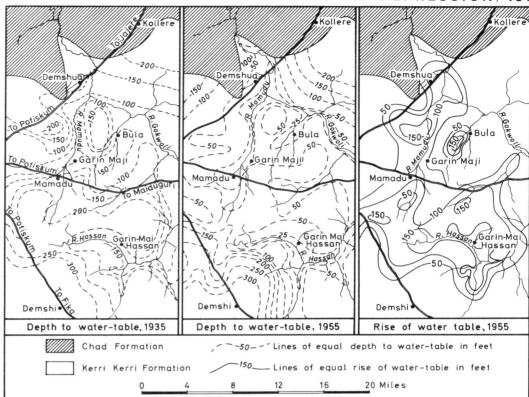

Figure 79. Recent Hydrological Changes in the Potiskum Division of the Chad Basin (after Canter and Barber)

such that water holes do not require pumps. Maintenance cost is therefore negligible and only simple precautions are necessary to safeguard the purity of the supply. At Maiduguri, a four-inch diameter borehole tapping the main acquifer yields about 3,600 gallons per hour with a head of twenty feet. A well such as this is capable of serving a small town and as many as 2,000 cattle. The present scheme, whereby the artesian reserves in Bornu are being exploited through deep wells sunk on roughly a ten-mile grid, is designed to combat the water problem of the area. It is hoped that with the provision of adequate supplies of water all through the year the local nomads will be encouraged to settle and cultivate the land. Cattle migration will be minimized and mixed farming made feasible.

Important hydrological changes which will have far-reaching implications on the water supply situation have been reported in the central parts of Potiskum Division. These changes consist of phenomenal rises in the level of the water-table resulting in the appearance of many new springs, streams and lakes (Figure 79). In the early 1930's springs appeared at Garim Hassan and near Garin Maji, and within the next decade these springs had gained in strength and were able to discharge sufficient water to support large perennial flows in formerly dry channels. Rises of over 150 feet have been recorded in the water levels in wells in the division, while substantial lakes have been formed at Garin Hassan. According to Carter and Barber, the level of the water-table is independent of the fluctuations in the annual rainfall but is related to the extensive deforestation and cultivation of vast areas.[1] The effect of deforestation and cultivation has been to reduce transpiration and evaporation while increasing the surface run-off. But since the ground is relatively flat the amount of water lost by run-off is not large enough to cause a significant fall in the water table. Rather the run-off enters the river systems which, being influent, are able to supply more water to the permanent groundwater. The view has also been expressed that in sub-arid deciduous thorny country such as is to be found in this area, as much as sixty-five per cent of the rainfall is lost by transpiration. In that case water gained as a result of reduced transpiration and evaporation consequent on deforestation will more than make up for loss due to increased run-off.

ASPECTS OF THE POPULATION AND SETTLEMENT

Bornu is inhabited primarily by the Kanuris, who numbered 753,000 in 1953. They constitute the ruling race and are thought to be of mixed Arab, Hamitic Kanembu and Tubu descent. Although many of the original tribal groups who inhabited Bornu before the Kanuri conquest have since adopted the Kanuri language, the Kanuri themselves have gradually become merged with the negro population of the region they conquered. Small pockets of pure Kanembu and Tubu population still exist in the central part of the Nigerian shores of Lake Chad and the Lower Yobe valley respectively. Next in importance to the Kanuris are the Semitic Arabs whom the Kanuris call Shuwas. In 1953 there were 99,000 Shuwa Arabs in Nigeria, most of whom inhabit the eastern part of Bornu. The Shuwa who migrated into Bornu at various

[1] Carter, J. D., & Barber, W., 'The rise in the Water-table in parts of Potiskum Division, Bornu Province' Records of the Geological Survey of Nigeria pp. 5–13 1956

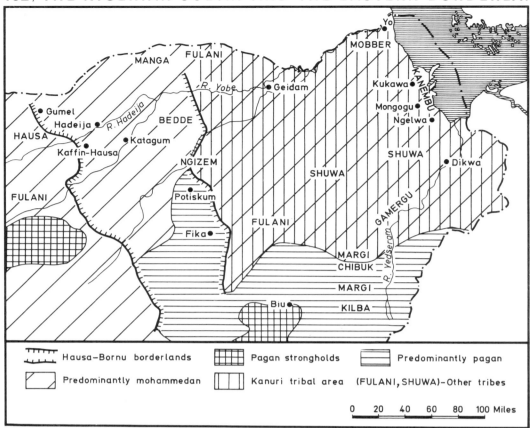

Figure 80. Elements in the Cultural Geography of the Chad Basin

times during the last five hundred years have lost most of their original traits excepting their language. Over the years, they have displayed a remarkable adjustment to their environment, and have changed their mode of life from wandering desert nomads to a settled agricultural people. Initially, according to Herr Schultze, they were obliged to breed cattle rather than camels with which their existence in the desert had been bound up. This change was found necessary since the climate of Bornu was not very suitable to camels, and today Shuwa cattle are used for transporting people as well as goods. Later, many of their cattle were decimated and the people found it necessary to settle down as cultivators. Today they are reputed to be the foremost indigenous group in Nigeria practising some form of rudimentary mixed farming.

Other ethnic groups found in Bornu include the Fulanis who are more numerous in the southern part, bordering on Adamawa, which is under Fulani rule. They are a race of wandering herdsmen, though some are now beginning to settle down. The Gamergu of the Middle Yedseram valley, a semi-pagan group who rear cattle and horses, the Mobbers of the Lower Yobe valley and the Mangas who occupy the plains north and south of the Middle Yobe valley are known to have settled in this region long before the Kanuri conquest. Further south, in the hill country west of the Mandara Mountains, are the Margi pagan groups, many of whom still settle on hilltops which provided them with adequate defence outposts in the days of slave raids by Bornu soldiers.

Most of the inhabitants of Bornu are Mohammedans

practising a rather liberal form of Islam in which women are allowed to participate in public affairs. The smaller ethnic groups, particularly those of the southern hill borderlands are still largely pagan. As in other parts of the far north Christianity has made very little inroad in Bornu, and the Christians found in such cities as Maiduguri, Bama and Dikwa are essentially migrants from the southern provinces of Nigeria. It is these migrants who direct the retail trade in imported consumer goods in these urban areas.

Kanuri villages consist of the usual round huts with conical roofs found over a large part of the Sudan. The walls may be of mud or wooden framework covered with grass matting and the roof is made of grass thatch or from the stalk of grains. Both in the villages and the towns the huts are arranged in groups or compounds which may be enclosed by a mud wall or a mat screen, which makes it impossible to see the inner yard from outside. Houses with flat roofs feature in the towns.

A common feature of all Bornu towns is the *dendal* or high street. These *dendals* form the main approach roads into cities like Maiduguri and Bama and are essentially very broad roads lined on both sides by shade trees. They provide, in addition to the market squares, centres for day-long activity, including lounging and gossiping.

The diverse peoples of this region are organized into the emirates of Bornu, Dikwa, Gumel, Fika and Bedde, of which Bornu is by far the largest and most populous. In the official ranking of chiefs in northern Nigeria the Shehu of Bornu comes second only to the Sultan of Sokoto. This list also shows that Bedde comes last in the ranking for Bornu Province.

The Chad Basin as a whole is very sparsely populated and much of it is still virtually uninhabited. Over most of the inhabited districts the density rarely exceeds fifty persons per square mile, excepting along the Bama–Maiduguri road where the figure rises to about 200 persons per square mile. The comparatively uniform spread of people in the habitable areas is striking, and so is the occurrence of an almost uninhabited belt in the region of the Hausa-Bornu borderlands (Figure 80). This border-land belt, which is sometimes referred to as the shatter-zone between the Fulani and Bornu empires, is the exact territory referred to on page 188 above. Its population history and pattern is very much similar to that of the middle belt of Nigeria. In the extreme north the influence of river valleys as tracts for population concentration is apparent.

CROP AND ANIMAL HUSBANDRY

The main occupations of the people are crop farming and animal rearing. There is sufficient land for everyone and the soil is fertile, particularly along the river flood plains. Even the *firki* soils which dry up suddenly, and become too hard to till, support good crops of cotton, millet and indigo. The limiting factor to crop farming is climatic, and various devices have been adopted to combat this. The rainy season is short (May to September) and permits only one cropping season, thereby creating a need for dry-season irrigation which the Kanuris and some other Bornuese tribes practise. The irrigated acreage is, however, limited and consists of small plots with rectangular beds which are irrigated by means of hydraulic contrivances from deep wells or from pools in the bed of rivers which have dried up at this time of the year. Only market-garden crops are produced on these irrigated plots, but there is a possibility of large-scale irrigation works in this region which is known to have plentiful supplies of underground water. It is now known that about 10,000 acres of land suitable for pumped irrigation exist immediately south of Lake Chad in the area lying on the left bank of the Ebeji River, and a scheme to develop another 10,000 acres along the Yobe River between Daya and Abadan has been in operation since 1960.

Staple food crops are grown exclusively during the rainy season and are therefore subject to the limitations imposed by the local rainfall. Crop failures may be caused by delayed rains or inadequate moisture. On the other hand excessive flooding may occur in the months of July and August, when crops are drowned and destroyed. Hence the need to construct ridges in the farms.

The common farming system in which fields are rotated around a fixed settlement is practised, but field sizes here are larger than in the forest belt. Crops grown for food include millet, sorghum, maize, groundnuts and seasame. Cotton which has been cultivated for many centuries in the Chad Basin is still grown for local use and for export. Crop production for export is so far not well developed in this region, its contribution to the cotton and groundnut exports being still very insignificant. Since the Kanuris and other groups inhabiting Bornu are very industrious and intelligent farmers, and since their soil is capable of producing good crops of cotton and groundnuts, it has been thought that the main problem facing crop expansion in this part of the country is undeveloped transportation. Hence the pious hope that the new Bornu railway extension would stimulate commercial farming in the area. It is true that the railway led to a rapid expansion of groundnut cultivation in the Kano area, but it has not produced similar results in the sparsely settled middle belt of Nigeria. The Bornu region is equally sparsely inhabited and it is not likely that the new railway will perform the wonders which its advocates dreamed of.

A rudimentary form of mixed farming is practised by the Shuwa Arabs, who still own large herds of cattle and are reputed to be the most intelligent farmers in Bornu.[1] The Shuwa Arabs were formerly a nomadic pastoral people but have since settled down to cultivate the land, although many of them are semi-nomadic in much the same way as their cattle are. During the rainy season, when the land is under cultivation, some of the cattle remain near the villages to graze on uncultivated patches, while a considerable number are driven to wet season grazing grounds in western Bornu. It is at this time that much of the manure used to spread on millet and maize crops is collected in large heaps. As soon as the dry season starts, that is about November, the cattle leave western Bornu to return to the Shuwa villages en route to dry season grazing grounds along the shores of Lake Chad and the Chad-Nigeria borderlands. Most of the cattle left crops is collected in large heaps. As soon as the dry season migration. The few herds left behind to provide milk and household manure are fed on crop residues including the straw of millet, guinea corn and maize as well as on oil cakes from groundnuts, seasame and shea butter nuts. Some degree of integration of arable and pastoral farming is thus achieved.

[1] White, S., 'Notes on Mixed Farming as Practised by Some Shuwa Arabs in parts of Dikwa Emirate' *Farm and Forest* Vol. 2 pp. 24–6 1941

Partly because the Kanuris and Shuwa Arabs were originally a cattle people like the Fulani or Masai, and partly as a result of suitable climate, stock raising has always received as much attention as crop farming in Bornu. Emphasis in recent years has been on cattle breeding with some households owning as many as thirty herds each. The cattle density of about twenty per square mile is only exceeded by that of the Kano close-settled zone although there are many more cattle per head of the population in Bornu than in Kano. The local cattle breed is named after the Shuwa Arabs and is a triple-purpose breed. It supplies milk for food, but this is scarcely made use of in the fresh state, being usually curdled first by mixing cow urine with it. The Kanuris also make butter from the milk, but the taste of their product is spoilt by this bad practice of adding cow urine to their milk. The Shuwa Arab is also used for pack transport, a bullock being capable of carrying a load of 175 pounds. It is also used for riding, particularly by Shuwa Arab women who may be seen riding their bullocks to and from Maiduguri market.

Considerable flocks of sheep and goats may be found in various parts of Bornu, but particularly in the south which is less suitable for cattle breeding. Camel and horse breeding are of long standing importance, although emphasis today is on the latter since camel breeding is found to be less successful for climatic reasons. Amongst other things these animals, together with the Shuwa Arab cattle breed, still provide the only means of transport between some settlements, particularly during the rainy season when many roads become impassable to wheeled transport.

GUM ARABIC AND OTHER FOREST PRODUCTS

Although the Sudan has supplied gum arabic to Europe since the early days of the Christian era, the collection of gum arabic in Nigeria is of recent origin, and the chief producing area is north Bornu, where the *Acacia senegal* (*Dakwara* in Hausa, *Kolkol* in Kanuri) which produces the highest quality gum grows in large numbers.[1] Early exports of gum arabic in Nigeria were based on collections from wild *Acacia campylacentha* and *Acacia seyal* in the region of the Gongola and Upper Benue, but the quality of gum from these trees is much poorer and today the industry is centred on the Bornu region. Gum arabic from Bornu is collected mainly in the dry season when exudation from the trees is greatest, and fortunately this is a slack season in the farming calendar.

A report on 'Gum Arabic in Bornu' for the Nigerian Government in 1930 indicated that after years of intensive propaganda to induce the people to exploit the gum, Bornu could produce about 2,000 tons of gum arabic per annum. In 1948, however, total exports from Nigeria were put at 700 tons valued at £40,000. The slow progress of the industry is best appreciated by realizing that about twenty per cent of the gum exported from Nigeria comes from the neighbouring francophone Republic of Chad. The response of the Bornu peasantry has been very disappointing and has been attributed to various factors including paucity of *Acacia senegal*, low prices and despoliation of gum crops by monkeys and thieves.

The other important product from the woods of Bornu is firewood which is very scarce in some areas, such as around Lake Chad, where lack of firewood for drying fish constitutes one of the problems of the lake fishing industry. In many areas it is even difficult to obtain wood for building.

TRANSPORTATION AND TRADE

Bornu is still very poorly served by land transportation and its road density is as sparse as that of the Middle Belt. The only trunk road with a good tarmac surface runs from Bama to Maiduguri while the Maiduguri–Bauchi road has so deteriorated that it is necessary to scrape off the entire surface before another tar coating is applied. The other trunk A roads are surfaced with laterite and may be closed to heavy vehicles for twenty-four hours after a heavy rainfall. As a result of this irritating practice a goods lorry from Maiduguri to Onitsha may take about one week to travel the three hundred miles between Bama and Jalingo. But even the car driver, who is allowed by regulation to proceed along these federal roads at all times, is often subjected to little fits of temper as a result of the annoying behaviour of the less responsible barrier keepers, who may go shopping in the local market with the keys in their pockets. Some of these federal roads, including that linking Maiduguri to Fort Lamy in the Chad Republic may be closed to all forms of traffic for a number of weeks during the rainy season. All trunk B roads in Bornu are dry season roads and are closed to motorized traffic in the rainy season.

In a situation such as this, one can readily appreciate why primitive forms of transportation have survived intact. The ubiquitous donkey is found near the villages, where they are used for carting loads from and to the farms as well as to the market. Local bullocks, horses and

---

[1] Macdonald, K. R., 'The Gum Arabic Industry in Bornu Province' *Farm and Forest* Vol. II No. 1 pp. 13–16 1941

Plate 49. *The Shehu's palace and mosque at Maiduguri.*

Plate 50. *The Maiduguri-Dikwa road. This road, which leads to Lake Chad, proved impassable in September 1965, because of heavy rains.*

camels are used for long distance travel, but by far the most common form of transportation is by foot.

Since it is situated in an area which is poorly served by land transportation, one would expect Lake Chad to be an important inland waterway. This is, however, not the case. Progress in crossing the lake is very slow and considerable difficulty is encountered in pulling vessels through the first mile or two of papyrus-choked channels before getting into open water. The shallowness of the lake, which rarely exceeds five feet, has necessitated the use of flat-bottomed vessels. Locally-made vessels are made of papyrus tied together in the form of a canoe, but in recent years flattish wooden canoes imported from Onitsha and Port Harcourt have come into use.

The new 400-mile Bornu railway extension is expected to solve the transportation problems of Bornu. The main argument for the railway was that the area through which it passes was inadequately served by road transportation and that existing roads were not able to cope with the agricultural production of the area at the time. As a result of this, the argument continued, the expansion of the cultivation of cotton and groundnuts in this rich agricultural area has been retarded. Hence the conclusion that the rail extension would vastly improve the economy of the area and the living standards of the people.[1]

Until the opening of the Bornu railway extension in 1963, cotton and groundnuts from this region were sent by road to the nearest Benue ports or the nearest rail-heads and from thence to the port of export. The region traded its fish and other products to the East Central State through Onitsha market, which in turn supplied it with imported goods. Supplies were held up during the rains as a result of poor roads and it is expected that the trade between Bornu and the south will increase now that there is a rail route to Maiduguri. It has also been estimated that the rail route will reduce by fifty per cent the cost of evacuating groundnuts and cotton from Bornu to the ports and that there will be a similar reduction in the transport costs of imported goods. Bornu's trade with Fort Lamy, which receives imported goods through Maiduguri, will still suffer some restriction as a result of the poor road between the two towns. The extension of the railhead from Maiduguri to Fort Lamy has already been suggested in political circles, although a good all-season tarred road would appear to be adequate.

Doubts have already been expressed about the wisdom of spending over £20 million on the Bornu railway extension which appears to have been built for political rather than economic reasons, poor transportation in Bornu and the above plausible arguments notwithstanding. A good road would have cost less and served a much greater area since road transportation is more flexible. These objections and others were however rejected by the advocates of the railway. It is yet too early to assess the impact of this railway on agricultural production along its immediate hinterland and it may well turn out that future developments will justify the hopes of those who pushed through the scheme. The projected freight traffic of 500,000 tons and the passenger traffic of two million persons annually may yet be achieved.

THE LAKE CHAD FISHERIES

Lake Chad possesses large reserves of fish and in recent years the Government has explored the possibility of expanding and improving the existing fishing industry. At present the lake fishing industry is confronted with a number of problems which are associated with the character of the lake itself. The large variation in the lake surface for instance limits the number of permanent good landing points, while the papyrus restricts movements from shore to open water to the extent that occasionally boats enclosed by papyrus get so entangled that they are abandoned. The shallowness of the lake is one of the problems facing future plans to develop the lake fisheries, since this will limit the type of vessels that can be used. At present the papyrus canoes which are propelled by punting rather than paddles rarely go out more than two miles from the shore, thereby seriously limiting fishing activities to the shores.

The common fishing method used on the Nigerian side of the lake is known as long-lining and consists of lines of up to 300 feet long tied at both ends to papyrus rafts or

[1] 'Bornu Railway Extension' *Nigeria Trade Journal* Vol. 7 pp. 20–3 1959

stout poles driven into the lake bed. Floats are attached to the line at thirty-foot intervals and unbaited hooks are suspended from stoppers every six inches. A few larger and baited hooks are also attached. Locally woven nets are commonly used, but tend to tangle easily when larger fish are caught, hence the rapid change to cast nets which are proving very successful. Most of the catch is flame-burned, smoked or dried and exported to the Southern Provinces. In recent years, the Northern Nigeria Fisheries Research unit at Baga has produced salted fish for sales to schools and institutions, but it is not known whether salting will prove an economic venture or whether there will be sufficient demand to justify it.

The main genera of fish caught in the lake include *Heterotis*, *Lates niloticus* (Nile Perch), *Synodontis* and *Tilapia*. *Hererotis* account for about one-third of the catch and *Lates* for about one-fifth. At present the neighbouring territories of Chad and Cameroon produce much more fish from Lake Chad, and this has been attributed to easier fishing conditions in the Shari-Lagone delta area. A considerable proportion of the forty to eighty thousand tons of wet fish produced yearly from the Shari-Lagone Basin is however marketed in Nigeria as dried fish.

For transportation to Maiduguri the fish are packed in all sorts of containers including tea chests, reed baskets and paper boxes, but from Maiduguri jute sacks are generally used. From the lake shore the fish are transported by head-load and animal transport to Maiduguri from where they are sent by road and rail to the south. The high incidence of infestation, resulting in the strong stench from the packages, is caused by poor storage en route to the markets, as well as poor communications which make for slow transportation of the fish. The present incidence of infestation is so great that as much as fifty per cent of its weight and about the same amount of protein content is considered lost by the time the fish reach distant consumers.

Since fish is a highly perishable product, future plans for developing the lake fisheries aim at reorganizing the industry from the catching to the distribution stages. A development company is to be set up to operate the scheme and the current Development Plan has made provision for 2,000 fishing boats in addition to £72,500 allocated to the Lake Chad Fisheries for housing, research and demonstrations. Experiments on new fishing techniques under local conditions are on foot and various types of boats are to be tested before large numbers are ordered. The use of ice to preserve the fish is under consideration and good landing places with permanent deep water have to be established. At present fuel shortage is a limiting factor to fish smoking, and for the future modern drying equipment will be required.

MAIDUGURI

Maiduguri (139,970 in 1963) is the name by which the Kanuri capital city of Yerwa is commonly referred to in commercial circles. Yerwa was founded in 1907 to replace the old capital of Kukawa which was rather remote and had suffered total destruction in 1893, when Rabeh captured the town. The new court of the Shehu of Bornu, which became the nucleus of the new town of Yerwa, was located close to an old village in Bornu called Maiduguri. In 1908 this small village was chosen by Lugard as the administrative headquarters for Bornu, and from then on the name came to be applied to both settlements. Today, with a population of over 139,000, it has grown up to become the premier town of Bornu.

The town has fairly good road connections with other parts of the north and is served twice every week by internal flights of the Nigeria Airways. It is a growing commercial centre serving a vast area as the only main market and administrative centre. The recent opening of the Bornu railway extension, the terminal of which is at Maiduguri, is expected to stimulate the growth rate of the town. The main products of Bornu, groundnuts, hides and skin, which were formerly carried by road to Jos, will now be railed mainly from the Maiduguri rail-head.

Works consulted and suggestions for futher reading:

1. Grove, A. T., 'A note on the former extent of Lake Chad' *Geographical Journal* No. 125 pp. 465–7 1959
2. Grove, A. T. & Pullan, R. A., 'Some aspects of the Pleistocene Paleogeography of the Chad Basin' in Howell, F. C. & Bourliere, F. (eds.) *African Ecology and Human Evolution* pp. 230–45 Chicago 1963
3. Nzekwu, O., 'From Maiduguri to Lake Chad' *Nigeria Magazine* No. 79 pp. 234–47 1963
4. Pullan, R. A., 'The Recent Geomorphological Evolution of the South Central Part of the Chad Basin' *Journal of West African Science Association* No. 9 pp. 115–39 1964
5. Stenning, D. J., *Savana Nomads: a study of the Wodaabe pastoral Fulani of Western Bornu Province* London 1959
6. Geological Survey Department 'Pressure water in the Chad Basin' *Nigeria Trade Journal* No. 7 pp. 147–50 1959
7. *The Industrial Potentialities of Northern Nigeria* pp. 110–18 Kaduna 1963

20 The Eastern Borderlands

The mountainous area which forms the boundary zone between Nigeria and the Cameroons is a distinct geographical region. At first sight the Nigeria-Cameroons boundary which passes through the region appears to be a 'natural' boundary, but a closer study of the area reveals that it is no less artificial than the Nigeria-Dahomey or the Nigeria-Niger boundaries. Indeed, the situation in this borderland region calls to question the idea that natural features like mountain ranges or river valleys are suitable political boundaries. Just as river valleys like the Lower Nile, the Euphrates and the Lower Niger, which constitute economic or cultural units, confirm the unifying rather than divisive influence of rivers, we find that mountain ranges like the Pyrenees or the Alps often sustain a special culture which transcends the political boundaries passing through them. So it is with the eastern borderlands of Nigeria which extend eastward into the Cameroons. Here man's adaptation to the hill environment has nothing to do with whether the district is being administered by Nigeria or the Cameroons. The Fulani cattlemen who find these fly-free uplands particularly attractive as grazing grounds are found on both sides of the border, while regional variations in climate, vegetation and culture depend largely on latitude and altitude rather than on political divisions. For this reason the highland area separating West Africa from Central Africa is considered as a natural geographical unit.

Most of this borderland region was once administered as part of the former German Cameroons. But the short-lived political unity of the region was disrupted after the First World War, when the Cameroons became a mandated territory with the western part under British administration and the eastern part under the French. The vote in 1960 by the northern part of the former German Cameroons to merge with Nigeria under the new name of Sardauna Province has ruled out the possibility of the region ever being administered again as a political unit. The region marks the eastern limit of Fulani settlement in the Sudan. It is a refuge environment and is rich in fragments of refugee culture.

Starting from the neighbourhood of Kumba in the Western Cameroons, the highlands making up this region run in a north-easterly direction to Gwoza in eastern Bornu, a distance of about 500 miles. A major break in the continuity of these highlands occurs between Garoua and Yola, where the Upper Benue breaches the range, dividing it into two unequal parts, a small northern component and a much more extensive and higher component in the south. A high level erosion surface is recognized in fragmentary form right through the region at altitudes varying from 3,000 feet upwards. In some areas this surface occurs as plateaux but in others it is so dissected that only isolated residuals or summit planes can be identified, and yet in some other districts it is buried with volcanic rocks which are very common all over the region. The varied topography of this region of granitic and basaltic rocks, of deeply incised river gorges and mountain grassland, presents a rather attractive landscape which contrasts markedly with the monotony that characterizes the open plains found in other parts of the country.

Some of the more prominent ranges of this region include the Mandarra and Alantika Mountains, the Mambila Plateau and the Bamenda Highlands. The main features of the relief of this frontier zone are described in the next few pages.

THE DISTRICT NORTH OF THE BENUE TROUGH (Figure 81)

Immediately south of Lake Chad the eastern borderlands consist of the vast *firki* plains already described under the Chad Basin. Extensive swamps and meandering water

Figure 81. Relief and Drainage of the Northern Part of the Eastern Borderlands

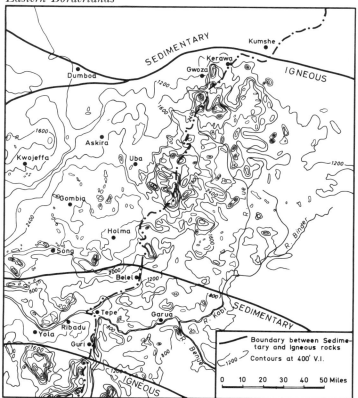

courses characterize the landscape, particularly during the rainy season when the black boggy soil of this region becomes plastic and saturated with rain water. Further south, at about a distance of one hundred miles from the southern shores of Lake Chad, the featureless plains of the Chad formation give way to a much higher and dissected countryside. The sudden change in the aspect of the landscape reflects a change also in the geological formation, for it is in this area that the rocks of the Basement Complex outcrop.

The northern limit of the mountain ranges which dominate much of this borderland region lies immediately south of geological boundary between the rocks of the Chad Group and rocks of the Basement Complex. Prominent hills, such as the Kerawa and Seledeba Hills, rise to over 3,600 feet in the vicinity of this geological boundary. North and east of Madagali the hills attain summits of about 4,800 feet, rising to well over 2,000 feet above the 2,400 feet erosion surface on which they stand. It is interesting that in this hilly area, as in other parts of the Cameroon-Adamawa Mountains, the highest elevation is found along or very close to the Nigeria-Cameroon boundary.

A belt of country which maintains a general elevation of 2,400 feet for over twenty miles connects these northern hills to the Mandara Mountains. The Mandara Mountains constitute the most prominent of the borderland ranges north of the Benue trough, and stretch for thirty miles from north to south, maintaining an average width of twenty miles. In essence the Mandara chain, which from the Nigerian side appears like a confused assemblage of enormous blocks of granite, consists of a dissected plateau surface at about 4,000 feet, but with summits rising to nearly 5,000 feet in many places. On the Nigerian side, where the mountains slope more steeply to the neighbouring plains, it is possible to discern the even crestline of the summits at various points along the Mubi–Bama road. The decline in altitude on the Cameroon or eastern side is less sudden.

West of the Mandara Mountains the borderland landscape consists of vast high plains dominated by massed inselbergs and isolated domes at various stages of disintegration, as well as restricted mountain ranges such as that at Uba. Farther west and also east of the Mandara Mountains the aspect of the countryside is similar, consisting of vast plains, above which rise such groups of hills as the Kilba Hills west of Mubi and the celebrated double basalt cone of Mendif on the Cameroon side. South of the Mandara Mountains the inselberg landscape of the crystalline plateau continues past the Basement

Complex/sedimentary boundary into the Benue trough. Important crystalline inselbergs which border on the Benue valley include the Zummo and Song groups of hills and the Fali Hills.

The Benue valley above Yola constitutes a part of the eastern borderlands. This part of the Benue trough consists of a synclinal basin filled with cretaceous sandstones which are covered with extensive flood plain and alluvial sediments deposited by the Benue and its affluents. At several places the sandstone outcrops near the river in various forms. The plateau areas rising above the plains to the north and south of Garua, the Bagele Hills (1,800 feet) opposite Yola and the hills of Gurin are some of the relief features developed on the cretaceous sandstones. Other features include the sandstone cuestas and ridges which occur mainly on the north side of the valley. A few small volcanic rocks have been found in this valley in the neighbourhood of Ribadu and west of the village of Wuro Boki. Both the ancient valley of the Faro and the eleven-mile-long gorge between Ribadu and Jobolio deserve mention at this stage. In the distant past the Faro flowed into the Benue just below Dasin pagan village and not at Tepe as is the case today. The origin of both features, the Upper Benue gorge and the diversion of the course of the Faro River, is connected with river capture and tectonic movements in the area. The proposed dam site for the Yola Reservoir (see page 138) at Dasin Hausa is located along this gorge.

Students of geomorphology will find a detailed study of the Upper Benue valley very rewarding. The Faro tributary displays several features of old age which include braided courses. Its valley is much wider than that of the Upper Benue gorge. But probably the most interesting topographical features of the Faro valley are the natural levees between which the river flows. At the village of Beka the river bed is at an elevation of over ten feet above that of the neighbouring ancient Faro-Benue valley. At the high-water season, when the levee wall is breached, the village, which stands on high ground, is often surrounded by water.

SOUTHERN ADAMAWA

The central part of the borderlands is that area lying between the Benue trough and the Donga valley in the south. It is an area of discontinuous mountain ranges and dissected high-level plateau surfaces, often separated by such major valleys as those of the Faro, Ini and Taraba Rivers. The numerous hills or groups of hills found on these

Plate 51. A Mountain Pass near Bambui.

plateau surfaces are much higher in elevation than those north of the Benue trough and the plateau surfaces are also more extensive.

Rocks of the Basement Complex reappear immediately south of the Benue in the Verre Hills and the Alantika Mountains, both of which rise abruptly from pediment slopes at the margins of the Benue Plains to heights of over 3,600 feet and 4,000 feet respectively. The Nigeria-Cameroon boundary follows the bend of the Alantika Mountains and continues along the Balakossa and Banglang ranges before taking a southerly direction. The sides of these highland areas are dissected by numerous steep-sided valleys, which radiate in all directions to join the larger river valleys such as the Deo, the Taja and Maio Faro. These wider valleys are given to sudden floods, which arise partly as a result of the heavy rainfall from these uplands. The eastern slopes of the Alantikas which overlook the Maio Faro are particularly steep, rising abruptly from 1,500 feet to 4,000 feet in places. The western slopes are not so steep, and in this respect the Alantikas form a contrast to the Mandarra Mountains which have steeper slopes on the western or Nigerian side and more gentle slopes on the eastern side.

An open undulating country, the Jada Plains (1,300 to 1,600 feet), drained by the Ini River, separates the Alantika and the Verre Hills from the more massive Shebshi Mountains in the west. Like the highland masses already described, the Shebshi consist of a high plateau surface rising from 3,300 feet in the south to 4,400 feet in the north. North of the Vogel peak (6,700 feet), the highest point on this plateau, there are numerous high hills with well-wooded upper slopes, but more open and badly eroded lower slopes. Many of these hills have flat tops and remind one of similar hills which, in the Jos Plateau, are associated with decomposed basalts of the Fluvio-

Volcanic series. The occurrence of volcanic rocks on the summits of the Shebshi Mountains, which are otherwise of crystalline Basement rocks, suggest that these flat-topped hills have the same origin as those on the opposite side of the Benue valley. Also like the Jos Plateau, the Shebshi Plateau constitutes a hydrographic centre with a well-developed dendritic pattern of drainage on the plateau surface.

South of the Shebshi Mountains the eastern highlands are breached by the valley of the Taraba River. Beyond this valley the highlands reappear as broken hill groups such as the Kungana and the Wanka Hills. Each hill area is bounded by steep scarps along which deep valleys have been cut. Wide, flat-floored river valleys with steep sides such as those of the Suntai, the Kam and the Mbam Rivers separate these groups of hills from one another as well as from the main massif of the Mambilla Plateau. Many of the hills, which have grass-covered flat tops, rise above 4,000 feet and some have peaks rising to more than 6,000 feet.

It is in the Mambilla Plateau that we come across the largest and highest of the several mountainous blocks on the Nigerian side of the borderlands. The plateau, which measures about sixty miles along its curved length by twenty-five miles, is bounded by an escarpment which in places is nearly 3,000 feet in height. The surface consists of gently sloping plains at 4,500 and 5,000 feet and is crossed by broad shallow valleys which contrast markedly with the ravines cut by the same rivers as they descend the scarp slopes to the broad valleys of the Donga, Kam and Mbam Rivers. Basalt flows, estimated to be about 500 feet thick, cover about 150 square miles of the plateau surface in the neighbourhood of Guroji. Elsewhere rocks of the Basement Complex, of which the plateau is built, are found.

Plate 52. A Crater Lake in Bamenda Province, Western Cameroon.

THE BAMENDA HIGHLANDS

The greatest extent of high-level surfaces along the eastern borderlands lies in the Bamenda Province of the western Cameroons, immediately south of the Mambilla Plateau. The highlands, which are in most areas bounded by steep scarps of over 3,000 feet, consist of gneisses and granites of the Basement Complex, which outcrop mainly at heights below 4,300 feet. Much of the highland area is about 6,000 feet or more above sea level, while the area north-east of Bamenda has numerous hills with summits exceeding 7,000 feet. Along the borders long spurs and isolated hills stretch in the direction of Obudu and Takum, while deeply incised valleys run far into the highlands.

Widespread volcanic activity has resulted in large-scale masking of vast areas of the Basement rocks by lava flows. As in the Jos Plateau three phases of volcanic eruption have been recognized. After the first phase in which basalt was extruded 200 feet thick in the Bansa area, the plateau was subjected to a long period of erosion in which valleys were cut through the basalts into the underlying rocks. The second phase featured the extrusion of volcanic lavas on a much larger scale such as that in the Oku area, and volcanic rocks accumulated to a depth of about 4,000 feet, making this area the highest part of the highlands. Another long period of erosion separated this phase from the most recent cones which are of local importance in that their lavas covered up the immediate locality of the cones. The highest points in the Bamenda highlands are to be found in these cones, many of which have well-preserved craters containing crater lakes as at Oku and Wum.

As a result of these series of lava flows the surface of the Bamenda Highlands is very irregular. A number of bevels or surfaces exist at different heights, the most consistent of which are the Basement surface at an altitude of 3,500 to 4,500 feet and a volcanic surface at 4,500 to 6,000 feet. The Basement surface is cut on the old crystalline rocks and is a true erosion surface. It occurs mainly along the margins of the plateau, since the central part is largely covered with volcanic rocks. A steep escarpment separates this Basement surface, giving rise to numerous waterfalls.

CLIMATE AND VEGETATION

Both the climate and vegetation of various parts of the eastern borderlands are influenced by latitude and altitude. The highest parts of this mountainous region are found near the coast and it is here that the heaviest rainfall in West Africa is recorded. Absolute totals decrease from about 400 inches per annum at Debunscha on the coast to 150 inches in the western parts of the Bamenda Highlands and less than 40 inches in the Mandara Mountains. There is also a corresponding decrease in the number of months having a minimum of four inches of rainfall, which is the quantity considered adequate for the growth of most plants in the tropics. At Debunscha every month of the year has at least four inches of rain, decreasing to nine and a half months at Bamenda and about five months in the region of the Mandara Mountains. The southern or Bamenda Highlands show a marked decrease in rainfall intensity from about 150 in the western slopes to 60 inches on the plateau and in the east.

The coastal area lacks any well-defined dry season but is characterized by consistently high humidity and temperatures. Further inland, in the Bamenda Highlands, there is a short but well-marked dry season which does not last more than four months. The higher plateau areas enjoy a much more temperate climate with minimum temperatures which often fall below 45° F. as compared with 71° F. and 72° F. at places like Calabar and Douala respectively. North of the Benue valley the borderlands have a long dry season (October to March) when very little or no rain falls and the relative humidity is low compared with that for the wet season. This is a season of very high temperatures and large diurnal range of temperature. Heavier and more regular rain, with a maximum in July or August, occurs during the wet season (April to September) when lower temperatures and smaller daily range of temperature are characteristic.

Line squalls occur all over the borderlands and are more frequent just before and after the wet season, due to the conflict between the harmattan blowing from the north-east and the south-west winds. They are often very violent with gusts up to fifty miles per hour, and are accompanied by thunder and lightning, causing much havoc to electrical installations and instruments. In the south they are most frequent about April, with a secondary maximum in September, but north of the Benue valley there is a long period of single maximum from June to August. No precise figures of the frequency of these line squalls are available, but in many places in the Cameroons as many as seven have been recorded in one month.

Violent wind storms occur in other parts of Nigeria but their character may well be described here. They may occur at any time of day or night and normally blow from east to west. The development of a line squall begins with a light west wind, the massing of dark rain clouds and thunder rumbling in the distance. This stage lasts for a few hours and is followed by a sudden change in wind speed. The winds become violent, upsetting canoes in the rivers or seas and damaging huts and crops. Torrential rain follows with the thunder and lightning persisting. There is a marked fall in temperature, and soon the winds become light, while the rain becomes gentler before ceasing eventually. When the rain stops, the sky clears and the cycle is completed.

The effect of altitude on vegetation is particularly noticeable in the south, where the Cameroon Mountains and the Bamenda Highlands display distinct altitudinal belts of vegetation. The coastal and lowland areas of the south have a natural vegetation of dense equatorial forest in which three plant communities may be recognized, mangrove woodland along the coast, a rather extensive area of evergreen forest and the more restricted areas of grass-woodland. Above the 3,000-feet contour the vegetation of Mount Cameroon and the Bamenda Highlands is a modified rain forest in which lianes are scarce, while tree-ferns and lichens are abundant. Above 4,500 feet trees

become smaller and less varied, but there is a common occurrence of temperate species. This zone of montane rain forest ceases at about 6,000 feet, but on Mount Cameroon it ceases at about 5,000 feet on the north side, and at about 8,000 feet on the south-west, this difference having to do with slope, drainage and exposure to fire.

On the upper part of the montane forest vegetation, woodlands give way to tall grasses of about two to three feet and isolated trees. On Mount Cameroon this montane grassland exists as a natural vegetation, but all over the Bamenda Highlands where the high rainfall suggests a forest vegetation, the tall grass cover which occurs above 4,000 feet is a biotic climax. This is confirmed by the existence of forests around villages, many of which have separate palm forests. Such forest outliers have been pre-served to supply building materials, wood and fruits and the trees growing there are both wild and cultivated. Apart from the oil palm, the most common cultivated trees in such forests include the kola tree and eucalyptus tree. Shorter grasses occur on higher elevations as well as in heavily grazed areas.

The dry and cool climate of the Bamenda Highlands is very similar to that of the Jos Plateau and favours the growth of many plants and garden flowers common to tropical and temperate climates. Green peas, asparagus and lettuces as well as strawberries and potatoes have done very well in the gardens of the Bamenda Highlands. Gallery forests which are common in the grassland country of West Africa are also found on these highland areas.

North of the Benue valley grass woodland predominates, giving way to thorn forests in the Chad depression. The highlands of Mandara and the granitic hills west and east of these highlands maintain a distinct assemblage of flora which is quite different from that of the surrounding plains. Many of the hills are covered with grass only, but in the frequently cultivated or permanently settled areas useful trees have been preserved to form orchards on the hills. Amongst such trees the most prominent are the shea butter tree, acacia albida and the boabab. Often the surrounding plains are more open than the hills.

THE PEOPLE AND THEIR WAY OF LIFE

The Nigeria-Cameroon borderlands are inhabited by dozens of small tribes such as the Margi, Kilba, Batta, Verre and Mambila, each of which is confined to a restricted but contiguous territorial district. These small indigenous tribes are predominantly pagans and may be distinguished from the Hausas and Fulanis who are essentially newcomers to the borderlands, even though the

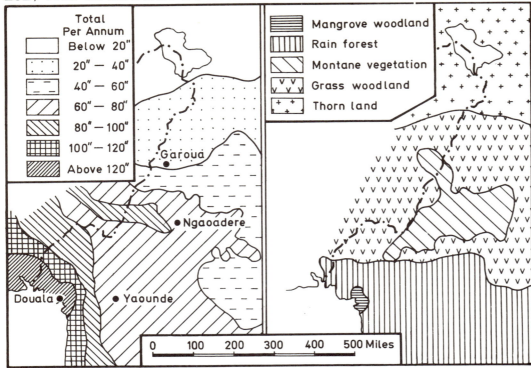

Figure 82. The Rainfall and
Vegetation of the Eastern
Borderlands

earliest record of Fulani presence in the region dates from about A.D. 1300. Although the Hausas and Fulanis are by no means the most numerous of the tribal groups found in the borderlands, they are the most widespread. The Hausas are here, not only as pedlars as is the case in other parts of the Central Sudan outside Hausaland, but also in well-established communities where they carry out other forms of economic activities including farming. Their main concentrations are in the grasslands of Adamawa and the Cameroons, where there are numerous Hausa colonies varying in population from less than one hundred persons to several thousands. In recent years, however, there has been considerable penetration into the forest belt, but here the Hausas settle as pedlars only.

Early migrations of the Fulanis, who are basically a pastoral people, were caused by their need for new grazing land rather than by any idea of conquest. As strangers, they paid grazing dues to the pagans in whose country they herded their cattle. By the end of the eighteenth century a large number of Fulani settlements had been established in the area south of the Mandara Mountains, but particularly in the Batta tribal area around Yola. It was during the jihad which swept the Fulani into power over a large part of northern Nigeria that Adamawa and parts of the northern Cameroons were subdued. When, therefore, the British and the Germans arrived on the scene, the northern part of the Nigeria-Cameroon borderlands was under the rule of the Fulani Emir of Yola. But the Anglo-German boundary arrangement placed certain Fulani-controlled territories under German Cameroon while the greater part remained in Nigeria. Many chiefs in the German area, however, continued to be subordinate to Fulani rulers in British Nigeria, and although the Germans were irritated by this they were unable to destroy Fulani native administration in the Cameroon. It is prob-

able that the situation today would be different if the Germans had stayed on much longer, but the vote in 1960 to merge with independent Nigeria was a clear demonstration of the existing ties between the peoples of this part of the Nigeria-Cameroon borderlands.

Thousands of Fulani cattlemen may be found scattered all over the upland grazings of the Cameroons-Adamawa highlands where there are at least 150,000 Fulani cattle. In these uplands the Fulani lead a semi-nomadic life, though most of them are becoming settled. All settled and even semi-nomadic Fulanis divide their cattle into two lots, the *horeji* or bush cattle, and the *sureji* or milk (homestead) cattle. The *horeji*, which constitute by far the greatest number of Fulani cattle on the Bamenda and Mambila Highlands, are placed in the charge of professional herdsmen and are kept always on the move in search of water and grazing. During the rainy season (May to October) the cattle population is widely distributed over areas which are relatively free from cattle disease. On the Bamenda Highlands the higher lava surface grasslands provide excellent grazing during the rains. In the dry season the cattle descend to the lower granite surface of the Bamenda region and to the Benue valley where adequate supplies of water and grazing exist along the main water courses. A few milk cattle are, however, kept around the homestead all through the year. Cattle management by the Fulanis of the eastern borderlands is, therefore, very similar to that of the Shuwa Arabs who live in the extreme north of this region.

Many of the pagan groups on both sides of the international boundary still live in the hills to which they retired during the period of Fulani domination of the surrounding plains. As in the case of the Angas of the Jos Plateau, many of these borderland tribes such as the Chamba and the Dakka of the Shebshi Mountains and foothills, may be divided into two classes, those who live in the plain and those who still live on hill-tops. The former were easily subdued and enslaved by the Fulanis with whom they now mingle freely. Fulani influence on these pagans of the lowlands is obvious in the houses they build, and in their clothing. Many have even adopted the religion of the Fulanis, but none have taken to cattle rearing, although all keep large numbers of goats and fowls. As in the Jos Plateau, the Fulanis found it difficult to conquer those groups who held themselves aloof on the hills. Rather, these hill pagans carried out sporadic raids on the Fulanis, whose cattle they carried off to their small villages which were built on apparently inaccessible heights. Henry Barth's observations of the situation farther north indicate that at the time of his travels the hill groups in the Mandara Mountains were able to maintain their freedom, while the Gamerghu people who live on the plain had been largely exterminated or subjected to heavy taxation by the Fulanis and Kanuris.

The hill pagans of Adamawa live in much the same way as those of the Jos Plateau. The neat pagan villages hidden at the foot of great granitic outcrops or set amidst cactus-hedged fields which are found within a few miles of Mubi and farther north remind one of the Birom villages of the Jos Plateau. Amongst the Margi and Kilba of Adamawa each wife is assigned three huts, just as is the case with the Angas tribe of the plateau. The working of iron which was a principal industry amongst the Chamba of the Shebshi Mountains was also known to some of the pagan groups of the Jos Plateau. We have already made occasional references to other similarities in the physical and cultural landscapes of both areas and we know that the pagan groups of the Jos Plateau and the eastern borderlands are amongst the most primitive people in Nigeria. A cultural gap created by the presence of more advanced tribes, and which corresponds with the Benue valley and the Bauchi High Plains, separates both regions of high relief and primitive culture. The pre-jihad connection between the pagans of the Jos Plateau and the eastern highlands, both of which suffered under the Fulanis, is still to be investigated. The Verre people who occupy the Verre hills south of Yola wear the penis-sheath which is also worn by the Bantu and semi-Bantu-speaking peoples of the Jos Plateau. In addition, the Verre speak a language which suggests some ancient connection with these other groups. Future research may yet establish that these peoples came from the same stock.

One of the most interesting pagan people in southern Adamawa are the Mambila tribesmen who inhabit the hilly country often referred to as the Mambila Plateau.

Like the pagans of the Mandara Mountains, the men wear a loin-covering of cloth while the women are completely nude. The distinguishing feature of this group is their technique of house-building, which is superior to anything seen anywhere in the region, and indeed in the entire northern provinces of Nigeria. Every Mambila hut has an upper storey which is used as a bedroom or a store. When used for storing grain the upper storey is reached from the outside through a hole in the thatch. The lower storey is used for cooking and flour-milling, for storing pots and occasionally as a bedroom. At night, a wood fire is lit in the lower storey to keep those sleeping in the upper storey warm. Two or three huts constitute a compound which may also contain one or two stone pens for goats or chickens. All compounds are neatly laid out and well drained by trenches and many of them contain groves of banana trees which remind one that one is approaching the Bamenda country.

Another important pagan group, this time on the Cameroon side of the border, is the Musgu who inhabit part of the flooded country of the Shari and the Logone Plains. They have much greater cultural affinity with the people of the Congo Basin than with the neighbouring tribes. Instead of using bows and arrows as their neighbours do, the Musgu hunt with the throwing-iron (spear), a weapon which is common in the Congo Basin. Musgu people are not very attractive to behold and the bad custom of disfiguring their features by the use of lipdisks forced into perforations in the lips, so that they project like beaks, tends to make them even more repulsive. According to the explorer Denham this fashion proved so disgusting to slave-dealers at Tripoli and Fezzan that they refused to buy Musgu women. They are a group of settled agriculturalists, who also keep large herds of cattle and, like other pagan groups, their clothing is both scanty and primitive. In spite of extensive slave raiding in the past, their territory is relatively very densely populated. It is the resultant pressure of population on farmland that has constrained the Musgu to make the most careful use of the soil by adopting a highly developed system of agriculture in which artificial manuring is important.

As in other parts of northern Nigeria, each town or large village has a district head who is responsible to the Emir for the collection of taxes and the keeping of peace. In Moslem villages there is always a mosque and in all Fulani dominated areas Moslem law is administered through the Alkali court. The system of indirect rule, which the British operated in northern Nigeria, has preserved much of the traditional administrative arrangement of the Fulanis. A rather conservative indigenous administration, which a local senior government official described as the most tolerant in Nigeria, was ushered in at independence in 1960 and has effected little economic and virtually no cultural change in the northern parts of the region, owing to its misguided policy of not wanting to force the pace of development in any part of northern Nigeria. Accordingly, there are very few schools in the area, while the people remain primarily as subsistence farmers who live and go about naked in the hills.

Like other parts of the eastern borderlands, the Bamenda Plateau displays great ethnic diversity. There are two major ethnic groups, the Bamileke, most of whom live in east Cameroon, and the Tikar, who live in west Cameroon. Each group is made up of many small tribes with different languages and customs. One of the best-known tribes in the area is the Bafut, which is a Tikar tribe, ruled over by the Fon of Bafut who is one of the most influential rulers in this region.

THE TRADITIONAL ECONOMY OF THE BAMENDA HIGHLANDS

Farming is the work of women and soils developed over the youngest lavas in the valley bottoms are particularly deep and productive. The interest, pride and amount of work the women put into farming is impressive and often they leave home at 7 a.m. and do not return till 4 or 5 p.m. Field preparation which begins in December and other farming activities are similar to those of any forest district in south-eastern Nigeria. Planting is carried out on mounds, as well as on ridges, the most important crop being the cocoyam. Maize, groundnuts, beans and sweet potatoes are also important subsistence crops. Farming practices have changed considerably in recent years. Mixed cropping of all or most of the crops already named has given place to single cropping and crop rotation is also practised.

Bamenda is the country of banana and plantains and the cultivation of these plants is the work of both men and women. There are many varieties of both crops and each can be made into a variety of dishes. The plants receive considerable care in this area as compared with Ibo and Ibibio country where the only attention given to the plantain grove consists of planting the sucker, providing a support in cases where a storm has done some havoc, and harvesting the ripe fruit. Cassava is another important crop, but yams are much less significant in this area.

With a population of about half a million the highlands are one of the most densely peopled areas of the borderlands. In areas around Jakari, Banso, Ndu and Nsop where many people are concentrated, the land is very heavily farmed. Cultivation on many uplands is commonly carried out on steep slopes where the crops are grown on ridges running up and down the slope, with ditches separating the fields. Yet gullying is not very apparent. The reader should, however, note the difference in hill farming as carried out by the hill tribes of Bamenda and that of such tribes as the Hill Angus or the Margi who build terraces and construct ridges along the contours rather than across them.

The tribes of this area are heavy drinkers, like the people farther north, but instead of millet or guinea-corn beer, the people here drink palm wine. Wine from the oil palm is considered to be better than that from the raffia-palm and is drunk by men, women and children as a staple drink at meals as well as on special occasions. The production of palm oil and kernels is also an important item in the cash economy. The method of preparation of the oil is similar to that of the Ibibio peasants of south-eastern Nigeria.

Meat is still a scarce item in the local diet, in spite of the large number of Fulani cattle that may be found in the area. Hunting with traditional weapons, spears and bows and arrows, as well as with the more modern flint-lock gun provides a major source of meat. The best time for hunting is in March, when the hillsides have been burned so that small game like monkeys, antelopes and cutting grass take refuge in the valleys. Hunting by individuals is common but sometimes the men hunt in groups of about eight. Hunting dogs are employed. Amongst the Bafut a communal hunt is held once every year when the men go out for several days to hunt for their traditional ruler, the Fon. This practice was once very common amongst the Yorubas and Benin people of southern Nigeria and may still be met with in the more rural areas of the country.

Most markets are held every eighth day and much of the trading is done by the women. Trade in imported goods is in the hands of professional traders who move around from one market to another. Ibo traders are found throughout the region and have the reputation of being able to undersell everyone else.

CULTIVATORS VERSUS PASTORALISTS

The well-watered, fly-free uplands of Mambila and Bamenda provide some of the best grazing in the region and the average density of about one hundred cattle per square mile in both areas is considered to be high for any part of Africa. There has been conflicting demands for land by pastoralists and cultivators, as the cattle population increases side by side with the human population. The highland pastures have since started to show signs of overgrazing, and although the Fulanis appear to be looking for more grazing they are in effect being forced to graze a lesser and lesser area. The reason for this trend, which has also led to overgrazing and soil erosion, is the spread of population and the encroachment of farmers on grazing land. The large nucleated village is giving way to dispersed farmsteads as people feel safe to migrate to cultivate distant farmland, and this extension of cultivation deep into the grasslands has meant a loss of grazing.

The nature of the problems vary from one area to another. In Mambila where the Fulanis have political power the situation is different from that in Bamenda where they are newcomers and essentially strangers. The soils of the Mambila Plateau are not particularly good for farming unless much fertilizer is used, but they support excellent grazing. This explains in part why the agricultural population of Mambila is relatively small (25,000) and why the intensity of stocking is one of the highest in the country. In Bamenda, on the other hand, the soil supports both good grazing and farm crops and many farmers are to be found in some of the best grazing areas. This encroachment by farmers on Fulani pastures is known to occur in other parts of the borderlands including the Maio Kebbi area, where dry-season grazing has been restricted by cotton growing. We come across similar problems again in Sokoto and the Lake Chad area. Indeed in some areas farmers are said to make farms in recognized grazing areas with the intention of gaining compensation from herdsmen for damage to crops.

It appears that the time has come when the Fulani cannot expect to gain more grazing in these areas, but there is a great need to define their rights more clearly in certain districts. In Bamenda, where the Fulani pastoralist is not the political overlord he is in Mambila, he is often at a disadvantage over the question of grazing rights. Yet the presence of large herds on the highlands is a source of much wealth to the Bamenda divisional treasury, which collects an annual tax of two shillings and six pence per head of cattle. In addition there is a ready supply of milk and butter as well as meat to the local population. Attempts so far made to demarcate grazing land in Bamenda Division have been unpopular with both the pagans and the Fulanis, because such demarcations infringe the customary rights of the former and restrict the movements of the latter. At present farmland lying fallow is also used for grazing, but a major step in tackling the problem appears to be the integration of cattle husbandry and crop farming.

RECENT DEVELOPMENTS IN AGRICULTURE

Agricultural development in recent years has taken the form of the introduction of new crops which are cultivated in plantations as well as in peasant holdings, improved methods of stock breeding and a pilot 'meat scheme'. As a result of these developments farming is no longer restricted to the women folk, although it is still true to say that food farming is the work of women. One of the crops which have been developed in recent years is coffee. Coffee trees are indigenous to the southern savanna areas, where the berries were widely used by the local people before European penetration. A few plantations existed in the francophone zone in the early 1930's, but it was only after the Second World War that coffee growing became important in the Bamenda Highlands following the introduction of *Arabica* coffee as a cash crop. Today coffee has been integrated with the peasant subsistence farming in much the same way as cocoa has been in western Nigeria. In many families it is the major source of cash income, and very often the expansion of coffee acreage has been along higher and steeper slopes of valleys, the lower slopes of which are devoted to food farms. Such expansion has created problems of soil erosion on the very steep slopes and has meant an encroachment on Fulani grazing. The adoption of contour ridging, which is advised by the Agricultural Department, has helped to reduce the incidence of soil erosion, but there is a growing tendency for the men to use the best soils for coffee growing, forcing the women to cultivate food crops on poorer soils. Coffee exports from the Bamenda Highlands stood at over 2,000 tons in the 1960's, as compared with only fourteen tons in 1947. Only a small fraction of this figure comes from the 1,200-acre Santa Coffee Plantation established in 1952 by the Eastern Nigeria Development Corporation.

Crops which have been introduced and are doing very well include bananas and cocoa in the far south, cinchona on the Bamenda Highlands, and potatoes, tomatoes and garden peas which have become increasingly important as a cash crop in the food farms. Banana and cocoa plantations, which were started before the First World War by German investors, are concentrated in Victoria and Kumba Divisions where extensive plantations of oil palms and rubber also exist. These plantations, which have since expanded, are now owned and managed by the West Cameroon Development Corporation and constitute a major source of revenue to the Government. Bananas and plantains, like the oil palm, are also grown for food as well as for export in peasant farms.

The cultivation of the cinchona, whose leaf is the source of quinine, was started in an attempt to lower imports and break a monopoly then held by Indonesia. The first plantations were established in 1929 near the plateau town of Tchang, which lies almost midway between Bamenda and Nkongsamba. An experimental laboratory at Tchang concentrates on the breeding of improved varieties adapted to local conditions, and nurseries from the Tchang plantations are still the major source of cinchona seedlings in the area. Both the yellow and red bark cinchona are grown, and locally-produced quinine has been in use in the Cameroons since 1938.

Tea was first introduced in 1928 by German planters who had been permitted to return to the Cameroons after the First World War. The main centre of production is at Tole near Buea, where a tea factory built in 1957 has been producing tea for the local market. In recent years tea cultivation has extended to the Bamenda Highlands, where there is a large tea plantation at Ndu. Local farmers have not yet taken to tea cultivation as they have done with coffee, but many under-employed farmers take up seasonal employment as tea pickers in the estate.

Considerable efforts have also been expended in developing the cattle economy of this region. Cross breeding of imported Montbeliard cattle from France with local zebu types has long been established by the French at veterinary centres and cattle farms at Ngaoundere, Nkongsamba, Tchang and Jakari as well as Bamenda and Obudu. The resultant breeds are usually dual-purpose animals with the accent more on beef than on milk production.

In west Cameroon, formerly administered along with Nigeria, where there is no rail link between the cattle highlands of Bamenda and the main meat-consuming centres along the coast as in Nigeria, cattle can only be transported on hoof. This results in loss of weight and lowering of the quality of the meat. The Cameroon meat scheme, started in 1959 for the production and distribution by refrigerated lorry of frozen meat, was directed at supplying consumers with good quality meat at reasonable prices. The scheme started with one cold store at Bali near Bamenda, but other cold stores have since been established at the main consuming centres like Victoria, Kumba and Tiko. Eastern Nigeria constituted a greater part of the market which the meat scheme was expected to serve, but this was lost in 1961 when west Cameroon voted in a plebiscite to break with Nigeria. Today the scheme is still faced with the problem of finding new markets which will make it possible for production to expand.

TRANSPORTATION AND THE MOVEMENT OF POPULATION

The Nigeria-Cameroons borderlands are very poorly served with transportation. The only railway runs from Duala to Nkongsamba in the forested south and was built as far back as 1911. Extension towards the north was once contemplated but later abandoned as a result of the mountainous nature of the terrain which would have made the cost prohibitive. Throughout the region roads are few and far between and are often poorly built. The hilly terrain and the numerous river gorges make road construction in many parts of the region an engineering feat. One of the most remarkable but expensive roads in this region is the road leading up to the cattle ranch at Obudu. Like the Mamfe–Bamenda road it winds through some of the most difficult terrain in west Africa. Occasionally the roads passing through the highland areas are blocked by fallen trees, landslides or disabled vehicles which cannot negotiate some of the high gradients. Problems posed by the practice of having to close major roads in northern Nigeria to heavy traffic after heavy rains have been referred to on page 194. Transportation along the Yola–Mubi–Bama road is particularly handicapped by this irritating practice. In the Bamenda District conditions are such that even such a main trunk A road as the Mamfe–Bamenda road caters for one-way traffic on alternate days. That is to say that journeys from Mamfe to Bamenda can only be made along this road on Mondays, Wednesdays and Fridays, while the return journey is restricted to Tuesdays, Thursdays and Saturdays.

In vast areas like the Mambila Plateau and the Shebshi group of hills the only means of transportation is pack transport making use of footpaths. The northern districts, which have the donkey and the oxen, are much better off in this respect than the forested south. Even canoe transport is precluded along the fast mountain streams, the courses of which are blocked by rapids and waterfalls. The only exceptions include the Benue and the Faro, but even here water communication is seasonal. In these circumstances it is not surprising that many communities have very little contact with the more developed parts of the country. Civilizing influences in such remote and out-of-the-way districts consist mainly of the Christian missions, but by and large the physical and cultural landscapes of such districts do not appear to differ from descriptions handed down to us by Henry Barth and other explorers who wandered past this region more than a hundred years ago.

Yet considerable changes have taken place in even the most isolated mountain areas. Pagans in the Shebshi Hills and other areas have been descending to the plains, though some still prefer the hill-tops. There has been increasing movements of population, involving the Hausas and Fulanis in particular, in the grassland areas, but also Ibos and local tribes such as the Ewondo (often known as the Yaunde) and the Bamileke from the south. Spatial movements of population in the south involve the migration of labourers from Bamenda, the Eastern States of Nigeria and eastern Cameroons to the vast coffee, banana and other tree crop plantations of Kumba and Victoria Divisions of west Cameroons. Tiv migrants from the Benue valley are also found in the plantations of southern Cameroons.

Works consulted and suggestions for further reading:
1. Bettany, G. T., *Barth's Travels in North and Central Africa* London 1890
2. Calvert, A. F., *The Cameroons* chapter on the Nigeria-Cameroon boundary London 1917
3. Crowder, M., 'Mambila Plateau' *Nigeria Magazine* No. 65 pp. 154–76 1960
4. Duckworth, E. H., 'Crater Lakes in Bamenda Province' *Nigeria Magazine* No 37 pp. 65–89 1951
5. Gleave, M. B., 'The West Cameroon Meat Scheme' *Geography* Vol. 50 pp. 166–8 1965
6. Grove, A. T., *The Benue Valley* Kaduna 1957
7. Kirk-Greene, A. H. M., 'The Hill Tribes of Northern Adamawa' *Africa* No. 26 pp. 369–79 1956
8. Meek, C. K., *Tribal Studies in Northern Nigeria* Vol. I London 1931
9. Pugh, J. C., 'Geomorphology of the Northern Plateau of Nigeria' Unpublished Ph.D. thesis, University of London 1955

The Nigerian
Political Scene
A POSTSCRIPT

Geographical Regions of Nigeria is written at a time when the country is fighting a bloody civil war and is very much in the news all over the world. An increasing amount of literature on the political situation, including cheap propaganda as well as sensational dispatches from news correspondents, is already in circulation and more is sure to appear sooner or later. Many writers have stressed the obvious fact that the events following the first military coup of January 1966 have resulted in a great and lasting change in the country. What many people do not appear to appreciate is the equally obvious fact that lasting peace in strife-torn Nigeria is only possible in the context of one Nigeria, not in balkanization.

When in 1960 the British left Nigeria for good the indigenous politicians inherited a most unwieldy federal structure in which one state, the Northern Region had a much greater area and more people than the other two states combined (Figure 83 and Table 15). In a country like Nigeria, where the basis of representation in parliament is population, and where political parties were organized on tribal and state basis, it meant that the Northern Region was in a position to dominate the country politically. There was a parliamentary opposition in each of the three state legislatures, but in Nigeria, as in other newly independent African countries, the ruling party always won in any election, and it was virtually impossible for opposition candidates to campaign for votes. Hence the fact that most representatives in the federal parliament from a given state always came from the government party in that state. And hence the importance attached to population figures by the various state governments.

The structure of the Federation was a source of fear and friction between the three major ethnic groups: the Ibos in the Eastern Region, the Yorubas in the Western Region and the Hausa-Fulani in the Northern Region. The two major southern groups feared the power which the north wielded simply because of its size, and wanted the country re-organized into smaller states. But the north also had cause to feel insecure and was certainly afraid of economic and bureaucratic domination from the south. The civil service, the distributive trade and other aspects of the commercial and industrial life of the Federal Government as well as of the Northern Region was manned by Nigerians from the south, simply because the north could not produce the skilled manpower to man these services. But there was another category of fear which both the British and the first generation of Nigerian politicians sought to dismiss lightly. This was the fear which minority ethnic groups in each state entertained.

It was a fear which was expressed in the sustained demand, by these groups, for the creation of more states in the country. It is proper to add here that the various minority groups in the country are together numerically superior to the three majority groups combined. It is also almost certain that if the demand for more states had been met the tragedy of today would have been averted.

Unfortunately the basic issues of the creation of more states, so as to make for a more balanced federal union, was not taken very seriously even by those who had been very vocal on the topic during the days before independence. The general attitude was to ignore the demands of minority groups, and the creation of the Midwest State in 1963 was only made possible by the political crisis in western Nigeria. For fifteen years Nigerian politics was dominated by leaders from the three main ethnic groups and all the main political parties were essentially tribal in outlook. Elections were a farce in a country which the world believed to be the model of western democracy in Africa, while local politicians wallowed in corruption and the suppression of any form of opposition.

The first six years of independence were a trying period in which distrust between the major tribal groups deepened. A national coalition government between a Hausa-Fulani dominated party and an Ibo-dominated party tended to alienate the Yorubas. The Yorubas became more apprehensive after the 1962 political crises in western Nigeria, the creation of the Midwest State from western Nigeria and the arrest, trial and imprison-

Figure 83. The Old Structure of Four Regions in the Nigerian Federation

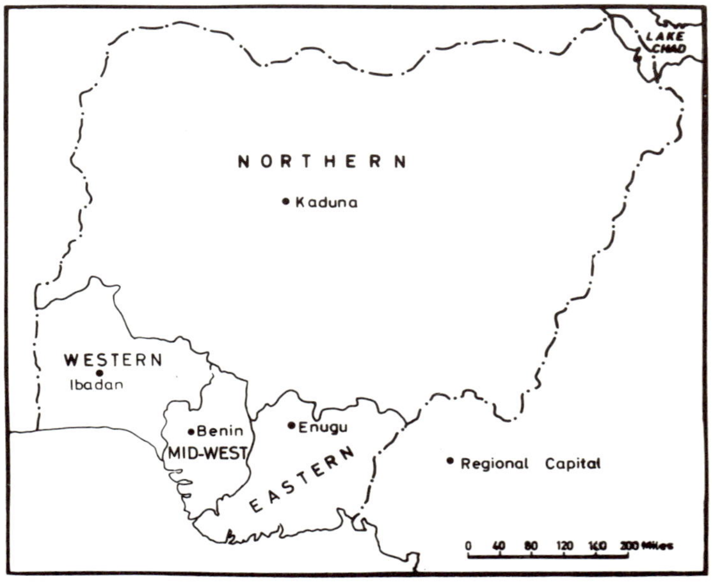

Table 15 AREA AND POPULATION OF THE FORMER STATES
OF FEDERAL NIGERIA 1948/66

State	Area in Square Miles	Populations in Millions		No. of Seats in Parliament	
		1953	1963	1953	1963
Northern Nigeria	281,782	16·8	29·8	174	167
Eastern Nigeria	29,484	7·2	12·4	73	70
Western Nigeria	30,454	4·6	10·3	47	57
Midwest Nigeria (1963)	14,922	1·5	2·5	15	14
Lagos (Federal Capital)	27	0·23	0·7	3	4
TOTAL	356,000	30·33	55·6	312	312

ment of the leader of the Yoruba-dominated Action Group Party, who was also leader of opposition in the Federal Legislature. Then followed the 1962–3 census controversy which contributed much to worsening relations between north and south, but particularly between the Hausa-Fulani group and the Ibos.

Table 16 AREA AND POPULATION OF THE NEW STATES OF FEDERAL NIGERIA (FROM JUNE 1967)

State	Area in Square Miles	Population in Millions	State Capital
North-western	65,143	5·7	Sokoto
North-central	25,954	4·1	Kaduna
Kano	16,630	5·7	Kano city
North-eastern	103,639	7·8	Maiduguri
Benue Plateau	41,744	4·0	Jos
Kwara	28,672	2·4	Ilorin
Lagos	1,381	1·4	Lagos
Western	29,100	9·5	Ibadan
Midwestern	14,922	2·5	Benin city
East-central	8,746	6·2	Enugu
South-eastern	13,730	4·6	Calabar
Rivers	7,008	1·5	Port Harcourt

During the 1962 census several southern politicians had hoped that the population of the southern states would exceed that of the giant north. They were greatly disappointed when the published figures showed the reverse to be the case, and proceeded to reject the figures, while calling for a fresh enumeration. The recount of 1963 confirmed the result of the 1962 census, vis-a-vis the numerical superiority of the Northern Region (Table 15). The importance of this census lay primarily in the 1964 elections which, true to expectation, were won by the government party in northern Nigeria.

It was in connection with the October 1965 Western Nigeria election that Nigerians witnessed the greatest rape of democracy by any ruling party. Through dubious and dishonest manipulations an unpopular government party managed to keep the tradition that the government party must win in a Nigerian election. The people reacted by burning and looting the houses of Government supporters. There was widespread confusion in Western

Nigeria and this confusion continued through December 1965 to the morning of 15 January 1966 when a group of young army officers carried out what turned out to be a partly successful coup, which overthrew the Federal Government.

The failure by the Federal Government to restore law and order in Western Nigeria, and the growing contempt with which the generality of the Nigerian public had come to regard the rich and corrupt politician, helps to explain the fact that the military take-over was received with a feeling of relief and general rejoicing even in Northern Nigeria. But this was short-lived. The people became disillusioned when details of the coup were known.

A feeling of fear and suspicion, much greater than the country had known before the coup, gripped the people. The leaders of the coup were found to be mainly of the Ibo tribe; the Yoruba and Fulani premiers of Western and Northern Nigeria respectively, as well as the federal prime minister who was Hausa were killed, while the two Ibo premiers of Eastern and Midwestern Nigeria were spared. The senior army officers who fell in the coup were all non-Ibos and General Ironsi, the head of the Nigerian army, whose responsibility it was to head the Military Government was Ibo. This was too much of a coincidence in a country where the major ethnic groups were already suspicious of one another. Indeed most Nigerians later came to see the coup as an attempt by the Ibos to dominate the country.

The author of this book believes that the leaders of the January coup were prompted by a genuine desire to reform the country's political institutions. The coup was, however, unsuccessful and those who came to power proved unequal to the task. Rather than break up the country into more states the Ironsi regime attempted to establish a unitary government. This proved disastrous because it was regarded as a sure sign of the road to Ibo domination, since the heads of most government services were certainly going to be Ibos. The barbaric rejection of the move to unify the civil services of the country by the Northern Region featured the slaughter in May of innocent southern civilians, largely of Ibo origin, living and working in the north. But this outburst did not change the political structure which was later accomplished by the overthrow of the Ironsi regime in July 1966.

At this stage the Ibo-controlled Government of Eastern Nigeria was already contemplating to secede from the Federation. The constitutional talks called by the new

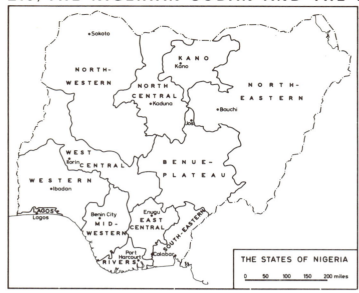

THE STATES OF NIGERIA

0   50   100   150   200 miles

Figure 84. The Twelve New States of the Federation of Nigeria

military leader, General Gowon (then Lt.-Col. Gowon), ran into trouble when the Eastern Nigeria delegation withdrew, following reports of more killings of civilians of Ibo origin in Northern Nigeria. This second barbaric outburst in Northern Nigeria followed an equally barbaric display in parts of Iboland, where people of northern origin were also killed as reprisals for the earlier killings in the north. In October 1966 the Ibo resolve to secede crystalized and all attempts at a peaceful settlement of the Nigerian crises were frustrated by the Government of Eastern Nigeria. A meeting of Nigerian leaders at Aburi in Ghana in January 1967 failed to resolve the crises and from March 1967 the Eastern Nigeria Government embarked on a policy of open defiance of the Federal Government.

Minority groups all over the country, but particularly in Eastern Nigeria became more vocal in their demand for separate states. On 27 May 1968, when it was clear that Eastern Nigeria was bent on seceding from the Federation, the Federal Military Government created twelve states in the country (Figure 84). This move was acclaimed by all Nigerians, except the Ibo leadership, as the most significant political event in independent Nigeria.

The Ibos rejected the new federal structure and proceeded to proclaim Eastern Nigeria as the independent Republic of Biafra. This was the immediate cause of the civil war.

Most outside observers appear to be impressed by the determination of the Ibos to keep out of Nigeria, but such observers appear to be ignorant of the determination of the eastern minorities to remain in Nigeria. These minority groups add up to five million as compared with seven million Ibos; but of more significance is the fact that the bulk of the crude petroleum, timber and agricultural resources of the former Eastern Region of Nigeria come from the minority areas now constituted into the Rivers and South-eastern States. The right of the Ibos to self-determination is indisputable, and so is the right of the peoples of the minority groups. The greatest case against the secession of Biafra is certainly its rejection by these minority groups. An independent Ibo state will not only be landlocked but will not be viable. The great task for the future is therefore one of re-integrating the Ibos into Nigeria. It is a difficult task, but it offers the hope of lasting peace in place of endless warfare which will result from balkanization.

Index